Valerie Anderson had a 30-year career in the NHS and university sector as a bio-medical and research scientist, after which she changed track to pursue a lifelong interest in nineteenth-century social history. After gaining her PhD from the School of Oriental and African Studies in London she is now an independent historian. Her decision to specialize in Anglo-Indian history was sparked by an inability to find satisfactory answers to her children's questions about their own ancestry and cultural heritage.

RACE AND POWER IN BRITISH INDIA

Anglo-Indians, Class and Identity in the Nineteenth Century

VALERIE ANDERSON

BLOOMSBURY
NEW DELHI • LONDON • OXFORD • NEW YORK • SYDNEY

BLOOMSBURY INDIA
Bloomsbury Publishing India Pvt. Ltd
Second Floor, LSC Building No. 4, DDA Complex, Pocket C-6&7,
Vasant Kunj, New Delhi 110070

BLOOMSBURY, Bloomsbury Academic India and the Diana
logo are trademarks of Bloomsbury Publishing Plc

First published in India 2022
Published in 2015 by I.B.Tauris & Co Ltd

This edition is published with permission from Bloomsbury Publishing Plc.
50 Bedford Square, London WC1B3DP

A catalog record for this book is available from the Library of Congress.
A catalogue record for this book is available from the British Library.

ISBN: 978-93-56401-00-6
For sale in the Indian subcontinent only

Exclusively distributed in the Indian subcontinent by
Manohar Publishers & Distributors
4753/23, Ansari Road
Darya Ganj, New Delhi 110002
Tel.: 23284848, 23289100
Email: sales@manoharbooks.com, manoharbooks@gmail.com

Typeset in Garamond Three by OKS Prepress Services, Chennai, India
Printed and bound in India by Replika Press Pvt. Ltd.

To find out more about our authors and books visit
www.bloomsbury.com and sign up for our newsletters.

For Glenn, Elizabeth, Edward and Elijah

CONTENTS

LIST OF TABLES

LIST OF FIGURES

ACKNOWLEDGEMENTS

I owe a huge debt of gratitude to Professor Peter Robb, whose thoughtful guidance has brought this work to completion. The South Asia History group at SOAS provided another layer of support and inspiration. The archivists and librarians of the National Archives of India, New Delhi; of the Oriental and India Office Collection, British Library; of Senate House Library; and of SOAS Library offered expert advice both on identifying sources and on negotiating their digital catalogues and other electronic resources.

Whilst in Delhi, I was assisted in so many ways by people who went out of their way to help a stranger. When you are thousands of miles from home, alone with a broken laptop and a contiguous welt of mosquito bites, a little sympathy goes a long way. Whether they were fellow researchers, staff at the archives, auto drivers, hotel staff, or fellow guests, they made my stay all the more memorable by their kindness.

Somewhere out there is an unnamed, faceless horde of transcribers and scanners, whose efforts to compile digital archives have brought to my laptop, now fully restored, unpublished archival material, rare books, photographs, and theses from every corner of the Earth, most of it completely free of charge. Two open-access digital archives that are particularly fabulous must be mentioned, Google Books and Archive.org, to which so many universities and archives have contributed material. Thanks to them, my research has not been constrained by opening hours or distance.

My greatest debt is to my family for their patience and tolerance. I have ignored their needs, disappeared for months of fieldwork, bombarded them with my thoughts and findings, and covered every household surface with unstable piles of books and papers. They learned to recognize when I was 'in the zone', provided endless cups of coffee and otherwise let me be. Even distance was no protection, as Australia and America are instantly accessible by e-mail and chapter drafts easily attached! Rather than a thank you, they all deserve an apology!

ABBREVIATIONS

BMJ	British Medical Journal
EAIA	Eurasian and Anglo-Indian Association
EIC	East India Company
EIR	East India Railway Company
FIBIS	Families in British India website
ICS	Indian Civil Service
IMS	Indian Medical Service
IOFH	The India Office Family History website
IOR	India Office Records
ISMD	Indian Subordinate Medical Department
MAS	Modern Asian Studies
NAI	National Archives of India, Delhi
NCO	Non-commissioned officer
ODNB	Oxford Dictionary of National Biography
OIOC	Oriental and India Office Collection, British Library, London
PRO	Public Records Office, Kew, UK
RAMC	Royal Army Medical Corps
TNA	The National Archives, Kew, UK
WO	The War Office

GLOSSARY

Anna	1/16 rupee
Ayah	servant responsible for child care
Batta	allowance
Babu	an Indian clerk literate in English
Bhestie	servant who supplies water
Bibi	Indian mistress
Boxwallah	a tradesman or merchant
Burra sahib	master of a family or department, senior official
Cranny	clerk
Dacoit	a bandit
Desh	one's native land or region
Durbar	court or government
Gentoo	a Hindu
Griffin	newly arrived government servant
Jaghir	hereditary landed estate
Jati	community
Kurta	a knee-length loose-fitting shirt
Languti	cloth used to cover a man's buttocks and genitalia
Masalchy	low-ranking kitchen servant
Maulvi	expert in Islamic law
Memsahib	European married woman
Mestizo	Portuguese term for person of mixed race

Mofussil	British India outside the cities of Madras, Bombay, and Calcutta
Munshi	a writer, secretary, or language teacher
Munsiff	small-causes judge in civil law
Native	ethnic Indian
Nauch	a dance performance
Nikah	Muslim marriage, both ceremony and legal contract
Nizam	ruler or sovereign
Pagoda	a Madras coin worth about Rs 3.5
Paise	1/4 anna
Pandit	expert in Hindu law
Purdah	women living concealed from men other than their closest relatives
Ryot	agricultural tenant
Saptapadi	Hindu marriage ritual in which the couple make their vows whilst taking seven steps around a sacred fire
Sati	self-immolation of a widow on her husband's funeral pyre
Sepoy	a native soldier in the Company or Indian army
Sirdar	high-ranking officer or leader
Statutory native	one born in India but of European, or part-European, ancestry
Sudra	the lowest of the four major castes of Hindus
Topasse	soldier of mixed Indian and Portuguese descent
Toty	low-caste labourer or messenger
Vakil	lawyer or solicitor
Writer	a legal clerk or junior East India Company servant
Zenana	part of a home reserved for women, especially those in purdah, or the women themselves

INTRODUCTION

HISTORICAL CONTEXT

That there were people of mixed European and Asian ancestry in India was not news to the colonial British; before their arrival in India there was an established Portuguese presence and a considerable number of Indo-Portuguese *mestizos*.[1] The British made use of them, as translators in their dealings with Indian rulers and traders, as *topasses* supplementing their own soldiery, as *crannies* to staff the administration, and as Christian wives and mistresses.[2] Despite the long history of cooperation between Britain and Portugal, Portuguese in general, and *mestizos* in particular, were always considered by the British to be their inferiors; Gilchrist described them as 'the most contemptible race to be found on earth',[3] Burton said:

> It would be, we believe, difficult to find in Asia an uglier or more degraded looking race than that which we are now describing. The forehead is low and flat, the eyes small, quick, and restless; there is a mixture of sensuality and cunning about the region of the mouth, and a development of the lower part of the face which are truly unprepossessing, not to say revolting [. . .] In personal attractions the fair sex is little superior to the other.[4]

Nor was Britain unaware that British men were fathering Indo-British children. The British had arrived in 1607 like the Portuguese, without women. They had been the dominant European presence since 1765, and yet the Eurasian of British ancestry as something 'other' than British, that had to be discouraged and controlled as a separate category of people, had not been a problem for almost 180 years. Little reference was made to their racial origins before the 1780s.[5]

The earliest name for children of Britons born in India was 'country-born'. According to Anthony, it was applied to those with solely European parentage as well as those of mixed ancestry, without distinction and, he claimed, with neither stigma nor derogatory sting.[6] That conclusion seems unlikely given the early belief in environmental determinism (the enervating and degrading effect of India's climate), even though that did not conform to racism in its later incarnations. There would have been no need to distinguish between the 'home' bred and the 'country-born' if that status was without stigma.

Besides Portuguese and British, numerous other Europeans were present in eighteenth- and nineteenth-century India and contributed to the growing Eurasian population, including French, Americans, Danish, Germans, and Dutch. Each had different policies and attitudes with regard to miscegenation and Eurasians. Each contributed to linguistic, religious, social, and cultural heterogeneity amongst Eurasians. However, increasing British political hegemony limited the impact of other European powers, subjecting many Eurasians to British influence and providing some opportunities for those anglophone, Christian, and appropriately educated.

Beginning in the 1780s, the exclusion of Indo-British Eurasians from both a European British identity and the separate 'domiciled' European category led to the formation of a distinct if never entirely separate community whose members, by an 1870 parliamentary statute, were labelled 'Statutory Natives of India'.[7] Thus, Eurasians became an Indian minority.

Throughout the nineteenth century, the British elite progressively distanced themselves from the Indian people and formed its own exclusive and privileged group, admitting members according to rank, pedigree, race, and behaviour. Race as a determinate of character, aptitude, and even morality became a central tenet of nineteenth-century British colonial thinking. In the late eighteenth and early nineteenth century, before the concept of race had firmly evolved along lines of colour and genotype (by about the mid-nineteenth century), 'environmental determinism' served to explain the putative vigour of Europeans and indolence of Indians. The 'enervating' Indian climate was seen as a danger to European health, character, and reproduction.[8] 'Society' attempted to ensure conformity within its own ranks by sumptuary rules, rules of precedence, standards of behaviour in work and leisure, by social pressure, and by sanctions in the workplace.[9]

For others domiciled in India whose only claim to privilege was to have been born of at least one European parent, the nineteenth century saw the introduction of increasingly draconian guidance and policing, as well as rewards for maintaining racial and cultural exclusivity. The lower orders had to be prevented from forming a bridge between the native and the European[10] if the image of European superiority, the legitimation of colonial rule, was to survive.[11]

Reforms to the East India Company (EIC), as it morphed from trading concern into sovereign power, allotted power and influence by race. Corruption, greed, 'nabobery', and even immorality would be minimized if Europeans in India retained their European culture and ties and the malign influence of 'natives' was reduced. A rigid and racialized social code soon emerged. Legislative reform in the 1830s and 1880s was grudgingly granted, allowing Indians some part in running their own country but only to the extent that it would appease (or buy off) liberal disquiet and Indian dissent.[12]

In this hardening socio-political context, Eurasians' racial 'hybridity' became a problem;[13] simultaneously too European and too Indian, they did not fit neatly into any European or Indian category. Early in the nineteenth century, a racialized colonial order effectively reserved significant posts (by law or usage) for Europeans. Later, opportunities were opened up to increasing number of

Western-educated Indians who provided tough competition for posts. There were opportunities for Eurasians in government employ where Indians remained excluded and Europeans could not be found, but the economic base of the community remained in a constant state of flux and full employment was never guaranteed.

Whether we talk of half-castes, East Indians, Eurasians, or in modern parlance Anglo-Indians, from the 1780s onwards they acquired a separate, contested and negotiated identity. It was an identity bitterly resented by some, prized by others, and vague enough to be manipulated to suit the ends of British colonial government. But, however loudly the British, from the start of the nineteenth century, protested that Eurasian 'half-castes' were 'the most rapidly accumulating evil',[14] almost a century later they were still 'to be found in every responsible office under government ... conspicuously employed & trusted'.[15] Eurasians therefore remained, paradoxically, an asset to British colonial government.

Empires have long since disappeared into history but Eurasians have not. In India today, the Anglo-Indian community is anxious to convey both nativity and loyalty to India but, stigmatized by past association with imperial oppression and 'Western' lifestyle, it is sometimes viewed as an unwelcome residuum of colonialism. At the same time, the diaspora is successfully integrating across the anglophone world but a plethora of internet forums and genealogical studies suggest widespread concern that their community history is fading from memory.

One author has quipped: 'Have you heard the joke about the Anglo-Indian national library? They lost the book.'[16] Certainly India's Eurasians attracted little attention from Victorian and early twentieth-century historians. Concentrating on the British elite, most Raj histories fail to mention them except, occasionally, as a problem.[17] It suited them to portray an exceptional breed, a handful of able and self-sacrificing Britons ruling an entire subcontinent. Arnold said: 'That, no doubt, was how the Raj chose to see itself.'[18]

The sparse Eurasian or Anglo-Indian historiography explores the community's early history but then jumps forward to the final decades of the nineteenth century and the last half century of British rule. Modern academic literature uses Eurasians to explore conceptual problems such as race, nation, and colonialism, concentrating on twentieth-century communities in India and those who now form a diaspora throughout the anglophone world. This large, liminal and marginal group, subjected to massive socio-political change (the end of empire, departure of the British, and life in independent India), has attracted the attention of sociologists and anthropologists exploring the lasting practical and psychological effects of colonial history on post-colonial Anglo-Indians. Works on poor Europeans and industrial relations in nineteenth-century India, and studies of the colonial Dutch Indies also include Eurasians.[19] But all of this has left a period of great change under-described.

My work examines significant issues in the nineteenth-century history of India's Eurasians, especially the anglicized predecessors of the Anglo-Indian community. It shows how growing British hegemony, and the racialized legitimation of the colonial state, caused Eurasians to be treated as an awkward reminder of an earlier alternative and more flexible scenario. It shows that Eurasians were presented with dilemmas affecting their freedom to mix European and Indian cultures, to associate regardless of race, to secure employment, and to claim a national identity, all of which was subject to scrutiny by the colonial state and its functionaries.[20] It shows why they could not generally favour their Indian ancestry and culture. I argue that their European-ness was reinforced by the colonial state, and that their agency to choose otherwise would have cost them both their identity and their livelihoods.

The first chapter re-examines Eurasian 'othering', concentrating on identifying the Acts, directives, and standing orders that first differentiated Eurasians from their colonial British kin. Exploring the effects these proscriptions produced, what motives have been identified, and what others have said about them shows that this approach identifies how but not why Eurasian 'othering' was achieved, since it looks at Eurasians in isolation, presuming them to be the main object of concern. Revisiting this ground, previously covered by Hawes and Goodrich,[21] was an essential starting point because recent developments in imperial history have shown that ideas travelled in both directions between the metropolis and the colony, and indeed between and across empires.[22] The fact that a British national identity was emerging simultaneously with Britain's Indian empire can no longer be ignored when examining both policy towards and problems within a colony.[23] Hawes touches on this, but I have put some of the policy-makers at the centre in order to show how their specific concerns for one part of the empire, whether a colony or within the metropolis, could affect a community in another part.

Chapter 2 therefore places Eurasian 'othering' in the wider context of British interests, home and imperial, to test whether Eurasians were the object of proscription or simply bystanders whose small numbers and lack of influence made them invisible and expendable. I look at three powerful men (Henry Dundas, Richard Wellesley, and Charles Cornwallis), showing how passionate interests outside India influenced their actions and priorities whilst they held powerful Indian offices. I conclude that, whilst Eurasians were 'othered', as a result of such men's actions, their motives must be understood and interpreted in a wider context than that hitherto adopted in Eurasian historiography, particularly with respect to evolving British identity.

It is impossible to assess Eurasian roles and status without approximate numbers, and impossible to make quantitative assessments without establishing a baseline, and so Chapter 3 attempts to enumerate how many Eurasians there were and how such a diverse category was defined and delineated. Every source yielded different figures, and all had problems in reliably identifying the Eurasian population.[24] However, I have been able to establish upper and lower limits for the size of the Eurasian population, and to highlight the artificiality of the concept of a single Eurasian community.

Chapter 4 explores the extent to which Europeans continued to form intimate relationships with Indian and Eurasian women. It is a comparative mass demographic study of India and England in one year (1881) drawn from marriage records, census, and military data from both countries. This approach minimizes subjectivity and shows that interracial relationships were unlikely to have disappeared at the rate that marriage and concubinage vanished from documentary evidence; it further shows that significant numbers of Eurasians, rather than forming a separate endogamous community 'mimicking' European culture, would have been regularly exposed to European culture and social mores by their husbands and fathers.

Chapter 5 investigates the nature of these intimate relationships, legal and otherwise. I explore marriage, as it was understood by the institutions of church and state, and how it was lived by different communities and classes, in Britain and in India. I contend that for the lower-class majority of Europeans and Eurasians, the simple division between legal wife and mistress or concubine was inadequate, was a cause of financial hardship, and was a source of prejudice against Eurasians.

The few Eurasian histories by Anglo-Indian authors offer interesting insights into how Eurasians viewed their own community or identity, and the political power shifts that affected relationships with the larger British and Indian peoples. However, shaped by political and ideological issues of their own times, these accounts are highly subjective.[25] I attempt to counteract this in the subsequent chapters by concentrating on quantifiable data, such as register entries, wages, and employment records, and show how infrastructural development offered a working solution in which Eurasians and the colonial state found mutual benefit.

The remaining chapters address aspects of Eurasian identity connected with employment. 'Employability' (Chapter 6) asks what work nineteenth-century Eurasians undertook or sought, what they had to do to get that work, how the British moulded 'useful citizens', and what agency Eurasians had in determining their own identity. I contend that Eurasians' cultural agency shrank as the British restricted Eurasian identity to those whose culture, education, and religion were considered appropriate to the employment opportunities they were willing to provide.

In Chapter 7, I consider the role of Eurasian women, once social pressures began to reduce the availability of European husbands, and their agency in directing their own lives. Concern amongst European men for the virtue of European and part-European women meant they could not be left to the mercy of Indian men. They were distinctive; Western dress, employment outside the home, mixing with men – all these aspects contrasted sharply with the popular nationalist trope of the compliant Indian housewife who embodied 'Mother India'. I show that there was a high rate of employment amongst Eurasian women, and that, unlike Indian and European women (unless of the lowest classes), Eurasian women continued to work after marriage, a financial necessity if Eurasian families were to maintain a European lifestyle.

Chapter 8 asks why the question of Eurasian military service was so contentious in the nineteenth century. I show that despite their demilitarization, the community remained anxious and able to serve in some capacities. Community leaders, the Indian government, the military and parliament all engaged in recurring discourses, ranging from the community's biological competence to serve, to its loyalty to Britain and the community's potential for economic and moral improvement through military service. This chapter, therefore, explores the construction and probing of what has been termed the 'internal frontier' of nationality.

Administrative expansion provided clerkships and survey work, appointments in the posts and telegraph services, customs, medical support roles, and railways. Existing Indian railway history comprises mostly facts and figures about miles of track, passenger numbers, goods moved, and finances. My Chapter 9 contributes a detailed comparison of Eurasian and European railway employment that complements Arnold's work on labour relations and Bear's ethnography of the Eurasian railway 'caste'.

This last chapter before my general conclusions asks what Eurasians got out of railway service, a sector of such significance that 'railwayman' became an alternative identity. I explore the diverse occupations and general benefits available to Eurasian railwaymen and their families, and life in racially segregated railway colonies that placed Eurasians alongside Europeans rather than Indians. I show that despite earning less than Europeans, the community gained security, status, acknowledgement that they were of European stock, and an opportunity to be of service to India. The price they paid was physical and social isolation from an Indian national identity.

Eurasians found roles for which their racial categorization was advantageous: government and quasi-government employment. The state acquired a subordinate labour force that was cheaper than Europeans but considered more capable and trustworthy than Indians. The disadvantage, in the longer term, was that Eurasians reaped such rewards only when (as Bear puts it) they possessed the right bio-moral character; that is, when they 'anglicized'. By examining a range of employment sectors, I show that close association with the colonial presence required anglicization, but that this has led other Indians (and even many Eurasians) to see Eurasians as indistinguishable from Europeans and therefore foreign.[26]

Shifting historical understandings of 'race' were deployed by the state and its representatives, and were particularly significant in determining how Eurasians were to be deployed, excluding and including them in British nationality as expediency dictated. British concerns about class, a major internal barrier almost synonymous with race, applied equally to domiciled Europeans and Eurasians. Both groups were subject to moral scrutiny, tutoring, and corralling in colonies to protect them from their own weaknesses and make them amenable to control. Racial 'degeneration', whether through environmental factors such as climate, through education, or through mixed ancestry, was an additional concern limiting the roles these 'hybrids' were permitted to play.

Hybridity would later exclude Eurasians from both the theory and practice of Indianization and Indian nationalism. Concerns over caste excluded Eurasians, as did their Christianity and lack of knowledge of (and pride in) India's pre-colonial and mythical pasts. The community's geographic mobility and lack of social cohesion also 'othered' them from Indian identifiers that centred on *desh* and *jati*. The association of Eurasian men with Raj employment, and the distinctly Western role and culture of Eurasian women, has left the community isolated in independent India.

Any study of a 'mixed' population under colonial rule cannot but show that the older histories' tendency to polarize rulers and ruled into distinct and separate enclaves simply rehashes colonial thinking. It is, however, important to keep colonial thinking in mind. It allows us to understand the difficulties presented by the deployment of convenient interpretations of what we now understand to be mutable concepts. Concepts such as race and nation, ill-defined as they were, were applied to people in the division of power and wealth; there would be no point studying Eurasians if that were not so.

CHAPTER 1

EURASIAN 'OTHERING'

Several authors have sought to establish how, when, and why the Eurasian *community* came into being.[1] All agree that the beginnings of a Eurasian community of British and Indian descent followed a series of 'proscriptions' formulated between the 1770s and the early nineteenth century.

The effects of legal proscriptions (Table 1.1) and informal 'usages'[2] were to deny Eurasians a fully British identity and the educational opportunities open to their European relatives, to restrict opportunities for employment and financial reward, to promote downward social mobility, and to lower their status. Authors vary on the 'proscriptions' they consider most important and what motives and effects they had, but all identify some of these directives as the 'push' that set Eurasians apart, causing them to come together into a nascent community.

This chapter reassesses the link between 'othering' and discrimination against Eurasians, and will comment on the interpretations provided in earlier accounts. I show how each change affected the community, but also that this approach cannot fully reveal the motivation behind the proscriptions.

1773: CONFUSION OVER NATIONAL STATUS[3]

The 1773 Regulating Act was identified by Hawes and Goodrich as the first Act to differentiate between Natives of India and British

Subjects.[4] The terms imply belonging to one 'nation' or other, neither of which had evolved a truly national identity. Nineteenth-century nationalities were nuanced by subcategories: e.g. martial Sikhs and Highlanders, 'primitive' Irish, and 'tribals'. 'British subject', a term that technically defined all within the British empire, was in reality shorthand for European 'whites' born in Britain or wherever their parents were temporarily domiciled. 'Native of India' meant non-European. Confusion resulted over what the terms meant for Eurasians, because their status was not addressed. For education, employment, defence, marriage, and access to law, Eurasians could be categorized simultaneously as European British Subjects, non-European British Subjects and Natives of India. In native states, they were never certain whether they would be subject to Muslim or British law. British administrators did not know whether to include Eurasians in returns on British subjects or not. There was no *official* designation for anyone of mixed race until 1827, when the inclusion of Eurasian widows (and continued exclusion of native widows) in Lord Clive's Fund prompted the British to define them.[5]

Uncertainty over Eurasians' nationality persists today, when many Anglo-Indians have adopted new countries, and others, despite Indian constitutional recognition as an Indian minority group, remain uncertain that they are accepted as 'native' by other citizens of post-colonial India. Eurasian national identity united Eurasians, in the sense that it posed a problem, but divided them along lines of language, ethnicity, gender, class, legitimacy, and other factors that define ethnicity or delineate community.

It is unlikely that the 1773 Act deliberately set out to strip Eurasians of British nationality since many Eurasians were still recognized by their extended British families, were still in government service, were still educated in Britain, and were in every sense British. The indecision of the next 50 years could have been deliberate, since it would have been easy to include a clause identifying them as either British subjects or natives of India. That lack of clarity was useful to the administration, which could include or exclude Eurasians as circumstances dictated. Later changes to the laws and regulations governing Europeans in India led to the

Table 1.1 Summary of Proscriptions Seen as Inimical to Eurasian Interests, 1773–1813.[6]

Date	Instrument	Effect/content
1773	Regulating Act[i]	Use of terms Natives of India *or* British Subjects. Eurasians not mentioned; status open to interpretation.
1786	Court of Directors' Directive, 14 March 1786[ii]	Bengal officers' illegitimate orphans cannot be returned to Britain. Many Eurasians but few European children illegitimate; severe effect on education, patronage, family connections for Eurasians.
1789	Recommendation of Cornwallis and letter from War Office[iii]	No officers or soldiers to be appointed as Europeans who could not prove that both parents were Europeans, 'without any mixture of the blood of natives of India'. Eurasians could not serve in regular army – limited employment and status.
1790	Court of Directors' Minute in 1790?[iv]	Ban on land ownership for Europeans and Eurasians from 1790 to 1837 – effectively confined Eurasians to Bombay, Madras, and Calcutta, the three presidency capital cities, and under British surveillance.
1791	Court of Directors' Directives, EIC[v]	Bar on covenanted Company service, marine, civil and military, for sons of natives (i.e. Eurasians) – further limited employment and status.
1793	Military consultations, Fort St George and London[vi]	Lord Clive's fund for EIC military and families specifically excludes Eurasians and natives from claiming benefits and is payable in Britain only – discouraging intermarriage and producing pauper families.
1795	Court of Directors' Minute, 1794[vii]	On recommendation of Cornwallis: no Eurasians to be combatants in EIC armies except as *sepoys* or musicians – loss of employment, and reduced status *or* military Eurasians led into service of native rulers.

(Continued)

Table 1.1 *(Continued)*

Date	Instrument	Effect/content
1790s	Court of Directors[viii] interpretation of Regulating Act of 1773	Eurasians increasingly seen by EIC as natives of India and not British subjects, and so could not serve on Calcutta juries – further 'Indianizing' Eurasians. Modified in 1827 to allow Christians to serve.
1803	Arthur Wellesley, August 1803, Military Proclamation[ix]	Recall of all Europeans (especially British but including Eurasians) in Maratha service. Eurasians now European when expedient, but could only serve Britain in 'irregular' service – EIC and regular army proscriptions against sons of natives remain in force.
1804	Regulations of Civil and Military Funds[x]	Benefits not available to Eurasian and native dependents. Financial hardship meant to discourage intermarriage, and benefits seen as encouragement to the sin of miscegenation.
1808	'Commander-in-Chief's Order'[xi]	All Anglo-Indians to be discharged from all ranks of the 'British Army' – evidence suggests that this did not happen.
1813	Charter Act, 1813[xii]	Hindus subject to Hindu law, Muslims to Muslim law, British subjects to law of England. EIC judiciary decision that the last-named meant 'British-born' left confusion over what law Eurasians subject to. Challenged in 1822 – legitimate Eurasians were British subjects, but usage as natives of India continued; Eurasian Christians had no access to civil law with respect to marriage or property.

increasingly frequent exclusion of Eurasians from the status of British subjects. The 1773 Act could, therefore, have been the first stimulus to Eurasian group formation.

1786: EURASIAN ORPHANS TO REMAIN IN INDIA[7]

In March 1786, the Company's directors resolved that the Bengal Military Orphan Society must not send officers' orphaned children to Britain for education unless they were legitimate[8] *and* of wholly European parentage. There had been arguments under this head in Bengal since the inception of the society. In November 1782, the managers asked Commander-in-Chief Eyre Coote to present their case to the governor and Council. They addressed objections already raised by persons unnamed 'whose opinions we have always respected very highly.' Amongst the objections cited, one was explicitly racial:

> the imperfections of the children, whether bodily or mental; that is whether consisting in their colour, their conformation, or their genius, would, in process of time, be communicated, by intermarriage, to the generality of the people of Great Britain; and by this means debase the succeeding generations of Englishmen.[9]

The managers counter-argued:

> it might, we conceive, be safely presumed, from the silence of the Legislature on this head, that the evil apprehended by some persons here must be altogether imaginary ... children of the same complection [sic] in the West Indies and America who have been educated in England, have neither proved chargeable to society, nor disgraceful to the human species.[10]

Several authors identify the 1786 Directive, and the discussions that preceded it, as significant because it heralded a divergence in prospects for European and Eurasian children.[11] Its effect was that Eurasians were excluded from following their fathers into Company service as 'gentlemen'. There was no law preventing a father purchasing a passage to Europe for his Eurasian children, and many continued to do so; racial categories remained flexible where there was wealth and influence. Once a boy was in England, however, his return to India could be blocked if it were contingent on Company employment. Thus, well-educated and wealthy Eurasians often stayed in Britain. A minority succeeded in gaining Company appointments and returned to India.

Employment prospects for those remaining in India as children were effectively blocked by their lack of a British public school education and influential patrons. Most Eurasians were, of course, unaffected directly by this order since, as the children of 'lesser men', most would have stayed in India anyway, and had only rudimentary education whether they were in England or India: their prospects were limited by class rather than access to patronage.

1789: ALL EUROPEAN CROWN ARMY[12]

When appointed governor-general in 1786, Cornwallis insisted on freedom to act as he saw fit and to overrule the Supreme Council when he wanted to. Burke objected when the bill was at committee stage: 'the principle of the bill was to introduce an arbitrary and despotic government in India'. He thought it unlikely that the decisions of one man could be fairer than the decisions of three (the Supreme Council). Nonetheless, the Bill was amended and the governor-general granted arbitrary powers.[13] Commanding all Crown regiments posted to India, Cornwallis banned 'officers and men born of black women' because of 'the injuries which would accrue to the discipline and reputation of HM's troops employed in India', and received retrospective War Office agreement.[14] Although Cornwallis was able to deploy Company troops as he wished without prior reference to London, it was two years (1791) before the directors banned recruitment of Eurasian officers for its armies.

The motives behind the exclusion of Eurasians from covenanted and commissioned posts were complex.[15] Valentia and, later, Stark cite fear that Eurasians would ape the 'mulattos' of San Domingo who led an uprising, a theory dismissed by Hawes since Haiti's revolution came later.[16] Fear of what could happen when colonists and settlers sought sovereignty was, however, a contemporary issue for many Britons and for Cornwallis in particular. He had, after all, been the commander of defeated British forces in America in 1781. He had first-hand, bitter experience of a settler army, aided by France and utilizing guerrilla warfare techniques adapted from Native Americans.

1790: RESIDENCE AND LAND OWNERSHIP RESTRICTED[17]

A ban on land ownership and rights of residence (cited by Anthony, Stark, and Hawes)[18] obliged Europeans and Eurasians to live within ten miles of a British settlement. Ross states: 'at this time no Europeans, except military officers and covenanted servants, were allowed to reside out of Calcutta, without a special license'.[19] The reforms determined:

> no British subject (excepting King's officers and the civil and the military covenanted servants of the Company) shall be allowed to reside beyond the limits of Calcutta, without entering into a bond to make himself amenable to the court of justice of the district in which he may be desirous of taking up his abode, in all civil causes that may be instituted against him by natives.[20]

Eurasians were included in this proscription; James Skinner's reward of a *jaghir* (for military services) was withdrawn because of it, and it was two years before government allowed him to exchange his pension for land near Delhi.[21] The ban was restated in the Charter Act of 1813, though the boundaries had been extended:

> nothing herein contained shall extend, or be construed to extend, to authorize the holding or occupying of any land or other immovable property, beyond the limits of the said several presidencies, by any British subject of his Majesty, otherwise

> than under and according to the permission of the Governments of the said presidencies.[22]

Eurasians sometimes used confusion about their nationality to advantage by asserting that they were not Europeans and were therefore exempt from this ban. Company policy, however, was to 'discourage' this 'troublesome' class.[23] George Sinclair was 'discouraged' in his ambition to become an indigo planter in a native state in 1832, because a Eurasian would likely be 'productive of future embarrassment'.[24] Since Sinclair later set up his indigo concern within Company territory, and ran it successfully for many years, the embarrassment did not reside in his business acumen.

The ban was relaxed in 1833[25] for those with government permission, and removed in April 1837:

> It is hereby enacted, that after the 1st day of May next, it shall be lawful for any subject of his Majesty to acquire and hold in perpetuity, or for any term of years, property in land, or in any emoluments issuing out of land, in any part of the territories of the East-India Company.[26]

That still did not allow Europeans or Eurasians licence to reside or work in native states, which were bound (or treated as though bound) by treaties requiring them to seek the express permission of the British before entertaining any 'foreigner':

> it is an important principle of Imperial policy that the entertainment by Native States of foreigners, whether European British subjects or other Europeans or East Indians, should be controlled . . . this principle is affirmed and maintained by the Government of India irrespective of our treaties.[27]

Government still considered Eurasians in Native states to be a 'troublesome' class, and it was easier to eject Eurasians than upset relations with the British. In 1882, the *Nizam* of Hyderabad was asked by the Resident by what authority he had employed a Eurasian called Butler; rather than answer, the *durbar* dismissed him.[28]

Whether to prevent access by native *durbars* to European expertise, to prevent exploitation of Indians by Europeans, or to discourage attachment to India, the effect was to urbanize the European and Eurasian population. Inclusion of Eurasians in the land ownership ban hit them disproportionately hard. Europeans could always buy property 'back home', whereas Eurasians born and bred in India, who were rarely wealthy, were unlikely ever to do so. It limited opportunities to diversify into employment or subsistence other than in commerce or government service. Thus, later proscriptions limiting government employment were particularly damaging to Eurasians.

1791: EMBARGO ON APPOINTMENTS TO COVENANTED POSTS

In April 1791, The EIC directors decreed 'no Person, the Son of a Native Indian, shall henceforward be appointed by this Court to employment in the Civil, Military or Marine Service of the Company'.[29] This order follows from the 1789 War Office order with respect to the Crown Army.[30] Hawes says that the order was not retrospective, although few Eurasians were henceforth appointed; those already in post continued to serve.[31] The wording of this order said no *appointments* would be made by the Court of Directors. A second order in November specified none could *serve*, but it was not retrospectively applied. Ricketts noted in 1830 that although the regulations were modified in 1827 such that for civil posts the embargo applied only to first-generation Eurasians, it continued 'by the established usages'.[32]

The Directors' motives were un-minuted, and there is nothing to suggest why being the 'son of a native Indian' should be a disqualification. What had changed was that the court had a new chairman and deputy, both Dundas' men, John Smith Burges and Francis Baring.[33] Appointed less than a week before, together with Manship, they also formed 'a Secret Committee agreeable to and for the purposes stated in the Acts of the 24th of His present Majesty's Reign Cap. 25 Sec 16 and of the 26th do. Cap 16 Sec 16 & 19'.[34]

These men were closely allied to politicians on the Board of Control, created by Pitt's India Act of 1784, who had sent Cornwallis to India to carry out reforms and 'clean up' Company service in India. Rather than the interpretation of Stark and Anthony that Eurasian exclusion was prompted by shareholder greed,[35] it is likely the decision was essentially political. Sons of natives might reasonably have been expected to have had at best divided loyalties.

1793: EURASIANS EXCLUDED FROM LORD CLIVE'S PENSION FUND[36]

Cornwallis used his executive powers in 1793 to decree that widows could not claim on Lord Clive's Fund, *in India*, unless they proved they were fully European.[37] Since by usage soldiers' Eurasian and Indian wives were not taken home 'on the strength',[38] and the men could not afford to take them independently, this excluded Eurasian families from the fund's benefits.[39]

The fund originally provided pensions to widows of soldiers of all ranks, with the proviso that they were 'widows or familys [sic] of such objects as the said Court of Directors shall in their discretions think fit'[40] but decisions had always been left to commanding officers, with the commander-in-chief and directors rubber-stamping their recommendations. From 1793, the directors insisted that payments no longer be made in India (except to widows proven to be Europeans).[41] They argued the fund was meant only for Europeans, that it would be expensive to pay Eurasians and Indians, and that payments would encourage vice.

This left native and Eurasian wives and children dependent on local charities. St Mary's Vestry, Madras said in 1805:

> The limitation with respect to Native Women is not specified in the original contract and ... the subsequent Regulations of the Court of Directors tend unequivocally to demonstrate that Widows of Officers and Soldiers of whatever denomination, were on producing the requisite Certificates, entitled to the Pension.[42]

The vestry argued there would have been no need for the fund in the first place if Eurasian and native wives were not to be included, since so few European soldiers were married to European women.[43] The rules were relaxed by 1824, after which pensions for all ranks could be paid in India by sanction of the governor-general but widows still had to produce marriage certificates.[44]

For Durba Ghosh, the debates and regulations of Lord Clive's Fund and the Bengal Military Orphan Fund (see above, 1786) were significant because they:

> contributed to the ruling apparatus in Bengal by providing an embryonic definition of the status of colonial subjects which would later feed into definitions of citizenship. Through the criteria for receiving financial benefits, ideas about who belonged to the world of British subjects in colonial India began to emerge.[45]

Ideas about who should be regarded as British were already circulating before this debate, but this fund's rules prompted a concrete contribution to official definitions. A Madras General Order, dated 15 June 1827, required widows claiming from the Lord Clive Fund to swear an oath that they were of European parentage *or* that they were 'country-born' or half-caste, terms rapidly amended to 'Indo-Briton' after communal protests. Before this, there had never been an official designation for people of mixed European and Indian descent.[46] The designation Indo-Briton was not universally welcomed; it implied a division of Eurasians into those of British and non-British descent: '[we] would prefer any [term] which embraces all Classes of our mixed race and thus obviate giving umbrage to any party.'[47]

1795: EURASIANS DISARMED[48]

In 1795, the governor-general banned Eurasian recruitment into the army, save a few non-combatant posts. Within three years, government was to reserve positions as musicians, in the

Company's native regiments, exclusively for wards of the various military orphanages.[49]

Sir John Shore succeeded Cornwallis in 1793, and was trusted to continue his reforms. Dundas told Cornwallis: 'Mr. Pitt and I ... agreed to recommend him to the Court of Directors as provisional successor to you',[50] and the king told Dundas: 'to be Governor-General at Bengal, no one could have been so properly thought of as Mr. Shore, who will certainly more explicitly follow the Civil plan Lord Cornwallis has laid down than any other person'.

Cornwallis was in London when, in 1794, Dundas asked for his 'opinion on the best mode of new-modelling the army in India, with a view to give safety and permanence to our Indian empire'. Cornwallis recommended that 'No persons who are not descended on both sides from European parents, can be admitted into the European branch of the service, except as drummers, fifers, or other musicians: nor can such persons be hereafter admitted on the establishment of European officers in Native troops, though those already in may remain ...'[51] In 1795, Shore implemented Cornwallis' policy barring Eurasians from military service except in non-combatant roles. Stark claims this policy was put into immediate effect, but his claim that 'Anglo-Indians in every branch of the army were *discharged* from service' was disputed by Hawes.[52] Stark and Anthony claimed the governor-general was forced into this action by greedy shareholders. Shore may well have been unwilling to implement this directive, since the Company army was already close to mutiny, but it originated with Cornwallis and Dundas rather than shareholders.[53]

The directive was a small part of wholesale reforms that Cornwallis and his faction were implementing. His larger aim was to ensure Company servants' loyalty to Britain by reducing their attachment to India:

> I do not conceive it possible that any system can be devised ... for the public good, unless, as a preliminary measure, the whole of our force in India ... shall be transferred to His Majesty's service ... it will be of essential importance to the interests of Britain, that Europeans should be discouraged [from] settling

> in our possessions in India, I look upon it to be highly expedient that it should be a fundamental principle in the new system, not only to relieve the corps of European troops frequently, but also to secure the return of all military men, who may be entitled to any provision from the public, to their mother country, by rendering all pensions and allowances to them after they... retire from the service, payable to those only who shall actually claim them in Europe.[54]

Since Eurasians usually lived and died their whole lives in India, and were of part-Indian ancestry, it is reasonable to conclude that Cornwallis saw them as irredeemably attached to India in a way that Europeans were not.

That he did not bar them from serving as other ranks in native regiments might argue against the interpretation that he was attempting to disarm the community, except that Eurasians would have been unlikely to serve as *sepoys*; they were paid considerably less than European troops and, at the time, were formed into corps with shared communal and religious roots. A further argument against this proscription as an attempt to disarm Eurasians was that they were still free to serve in native states, sometimes achieving positions of great power and influence. Whether this was because the British were not in a position to impose their will in these states or because they believed their own prejudice that Eurasians were not a martial race and therefore no threat, remains a moot point.

Under the British, whilst employment as bandsmen offered some security to Eurasian men, including pensions and, for their sons, education and future employment as bandsmen, these were limited opportunities for advancement, especially if serving with native regiments.[55]

1790S: EURASIANS NOT BRITISH ENOUGH TO BE JURORS

The disqualification of Eurasians from jury service stemmed from an increasing tendency to see them as *not* British subjects. The 1773 Regulating Act had specified that in Calcutta's Supreme Court

British subjects would be tried only by 'British subjects resident in the town of Calcutta, and not otherwise'. Better-educated Eurasians had at first been treated as eligible British subjects, but by the 1790s they were usually disqualified from jury service.

The official approach to Eurasians' qualification to serve on juries was confused and inconsistent because the 1773 Act used the terms 'British subject' and 'native of India' but did not indicate which Eurasians were. Opinion settled at some point in the 1790s when, with respect to jury service, Eurasians were invariably considered by usage to be natives of India even though in an 1822 ruling (Charles Reed *vs.* Byjuant Sing) the Supreme Court implied that legitimate Eurasians were British subjects.[56]

Government servants always enjoyed a higher status than non-officials even when of similar wealth and background, so exclusion from covenanted and military service had lowered Eurasians' social status. The growth to maturity of more Eurasians who were denied a European education also promoted downward social mobility and further coloured perceptions. Thus, social attitudes and usages rather than regulations or laws now restricted the acceptability of Eurasians as British subjects. In 1827, jury service was widened to include Christians, and thus Eurasians, but the latter still only as non-British subjects.[57]

1803: RECALL FROM NATIVE STATES[58]

Wellesley's 1803 proclamation is cited in letters from European and Eurasian officers in their appeals to government for pensions they believed it had promised them.[59] Many Eurasian men wanted to follow their fathers as military officers, but with Crown and Company armies closed to them could only serve in the armed forces of native states. Whilst such states and the British were at peace, many Eurasians rose to positions of responsibility and status.[60]

Grey estimated that there were upwards of 1,500 European and Eurasian officers serving native states in 1792,[61] and Hyderabad Records from 1806–7 show substantial numbers served in the ranks too, especially in the artillery.[62] Military service in native states was therefore an important source of employment and status for both Eurasians and Europeans.

Maratha hostilities prompted Wellesley's proclamation of 29 August 1803 recalling Britons and Eurasians from several Indian states. If they refused to return to British lines they were to be considered traitors, expediency having dictated that Eurasians were once again British subjects. Many Eurasian soldiers were subsequently briefly employed by the Company as irregulars, many units of which were disbanded at end of Maratha hostilities or in the Company army's reductions of 1808.[63] Hawes states that the last to go were those Eurasians who were in the *Nizam* of Hyderabad's employ. From Sydenham's reports on the *Nizam's* armies in 1807, some had previously been in Maratha employ then in irregular British units serving the *Nizam's* court.[64] They were finally replaced by seconded Company men in the 1820s.[65]

Increased British influence over native states further reduced opportunities for military service. Eurasians could continue in the service of Indian princes, but the requirement for permission of the Company was more often extended to include Eurasians than it had been previously. Native rulers, who in the past might not have been required to seek British sanction before employing Eurasians, found themselves having to explain why they had not sought permission before employing them.[66] Even the most powerful native states were subject to Company policy, albeit softened by diplomatic considerations: 'conduct towards the state of Hyderabad must be regulated by principles of peculiar delicacy and care'.[67]

Where it was impossible to enforce removal of Eurasian or European officers, they could be removed by less formal means, such as a bad character assessment leading to dismissal and replacement with the 'right sort' of man. The British advised the *Nizam* in 1806–7 on the reform of his armies. Of Rodriguez, Captain of the 5th French Corps: 'He is of a cruel disposition and bears a bad Character. He is of a very Low origin...' Of Adjutant Martine: 'He bears a very bad character and is of a turbulent and refractory disposition.' Terribio, an Indo-Portuguese captain, was described as quarrelsome.[68]

The significance of the 1803 proclamation is obvious: whenever British rule was under threat, Eurasians' British-ness was acknowledged. That status was removed, renewed, or left in abeyance as expediency dictated.

1804: CHARITABLE FUNDS CONTROVERSIES

From 1804 onwards, rules for the various civil and military charitable funds excluded from benefit native and Eurasian wives and children (regardless of marital status or legitimacy) in the belief that financial hardship would serve to 'discourage vice and ... connections with native women'; benefits 'would encourage sin'.[69]

Rather than exclude natives and Eurasians, the Bengal Civil Fund (1804) assumed all civil servants' children and widows were European and legitimate. Calcutta society was split, with the old guard arguing that illegitimate children should be included and younger men educated at Fort William College (such as Charles Metcalfe, who later fathered three illegitimate Eurasian sons) claiming:

> the Civil Fund, if loaded by the proposed extension of its objects to illegitimate Children, will tend to the destruction of public principles, the overthrow of established and sacred institutions, to the encouragement of prostitution and vice, to the disgrace of the character of this Settlement, and to the injury of the interests of our country.

Opinion was divided equally, but Governor-General Wellesley, with Court of Directors' support, ruled against the inclusion of illegitimate children.[70]

Persons entitled to benefits from Madras Military Fund regulations (1808) were:

> [1.] All widows and legitimate children of marriages contracted before 1st April 1808. [2.] With regard to marriages contracted subsequent to the 1st April 1808, it shall be an indispensable

> qualification that both the parents of any and every claimant shall have been . . . of unmixed European blood . . . four removes from an Asiatic or African being considered as European blood. [3.] Legitimate children of those who were married subscribers on the 1st April 1808 (provided they be the offspring of such marriages), as also the legitimate descendants of those children, shall be entitled to the full benefits of the fund, either as orphans or hereafter as widows, notwithstanding the restriction contained in the preceding article. [4.] Marriages subsequent to the 1st April 1808, with persons of mixed blood . . . exclude the widow and children from the benefits of the fund . . .[71]

A review in 1824 prompted Munro, Governor of Madras, to say 'the proposed allowance to half-caste wives and children of European soldiers is in my opinion highly objectionable'.[72]

The Bombay Military Fund had similar regulations from November 1816. All marriages and legitimate children before that date qualified, but only the 'unmixed' or 'four removes from the Asiatic' qualified thereafter. Bengal's Military Fund admitted illegitimate children, but required fathers to make reasonable provision or risk their exclusion. It also expected men to provide for the mothers a monthly sum of 30 sicca rupees for native and 50 for European women.[73] The Bengal Mariners and General Widows' Fund was less squeamish, stating: 'This Fund affords provision to the widows and legitimate children of subscribers* belonging not only to this Presidency, but all British settlements . . .' The asterisk is followed by a footnote explaining 'Members of this Institution are generally persons in the middling class of Society, and individuals employed in the different public offices and other situations under Government.'[74]

The King's Military Fund (for Crown forces) stipulated:

> Every lady seeking relief from the Fund, on becoming a widow, at either of the three Presidencies, is required to embark for Europe, within two months, (or earlier if possible) from the death of her husband, after which period, the maintenance

> allowance ceases, unless it shall satisfactorily appear to a General or Regimental Committee, that no opportunity of procuring a passage to Europe has occurred at such Presidency, within that time, in which case, an additional award may be obtained from the Committee to the period of the earliest possible departure of such widow. On the death of a subscriber at out stations remote from the several Presidencies, his widow is allowed a period of four months to repair to the nearest Presidency.[75]

Eurasian wives and children were thus excluded by the insistence on a return to Europe.

Besides restrictions on charitable funds, the Company's soldiers' marriage allowance from 1810 was only payable if the wife was of British birth. This rule was rescinded in 1824 but the allowance was then paid at half the rate of the pension, and marriage allowance paid to Europeans and only for Eurasian (not native Christian) wives.[76]

Goodrich identifies the 1804 Bengal Civil Fund debate as crucial; prior to this, discrimination against Eurasians had come from London, with Company servants in India largely wanting all their children treated equally.[77] However, two points suggest otherwise. Firstly, the directive on Bengal orphans, with objections raised in India, predate the debate by two decades. Secondly, Cornwallis' reforms disbarring Eurasians from covenanted posts, civil and military, predate it by a decade. Both proscriptions rapidly decreased the status and wealth of Eurasians, and so in a society where position and connections meant so much there was already discrimination towards Eurasians prior to 1804.

1808: The Company Discharges Last Serving Eurasians?

Anthony claims an order was issued in 1808 discharging Anglo-Indians from all ranks of the British army.[78] Stark also mentions that 'Anglo-Indians were thrown out of military service', citing (without a source) an order from the commander-in-chief.[79] Perhaps both authors were referring to the discharging of men recruited to Company, Crown, or irregular units that had been temporarily expanded during the Maratha crisis and later disbanded. These were units in which Eurasians would have figured prominently, but there is no evidence that discharges targeting Eurasians occurred at this date. Hawes found many who remained in post,[80] and I have found evidence that in Madras Eurasians continued to serve in the Company's military.[81]

1813: CHARTER ACT

The 1813 Charter Act decreed British subjects were subject to English law, leaving Eurasians concerned about their legal standing. In Ricketts' words: 'We are not recognised as British Subjects by the Supreme Court of Calcutta, if residing in the *Mofussil*.'[82] They were subject to Muslim criminal law, but no civil law governed Christian marriages, property or succession. The Calcutta Supreme Court considered legitimate urban Eurasians to be British subjects, but normal usage conflated Eurasian with illegitimate and continued to assume that 'British subject' meant European British to the exclusion of all Eurasians.[83]

The situation was no clearer to *mofussil* administrators. They consulted the judicial department on the legal standing of Eurasians and Europeans, with respect to criminal proceedings, divorce, vagrancy, and (frequently) employment.[84] The answers they received indicate that the power, influence, or importance of native rulers could affect how individual cases were handled. Hyderabad, for example, had to be treated as an exceptional case because 'it could go against British interests to upset the Nawab' who talked directly with the viceroy.[85] The widowed Eurasian wife of Awadh's King Ghazi Uddin Haidar spent 12 years petitioning the British Resident for assistance to leave Lucknow; he did nothing rather than risk accusations of interfering in the royal household.[86] Eurasians were left in a difficult position because they could never be certain whether they would be treated as British subjects or as natives of India.

MOTIVES

It is tempting, because the proscriptions were collectively inimical to Eurasian interests, to infer deliberate and malicious intent, but the motivation behind individual proscriptions is not always obvious.

Fear of Eurasians' racial 'degeneracy' seems an unlikely motive. If it had been a factor, then legislation to discourage intermarriage and miscegenation should have been seen throughout the empire. Fear of Eurasians as likely leaders of a revolt is implausible. Firstly, the revolts in Spanish America had not yet occurred, so the scenario of 'mulatto' leaders siding with blacks was yet to happen. Secondly, they were not feared as potential leaders of natives because the British believed Indians despised Eurasians. There was, however, fear of settlers *per se*. This had less to do with race than with maintaining allegiance to Britain. The fear was that European settlers and Eurasians together, aping American settlers, might take India for themselves. Once European loyalty was secured, then Eurasian's potential disloyalty could be ignored.

Since Company shareholders would have wished to maximize their profits greed is often cited as a motive for the proscriptions, but this would not have been served by reducing the Eurasian and Indian workforce; that only increased the number of expensive Europeans needed. As for disbarring Eurasian and native claimants against charities, that money would never have found its way into the pockets of shareholders wanting better returns. Where greed for patronage is suggested then, again, nothing was served by removing Eurasians or Indians from subordinate posts. Shareholders were not looking for such lowly posts for their relatives and friends. Administrative reform was an important motive behind many changes instituted in the 1773 India Bill and in subsequent parliamentary legislation. British public opinion believed Company servants were enriching themselves dishonestly and fighting expensive wars and battles for that purpose. There was also concern that India itself, whether through climate or native influence, caused Europeans' characters and constitutions to degenerate. Perhaps Eurasians were targeted by this motive too – except that the despised nabobs and warmongers were Europeans, not Eurasians.

Legitimation of rule is also linked to reform. If every European was the embodiment of racial superiority then controlling behaviour, through regulations, social usage, and coercion, was necessary. The right to reside in the *mofussil* was limited to the most senior officers because they had the most to lose if they failed to perform as *burra sahibs*. A privileged few non-officials could join them only if their characters and ancestry passed muster. Confining 'lesser' Britons and Eurasians to cantonments and the main cities made them easier to control. Eurasians' nativity made their movements less controllable until later when British hegemony was more widespread and compliance might more often be rewarded with employment. The 'civilizing mission' also influenced events around this time. Certainly some wanted to proselytize the 'heathens', calling for missionaries to be allowed into India, though these were hardly welcomed by the Company. However, the influence of those who wished to civilize the behaviour of Britons, both at home and in India, was contemporaneous and consistent with the proscriptions. The difference of opinion between the older and younger men over the Bengal orphans illustrates a change in standards of public behaviour in the officer cadre. The proscriptions might be viewed therefore as a move to prevent Indian acculturation of Company servants.

Charity and protection for the poor was a moot point, whether in Britain or India, but one Madras governor was in no doubt:

> It is easy to appeal to humanity; but it is often the harsh duty of Government to resist its call, ... If we leave the half-caste people to themselves, they will go on ... increasing slowly, according to their means of subsistence. They will seek employment as servants, mechanics, shopkeepers, and merchants ... When there is no longer room for them there, succeeding generations will be forced to look for a subsistence as bullock-men, peons, labourers, and *ryots*. This is what has happened to the descendents of the Portuguese on the west coast, and there is no reason why the same thing should not happen to the descendents of English soldiers, if it be not prevented by imprudent interference.[87]

Was it a Christian duty to help Eurasians and poor whites, or did that make them dependent and remove the incentive to work? Did a safety net for soldiers' families encourage men to marry without permission? First-generation Eurasians were also likely to be illegitimate, and were those born 'in sin' entitled to be treated as 'deserving' poor?

If parliament's 1773 and 1813 Regulating Acts were meant to be directed against Eurasians, then they would surely have mentioned them. Their exclusion from Calcutta juries by the 1790s was a matter of usage not legislation. Attempts were made to assign native status based on illegitimacy, but Eurasians were not formally defined as natives of India until much later.

The directive banning repatriation of Bengal officers' orphans unless legitimate and wholly European appears to target Eurasians, but legitimate and wholly European children of lower-class whites were also left in India.

The requirement that officers of the king's regiments be wholly European was directed at weakening settler ties – embodied in the Eurasians 'mixed' blood. The ban on land ownership for Europeans and Eurasians was in keeping with other reforms designed to clean up the Company's reputation – reducing opportunities for warmongering and personal gain. It was never certain that Eurasians were meant to be included, and generally in this early period they were not. The 1791 directive barring sons of natives from covenanted Company service was justified by the presumption of Asiatic dishonesty.[88] But race was assessed on appearance. If a fair-skinned Eurasian presented in Britain, and no one mentioned or even knew his mother's ethnicity, how could the ban have been enforced?

Changes to the rules of both civil and military funds excluded both Eurasian and native claimants. But most private soldiers' families in Britain were similarly ignored by the army and thrown back on 'the parish'. That Europeans in India were supported was the unusual part.

Cornwallis' 1795 decision that no Eurasians could be combatants in Company armies was not intended to disarm them because it left them free to serve native rulers. Rather, it anglicized the Company's European force. Nor did Wellesley's 1803 proclamation disarm

Eurasians; he used them extensively as irregulars. The elusive 1808 order discharging Eurasians from the 'British Army' is probably a misreading of a peacetime reduction of irregular corps.

COMMUNAL RESPONSE

Withdrawal of recognition and assistance by the British authorities, increasing social distance between Europeans and Eurasians, and the growing numbers of distressed Eurasians necessitated an organized response from the Eurasians themselves. They had no choice but to band together to help one another, prompting prominent men in Calcutta and Madras to form associations representing the interests of Eurasians to government, organizing charitable support, educating their young, and promoting employment. The better-educated, wealthy and philanthropic emerged as informal leaders, and a Eurasian press grew to serve the community.[89] Some churches, formally or informally, became predominantly Eurasian establishments.[90] Adversity drew Eurasians together into a nascent community with its own values, issues, and institutions.[91]

In 1805, the benefaction of St Mary's Church in Madras was amongst the earliest visible signs of communal activity, with the vestry supporting the native wives and Eurasian children of departed soldiers.[92] By 1823, the vestry supported 7,623 persons. Besides contributions from the congregation, it had benefited from large donations from three men representing the diverse roots of the Eurasian community. Charles Weston was an Indo-Briton, Claude Martin was French, and John Barretto a prominent Indo-Portuguese.[93] All three were renowned philanthropists.

Education was a major communal concern because so few could travel to Britain. Elementary provision, provided by small private schools or churches, delivered basic literacy but did not equip Eurasians (or poor whites) with the education required for advancement. Government initiatives addressed Muslim and Hindu education by providing government-sponsored English-medium schools – but these tended to be in the wrong parts of town for Eurasians, who lived alongside Europeans.[94] The community established the Christian non-denominational Parental Academy in Calcutta. Set up in 1823, it was the earliest of the major private English-medium and overtly Christian schools, and was intended primarily to educate its own community. It was quickly followed by Calcutta Grammar School, which was expressly Church of England.[95]

Political organizations formed to represent the community, though this was always problematic since so many Eurasians were government employees. An association of a few dozen men had petitioned the government in 1818, thereby proving to those who wished to interpret it that way that Eurasians were troublesome and dangerous.[96] In Madras in 1827, over 200 Eurasian men were able to sign a petition to the governor over the name by which they were to be designated.[97] However, they did not represent all Eurasians and the government heard from another Madras group claiming to represent a section of the community who held a different view. In 1830, John Ricketts was dispatched from Calcutta to London to present a petition with over 600 signatories, against the wishes of another faction within the Calcutta Association who publicly denounced the action.[98]

In these few examples the existence of an emerging Eurasian community can be seen. No one has argued otherwise. The question that remains unanswered is what were the motives behind orders, laws, and 'usages' that caused such a dramatic change in the circumstances of India's Eurasians?

PROBLEMS OF INTERPRETING MOTIVES

A recognizable community of Anglophone, 'mixed-race' Christians came into being as a result of the series of measures around the turn of the nineteenth century that excluded Eurasians from a fully British identity. The motivation of the Company's directors in effectively 'othering' Eurasians has provoked much discussion. Disagreement between authors who have explored Eurasian othering centres on emphasis and motives rather than effects, but the true motives behind the proscriptions leading to Eurasian 'othering' are hard to find. The brevity of directives recorded in the directors' court minute books, of army regulations, and of the governor-generals' standing orders obfuscate underlying motives, dissent, and discussion prior to their enactment.[99] Near contemporary collections of the writings of Wellesley and Cornwallis (both include Dundas' writings) are more illuminating, revealing larger plans of which these 'laws' were a small part,[100] but even here, authors deliberately omitted names, said certain topics were best left for private discussions, or referred to topics (unspecified) which they had already discussed and did not commit to paper.

Departmental records from India are a rich source of information on how such laws were to be interpreted and enacted, revealing custom and practice, confusion, and prejudices as well as the flexibility necessary in everyday administration. What they do not reveal is motivation. 'Humble petitions' from Eurasians, sometimes included in departmental records, reveal which issues led to concerted group action or caused division and dissent. Petitions, from individuals, such as the soldiers who left Maratha service in 1803, reveal the effects of the governor-general's proclamation on their military careers and financial security. Again, these are unhelpful for establishing motives for the proscriptions discussed above.

There has been no work on the beginnings of the Eurasian community in India since Hawes' book was published in 1996. Since then, recent works on the British Raj have recognized that the relationship between metropolis and colony worked both ways; British identity was itself undergoing rapid change, and lessons learned in one part of the emerging empire might shape actions in another.[101]

Addressing issues and personalities at home and elsewhere in the empire may help us better understand the motives behind the proscriptions that effectively turned Eurasians from British subjects into 'others'. In the next chapter, therefore, three men (Henry Dundas, Richard Wellesley, and Charles Cornwallis) have been selected for discussion from the many whose influence was felt in India around the turn of the nineteenth century. These three illustrate how events, priorities, and personal experiences, at home or elsewhere in the empire, informed and affected what they did with regard to Indian reform; placing their actions in a wider context may throw light on their motives for actions that affected the Eurasians.

CHAPTER 2

HIDDEN AGENDAS

The legal proscriptions discussed in the previous chapter barred many Indians and Eurasians from EIC employment, and were the method by which Eurasian 'othering' was initially achieved. At the time, the priorities of the Board of Control and the Company's Court of Directors were to firmly affiliate Company servants to Britain, improve Company profitability, and – by removing native influence, believed to be a source of corruption and greed – to improve its image. Claims of 'oppression' and 'cruel measures enacted against the Anglo-Indian race', whilst describing the effects of the proscriptions, do not fit comfortably with this picture; more likely, the damage caused to Eurasians was incidental.

Other than noting the rise of evangelical Christianity and the moral resurgence in Britain, no study has yet considered the effects of other profound changes within metropolitan Britain in relation to British treatment of India's Eurasians. Some of these comprised the specific interests of influential and powerful men. Classes of British people, who had previously played little or no role in empire, were beginning to find themselves included. Scots demanded, under the terms of the 1707 Act of Union, greater access to English markets abroad. The 1800 Act joining Ireland and Britain came with the expectation of Catholic emancipation and inclusion. Ireland and Scotland had huge economic problems and large dissatisfied populations that threatened the integrity of the United Kingdom.

Britain was also rocked by two events of enormous political importance; the American Revolution and the protracted war with revolutionary France. All of these contributed to the reshaping (perhaps invention)[1] of a British identity, and to the mind-set of those who served in the wider empire, at the moment of Eurasian exclusion. The loss of the north American colonies and the huge upheavals in Spanish America where settler, mulatto, and native populations rose against their European masters in Haiti, Mexico, and Peru contributed to an anxious reappraisal of Britain's imperial endeavours. Few previous studies have considered the personal interests of individual players, whether in parliament, or amongst the Company's directors, or in India itself, and how their personal agendas brought contemporary British issues such as these to bear on Company and government policy towards India, and none have explored these issues in relation to the Eurasian population.

It is significant that the Eurasian 'problem' surfaced around 1784, when the parliament-dominated Board of Control was set up to direct the Company. Whilst the Company's directors may always have made decisions with their own pecuniary interest to the fore,[2] the same cannot be said of many British parliamentarians (other than the India interest group) for whom, even when deputed to oversee the Company, apparently unrelated issues were just as pressing. Henry Dundas, for example, chaired the Board of Control but was also deeply committed to extending Scottish interests within the empire, subverting Irish Catholic disaffection,[3] and strengthening Britain's commercial pre-eminence globally.[4] Governor-General and Commander-in-Chief Cornwallis' experiences in America, before he ever set foot in India, shaped his distrust of settler communities, whose loyalties to Britain he distrusted. But, like Dundas, he thought Catholic recruitment would reduce dissent in Ireland and was happy to encourage raising Irish regiments for service elsewhere, including India, because it brought employment and incomes. Governor-General Richard Wellesley, also a Board appointment, was an Anglo-Irish peer and later Lord-Lieutenant of Ireland. He believed empire was best served by stability at home, so unrest in Ireland was high on his list of priorities. He championed Catholic emancipation and any moves likely to improve the lot of impoverished Irish Catholics, in order to bolster their loyalty.

This chapter considers these three men and their involvement with some of the aforementioned issues, thereby offering new insights into the motives for, and the timing of, the apparent *volte face* with regard to the place of Eurasians in India. They were in positions of great influence at this crucial point in the history of India's Eurasians, but it is possible to show that other considerations were far more pressing to these men, and much of contemporary Britain, than the effects their actions had on Eurasians. This approach, broadening the historical context, allows a more objective assessment of the motives behind the actions that set Eurasian 'othering' in motion.

CHARLES CORNWALLIS AND SETTLERS

Cornwallis was a soldier from 1756 until his death in 1805. He held several military and civil positions, including second-in-command of British forces in the American Revolution, Governor-General of India, and Lord-Lieutenant of Ireland. In India and Ireland, he was given plenipotentiary powers to represent Britain's interests.[5] In Ireland in 1798, his 'great object' was 'consolidating the British Empire'.[6] The same held true in America and India. His remit in India was to reform the Company armies and civil service, end corruption, and 'anglicize' the British presence. His powers to act independently meant he did not hesitate in decisions about deployment of the Company's civil and military personnel, and in making war with Mysore. Even the 'permanent settlement' of land revenue in Bengal, referred back to the Board for decision, had already been discussed with Dundas prior to his departure for India.[7] Cornwallis' personal experiences and prejudices had a marked effect on the administration of British India,[8] and the official 'othering' of Eurasians of British descent began during his tenure.[9]

During the American Revolution, Cornwallis had been the local commander who surrendered to combined American and French forces at Yorktown. Despite local military superiority there, loyalist militias, who could have significantly altered the course of the war, were disregarded by British commanders, including Cornwallis. He was never publicly blamed for the loss of America, but as a professional soldier felt humiliated by defeat at the hands of the rebels' commander, George Washington, who, to him, was a mere militia man. Cornwallis sought success elsewhere to recover and enhance his reputation, though he portrayed his offices as a painful 'duty' he would rather have avoided. His experience of rebellions in India, Ireland, and colonial America had a lasting effect, colouring his attitudes towards anyone who might usurp British power. Bayly noted he had 'disliked and distrusted settlers, having no time for either loyalist or republican 'banditti'.[10] He felt much the same about European *boxwallahs*, Indians, and any corrupt British officials.

For many Britons, America, like India, had represented a chance for second sons to amass a fortune, or to gain land and establish themselves as settlers. Its loss removed those opportunities, unless they were willing to serve under a now foreign government. There were also 'redcoats' who had fought in America, who needed to be disbanded or redeployed. On top of that, many American loyalists had been ejected from the United States, some left for the West Indies, Britain, or India, and 40,000 crossed into Canada. Its American defeat also dented British confidence in its role as a world power. If a justification or explanation could assuage embarrassment, then it was that the rebels were themselves of British descent; there had therefore been no defeat by a foreign people. This logic can be seen as a beginning of racial justification for British rule elsewhere. For Britain and Cornwallis, India offered the chance of recovering dented pride and reputation as well as a role for those Britons and loyalists who could no longer be deployed in America.

Whilst in America Cornwallis was twice offered India but declined,[11] until parliament granted the governor-general full powers without prior reference to London or the Supreme Council in India, and he was made commander-in-chief of the armies, regular and Company. In February 1786, Cornwallis wrote about his appointment to India: 'much against my will, and with grief of heart, I have been obliged to say yes, and to exchange a life of ease and content, to encounter all the plagues and miseries of command and public station'.[12] We can safely conclude India was not his first love. He was governor-general from 1786 to 1793, during which time Dundas was always the moving force behind the Board of Control, despite its having three successive presidents. Cornwallis' remit was to devise and implement administrative reform, civil and military. He could not entirely avoid warfare, nor, without provoking a mutiny, was he able to enact many of the military reforms that he thought necessary. Nonetheless, he did institute widespread measures to 'clean up' the Company's reputation. The direction these reforms took was agreed with Dundas before he set sail,[13] but he brought his own 'baggage' too, especially his distrust of colonists and settlers. He was determined to unite the Indian military under one head because in America he had seen the effects of divisions within British command structures.[14] He also brought 25 years' experience of the regular army's distressing attitudes to camp followers, marriage, and soldiers' families, as discussed below.

Cornwallis was determined to fight corruption in India, and, since he believed all 'natives of Hindostan' to be corrupt and distrusted those Europeans with close Indian connections,[15] his solution was to exclude Indians and anglicize the service. Anglicization also meant change for British men, to weaken their connections with India in whatever form they took. As early as 1787, Cornwallis wrote to Dundas about the Resident of Benares; together with a salary of Rs 1,000 a year from the Company, he was making Rs 400,000 a year in 'emoluments' and held a complete monopoly over commerce. Cornwallis did not believe this Resident to be unique; almost all collectors, he said, were deeply involved in private commerce through a third party, either a relative or friend, not in Company service. To decrease corruption and stop company servants' distraction with private trade, he insisted they be paid well enough to rise above considerations of personal advantage and profit. Higher salaries allowed Company servants an honest means to accumulate a 'pension pot', shorten their stay in India, and facilitate their rapid return 'home'.

Cornwallis separated judicial and revenue-collection functions into distinct branches of government. Ross, paraphrasing Cornwallis' attitude and describing the legal system before his reforms, said European's deficient 'knowledge of the language or the habits of the natives' meant that because 'natives were the sole judges corruption generally prevailed to an unlimited extent'. Judicial reform included restricting native judges to cases of Rs 50 or less, and insistence that other civil and criminal cases must be heard by Europeans.[16]

British public opinion believed Company wars were motivated by its military officers' desire for prize money and booty. Cornwallis believed anglicization of European military servants, paying them properly, and addressing issues of status between the Company and regular armies would focus their ambitions firmly on returning 'home'. In 1783, British officers in the Company's armies were complaining their pay was lower, and promotion slower, than in Crown regiments.[17] In 1789, fearing a settler community whose interests differed from those of Britain (like his nemesis, the American rebels), Cornwallis wrote to the Directors:

> it ought to be part of the political system for the management of India to discourage and prevent Europeans ... particularly European officers, from colonising and settling in this country; ... when they have reconciled their minds to relinquish all thoughts of returning to their native country, they will soon become indifferent, or ... even hostile to its interests; and many circumstances might in time arise ... in which a number of men of such dispositions might have it in their power to create serious embarrassment to Government.[18]

Although Cornwallis did not succeed in merging Company and Crown armies, he did anglicize all ranks by barring 'sons of natives' from European regiments except in the lowliest positions.[19]

The gradual change in status of Eurasians from European to 'native' follows from Cornwallis' anglicization policies. He considered Eurasians both settler and Indian, so they were doubly repugnant to him. The directors' decision that Bengal officers' illegitimate orphans (usually Eurasians) could not be returned to Britain came soon after Cornwallis agreed to go to India.[20] Debarred, from Company service, from an English education (for most), increasingly from jury service, and later from Fort William college and the best tutors, a racially-motivated gap was first created between Eurasians and Europeans in Bengal.

The relevance of race to some of the proscriptions inimical to Eurasians is complex. So far as Cornwallis' attitudes can be determined, race was a factor but so were cost, military efficiency, and strengthening company servants' allegiance to Britain. Cornwallis' background as a career soldier must also be considered; he had been a regular army man for 25 years before he set foot in India and had a reputation as someone outstanding at logistics, going on to become Master-General of Ordnance when he returned to Europe. To a logistics specialist, anything (including families) not directly connected with the deployment of fighting men was a drain on military resources and efficiency.

It was never clear on what basis the 1790 ban on land ownership for Europeans[21] applied to Eurasians, except that it was Company policy to control the image and influence of their European kin. Though undoubtedly framed in racial terms, two further proscriptions from Cornwallis were aimed at anglicizing the Company's servants by discouraging intermarriage and settling, rather than at punishing their progeny.

His 1789 recommendation that no military officers or soldiers with 'the blood of natives of India' could serve in the regular army[22] was by definition racially explicit, as was the directors' decision in 1791 to exclude sons of natives from all covenanted Company service.[23] It may seem odd that Cornwallis did not bar Eurasians from military service in the princely states, because superficially this decision undermined his anglicization policy. It was, however, very useful; it provided intelligence about the princes and placated the fathers of Eurasian sons. He went on, after leaving India, to recommend that no Eurasians should be combatants in European regiments but they could serve as *sepoys*. Again Cornwallis' motivation was not simply race; it was the Eurasians imagined split allegiance as Indians and settlers.[24]

The 1793 changes to Lord Clive's Fund may appear solely attributable to race, but were far more complex. Many Eurasian and native dependents were reduced to pauperism by them, but the proscription on payments in India to Europeans clarifies the real motivation.[25] Whilst legally free to marry, any soldier who did so 'off the strength' was treated as single and (regardless of race) no provision was made for his family.[26] This was just as callously applied in England as anywhere else. In Cornwallis' time, England's military families relied on Poor Law and parish relief whilst their husbands were away; the army refused to accept any responsibility for them or even recognize their existence. No doubt Cornwallis would have wished to treat all 'off the strength' families in India in precisely the same way; he would have seen this as military efficiency. However, there was no Poor Law or parish relief in India to care for European women and children, and the British could not be seen to abandon their own. The paucity of European women, along with Cornwallis' desire to discourage settlers, meant that repatriation, with payments from Clive's fund in England, was expedient. Whilst the abandonment of Eurasian and native dependents was harsh, it was meant to discourage European men from further miscegenation and settling. The treatment of Eurasians and natives was entirely in keeping with the army's attitude to all 'off the strength' families and followers. It was the support for Europeans that was unusual.

With his reputation as an administrator further enhanced, Cornwallis returned from India in 1795 and was appointed 'Master-General of the Ordnance', a cabinet-level but military post with responsibility for military logistics, engineering, procurement, and field hospitals. He retained this office even whilst serving as Lord-Lieutenant of Ireland, and continued to be involved with Indian affairs until his return to the subcontinent and untimely death there.[27] Even when he was not in India, his interests and experiences are therefore relevant to this discussion.

Writing to his friend Ross, days after arriving in Ireland as Lord-Lieutenant, Cornwallis described his new post as 'my idea of perfect misery'. He could please neither the Protestant ascendancy nor the Catholics. Of the Protestants, he complained: 'the violence of our friends, and their folly in endeavouring to make it a religious war, added to the ferocity of our troops who delight in murder, most powerfully counteract all plans of conciliation'.[28] He believed, like Wellesley, that severe treatment of Catholics by the Protestant ascendancy provoked Catholic dissent in Ireland. Protestants resented his failure to 'understand their difficulties' and Catholics resented the proscriptions he imposed on them and his harsh treatment of captured rebel leaders. Unlike Wellesley, who was motivated by a desire to improve the lot of Irish Catholics, his motivation was pacification and the rule of law.

In 1797, before he had set foot in Ireland, Cornwallis was pessimistic about Britain's ability to resist a French invasion: 'Torn as we are by faction, without an army, without money, trusting entirely to a navy whom we may not be able to pay, and on whose loyalty ... no firm reliance is to be placed.'[29] And yet by 1805, French hostility had prompted the staggering figure of one in five British men to enlist.[30] Once in Ireland, he was immediately faced with violent rebellion (amounting to civil war) and a republican faction who saw their best hope for emancipation in a French invasion.[31] He wrote to Pitt that he distrusted the Irish Light Infantry, thought the militia formidable only to their friends, and that the regular army regiments were skeleton forces of raw recruits.[32] He was even asked what troops he could spare for India. It is not surprising that he felt miserable. Cornwallis had pressed for the Act of Union of 1801 as a means to encourage Irish loyalty, not to provoke further revolt, but his continued involvement with Indian affairs was to provide a convenient and immediate 'safety valve'. If he could not spare loyal troops, and Catholic troops were of suspect loyalty when in Ireland, Richard Wellesley and Henry Dundas were happy to recruit them for service in India. Cornwallis had wanted more European troops there anyway, and he shared the views of the other two that greater involvement of the Irish in British affairs would build loyalty to king and country. Irish recruitment is considered more fully in my discussion of Richard Wellesley.

After Ireland, and negotiating a brief peace with France, Cornwallis returned to India for a second term as governor-general, but promptly died. Shore and Wellesley had continued his reform policies, and his second-term priorities were to have been peace with the Marathas and Company debt reduction.

Cornwallis is described by Bayly as a transitional figure, rooted in old-fashioned unquestioning devotion to the monarchy but pointed forward to the new Victorian type of Crown servant.[33] His numerous references to his personal sacrifices for the sake of duty, taken together with his reforms of the Indian administration, would support this view. His obvious belief in European superiority can, perhaps, best be understood as a form of patriotism rather than racism as we understand it today. His belief in Indian inferiority underlay his policies designed to remove Europeans from their 'corrupting' influence. What is less clear is whether he saw Indians' 'corruption' to be a biological, racial quality or a cultural one inherent in non-Christian society. The fact that during his administration, and afterwards when he was still consulted on Indian affairs, so many barriers excluded Eurasians from responsible government posts and European society suggests the former. His belief that Europeans were corrupted through association with Indians suggests the latter.

RICHARD WELLESLEY AND IRISH CATHOLICS

Wellesley was an Anglo-Irish landholder, peer and MP, who served as Governor-General of India from 1798 to 1805, as foreign secretary from 1809 to 1812, and in several high Irish offices from 1821 to 1835.[34] Though a prominent member of the Protestant ascendancy, he was a long-standing champion of Catholic emancipation. In a letter to Lord Liverpool on the subject, he said:

> At the remote period of the year 1797, upon the eve of departure for India, I stated to the late Mr. Pitt my solicitude that he should direct his attention to the settlement of Ireland; and I expressed to him my conviction that Ireland could neither be happily settled, nor firmly united to Great Britain, without a concurrent settlement of the claims of his Majesty's Roman Catholic subjects.[35]

He made an impassioned speech in January 1812, stressing Catholic emancipation as vital to the safety of the empire.[36] That spring, he resigned his post as Secretary of State for Foreign Affairs because he was 'resolved to stand or fall with the Catholic cause'.[37] The prince regent invited him to form an administration. He failed to gain enough support because he prioritized 'the state of the laws affecting the Roman Catholics, with a sincere and earnest desire to bring that important question to a final and satisfactory settlement'.[38]

As Lord-Lieutenant of Ireland from 1822 to 1828, he fought tirelessly for full Catholic emancipation. He was welcomed by all, Catholic rebel and Protestant landowner alike, as the best hope for an end to insurrection and oppression.[39] In 1828, he and his brother Arthur, Duke of Wellington, disagreed over the 'coercion bills', with Wellesley claiming that draconian laws and oppression were the cause of insurrection and Wellington claiming that such laws were the only protection against the rebels.[40] Even after he resigned his post as Lord-Lieutenant of Ireland, and after the Catholic Emancipation Bill had passed into law (1829), he continued to fight for Catholic rights until his death in 1835, complaining:

> Entitled, by law, to admission into almost any office in the state, they have been, and are still, practically excluded from almost every branch of the executive administration of the Government ... It is impossible to suppose that a whole nation can repose confidence, or act cordially, with a Government, when so large a portion of the people are practically excluded from all share in the higher offices of the state, while their right to admission is established by law.[41]

The Irish 'question' was a long-standing matter of national security. Whilst Irish Catholics could not serve in a British army, they could and did choose to serve in other armies. Albrecht Dürer sketched Irish mercenaries in 1521,[42] and tens of thousands had formed Irish regiments serving foreign powers (particularly Catholic Spain and France) against Britain. In Napoleon's army, many officers and men were Irish Jacobite recidivists and prominent freedom fighters; he had an Irish legion earmarked to lead an invasion of Ireland. But for all their apparently treasonable sentiments, once recruitment into the British army was opened to Catholics they readily took up this option and far fewer were to be found serving in the armies of European Catholic powers. The motivation for most was, therefore, an economic one.[43]

Even for some who did not support Catholic emancipation, Wellesley's passion for Irish recruitment would have had other appeals. They were not Anglo-Saxons[44] but the Irish were Europeans, and the Company was always short of those for its European regiments. As he and Dundas argued, if the Irish took the king's shilling then they would not be available to fight for Napoleon. Nor could they foment trouble and rebellion in Ireland if they were sent elsewhere. To Anglo-Irish landholders, each new regiment meant up to a thousand fewer starving peasants on their estates. With army discipline, regular work, food, clothing, and pay, Irish Catholics might even become useful citizens! Each new regiment also represented another dozen commissions for sons of the Protestant ascendancy, with the chance to cover themselves in glory and prize money. Nor could it harm one's reputation if one offered to raise a regiment; men were ennobled for less.

Wellesley continued to fight for more Catholic emancipation by the series of enactments between 1778 and 1829 that opened many previously closed doors to Roman Catholics for the first time in centuries. From 1793 onwards, huge numbers of Irish Catholics were recruited into the British army for service throughout the empire.[45] In 1794, for example, 22 Irish regiments were raised including some EIC battalions; by 1813, a third of the British army's manpower was Irish.[46] With such a large increase in numbers, limitations on where they could be deployed, and a governor-general actively seeking a role for the Irish in the wider empire, Irish manpower in India rapidly became quite considerable.

The number of European troops in India increased from 13,000 in 1796 to 24,500 by the end of Wellesley's tenure, and that was on a peacetime footing. The size of the Company's native army, officered by Europeans, also increased, from 57,000 to 130,000, representing a substantial increase in the number of covenanted posts, which now included Irishmen (although rarely Catholics). Irish regiments, and others reinforced in Ireland with large Catholic contingents, were more likely to be posted abroad because there was opposition to having armed Catholics on home turf; Scottish and English regiments replaced them in Ireland. Those remaining in Ireland, portrayed by Dundas and Pitt as a demonstration of Catholic loyalty, were posted away from their home counties, near English regiments who could keep an eye on them. Regiments with large numbers of Catholics were carefully deployed abroad; not used in America in case they joined the rebels, nor in Canada in case they supported the French, they were deployed in Europe, and the East and West Indies.[47]

Wellesley went to India to continue the policies of Dundas and Cornwallis, cleaning up the administration, anglicizing government and its servants, reducing costs, and improving profitability. His seven years in India were marked by disagreements with Dundas, Castlereagh (Dundas' successor) and the directors, over his support for private trade, country-built shipping, and the expense of territorial gains.[48] But in 1841, the Company erected a statue in his honour and discussed his governor-generalship in glowing terms; he had brought peace and tranquillity to British India by adding 140,000 square miles of territory, yielding net annual revenue of over £1 million sterling. He had:

> ... laid the foundation of all good government by training up a class of men who would be found adequate to the fulfilment of the high and responsible duties committed to their care. The foundation of the College of Fort William was indeed a master-stroke of policy.[49]

Wellesley was wrongly credited with founding the first Christian church in Calcutta and supplying it with ministers, at a time when 'the natives of India were unaware whether we had any religion or not'.[50] He encouraged Company servants to improve their own behaviour, with regular Church parades and a public show of piety and morality. Insisting on observance of the Sabbath, and even banning the publication of Sunday newspapers, he left no doubt that the British were a Christian people.[51] He discouraged informal relationships with native women; if officials had to have female companionship then it should be in a Christian marriage, preferably with a British woman. He supported the exclusion of Eurasian and native dependents of British men from the benefits of the various civil and military pension funds, and, with the Court of Directors' support, ruled against the inclusion of illegitimate children. The opinion that financial hardship would discourage intermarriage and that miscegenation was a sin was most strongly voiced by the young men trained at the institution that constituted his brainchild, Fort William College.[52] Wellesley's college, a logical further step in anglicizing the European presence, ensured that young recruits to the service were taught the dangers of reliance on Indians. Native tutors at the college, though necessary, were barred from teaching anyone but its students. The *griffins* were overseen by their seniors and the clergy to ensure that they retained European values.

Eurasian appointments to civil and military offices, and to positions as combatants in the Company's armies, had already been proscribed before Wellesley's tenure, but Cornwallis and Shore had sanctioned Eurasians' continued employment in native states. At Hyderabad: 'The corps of Boyd and Finglass were taken into the service of the Nizam ... under the sanction of the Government of Bengal ... with a view of forming a counterpoise to the corps of Raymond.'[53] Wellesley began closing that door. These two commands, under an American and an Irishman, to balance the French influence of Raymond included Eurasian men at every level, though Wellesley described them all as 'Europeans'. Even before his arrival in India, he expressed to Dundas his doubts about the policy of relying on such adventurers.

Rather than follow his informant Kirkpatrick's suggestion, that French officers in native *durbars* (meaning French Eurasians too) be excluded and replaced with acceptable British subjects, Wellesley proposed sending in official Company detachments which *per se* excluded Eurasians. Gradually, this policy was implemented in all princely states bound by treaty, squeezing Eurasians and non-official Europeans out of employment in the independent states. These men, Wellesley felt, could not be trusted because: 'I much fear that many British subjects might be found in India whose spirit of adventure would rather direct them to seek a new order of things, than to contribute to the maintenance of our power . . . [and] there is scarcely a native court in India without its establishment of European officers.'[54] His doubts even extended to Company men with a proven track record if their associations with natives were deemed to be too close. He soon initiated a secret enquiry into the conduct of the Hyderabad Resident, James Kirkpatrick, who had been his informant whilst he was *en route* to India. Wellesley's brother Arthur had heard from an out-of-favour Hyderabad official that Kirkpatrick 'was so completely under the influence of the [prime] minister it was to be expected that he would attend more to the objects of the Nizam's court than to those of his own government'.[55] Being at home with native customs and people, especially if that involved family ties, was now a cause for concern. Dalrymple noted that an old culture, in which men like Kirkpatrick lived and worked as part of an Anglo-Mughal accommodation, was being replaced with growing anglicization. Spreading from the presidencies outwards, the change was beginning to be felt in the *mofussil* even before Wellesley's time.[56]

Unlike his brother the Duke of Wellington, who lurched from passionate support of Catholic emancipation, to coercion laws, and back again, Wellesley never wavered in his support for Catholic emancipation, removal of legal proscriptions, and full Irish participation within the British empire. His championing of this group, by increasing the number of Irishmen in India, would have taken jobs and opportunities away from Eurasians.

Since any disaffected group of subjects could represent a threat to the empire, Wellesley's arguments (for inclusion of the Irish) applied to all Britons. He would not have considered isolating and embittering Eurasians by legal proscription if he thought of them as British. Eurasians were a tiny minority in India but represented a majority of those of European descent. He could not fail to have been aware of the hardship his treatment of Eurasian and native dependents was causing; their suffering was designed to discourage British men from entering into such relationships. He must also have noticed that half the Eurasians were Roman Catholics, a group normally dear to his heart. If, as he argued, the British empire would be strengthened by the inclusion of Irish Catholics, then it is improbable that he would have deliberately excluded another group of Catholic Britons. He could not, therefore, have felt that Eurasians, even those of Indo-British descent, were as British as the troublesome minorities at home.

How much race influenced Wellesley's attitude to Eurasians is hard to assess. Ingram detected no evidence that Wellesley was in any way influenced by the doctrine of racial superiority. In conquest, Ingram held that Wellesley was 'morally neutral', believing in force of arms to subdue a conquered people. Power, personal and national, was his justification and motivator.[57] Whilst he may have eschewed the racial justification for British success in India, perhaps it was power, or rather their lack of it, that allowed him to disregard the increasing hardship and disaffection his policies caused for Eurasians.

HENRY DUNDAS, HIGHLANDERS, AND OTHER SCOTS[58]

Two major Scottish issues must be considered because the man central to all things Scottish at this time, Henry Dundas, was also the driving force behind the Board of Control for Indian Affairs. The first issue concerns the Scottish gentry; the Act of Union of 1707 promised them a greater share in empire and global trade, yet few had benefited. Highland gentry, dispossessed because of their support for 'the '45' (the Jacobite rising of 1745), and clan chiefs affected by social change also sought new purpose. The second issue was that the clearances (highland and lowland), though of little interest to the Company's directors unless they too were Scots, were of great importance to the government, to Dundas, and to others on the Board of Control. The British army was begging for manpower whilst Scotland's manpower was bleeding away to settle in the colonies. Attempts by Dundas and others (such as Prime Minister Pitt) to increase Scots' participation in the empire were therefore aimed at embedding Scotland firmly within a British identity. Dundas and Pitt sought to 'promote patriotic feelings, and overawe any disaffected elements' through military discipline in militias, volunteer units, and the army. Noam Chomsky has said 'volunteerism means a mercenary army of the disadvantaged'.[59] To Dundas, these 'disadvantaged' were Highland Scots and Irish Catholics, who might otherwise cause trouble; those who were excluded from 'bearing arms on the right side' might otherwise 'become prey to the intrigues of traitors and enemies'.[60]

Cookson paints a portrait of Dundas on the world stage. Whether quelling Irish rebellion, stemming Highland disquiet, or defending the empire from French aggression, his strategies interlocked, harnessing possible sources of unrest and redirecting them to serve British interests.[61] Ingram selected a quote from George Canning to characterize him: 'Dundas is more active and diligent than any other, but also selfish and Scotch. [His interest is] pillage and patronage; pillage by conquest and patronage at home.'[62]

Dundas served on the Board of Control from its inception in 1784 to 1801, but was an influential expert on Indian affairs for much longer.[63] He had been intimately involved with writing Pitt's 1784 India Bill and in getting it through parliament.[64] Even before he became President of the Board, he 'consolidated his position', often taking the chair, hand-picking his staff, and provoking resentment from the Board's official president, Lord Sydney.[65] Dundas headed the Secret Committee (of the most senior directors) from 1784 and served as President of the Board from 1792 until 1801, but already 'by 1787, his ascendancy was openly recognized in numerous pamphlets, in newspapers and in parliament'.[66] His influence continued even after he left the Board, through his son Robert, until his death in 1811. Besides the Board, Dundas had been an MP since 1774, was Admiralty treasurer between 1782 and 1800, home secretary in 1791, and, concurrently with heading the Board, Pitt's minister for war from 1794 to 1801. He returned to the Admiralty as First Lord from 1804 to 1806. He was also Keeper of the Privy Seal of Scotland from 1800 until his death in 1811.[67] Dundas was impeached in 1806, accused of misappropriation of funds, but acquitted.

Dundas' career in public office spanned 37 years, and, friend or foe, all agreed that he had a remarkably full political career. Some thought power had made him arrogant, others that his career was 'a slavery mocked by the name of power'. James Mill characterized his contribution to Indian government as merely the appearance of a great share but that any advice he gave was either very obvious or wrong.[68] What is certain is that Dundas, as the main source of patronage for Scots, was able to supply them with increased opportunities in Britain and the empire.[69] His efforts were not limited to his own family or class. He sought employment for the masses, emancipation for Catholics, and promoted the interests of the Scottish gentry in London, suggesting Scots for offices, patronizing their sons, and supporting their efforts to raise regiments, thereby increasing their influence still more. His Scottish interests did not go unnoticed, though he rebuffed claims that he exercised undue partiality.[70] He claimed to have no more patronage than anyone else.[71] Whilst that was true, his position gave him great power to further the interests of others who might benefit in return for following his 'recommendations'.[72] Dundas was not alone amongst the English; there were ten Scots in the Directors' Court during his tenure at the Board of Control,[73] and several fellow Board members were also relatives or friends who would have shared his interest in furthering the same family or acquaintances. Also, his cumulative *direct* patronage was greater than most because he spent almost four decades in public and political offices, including 17 years on the Board.[74] Lovat-Fraser said:

> He knew the qualities of his countrymen and recognised that he was safe in placing them in positions of responsibility . . . they had those habits of command, that unlearnable self-estimate, which insensibly exacts obedience.[75]

Like Cornwallis and Wellesley, Dundas also saw empire as a safety valve for Irish disaffection.[76] He felt that enfranchising Irish

Catholics, giving them freedom of religion, and improving their prospects by employing them within the empire[77] would relieve tension and unrest. Rather than look to republican France, Irishmen would be grateful for their new freedoms and become useful to Britain. He argued for Catholic emancipation, in Ireland, attracting the king's ire, and sparking Gordon to incite destruction in Edinburgh and anti-papist riots in London.[78] Dundas believed Britain's global commercial pre-eminence was essential to avoid national bankruptcy. [79] With the loss of the American colonies, India became more important than ever. Dundas' guiding principle was to reduce costs,[80] but he also took the military threat from European competitors for India very seriously[81] and sought military reorganization with an increased deployment of British troops. Whilst he would not have supported the aggressive land-grabs of Clive, he did urge the governor-generals to secure British interests, particularly from potential French incursions. At a time when English troops were spread thinly in India, the West Indies, and in Europe, there was, therefore, scope to increase Scottish, Irish and Catholic participation.

During Dundas' Board tenure, each governor-general was picked to carry through administrative reform.[82] Cornwallis, Shore, and Wellesley all understood the expectations of the Company's directors, Pitt and Dundas.[83] All communicated frequently with and supported Dundas and, when carrying through India Office reform priorities, were supported by him in disagreements with the directors.[84] This did not preclude disagreements when governor-generals made decisions over situations requiring pragmatic local solutions, such as Wellesley's use of country-built ships. Some directors had a vested interest in British-built Indiamen, and had countermanded his orders. Parliament, anxious to protect shipbuilding in Britain, agreed with them. But Indiamen were not always available when private traders (of many nationalities) needed to move profitable goods. Wellesley believed country-built shipping sailing to London offered a better return than leaving them to trade with foreign ports.[85]

Dundas was the only Scot on the Board of Control until Lord Campbell joined him in 1790. They were joined in 1791 by the

Duke of Montrose, and Scots now made up half of the Board. By 1797, there were ten commissioners; three were Scots[86] and one Irish. Over the next decade, 40–50 per cent of commissioners were Scots or Irish.[87] Still more had Scottish connections through marriage. Scots were also well represented amongst the directors. Six of the 24 directors in 1790 were Scots.[88] Dundas' kin were prominent on the Board and in parliament too.[89] In 1799, Dundas, his son Robert and two nephews by marriage, Caning and Portland, were all at the Board of Control. The Duke of Portland, an MP who joined the Board from 1795 to 1805, was married to Dundas' niece, Henrietta. Another niece, Joan, was the wife of George Canning – MP, Board member, foreign secretary, forces paymaster, and eventually President of the Board, and prime minister. Dundas half-brother Robert, Lord Arniston, was an MP from 1754 to 1787. Arniston's son, Robert, was an MP from 1790 to 1796, and his second son, William, served as secretary for war from 1800 to 1804. Dundas' own son Robert was his private secretary from 1794, a Board commissioner from 1797 to 1802, and president from 1807 to 1811. Nephew William held senior Scottish legal positions. Also in Scotland, the Earl of Moray, a freemason and holder of various high offices, was married to yet another niece, Lucy. Dundas was not only advancing relatives out of a sense of filial duty; they could also be useful. He remarked to Cornwallis in 1799 that things were easier on the Board with both his son and his nephew with him. He also remarked that in Hugh Inglis and David Scott, variously Chairman and Deputy Chairman of the Directors' Court between 1795 and 1801, it would be easier to get the Company to agree to his (and Cornwallis') priorities.[90]

There had long been concern in the press about 'Highlanders, determined to immigrate to America to assist His Majesty's rebellious subjects in that bloody Region'.[91] War ended in September 1781, but the peace treaty was not ratified until January 1784 and relations between the two nations remained poor. In 1791, still concerned that disaffected Scotsmen were embarking for America, where they might take up arms against Britain, Dundas forbade ships carrying them from leaving port if they were bound for North America.[92]

Military service provided employment for both Highland and Lowland Scots displaced by agricultural improvers in the clearances.[93] The Napoleonic wars had provided a respite, mopping up vast numbers into the military and militias, but with peace, many regiments were disbanded and men were again unemployed. The numbers were massive and the problem long lived: statistics of emigration published in 1853 showed 'since the conclusion of the war, thirty eight years ago, there have left this country 3,463,292 emigrants'.[94] With so many desperate men leaving, the viability of the Scottish nation was at stake.

At least seven Highland regiments were formed whilst Dundas was President of the Board, absorbing several thousands of Scotsmen who might otherwise have emigrated.[95] Dundas believed Highlanders to be an untapped source of 'martial' men.[96] The first Highland regiment raised was the 79th. Formed by an exiled American loyalist, Alan Cameron, on Dundas' suggestion, specifically for service in India, it comprised 98 per cent Highlanders.[97] Other Highland regiments are known to have served in India during Dundas' tenure. Not everyone was convinced. Eyre Coote, commander-in-chief in India, expressed doubts about Highlanders' suitability for service there. McLeod's Highlanders arrived in 1782 and Coote complained: 'on the first march ... after they arrived in the country, most of them were knocked up by the heat of the climate, which did not agree so well with regiments composed of men born in the North, as with regiments of men born in a more mild climate'.[98] Coote asked that no more Highland regiments be sent but was ignored, and Montgomerie's 77th Highlanders were due to embark for India in January 1783.[99]

There is no indisputable evidence that Dundas abused his position to favour Scots, but his long tenure, immense influence, care for his kin, and concern for his own nation, whether Scotland or Britain, did coincide with an increased Scottish, Irish, and Catholic presence in India and throughout the empire. His aims, besides patronising friends and relatives, were to unify Britain and defuse dissent through a policy of inclusion.

There is no evidence of any attempt to exclude any British group; that would have run counter to his professed aims. But his stress on unity and the inclusion of all British identities – Catholic, Scottish, Highland, and Irish – necessitated the exclusion of someone else. The obvious and much vaunted 'others' of the time were republicans, the French, and Indians. The first threatened the British state, the second her independence, and the third her empire. If Dundas did not suggest that Eurasians were 'foreign' and dangerous, he appears to have done nothing to dispel the idea. If scope was to be found for more home-grown men to serve, then, even with expansion, someone had to make room. Eurasians were part-Indian, sometimes part-French, some were Muslims, many were 'born in sin', and some even looked foreign. The objections of their fathers were easily dismissed; they were the 'nabobs', corrupted by the East, men who kept heathen women – sometimes more than one. Eurasians could not fight back; they were unorganized and too heterogeneous at this stage to be a united threat. If the directors proclaimed that no sons of natives could serve the Company, that illegitimate children should not be supported by the Company, there was no one to argue otherwise.

GENERAL DISCUSSION AND CONCLUSIONS

From the previous chapter, it is clear the Eurasians and Europeans in India drew apart between 1786 and 1813. This was the point at which the 'half-caste' of India became 'visible' in England, and at which signs of an emerging Eurasian community in India can first be detected. Reactions to 'racial mixing' were often strong and usually negative, but whether that translated into official action to deliberately disadvantage Eurasians in India remained unclear. The historiographical discourse, particularly from Anglo-Indian authors, is unconvincing because motivation cannot be established from the proscriptions, most of which do not mention Eurasians. Equally, inferring motivation from effect is not valid. The broader approach of this chapter was necessary, exploring the interests and motivation of key decision-makers in Indian affairs, to determine whether the proscriptions they enacted (regardless of effect) were aimed at Eurasians, or not.

In this period metropolitan minorities were beginning to be integrated within an evolving British identity, and greater attention needs to be paid to this change. Irish insurrection and Scottish dissent threatened the integrity of Britain from within. Three men with great influence over Indian affairs, Cornwallis, Wellesley, and Dundas, were in positions from which they could serve British interests that each held dear. Each used India as a conduit through which various disaffected elements might emerge as useful and loyal Britons. Pitt's India Act gave them the power to act virtually independently of the Company, and, important as trade was to Britain, the act meant they also viewed India as an extension of the British state.

In promoting wider British interests, Cornwallis, Wellesley, and Dundas added significant difficulties to the position of India's Eurasians. Each promoted his own interests in indigenous British minorities by creating employment opportunities for them within the wider British empire. The motives behind the apparent 'othering' of Eurasians are therefore shown to be complex. Legislation or directives that appear to have been designed to hold Eurasians back may rather have been intended to promote other groups, or simply to reform the colonial British themselves. Similar motives informed other decision-makers who were reshaping Britain and British India, but they have not previously been factored into discussions about the proscriptions and the beginnings of a Eurasian community. Their relevance only becomes apparent when the interests and personal missions of such men are considered in this broader context.

Once the proscriptions were enacted, whatever the motivation may have been, their effects were especially inimical to Eurasians, who, at the time, were isolated and without community support. They created the Eurasian 'problem'. Extremist voices were also rallying ill feeling towards Eurasians and calling for measures to exclude them from Britain and from British society in India. Authors began to write about Eurasians as 'a problem'. Maria Graham, writing in 1813, noticed Eurasian numbers in Calcutta and Madras: 'the numbers of half-caste, and therefore (if I may use the expression), half-parented children, exceed what one could imagine'.[100] Valentia constructed connections between racial degeneration through miscegenation, and Spain's inability to hold on to its empire.[101] Williamson's guidance to *griffins* warned that Eurasian beauty was short-lived and Eurasian women were prone to madness.[102] Gilchrist's reworking of Williamson removed his advice to *griffins* to take a *bibi* to help them learn the customs and languages of India.[103] Anglo-Indian genre fiction began to feature duplicitous 'half-castes',[104] dusky sirens, scheming Indian relatives, and plucky British chaps (or white women) 'ruined' by association. Travelogues (such as those by Valentia and Graham) reported the degraded condition of 'half-castes' without reference to its cause, and advised that an English education was unnecessary or unkind because it raised their expectations and made them miserable.[105]

Jon Wilson's *The Domination of Strangers* has suggested that to establish their colonial dominance the British cast Indians in the role of the stranger.[106] Such psychological distancing was not unique to India, or even to subjugated colonies generally. It allowed the British to include those in their midst who had previously been strangers; Catholics, the Irish, and the Highlanders were white, and born and bred in Britain. In India, the 'stranger' role was also applied to others; neither white settlers, who, without a home in Britain, did not conform fully to notions of Britishness, nor Eurasians, whose mixed descent was an additional problem, could be fully included if Britishness meant attachment to the British Isles. The two-stage domination described by Wilson, quite evident in the rules described in the last chapter, was to systematize laws, regulations, and boundaries, and to impose a colonial (and foreign) viewpoint on India – supposedly rewarding Indians with long periods of peace, prosperity, and progress – and was essentially impersonal. Its aim was to 'cultivate' in India's diverse cultures a utilitarian society of colonial subjects fit for Britain's purpose. The three men discussed in this chapter had personal agendas – but if the effects of their legislation appeared personal to those affected, this was incidental.

The official proscriptions were short-lived, with almost all removed by 1833, but they brought about a far more racially hierarchical colonial society than before. The basic necessities for being trusted with high office were a British education, firm links with 'home', and unsullied European values and interests. Eurasians with neither a British education, nor property, and with Indian ancestry, were perceived to be inferior. Social mores were deployed to promote European-ness and preserve European advantage. Through these means, even after official barriers to Indian and Eurasian employment were removed the Eurasian remained 'a problem'. The community began as the Eurasians' own solution to that problem; its continuance and its form were, as will be seen in the following chapters, a pragmatic amalgam of the needs of its members, and the expediency and exigencies of the Raj.

CHAPTER 3

POPULATION STATISTICS

It is impossible to assess Eurasian roles and status, or to make any quantitative assessments, without establishing a baseline for their approximate numbers. But enumerating British India's Eurasian population, even with the Raj bureaucracy's extensive records, is surprisingly difficult. Census returns of Eurasian numbers, reports by the clergy, historians, and other government sources such as education reports and employment enquiries all had problems in reliably identifying and defining 'Eurasians'. Later census efforts acknowledge their own inaccuracy, and suggest reasons for the difficulties. The fact that figures are so unreliable, and that they were so difficult to collect is of itself, informative. Exploring the sources reveals both the difficulties in collecting the data and the artificiality of the concept of a monolithic and separate Eurasian population, whilst establishing a range within which the baseline figure must fall.

CENSUSES AND OTHER ESTIMATES

In 1813, the Scottish missionary and clergyman Claudius Buchanan was employed as a Company chaplain and served as vice-principal at Fort William College. He criticized the Company's attitude to the spiritual needs of people of European descent and Protestant persuasion in India; it provided 488 surgeons and assistant surgeons but only 35 chaplains across British India. He was particularly concerned for the unofficial population, for those in small stations, and for the Eurasians of British descent. He put the number of 'half-cast descendants of the English' in India at '100,000, and upward, most of whom are brought up, at least nominally, as Protestant Christians'.[1] We know that around half the Indo-British Eurasians were Catholics and that Buchanan excluded them from his calculations, so this gives a figure of 200,000 Indo-British Eurasians in 1813. Besides these, there was a large Catholic Indo-Portuguese population, a smaller number of Indo-French, and other mixed populations in British-controlled territory. In the Bombay presidency, Buchanan found 27,783 Protestants, including 20,000 Eurasians, but quotes an 1811 study including Catholics that showed 65,100 Christians in the same territory.[2] Buchanan's estimate of Protestant, Indo-British Eurasians was larger than any other, but not impossibly large. His estimates were still respected and quoted as late as the 1870s.[3]

Another early report, on Bombay Island in 1826, was reprinted by Martin in 1837.[4] It gives some idea of the number of Indo-Portuguese in British territory. In the same volume, Martin states that in the Bengal, Madras, and Bombay presidencies:

> [T]he Roman Catholics (descendants of the Portuguese and French, or converts to their faith) amount, it is said, to 600,000: they are sunk in a state of idolatry not far removed from Hindooism. There are 50,000 Portuguese, or converts to their religion assuming Portuguese names, in the territories under the Bombay Presidency.[5]

Of these, 8,020 were identified in 1826 as Indo-Portuguese[6] and the rest as converts.

The British were distributed across the Bengal, Madras, and Bombay presidencies roughly in the proportions 5:4:3[7], so it is safe to assume that the Indo-British (and the Indo-Portuguese, seeking work) would have been distributed in the three presidencies in similar proportions. Applying these relative proportions throughout the three presidencies, 8,020 Indo-Portuguese Eurasians in Bombay would equate to 96,240 in 1826 British India. Bearing in mind that Portuguese Eurasians may have had more freedom to seek work in native states, this might well be an underestimate of their total numbers. Eurasians of British descent are not recorded in the 1826 Bombay census, but they were certainly present; the orphan schools at Byculla had 284 children on their rolls at a similar date, most of whom were Indo-British Eurasians.[8]

Martin also reprints an 1837 census of Calcutta,[9] though it excludes the outlying suburbs of Kidderpore (where the orphan schools were full of Eurasian children),[10] Gardenreach, Seebpore, Howrah, Cossipore, Sulkea, and 'the other side of the Mahratta Ditch'. It was conducted by house tax assessors.[11] This census, unlike the earlier one of Bombay, acknowledges the existence of Indo-British Eurasians. If Calcutta was home to half of Bengal's mixed Indo-British,[12] then in 1837 the Indo-British Eurasian population (applying the proportions used above) would have numbered about 22,781: 9,492 in the Bengal, 7,594 in the Madras, and 5,695 in the Bombay presidencies. These are low totals compared with Buchanan's.[13] Even official decentennial censuses from 1871 onwards recorded more than twice that number, and the population had not grown that quickly. Calculating the Indo-Portuguese population from this 1837 census, the numbers would be 6,362 (Bengal), 5,089 (Madras), and 3,818 (Bombay), giving a total of 15,269. Again, this total is unrealistically low; compared with the figure extrapolated from the 1826 study above (96,240), and the total (30,272) identified in the 1871 census. The Portuguese had been in India for over three centuries and, without European wives, had intermarried freely, so the number of Indo-Portuguese cannot have been so low. For these reasons, this census is not included as a source for my calculations.

A census of Bombay *mofussil* Europeans in 1851, like the 1826 Bombay Island census, is reticent on the subject of Indo-British Eurasians, perhaps because they were considered to be outside its remit. Only one 'East-Indian' wife appears.[14] Europeans and Eurasians were spread throughout the Bombay presidency and, besides those in Bombay proper, there were European populations at 24 *mofussil* 'stations' in the presidency. We know from other sources that one of them, Karachi, had a sizable enough Indo-British population to warrant a government-assisted school.[15] It is unclear why Eurasians were not separately enumerated in this census, their number being integrated with the European or native communities, but, obviously, this census cannot be used as a source for Eurasian numbers.

The 1871 and later censuses (Table 3.1) attempt to show geographical distribution and number of Eurasians (meaning, in this context, Indo-Britons) and Indo-Portuguese. Indo-Portuguese were a separate category, but their low total (30,272) and absence from Bengal and Madras indicates a problem with these classifications. Indo-Portuguese who did not recognize distinctions between themselves and other Portuguese would have identified themselves as European,[16] and some – especially government and railway employees, aware that their employers classified them as Eurasian – were believed to have returned themselves as such.[17]

The distribution of Indo-British Eurasians in 1871 also seems unrealistic, since the ratio of returns from the three presidencies was Bengal 5: Madras 6: Bombay 1. Bombay returned just 3,671 Indo-British Eurasians, so many were probably being recorded amongst the 29,737 Indo-Portuguese. The Bengal count (20,195) is also low compared with Madras (26,426), but if other north Indian provinces (Awadh, Punjab, and the North-West Provinces) are included with Bengal, the count is 25,445 and the relative proportions are more realistic. The category 'other mixed races' (14,279) included those of Indo-European descent other than Portuguese or British, but also many other 'mixes' of Indian and foreign ancestry. Almost all of these were returned from Bombay.

All the 'mixed race' categories together yield an 1871 total of 108,402. This is low compared to my calculation, based on the 1826 Bombay census, of 96,240 Indo-Portuguese in India, and Buchanan's earlier estimate of 100,000 Indo-British Protestants. It also implies that 44 per cent of all mixed-race people lived in Bombay presidency. The figures, however, were not challenged by the Eurasian and Anglo-Indian Association's own estimates.[18] This association, in protecting the status of the largely Indo-British community it represented, was careful about whom it considered to be 'Eurasian' and readily discounted the illiterate, the non-Anglophone, and even the illegitimate. It would have had no interest in inflating the numbers when government support was inadequate for those already classified as Eurasian.

The enumeration of mixed-race categories in British India showed that numbers had dropped from 108,402 in 1871 to 62,085 in the 1881 census. Commenting on the Bombay count, the returning officer stated: 'The Eurasian community is, I believe, much more numerous than here represented ... there is great confusion between this class and the European.' Certainly the census wording had caused problems in distinguishing between the two. Europeans born in India were meant to be recorded as 'European British subjects' but many entries were abridged to either 'British Subject' *or* 'European', including, it was believed, many cases 'in which the persons concerned were of distinctly mixed race'.[19] That would not have been an issue unique to Bombay.

Even more significantly, the 1881 census does not report any Indo-Portuguese in India after lumping most of them in with native Christians or 'Goanese'. It was claimed that few would have identified themselves as Indo-Portuguese anyway. The change may have been sparked by petitions from the Eurasian and Anglo-Indian Association (EAIA), complaining that Indo-Portuguese, styling themselves 'Eurasian', were mostly native Christians or the descendants of manumitted slaves with Portuguese names.[20] Their remit was to promote the interests of the Anglophone and largely Indo-British Eurasians. At the time, government was undertaking another review of schooling and education provision for the domiciled European and Eurasian population, and so it was in the EAIA's interest to focus government attention and funding on their community. Downplaying Indo-Portuguese claims to a European heritage was therefore beneficial, and the British agreed: 'Goanese' conveyed to the British a population of cooks and domestic servants, uniformly Roman Catholic, in Western dress, but essentially native Christians with no real claim to a mixed-race status.[21] There were 47,038 Goanese recorded but this was a geographic and language category, not a racial one.

Bombay's 'Indo-Portuguese' were redefined as two classes of native Christians: a higher class whose education and employment had allowed them parity with the Portuguese, and a lower class whose native ancestors had been forcibly converted.[22] We know from their names that some Indo-Portuguese became (through marriage, education, and employment)[23] part of the 'Eurasian' community, but the total number of Eurasians in 1881 (62,085) is not proportionately increased from the 1871 count of 63,685: 30,272 Indo-Portuguese and 14,445, classified in 1871 as of 'others mixed race', disappeared into the category of native Christian.

In Baine's report on the 1891 census, many Eurasians were enumerated as natives and the report demonstrates the central importance of religion in the government's perception of Eurasian identity. The author of the Madras report listed every caste name entered in the schedules including 'Eurasian Hindoo'. But '. . . caste terms . . . modified by prefixes or affixes . . . [were not] considered satisfactory'.[24] Thus, any Eurasians who thought themselves Hindu had to be returned either as Eurasian or Hindoo, not both. The idea that a Eurasian might profess another religion was met with incredulity, and removed from the records:

> . . . there were a few instances, altered on scrutiny, of Buddhists amongst European and Eurasian Christians. Some . . . may be set down, perhaps, to the example of a high official, who pronounced for Buddhism, on the ground that there was less to be said against it, he thought, than against any other form of religion.[25]

There was continued confusion over terminology such as 'Portuguese' and 'East-Indian'. Both terms were still widely used, and yet enumerators were instructed that 'Native Christians, for instance, may be returned as Portuguese, East Indians, Madrási, or by their caste if recognised.'[26] So any Eurasians still using the terms 'East-Indian' or 'Portuguese' would have been enumerated as native Christians. The term 'Goanese', again lumping the Indo-Portuguese and native Goanese together as 'natives', continued in use for this census.

The 1891 count of Eurasians, which Baines assumed was correct, was 79,790. He did not find it surprising that Madras Eurasians (26,600) outnumbered those of Bengal (15,000), but remarked that in Bombay (total 8,500) 'there are no doubt a good many Goanese or others with Portuguese patronymics'.[27] Baines thought it would be interesting to compare the last two enumerations to see if the Eurasian population was increasing, but did not attempt to do so.[28] However, the 1881 total of 62,085 compared with 79,790 just ten years later, representing a spectacular growth rate of 2.54 per annum. Since in the same period the UK population was growing at 1.3–1.5 per cent and India's at 0.4 per cent (see below), this improbable growth rate illustrates the inaccuracy of censuses.

GROWTH

We cannot gauge accurately the size of the Eurasian populations in nineteenth-century India, but it is worth establishing a range of possibilities from published figures and possible growth rates. Blussé and Booth state that India's population grew slowly in the nineteenth century due to famines and epidemics, such as malaria in the north, cholera in the south, and smallpox at the earlier dates. They estimate annual growth of India's population at only 0.4 per cent until 1920 and 1.5 per cent thereafter.[29] It would be pointless to estimate the Europeans' growth rate, as they were largely transient, but annual population growth in England between 1841 and 1851 was about 1.3 per cent. It is likely the Eurasian population (without allowance for exogamous marriage) would have grown faster than the indigenous Indian population but not as fast as populations in Europe. I am, however, looking for a baseline, so the following calculations use the low population growth rates of India. Taking Buchanan's figure of 100,000 Protestant Eurasians, without making allowance for the Roman Catholics he ignored, and adding in 96,240 Indo-Portuguese gives a starting figure for 1813 of 196,240 Eurasians (British and Portuguese), which has been worked forwards to 1911, increasing year on year by 0.4 per cent. Besides these, the census totals for 1871 and 1881 are worked both forwards and

Table 3.1 Census of India; Eurasians Enumerated by Province, State, and Agency.[30]

	Number of Eurasians			
	1891	1901	1931	per cent growth 1891–1931
Provinces	71,877	73,879	114,154	58.8
Ajmer-Merwara	636	341	1,232	93.7
Andamans	111	71	–	–
Assam	383	575	650	69.7
Baluchistan	147	124	379	157.8
Bengal	15,162	20,893	27,573	81.9
Bombay	8,809	6,889	16,219	84.1
Burma	7,022	8,449	19,200	173.4
Central Provinces and Berar	2,525	2,605	5,065	100.6
Coorg	212	295	84	–
Madras	26,671	26,209	28,694	7.6
Punjab and North-West Frontier	3,155	2,498	3,786	20
United Provinces	7,044	5,230	11,272	60
Birar and Orissa	–	–	6,638	–
Delhi	–	–	1,010	–
Gwalior	–	–	131	–
Sikkim	–	–	2	–

Western Indian States Agency	–	–	428	–
States and Agencies	8,167	13,151	15,936	95.1
Baroda State	108	57	63	–
Central India Agency	373	572	736	97.3
Cochin State	270	1,494	1,717	535.9
Hyderabad State	2,507	3,292	3,370	34.4
Kashmir State	5	23	123	–
Mysore State	3,931	5,721	8,309	111.4
Rajputana Agency	441	503	828	87.8
Travancore State	532	1,489	790	48.5
ALL INDIA	80,044	87,030	138,298	72.8

Table 3.2 Estimating Eurasian Population Growth – All India.[31,i]

Year	Calc. from Buchanan and Martin		Calc. from 1871 census[ii]		Calc. from 1881 census[iii]	Caplan and Buettner[iv]
	Indo-Portuguese[v]	Indo-British Protestants[vi]	Indo-Portuguese	Indo-British	Indo-British	Anglo-Indians
1813	91,354	100,000*	24,021	48,773	45,691	
1821	94,331**	103,245	24,800	50,356	47,170	
1831	98,180	107,450	25,809	52,617	49,288	
1841	102,179	111,826	26,859	54,540	51,090	
1851	106,340	116,381	27,951	56,762	53,171	
1861	110,671	125,464	29,089	61,193	57,313	
1871	115,179	13,0573	30,272#	63,685#	59,646	
1881	119,870	141,305	31,505	66,279	62,085##	
1891	124,752	147,061	32,788	68,979	64,614	80,000[vii]
1901	129,833	153,049	34,123	71,788	67,246	87,000[viii]
1911	135,120	159,283	35,513	74,710	69,985	100,400[ix]

* Buchanan's figure for 1813.
** Calculated backwards from 1826 Bombay Census.
\# From 1871 census report.
\## From 1881 census report.

backwards to reveal figures for each decade from 1813 to 1911. Other figures are included for comparison, but not worked through to other dates. Reading across Table 3.2 (above) then reveals the range within which the size of the Eurasian population would likely have fallen at that date.

RESULTS

Table 3.2, constructed using statistics gleaned from the sources discussed above, and extrapolating over time, has allowed for comparisons that illustrate some of the inconsistencies in the censuses, as well as allowing the production of a range, at any given date, for the size of the Eurasian population of India. In 1813, there were between 45,691 and 100,000 Indo-British and between 24,021 and 96,240 Indo-Portuguese, giving a Eurasian total of between 69,712 and 196,240. A century later in 1911 there were between 69,985 and 159,283 Indo-British (newly renamed Anglo-Indian) and between 35,513 and 135,120 Indo-Portuguese who had disappeared as a category from the census returns, together totalling between 105,498 and 294,403 Eurasians. Applying Blussé's and Booth's population growth rates for India to Eurasian groups shows growth over the century of at least 59 per cent. Official figures from censuses (see Table 3.1) confirm that this is a conservative estimate; many states and provinces exceeded this figure in just 40 years.

However unreliable the counts may be, they yield a range within which the true figures are likely to lie. But importantly, examining census reports has also illustrated how, in a supposedly racial classification, culture and religion became increasingly important. We know the British administration was concerned about the 'Eurasian problem', but by reclassifying the Indo-Portuguese and non-Christian Indo-Britons as natives, 'half the problem' disappeared.

CHAPTER 4

EUROPEANS AND MISCEGENATION

> In thim times a man lived an' died wid his Rig'mint;
> an by natur' he married whin he was a man.[1]

Many men, in Europe or India, sought nothing more from women than they got from prostitutes, and military authorities worked on this premise; 'celibate' meant unmarried rather than chaste. There were many such women kept exclusively by the better off, shared by a few men, on the street, or in brothels. Lock hospitals, where prostitutes were examined and treated for sexually transmitted diseases, were not peculiar to India. Venereal disease attracted attention from government and military authorities because it reduced the efficiency of their armies. Thus, women in port and garrison towns in England were also subject to confinement and inspection under contagious diseases legislation between 1864 and 1886.[2] Increased venereal disease rates amongst British troops in India are taken as evidence that more men there turned to prostitutes. But this does not necessarily follow since counts are based on treatment episodes, not the number of men, and, even if they were, statistics do not necessarily reflect behaviour. Treatment episodes would still have increased or decreased with fluctuations in prevalence and virulence over time, and probably with changes in sanitary arrangements and climate.[3] Besides, there was no shortage of prostitutes in England: 75,000 are thought to have worked in London, and every garrison town had a good supply; yet, as I show in this chapter, the number of soldiers in England who chose marriage was more than the army permitted.

Arrangements with prostitutes are not my concern in this chapter; men who relied on prostitutes in England would do so in India. I am concerned with longer-term relationships that had they occurred in Britain, might have been considered equivalent to marriage. My aim is to consider one aspect of the Anglo-Indian community's identity that its members hotly contested: the alleged irregularity and illegitimacy of its origins. I show roughly how many there were who might have had regular relationships with Europeans. This establishes, for the discussions of later chapters, one route for Eurasians to be influenced in behaviour and standing by intimate and continuing connections with the British. A further chapter examines the norms of cohabitation.

Despite social mores, political pressure, and legal impediments putting distance between them, Indians, Eurasians, and Britons continued throughout the nineteenth century to form intimate relationships, many lifelong, and to produce Eurasian children. Historians variously describe the majority of these women as mistresses, prostitutes, servants, and even slaves. Many intercultural and interracial relationships do not figure in official sources, and therefore are not recognized as marriages. Marriage forms acceptable in some parts of Britain, or in some strata of British society, or made available under British law at home, were not recognized in British India. But for official attitudes to miscegenation, many such relationships could or even should be considered irregular but valid marriages. Therefore, where appropriate, the words 'marriage' and 'wife' are used in that sense in this chapter.

The disappearance of native and Eurasian mistresses and wives from the wills of British officers and civil servants has been well noted, and cited as evidence that interracial relationships fell dramatically after the first decades of the nineteenth century and were never again frequent occurrences.[4] Whilst this may have been the case for the upper echelons of British-Indian society, it is likely that such relationships continued unabated amongst the 'lower orders' that formed the majority. Rather, as legislation and regulation increased and racial attitudes hardened, recognition fell away and relationships became far easier to dismiss as insignificant.

Most of the British in India had no social standing to speak of, no political power to lose, and no lucrative promotions prospects to damage by associating with Indians.[5] Nor would they have had much to bequeath; they were common soldiers (Table 4.1), many of whom would never return home even had they wished to. They were neither the public face of the Raj nor its ambassadors. Lack of social standing and the paucity of European women means relationships between Indians Eurasians and Europeans must have continued. British attempts to 'other' Eurasians, and classify them as statutory natives of India, were never going to cast them completely from the British sphere as long as there were Britons who had nothing to lose, and Eurasians or Indians who had something to gain, by continuing to associate with the other.

In 1858, 12 per cent of soldiers in India could expect permission to marry.[6] The same stricture applied in 1881, when 3 per cent of 'other ranks' arriving in India and 6 per cent of those leaving were accompanied by wives.[7] Soldiers in Britain were subject to similar regulations, and yet calculations based on 1881 England census data (Table 4.2(a)) show army proscriptions on marriage were only partially successful; regulations were not uniformly applied by commanding officers, and soldiers often married, against regulations, 'off the strength'. Further, the age demographic of soldiers in India was different to that in England and, since regulations differed by both

Table 4.1 British Soldiers in India – Crown and Company Armies.[8]

Year	Men	Year	Men
1794	16,000	1857	39,800
1805	24,500	1881	59,000
1837	37,000	1906	74,500

age and rank, this must be taken into account when considering marriage in India.

Data has been collected for England from an online database that includes both indexes and scanned images of enumerators' returns of the 1881 census. This was queried using simple filters such as 'male', 'married', and 'soldier'. Comparable data for India has been collected from 1881 census reports, army returns, and other official statistics for India.[9]

Army regulations and commanding officers' attitudes do not describe the reality for soldiers serving in England. There was no legal impediment if a soldier wished to marry without permission. Stocqueler said in 1857, 'I have seen many means adopted to prevent men marrying: I have known officers reason with, persuade and threaten, nay, as a precautionary measure, actually confine, but generally speaking to no purpose; the deed [marriage] is but rarely postponed, and still more seldom is the inclination subdued.'[10] Official returns, likewise, could not describe the situation in India where the proportion of soldiers older than 20, and so more likely to want to marry, was higher than in England. We cannot use the regulation figure of those married 'on the strength' to project actual marriage statistics for enlisted British soldiers serving in India. If soldiers in England married without permission, then they must also have done so in India. 1881 Census data for India records the number of British-born men, soldiers, or otherwise, and of British-born women. Army returns give figures of soldiers, their wives, and children 'on the strength'. Neither shows the number of wives not 'on the strength', and not British born. Ecclesiastical returns also tell only a partial story since they record only one form of marriage – one that, even in Britain, many did not subscribe to (see next chapter).

I argue that marriage rates for soldiers in India are likely to resemble those of soldiers in England, corrected for age. Any disparity between this projected rate and marriage entries in the ecclesiastical returns from India then demands some consideration of alternative scenarios. There was a shortfall of European women in India, both for the number of men who formally married and for the number of men who may have wished to marry, but this does not mean they found marriage impossible. Whilst many without a European wife would undoubtedly have been content to use prostitutes, keep mistresses, pray, drink, or go pig-sticking, these were not the only alternatives. There was no shortage of Indian and Eurasian women. Whilst they may have been invisible, unthinkable, or embarrassing to the Victorians who recorded the nineteenth-century Raj, the silence on this subject now seems rather loud.

I have therefore looked at European numbers and demographics (military, civilian, and female), established how many men were permitted to marry, how many European women were available, and how many marriages appear in ecclesiastical returns. I go on to compare the demographic of European men in India with their counterparts in England to explore how many were likely to have entered into marriage-like relationships with Eurasian or Indian women. The reasons for discrepancies between these figures and the number of marriages recorded in the ecclesiastical returns are then explored in the next chapter.

SOLDIERS – OTHER RANKS

Excluding boys under 14 and men over 60, the 1881 census of England and Wales returned almost 7 million adult males in the general population, amongst whom almost 30,000 individuals were described as 'soldiers'.[11] Since this excludes those returned by their rank or trade (e.g. captain, bombardier, sergeant, or gunner) it is an underestimate of military men, but when seeking a minimum figure this inaccuracy can be accepted. Over half of all adult males were married, against one in seven soldiers (Table 4.2(a)),[12] showing that serving soldiers were far less likely to marry than civilians but the figure was still higher than the 6 per cent (allowing for rank and age) that regulations permitted.[13]

Excluding the youngest soldiers radically changed the figures; two in five soldiers over 30 years of age were married (Table 4.2(b)). Alternatively, restricting the search parameters to specific areas or garrison towns revealed further differences. One in seven nationally but one in six soldiers in Yorkshire were married. Two in five of those

Table 4.2(a) Marriage Rates and Age for 1881 – General Male Population and Soldiers.[14]

		Genl. male Population England			Soldiers in England			Soldiers in India		
			Married			Married			Predicted married	
Birth year	Age	All	Number	Per cent	All	Number	Per cent	All*	Number	Per cent
1867	14 yrs	265,011	189	0.07	127	0	0			0
1864–6	15–17	729,785	1,067	0.15	781	2	0.26			0.26
1861–3	18–20	684,094	20,568	3.00	6,286	26	0.40	1,255	5	0.40
1851–60	21–30	196,6386	913,557	46.46	14,718	1,353	9.19	43,927	4,037	9.19
1841–50	31–40	1,477,531	1,181,774	79.98	5,448	1,925	35.33	12,267	4,334	35.33
1831–40	41–50	1,102,520	922,886	83.16	1,249	669	53.56	828	443	53.56
1821–30	51–60	772,339	625,511	80.99	240	119	49.58	74[15]		49.58

Table 4.2(b) Marriage Rates for Age Ranges – General Male Population and Soldiers.

1821–67	14–60	6,997,666	3,665,552	52.38	28,849	4,094	14.19	57,096	8,856	15.51
pre 1861	21–60	5,318,776	3,643,728	68.51	21,655	4,066	18.78			
pre 1851	31–60	3,352,390	2,730,171	81.44	6,937	2,713	39.11			

Table 4.2(c) Age Demographics – General Male Population and Soldiers.

	General population	Soldiers in England	Soldiers in India
Percentage of population under 21	24	25	2.20
Percentage of population aged 21–30	28	51	77

garrisoned at Colchester, but only one in five at Aldershot garrisons were married. Aldershot had many raw recruits undergoing basic training, whereas guards' regiments were garrisoned at Colchester. There were, therefore, great variations in marriage rates with age, regiment, and type of army establishment.

In England, about a quarter of all the men aged 14 to 60 years were under 21, an age at which around 3 per cent of civilian men, and a mere 0.4 per cent of soldiers, were married.[16] The age demographic of European soldiers in India, however, was quite different to that in England: the 1881 census of India shows that only about 2 per cent of European soldiers serving there were under 21 (Table 4.2(c)). To get a baseline to which we can compare European marriage rates in India, it is therefore necessary to put teenagers to one side. Of men over 20 in England, around 70 per cent were married, as were 20 per cent of soldiers; and for men over 30, the rates were nearer to 80 and 40 per cent respectively.

English civil registers for 1881 record 200,600 marriages (about 3 per cent of the adult population) in that single year. Since 70 per cent of the general population aged over 20 were married but only 20 per cent of soldiers in the same age range, their marriage rate would have been less than 1 per cent annually.

There were 59,000 European British troops in India in 1881, with a 10,000 annual turnover on troop-ships.[17] Only 3 per cent of soldiers (excluding officers) took wives with them,[18] but 6 per cent left India with wives. Figures for the years before and after are similar, suggesting that 6 per cent had wives 'on the strength' when they left India after a six-year tour of duty. Half of soldiers' wives going to Britain, an extra 1,720 women, were therefore married in India.[19] Who were they? Some were daughters who, having travelled out with their fathers matured and married whilst in India. But 75 per cent of soldiers were under 30, so their daughters were unlikely to be the source of many of these extra wives.[20] That 170 army daughters reached India in 1881 but 850 daughters left is testament to their parents' youth.[21]

Even had all soldiers' daughters matured enough to marry 'on the strength' in India, this would still account for less than a thousand of the 1,720 extra wives after a six-year tour. We are left with a minimum of 700 women, every six years, who can only have come from outside the regimental families. Further, if the soldiers behaved as we know their counterparts in England did, and married without permission, then we might expect that, after correcting for age, almost 16 per cent of British soldiers in India, that is 8,600 excluding officers, would have enjoyed some form of family life in 1881, giving a total of 5,313 (886 per annum) wives, neither British-born nor 'on the strength'.

Besides age, rank affected a soldier's right to marry. Most European regiments in India were infantry and their structure did not vary much, so we can look at a single regiment to get an idea of how many European non-commissioned officers (NCOs) of each rank there were in India. As their rank rose, army regulations (and earnings) permitted marriage for a larger percentage; all first-class NCOs (warrant officers), half of sergeants, a quarter of corporals, and 10 per cent of privates who had completed a first tour, could marry 'on the strength'.[22] According to the UK Defence Forum, about a third of the current army comprises NCOs,[23] but the nineteenth-century army had fewer because there was less need for technical experts.

An 1804 muster roll for the 94th Regiment (The Scots Brigade) included 53 commissioned officers, four NCOs 1st Class (later styled 'warrant officers'), 66 sergeants, 84 corporals, and 817 privates and drummers.[24] The relative proportions of each rank changed little over the century. Thus, in 1881, one in six of the 59,000 European other ranks would have been NCOs (230 first-class NCOs, 3,800 sergeants, and 4,840 corporals), amongst whom about 3,500, by virtue of rank, could have expected to marry 'on the strength'. Besides these, a further 2,000 privates amongst the 20,000 who had completed their first term of engagement were eligible to seek permission to marry. Rank and experience would, therefore, have allowed about 5,500 'other ranks' to marry 'on the strength', representing about 9 per cent of 'other ranks'.

We now have a considerable disparity between several alternative figures: the 6 per cent returning to Britain as married men, the 9 per cent permitted to marry by rank, the 12 per cent maximum permitted by army regulations, and the near 16 per cent (over 9,000) that their counterparts' behaviour in England suggests might have been family men regardless of regulations.

Some of these men would have left wives behind in Britain before they set sail for India but, because of the men's ages, this would not have been many. Four in five British soldiers in India were still under 30, and half of those under 25. Three in five had been soldiers for six years or less, and (with up to 10,000 of 59,000 moved and replaced annually) many would have served most of that time in India.[25] Working from the army regulation maximum marriage rate of 12 per cent overall for 'other ranks', assuming that the army transported all 'on the strength' wives and children back to Britain when their husbands left, huge numbers of potential wives are missing. If 12 per cent of 'other ranks' had married but only 6 per cent took wives back to Britain, this would suggest a figure of around 3,500 missing wives. The figure was probably much higher, if soldiers in India behaved as their counterparts in England did: the 14 per cent of soldiers of all ages who were married and in England, would translate to 16 per cent in India (because of the narrower age demographic), leaving about 5,500 female partners (and partnerships) unaccounted for. It is not reasonable to accept that such a large number of men, whose counterparts in England claimed to be married, would have been blind to all possibilities except prostitutes or temporary mistresses. These were, after all, readily available in England too, but many there still chose marriage.

CIVILIANS AND OFFICERS

Besides military other ranks, there were 90,000 Europeans in 1881 India (army officers, government and quasi-government officials, non-officials, professionals, missionaries, women, and children), amongst whom the British-born numbered 14,000 civilian men (over 21), 9,600 women (over age 14), 4,811 boys and 3,297 girls, and a further 50,000 other British subjects, men women, and children, who were born outside Britain, most likely in India.[26]

The 12,600 males and 6,498 females who spoke European languages other than English were likely European nationals, but amongst these 6,306 males and 4,217 females were Portuguese speakers, the majority Eurasian of Indo-Portuguese ancestry. The number of males and females born in continental Europe, therefore, would probably have been closer to 6,300 and 2,300 respectively, but I have not attempted to identify and remove Portuguese Eurasians from my calculations.

Excluding children, military 'other ranks', and their wives 'on the strength', this gives an adult European civilian population of about 49,000 men over age 21 and not subject to military regulations, and 24,500 women over age 14. In England, of men between the ages of 21 and 60, two-thirds were married.[27] If those in India behaved in this way, then civilian Europeans and army officers would have taken around 33,500 wives, marrying 963 of them in 1881 alone, a shortfall of 9,000 European women. Brown's statistical study of marriage rates in 1864 suggests Europeans in India of high social status were more likely to marry than their counterparts in Europe. Comparing the general population and the peerage of England to members of the Bengal Civil and Madras Military Funds, Brown found army officers in India married later, but a higher percentage married than in the general population in England, and civilians in India were also more likely to marry and did so at a younger age.[28]

EUROPEAN WOMEN

Having looked at the size and demographics of the European male population of India, the number of married men, and the number who might be expected to marry, I now turn to the pool of European women available to them, to quantify any shortfall. This presupposes that, all else being equal, a European man's first choice would always be a European wife, a premise far from proven!

Some European men arriving unaccompanied in India were already married. Soldiers' wives not 'on the strength', and many who were, were left behind and could not afford to make their own way to India, and many wives of the wealthy preferred in live in Britain. The existence of a wife in Britain would not, necessarily, have prevented husbands from seeking long-term alternative arrangements in India, but we should, perhaps, exclude such men from our calculations of those seeking a relationship akin to marriage.

To get an idea of how many wives were in England whilst their husbands might have been in India, in the absence of a direct method of enumerating them, I looked at figures for India-born children in the 1881 England census. This does not represent a total for such wives, but many would have had children in India and those who remained in England were often accompanying them. Some would have been childless or mothers of adult children, but these cases were probably a minority since they had less need to live apart from their husbands.

There were 13,175 India-born children in the 1881 England census.[29] I examined households of a 5 per cent sample and found two children per woman, an average family unit in 1881.[30] Two-fifths of India-born children in England were living with neither parent,[31] a third lived with both parents, and 17 per cent were with mothers but not fathers. This suggests that 1,120 men, probably still in India, left wives in England.[32]

Most European men went to India young and single. Corrected for age and whether military proscription applied or not, two-fifths might have been expected to marry if they behaved as men in England did.[33] But there were comparatively few European women present, married or single[34] – about three (if we include the wives living in England) to every 11 men (Tables 4.3 and 4.4). Even if every adult European woman in India were a wife, it would mean only two-thirds of men who would have married had they been in Europe, i.e. 27 per cent of all the European men in India could anticipate marrying a European woman. The remaining roughly 14,500 likely

Table 4.3 European Population of India, 1881.[35]

	Men over 21	Women over 14	Boys <21	Girls <14
British born (other ranks)	59,000	9,600	4,811	3,297
Others – British born	14,000			
British but born elsewhere[36]	25,000	13,500	6,785 est.	4,715 est.
Other Europeans[37]	10,128 est.	4,770 est.	2,487 est.	1,728 est.
Subtotal	**108,128**	**27,870**	**14,083**	**9,740**
Total	159,821 persons			

Table 4.4 Shortfall of European Women in India, 1881.

All European men	108,128		
All European women	27,870		
	Number	**Expected per cent married**	**Number expected to marry**
Soldiers	59,000	15.51[38]	9,151
Other European men	49,128	68.51[39]	33,657
Total number of European men who might be expected to marry (percentage of total)	42,808 (40.5 per cent)		
European women in India	27,870		
Wives in England	1,120		
Shortfall	**13,819**		

to have sought a wife had to make other arrangements. This is an underestimate, since we know some European women remained unmarried. They travelled to India at great expense, often with the aim of finding a husband, but those who did not succeed returned to Britain as the 'returned empties'.[40]

Williamson's 1810 *Vade Mecum* estimated the annual outlay on a European wife (for a 'man of quality') at about £600, whereas a native woman suitable for a longer-term relationship could be kept well for £48 a year.[41] Innes Munro's estimates were £360 and £30–48 per year respectively. Munro said a whole *zenana* of Indians would be cheaper than one English 'lady'. The idea of a *zenana*, exclusive and accommodated in a household, suggests he was costing a long-term arrangement rather than one involving prostitutes.[42] Neither Williamson nor Gilchrist mention the 'bargain basement', at the military orphanages, of officers' daughters, European or legitimate Eurasian, who came with an orphan's 'marriage portion' of one or two thousand rupees.[43] Nevertheless, amongst the younger European elite yet to earn a good wage, there was still considerable scope and incentive for relationships with Eurasian and Indian women.

The presence of 'fishing fleet' women was irrelevant to common British soldiers who, like Indians, belonged (socially) to another race.[44] Amongst poorer European men who might have wanted a European wife, choice was severely limited by the policy of Company and Crown to keep working-class European settlement to a minimum:

> India offers no field for popular emigration ... A settler in the East Indies may be said to resemble in many respects a planter in the West. He introduces capital and skill, but avails himself of native labour. Colonisation, in fact, must originate in India from the upper and not from the lower classes of society; and the true function of a European there, is not that of a labourer but as a director of labour.[45]

Government had little choice but to import working-class men as soldiers, but did not want a surfeit of working-class European women. There was never an adequate supply of such women, not even after travel costs dropped with the opening of the Suez Canal.

The low pay of soldiers restricted their ability to support a family, but did not necessarily discourage them. Whether European, Eurasian, or native, working-class women often earned their own keep and contributed to the family income. In England, this was shown to increase marriage rates.[46]

There were several ways, besides resorting to regimental daughters, for European other ranks to find European wives in India. The widows of crown troops were obliged to remarry within six months because the army ceased to support them after that.[47] But Quinney's account says private soldiers found it hard to compete: 'The [private's] widow ... evinced early symptoms of an anxiety again to enter the matrimonial state, but nothing under the rank of a conductor seemed good enough in her estimation, and one of that rank she actually obtained.'[48]

Also near the garrisons were predecessors' discarded 'wives', left behind when a regiment redeployed. Whether these were mistresses or wives is a matter of semantics and class perspective. Serial monogamy was perfectly acceptable amongst the 'respectable' working classes in England, especially in garrison towns and ports where men came and went, often for many years, leaving their 'wives' and children to cope as best they could. As Walkowitz put it: 'Poor residents [of Plymouth] ... adhered to standards of sexual and social behaviour that were in sharp contrast to conventional Victorian mores.'[49] In the later decades of the century, railwaymen's daughters and widows were also available. At all dates, single working-class women arrived in India as servants to wealthier families:

> Whenever a lady has carried out an European female servant, whether old or young, ugly or beautiful, a speedy separation has usually taken place: many, indeed, have deserted their mistresses while touching at Madras ... Bonds, contracts, or agreements, are all cancelled ... the necessity for upholding the British character, however much formerly neglected by some

> persons in power, is now so well understood, that, without absolute compulsion, no magistrate would commit an European woman upon a charge of neglect of duty, inebriety, insolence, or other such impropriety.[50]

It is reasonable to conclude since most European women in India were either already married, of a higher social class, or looking for a wealthier catch, that common soldiers might look for relationships with Eurasian or Indian women.

EURASIAN AND NATIVE WOMEN

I have identified a shortfall of European women of about 14,500 in 1881, and suggested that since so many men had little hope of returning to Europe they sought family life in India. They had plenty of opportunities to meet and marry Eurasian women. Stanley said: 'Soldiers coveted marriage as a route to both solace and respectability.'[51]

Men visited orphanages to find wives amongst the older girls. Anthony said most European men in India found wives amongst the orphan girls who were all raised with that purpose in mind.[52] William Butterfield chose his wife Elizabeth Daniels when visiting Madras Military Female Asylum in 1834.[53] Eliza Gaghan, Margaret Garvey, Mary Gibbons, Elizabeth Gill, and Elizabeth Grimes were also removed for marriage, although no record appears of these events in the ecclesiastical returns. Staff Sergeant Thomas Quinney, however, who visited Bombay's Central School, said:

> When the children are orphans they frequently become the wives of young men who manage to obtain a character from their commanding officer, and are thus introduced to the secretary (generally the chaplain . . .), who admits them to the school-room as casual visitors. This usually ends in a matrimonial engagement. In such instances, however, the girl must be married before she is allowed to leave the establishment.[54]

Not only was there plenty of opportunity to meet Eurasian girls, some came with a financial sweetner. Of the Lower Military Orphan School, Bengal, Lushington reported in 1824:

> The female wards, when arrived at a suitable age, are chiefly disposed of in marriage to Non-Commissioned Officers, and Privates, Drummers, &c. in the King's and Company's Regiments, and to other persons of reputable character. To those who become the wives of Soldiers, an allowance of four rupees per mensem each is paid from the public Funds.[55]

Soldiers (especially NCOs) were invited to Railway Institute social events: 'Some BORs [British other ranks] fought both army regulations and prejudice to marry Eurasian girls, usually encountered at the Railway institute dances that did much to lessen the isolation of the British soldier'.[56] It was harder to meet native women, with native settlements and town bazaars usually off-limits to soldiers, but contact with the Eurasian community was not curtailed. The social gulf between British other ranks and railway families was easier to bridge than that between these men and European 'society' ladies. Railway girls and orphans were obvious and readily available sources of female companionship for British soldiers.

There is evidence to suggest that fewer Europeans, even of the lower classes, married Eurasians towards the end of the nineteenth century. In 1881, troop-ships brought 375 women to India with the other ranks, and returned 628. Thus, 253 wives had been added to 'the strength' whilst in India, who, for economic reasons alone, are unlikely to have been Europeans. Numbers were similar in the next year, and are likely to have been comparable in the previous decade, but in the subsequent three years more wives were brought out from Britain and the extra numbers returning declined to under 100.

Officers' wives who arrived on troopships left in similar numbers, with no change in pattern over time.[57] No regulations restricted officers' marriages, and wives were entitled to travel with them, but there were social pressures that discouraged senior men from choosing 'unsuitable' Eurasian or native wives. Moreover, officers and covenanted men were entitled to furloughs 'home', during which many acquired their European wives. The opening of the Suez Canal also contributed to the practicability of taking a European wife. These factors support the view that interracial relationships amongst the upper echelons of British society fell away at an earlier date than they did for others.

ECCLESIASTICAL RETURNS

The European demographic in India, allowing for age, rank, and occupation, suggests 40 per cent of men would have wished to marry (see Table 4.4). To maintain such a rate would have required about 1.7 per cent to marry each year; in 1881 India that represents about 1,800 marriages per annum, but there were only about 1,500 marriages in the ecclesiastical returns. This figure, over time, would maintain only a 34 per cent marriage rate for European men within India.[58]

The difference between the two-fifths predicted and the third recorded may represent a failure to marry, but contemporary sources suggest Europeans in India were more likely to marry than their counterparts at home.[59] Most men went to India before marriage, and those who married on furlough returned with wives, at least until the children were sent home, and so their spouses are accounted for. The disparity could therefore signify irregular marriage forms not recorded in ecclesiastical returns. But, even leaving aside predicted behaviour based on that of men in England, we are left with the fact that the number of marriages in the ecclesiastical returns for India exceeds the number of European women there. About 7,600 men in India, 7 per cent of them all, were therefore in legal marriages that could only have been to Eurasians or Indian Christians.[60]

These figures could be reduced by the presence of endogamous Eurasian marriages amongst the returns, but Eurasians were classed as statutory natives and, as such, unless marrying a European, most would have been entered in registers of native Christian marriages.[61] Since these remained in district offices all over India, and many native Christians acquired European names, exploring these registers would be neither practical nor helpful.

The 1881 India census counted 62,085 Eurasian men, women, and children.[62] Working on a total marriage rate of 52 per cent, as in England, for the adult general population, we can infer that amongst 20,695 Eurasian males, 10,761 could have been married.[63] To maintain that number would have required 311 marriages per annum, spread across the European and native Christian registers. Race is rarely recorded in indexes of the ecclesiastical returns, but careful examination of individual records for 1881 identifies some endogamous Eurasian marriages and further reduces the percentage of Europeans legally married whilst in India. However, this inaccuracy, a maximum of 311 entries per year, will only serve to increase the likelihood of irregular marriages of Europeans.

COMPARISONS

Suresh Ghosh found 1,581 'European marriages' in Bengal returns to the Court of Directors between 1757 and 1800, amongst 2,626 *writers* and cadets, 3,500 non-officials, and about 10,000 European troops. About a quarter to an eighth of all European men in Bengal, therefore, formally married there. Rates of marriage, by status, were: one in four *writers*, one in ten cadets, between one in ten and one in 45 military other ranks, and an eighth of non-officials.[64] The wording 'European marriages' is carefully chosen since Ghosh describes the ubiquity not of celibacy but of 'marriages in all but name'. The fact that amongst 100 men the author found one in eight married and I found three or four in every ten to be married, including one in eight definitely married to Eurasians or Indians, is not necessarily contradictory, since we are concerned with different time periods. In this earlier period, there were even fewer European women, a lack of clergymen who might have performed marriages, and more likelihood of interfaith relationships precluding 'European' marriages.

My figures are in keeping with those of Thomas Munro, Governor of Madras, for those who would marry if they could afford to. In his 1824 argument against pensioning 'half-caste' women, he stated:

> If we change that system for one of giving a permission not only upon marriage, but upon the number of children, we shall encourage the production of a great and helpless population, and increase a hundredfold by our ill-judged humanity the distress it was meant to diminish. If we suppose that a half or a third of the European soldiers marry half-caste women, there will be in India ten to fifteen thousand wives with their children to maintain at the public charge. But this is not all – there will in twenty years be several successions, because the number of men will be renewed two or three times over in twenty years.[65]

Munro's comments were written in the year that Eurasian wives were admitted to some military pension funds.[66]

CONCLUSIONS

In 1881, the number of European men formally married to Eurasian and Indian women was at least 7,600, with a similar number, if they behaved like soldiers and civilians in England, cohabiting. This would mean, late in the century, that one in seven European men continued to form interracial relationships.

I have shown that in England rates of marriage amongst soldiers, whilst less than those amongst the general population, were higher than army regulations permitted, and I conclude that, if they ignored regulations to marry, so too would soldiers in India.

I found only sufficient European women in India and wives in Europe to partner a quarter of the men, and yet the ecclesiastical returns show legal marriages sufficient to maintain a 34 per cent marriage rate. The difference, therefore, indicates marriages with non-European women. In reality, this figure would be higher since no allowance was made for unmarried European women in India.

From the behaviour of their peers in England, I expected to find in India up to one in six of privates and NCOs and over two-thirds of other men married – about 40 per cent of European men. I found just over a third married according to ecclesiastical returns. It is possible that the difference represents European men in India sacrificing a basic human need for home, family, and companionship, completely changing their behaviour compared with their counterparts in England, and remaining unmarried. More likely, this portion of European men in India formed *de facto* marriages, with Eurasian and Indian women.

One in seven European men in 1881 was likely to have had a Eurasian or Indian spouse, half of them legally married and documented and the remainder living as man and wife. These figures represent a tiny proportion of Indian women but, even if *de facto* marriages are excluded, a substantial proportion of the much smaller Eurasian community. Exogamy therefore facilitated close and continuous cultural ties between the European and Eurasian populations.

The speculation about numbers involved in 'regular' relationships matters because a norm of respectability, in parallel with Europeans, was keenly espoused by later generations of Eurasians. Further exploring the basis for this, two main questions arising from this chapter will be addressed in the next. Firstly, what was understood by the concept of marriage? Because different races, faiths, denominations, nationalities and social classes were involved, I will explore various understandings of 'marriage' besides the legal and practical issues. Secondly, what happened to Eurasian and Indian women and children when a husband died, when he was posted elsewhere, or when he could not or would not continue to support them?

CHAPTER 5

LAW AND MARRIAGE

Marriages between Eurasians of the same denomination were easily achieved, but a common assumption is that mixed unions in nineteenth-century India were overwhelmingly *un*-married relationships. Anthony insisted: '... nothing is further from the truth. The Community has developed along quite formal and legitimate lines.'[1] Anthony's perspective was informed by a wish to rescue his community's reputation from stereotyping;[2] Eurasians were no more or less moral than the European British.[3] Elite British men in India drafted the laws defining marriage, and thus where the line between mistress and wife was drawn – but even an accountant-general admitted, regretfully, that after many years in India, 'we lose our English ideas, and our English affections; until, in fact, we forget the distinction between a concubine and a wife'.[4] This blurring of boundaries means that, rather than applying to all marriages a middle-class, European template, the concepts of marriage,[5] wife, and mistress need a re-examination for our purposes.

Restricting marriage to something accepted in law, or by the established church, does not bear scrutiny even when applied to marriage forms in Britain. Scotland accepted an informal exchange of vows before witnesses into the twentieth century, when at least 12 per cent of valid marriages had neither documentation nor clergy involvement. Nor were these civil marriages; there were none in Scotland until 1939![6] Civil marriage, possible in England and Wales from 1837, could be an unpleasant ordeal as registrars' offices were normally sited in workhouses. Nonetheless, in 1864 this route was chosen by 23 per cent of Welsh couples and 3 per cent of Londoners, and in 1880 by 40 per cent of couples in Northern England.[7] But this marriage form was not available in colonial India.[8]

Elsewhere in Europe there were valid, legally binding forms of wedlock, such as the 'German left-handed marriage' between couples of unequal social standing. A British variant, whereby mixed-race or working-class women might be selected by British 'gentlemen', sometimes even sanctioned by court order, was found in West Indian colonies, at least prior to 1830.[9]

Thomas Metcalf describes interracial relationships in India thus:

> Before the mid-nineteenth century a high proportion of army officers and civil servants kept Indian mistresses. Books of guidance for young men going to India assumed that they would do precisely that. Critics of what was alleged to be the prudery of later generations have assumed that liaisons were conducive to good race relations. Some well-documented instances do indeed leave no doubt of deep mutual affection, but in many cases such relationships were highly exploitative of the women involved, since offspring were usually not recognised and the man abandoned the woman when he returned to Europe.[10]

No doubt Metcalf's view is correct with respect to Victorian prudery and exploitation of women, although others dispute his assertion that children were usually not recognized.[11] Metcalf's view of the British would not apply to all, without regard to class heterogeneity; Stanley, also describing the first half century, claimed: 'The Company's soldiers had always demonstrated a greater willingness to stay in India after discharge, partly from having married Eurasian or native women' and Kipling's returning soldier pined for his 'neater, sweeter maiden in a cleaner, greener land'.[12] Stanley and Kipling portray working-class British soldiers, the majority of the British in India.

By the application of Metcalf's views to all British in India, a reader might infer that man and mistress was the only relationship possible between European men and Indian or Eurasian women. Of course, there were sex workers: street prostitutes available to anyone; brothel prostitutes for casual hire or attached to specific regiments; and exclusive prostitutes reserved for specific customers. Whether *bibis* should be regarded as sex workers is questionable; their condition is only considered dissimilar to marriage because their contracts were temporary and they lacked acceptability in British 'society'.

Post-Mutiny, political change denied many ordinary British men the stability of Stanley's Company soldiers who had enlisted for long Indian service. Short-service enlistment became common and regiments, all now Crown regiments, were more frequently redeployed worldwide. But it does not follow that such changes would necessarily have altered personal behaviour. If men could not marry with permission, could not afford for their families to travel, had not served their time, and the army refused to allow them to transfer and remain in India, what else could they do but abandon their families? The charge of exploitation might more properly be applied to the government that made the laws and policies, than to men who were just as exploited as Indian and Eurasian women.

Even limiting Metcalf's view to the class he was considering, army officers and civil servants, he does not take into account different conceptions of marriage, different understandings of the social standing of 'mistresses', or what the women themselves may have thought their particular relationship signified. Indian women did not necessarily share the middle-class European view that a mistress was not a wife. Nor does Metcalfe's view highlight the legal and social impediments to interfaith and interracial marriage.

The influx of evangelical Christians after 1833 magnified the problem; to them, marriage was a religious institution, a contract with or before God, or even a sacrament, so it could hardly include a 'heathen'. Their voices were prominent in metropolitan society and parliament. The 'moral laxity' of the previous century became unacceptable in genteel society. The morality of the country's representatives in India became a public concern, and not simply for the sanctity of a Christian institution.

Company directors in 1784 expressed disquiet over the 'imperfections' of the children of European men by Indian women: '... whether bodily or mental; that is whether consisting in their colour, their conformation, or their genius ...'.[13] There was a perception that the moral laxity of their progenitors was an inherited characteristic of a whole community. The mantra that 'half-castes' exhibited the worst characteristics of both parent races, and few of their virtues, was common in contemporary literature. Hyam claims that this attitude sprang from the Cornwallis and Wellesley reforms, which discouraged miscegenation and increased the social gulf between Britons and Indians.[14] It was later fed by 'scientific' racism. Darwin stated, '... the degraded state of so many half-castes is in part due to reversion to a primitive and savage condition, induced by the act of crossing, as well as to the unfavourable moral conditions under which they generally exist'.[15]

The heterogeneity to be found in Eurasian ancestry added further layers of discrimination. Raikes, former North-West Provinces' commissioner and judge, spoke with authority and long Indian experience. On the failings of Indo-Portuguese clerks, he claimed, 'anywhere in India ... [they are] vegetating rather than living, with the vices of the European added to the superstitions of the heathen'. Rather than limit himself to personal experience, he also pronounced on events a century before: Madras had been lost to France because the British force was half composed of *Topasses*: '... a black, degenerate, wretched race of half-caste Portuguese, utterly destitute of fighting qualities'.[16] 'Eurasian' became shorthand for illegitimacy, immorality, weakness, and criminality – more so when of Portuguese stock. This stereotyping served to justify Eurasians' exclusion from high-ranking positions, and diminished their worth in Indian eyes.

The conflation of immorality with 'Eurasian' rested on three premises: that Europeans in India subscribed to contemporary middle-class values and marriage practices, and Eurasians did not; that illegitimacy was so widespread amongst Eurasians that the labels were effectively interchangeable; and that since interracial sex was unnatural,[17] the products of such unions were also unnatural. Such stigmatizing led to resentment and social difficulties.

The must numerous British men in India were enlisted working-class privates and NCOs. In 1895, besides Royal Artillery, engineers and cavalry, there were 51 British infantry battalions in India.[18] There were also skilled working-class civilians, supervising and implementing infrastructural change. In 1881, at least 4,500 British-born working men were employed across the Indian railways.[19] Raj reportage was shaped by the values of an elite (numbering only 3,000 to 4,000), but it is the 65,000 working men whose behaviour represents the lived experience of the British in India and their interactions with Indians and Eurasians.

This chapter explores various 'marital' relationships formed between British men and Indian or Eurasian women. Beginning with marriage law, customs, and practices, rules governing or applied to Indians, Europeans, and Eurasians are explored. The last section considers the implications of these findings for the Eurasian community. What emerges, in a Raj filled with common soldiers and railwaymen rather than gentlemen, is a sizable 'grey area', in which many marriages were neither legally sanctioned nor void. As in England and Wales amongst the respectable working classes, and in Scotland across all classes, these relationships sat between legal marriage and the world of mistresses and prostitutes.

LEGAL MARRIAGE

Legislation

The Government of India, Company and Crown, divided the population into Europeans and Eurasians, exclusively Christian, and Indians who professed indigenous religions or were converts. It recognized pre-existing codes of personal law, customs, and practices signifying marriage, studied Hindu and Islamic law, and consulted with *pandits*, *maulvis*, and *vakils*. Armenian and Syrian Christianity was considered indigenous, Roman Catholicism and Protestantism were not. The Indian Marriage Act, applicable to Europeans and Eurasians, appeared in 1851, but its scope was limited to prevention of the clandestine marriage of minors and clarifying the legal powers of registrars to conduct marriages. The governor-general decided, case by case, whether he 'thought it desirable that evidence should be transmitted to England', and the validity of dissenters' marriages by nonconformist ministers was not addressed.[20] The Marriage Act of 1872 still left confusion over the validity and legality of many marriages involving Europeans or Eurasians in India.

The English Marriage Act of 1753 (the Hardwick Act) was the first to stipulate the conditions of a legal marriage in England: '... with banns or a license, with parental permission for minors, before witnesses and an authorized clergyman, in a church, during specified hours, and by recording the event in a Marriage Register'.[21] Authorized clergymen had to be ordained by an established church bishop. The only exceptions were Quakers and Jews. Scottish irregular marriage continued to be legal, a loophole attracting English couples to Gretna Green.[22] Catholic recusant and nonconformist marriages, though valid, were not legal unless performed by an Anglican clergyman with established church rites. Civil registration of English marriages, introduced in 1836, remained unenforceable before 1855. Anglican canon law recognized publicly exchanged vows (spousals) and cohabitation as valid marriages, but English civil courts recognized only church marriage and most people mistakenly believed a clergyman was needed to perform a valid marriage.[23] In England pre-Hardwick, what constituted marriage was confused and that confusion was exported to India. However, contrary to much of contemporary opinion, the Hardwick Act did not apply there.

Buchanan, an Anglican clergyman, highlighted confusion over the validity of British marriages in India, in 1813, claiming the majority did not meet the requirements for a legal English marriage.[24] He may have been unaware that there was no legal requirement that they should.

The Justice of the Peace and Parish Officer aimed to supply its readers 'with as much law as is necessary for the execution of their respective offices'.[25] Its editors, barristers and legal writers of great repute, addressed the legal status of British subjects marrying in India.[26]

Finding no specific legislation governing such marriages, they concluded: 'A marriage celebrated out of England, according to the *lex loci* [or law of the place] is recognised in this country as a valid marriage, and not affected by the marriage Acts. What is called the Marriage Act does not follow subjects to foreign settlements.'[27]

This assessment still stood in 1850, when Buchanan's concerns were echoed by the Parliamentary Commission on East-India marriages: '. . . questions of a very serious character arise with respect to the validity of marriages heretofore solemnized; and, consequently, doubts may exist, both as to the *status*[28] of individuals, and rights to property'.[29] Despite the commissioner's plea for legislation only the limp provisions of the 1851 Act resulted, and, since it did not say otherwise, marriage under Indian personal law or pre-Hardwick English law remained valid under contemporary English law.[30] Whether Company or Crown government honoured this is another matter. Although not required by any law, both expected sanction to be sought before a European British subject married. The Chittys discussed the validity of a Catholic marriage between British subjects at Madras, for which no governor's licence had been sought:[31]

> the question . . . is whether it would have been a valid marriage here [England] before that act passed. And his lordship [sic] lays down, that 'a marriage between British subjects, celebrated in a British settlement, according to the laws of this country, as they existed before the Marriage Act,' is . . . valid.[32]

British (or English) authorities accepted Catholic marriages of British subjects in India on the same basis as in mainland Britain; before Catholic emancipation (pre-1829), such marriages were considered valid but not strictly legal.

The Chittys also claimed marriages between Catholics and Protestants were void if conducted by Catholic priests.[33] In India, where Anglican clergy were few, Catholic priests easier to find, and half of Eurasians were Catholic, many marriages may have been voidable. The Chittys also made passing reference to *de facto* marriage, legally defined as 'in practice but not necessarily ordained by law'. Various forms of *de facto* marriages, recognized and practised amongst the English working classes and in garrison towns and ports, would have continued amongst soldiers in India, even though government refused to recognize them.[34]

Whereas interfaith couples could undergo civil marriage in England from 1837, there was no such facility in British India. Registrars, officers, and magistrates there could only conduct marriages according to Anglican rites. There was never a British-Indian law enabling marriage between European Christians and any Indian other than another Christian, and even then most clergymen would expect a couple to belong to the same denomination.[35] Officers (civil and military) could also refuse to marry a couple based on their assessment of the character of groom or bride, some believing Indian or mixed 'blood' to be a sufficient character flaw. Gilchrist lamented Eurasian women's tendency towards insanity,[36] and the Eurasian woman of easy virtue was a widespread stereotype. Some officers were against soldiers' marriages *per se*, believing families were a nuisance.

Two further differences between lawful marriage in India and England are also documented by the Chittys; an English Act of 1828 made some fundamental differences to the effects of long-term spousal absence and to what constituted bigamy in England.[37] Previously, anyone whose spouse, even if living, had been abroad for over seven years was free to remarry.[38] After 1828, a missing spouse had to be dead or else a second marriage was considered bigamous.[39] Before 1828, second marriages occurring outside the jurisdiction of English law were not punishable as bigamy; after the Act, they were.[40] The difference in this and the previous point is that there was no qualifying period; the 'missing' spouse could marry as soon as they left English jurisdiction. The Chittys claimed the 1828 Act had not been extended to India. The British, in Indian presidency towns, were subject to English law but only as it applied when those settlements were founded. Since the 1828 Act was not extended to India, married English men and women were free to remarry there and, provided they stayed abroad, were not bigamists.[41]

Clergymen

Early in the century, Anglican marriage could be difficult because there were few Anglican clergymen in India. Buchanan said, 'Of fifty one stations only eight are supplied with Chaplains', and so civil magistrates or army officers conducted marriages and burials, and baptism was frequently deferred. He suggested: 'It is possible, that some circumstance may arise which will make it necessary for an Act of Parliament to pass, to give validity to the marriages in India, solemnized by laymen, for the last fifty years.'[42] Buchanan identified only 35 Anglican chaplains serving in British India. In 1836, a report on the ministry in Bengal in *The Times* claimed:

> It appears by an official statement, that in the presidency of Bengal there are, exclusive of the chaplains paid by the Government, 31 Roman Catholic ministers and missionaries; 28 Episcopalians; 21 Baptists, connected with the Serampore mission; 15 Baptists, connected with the Baptist Missionary Society; 10 Independents; 9 American Baptists; 7 Armenians; 3 General Baptists; 3 Presbyterians (Scotch); 3 Presbyterians (American); and 2 Greek; making, altogether, 132.[43]

By 1881, the situation had changed little; there were then 381 British clergymen to cover all of British India.

National Status

How a marriage was recorded depended on denomination and, later, national status. The terms 'British Subject' and 'Native of India' were introduced in the Regulating Act of 1773, leaving the question of whether Eurasians were British subjects or not open to interpretation because the Act said nothing about their status.[44] Inconsistent interpretation created problems for Eurasians after 1872, as it determined where their endogamous Christian marriages might have been registered. The Act required two registers: one for marriages of British subjects, from which ecclesiastical returns were transmitted to London; the other, recording marriages of native Christians, stayed in India at district level. There was no separate register for Eurasian marriages. The only guidance in the Act was that those born, naturalized, or domiciled in Britain and their legitimate children and grandchildren were British subjects. Illegitimate Eurasians were not considered British under this Act. If one parent had been a Eurasian, if British-born antecedents were further removed, or if the necessary paperwork to prove legitimacy was not produced, then the question of which register to use depended on an individual clergyman's decision. Eurasian endogamous marriages could therefore appear in either register.

THE CHURCH

Even marriages between two European Christians could be problematic because of inflexible laws, and doctrinal and political differences between denominations. At the beginning of the nineteenth century, the established churches of Britain still presumed everyone was a member of the established church even though the days of 'church as state' had gone. But differences in doctrine, in the way marriage was accomplished, and in its significance were, to an extent, dealt with by the introduction of civil marriage in England and Wales and by greater flexibility in Scotland. This did not hold true in British India.

Divisions amongst Scottish Protestants, particularly the absence of bishops in the Free Church, posed special legal difficulties requiring a more flexible understanding of the concept of marriage, but despite the presence there of large numbers of Scots, including many lawyers, this was not extended to India.

Besides Britain's reluctance to recognize marriages outside its own established church, Roman Catholic and many foreign, indigenous, and nonconformist churches were reluctant to make returns to British authorities, and so data is missing from the ecclesiastical returns. The Syrian, Armenian, and Goan Catholic Churches were considered indigenous religions, so provided a couple were also indigenous their rites were respected in the same way as those of any other indigenous religion, unless one or both parties to a marriage were European. But besides British nonconformists there were many

American, Danish, German, and other foreign Christian churches with European and Eurasian followers in India.

The Established Church and Other Protestant Denominations

Before 1833, the Company rarely allowed British missionaries into India. Its own chaplains were there to minister to the official community, which often left non-officials, Eurasians, and officials in remote stations with little access to clergymen of their own. The gap was sometimes filled by Catholic priests; alternatively, there were some Baptist, Armenian, and Lutheran clergy, who conducted marriages. However, on-going theological debates in the Anglican Church about the status of Lutheran bishops and the apostolic succession meant the validity of marriages performed by Lutheran clergy ordained by German bishops was in doubt. Thus:

> The Reverent Reichardt [of Heidelberg] ... in 1825 ... was ordained by Bishop Heber. Having been previously a Lutheran minister, he received ordination from the Bishop, in order that he might be a recognised minister of the English Church, and also that his ministerial acts might be of legal force, as in India the marriages of Dissenting ministers are not considered valid in point of law.[45]

Reichardt was not alone, but many nonconformist clergy would not have taken such a step.[46]

As in Britain, dissenters, Catholics, and Jews sometimes married, and had their families baptized, in the established church to ensure their status did not prove problematic for marriage, legitimacy, inheritance, or work. John Hammerdinger was baptized in Buxar in January 1818 although his parents are described as Jews, not converts. In Calcutta, Martha Isaacs renounced Judaism and was baptized in 1779, four days before she married Alexander Higginson, a member of the Board of Trade. Three adults – John Vendrick in 1789, Paul Raphael in 1844, and John Charles in 1766 – all renounced Judaism and were baptized Anglicans. Since these baptisms were not followed by marriage, their motives may have been work related. William and Louisa Caustaut, though already married in a Catholic ceremony in Chandernagore, had an Anglican marriage in 1823 at Dum Dum.[47]

For non-Christians, sudden conversion could be a pragmatic step. Helen Beg, 'mistress' of Alexander Speirs (British Resident, Gwalior,1847) bore him eight children, remained Muslim during their 30-year relationship, but was finally baptized and married under British law, an act which would certainly have simplified probate. Speirs had intended returning to Scotland with his family just before he died,[48] and under Scottish law children became legitimate on their mother's marriage.

Catholicism

Most Irish soldiers in India were Roman Catholics. Whereas Catholic marriages in England, Scotland, and Wales were not fully recognized in law until 1829, they were legal in Ireland long before: they were a matter for the Church and not subject to the same laws as they were elsewhere in Britain. In an 1817 House of Lords debate, an Anglican bishop complained:

> ... the Roman Catholic clergy of Ireland, with respect to marriages, exercise a power which the Protestant clergy are forbidden by law to exercise ... A Roman Catholic clergyman marries his parishioners without any banns, and is liable to no penalties.[49]

Catholic emancipation came to England in 1829.[50] The Emancipation Act removed: 'certain Restraints and Disabilities ... imposed on the Roman Catholic subjects of His Majesty, to which other subjects ... are not liable'.[51] It was meant to quell Irish discontent by allowing Catholics to sit as members of parliament and to hold civil and military offices. It also meant that British Catholics going to India were now more socially diverse and could include officers and covenanted servants.

Divisions within the Catholic Church affected the validity of marriages in India. Portugal's monarch had papal authority in all matters relating to eastern dioceses, including appointing clergy, but against the wishes of Portugal the Pope's Vicars Apostolic were also in India, and they established an alternative Catholic clergy. British authorities in India left congregations to choose which they recognized, but the Vicars Apostolic declared marriages under Portuguese authority invalid. Since the Company paid many Portuguese priests to act as civil and military chaplains, this had serious implications for the legality of many Catholic marriages.[52]

The India Office Library's description of marriage returns cautions that they are incomplete, and this is especially true of Catholic returns. These only began in 1835, 130 years later than Anglican ones.[53] Even then, Catholic clergy were often French, Italian, or Portuguese,[54] and may not have felt obligated to make returns to the British government. A glance through the French marriage index from Chandernagore, for example, shows marriages which are included in Bengal returns but also many which are not recorded elsewhere, even though they involve British subjects.[55] Likewise, marriages at St Thomas Mount Portuguese Mission Church, some involving serving British soldiers, are usually not included in British ecclesiastical returns.[56]

In 1852, the Company government offered an extra Rs 200 per month to Catholic bishops in India who made 'sacred returns', but even this sizable incentive moved only four of the 16 bishops to comply.[57] At most, therefore, a quarter of Catholic marriages and births were returned.

Scottish Understanding

British law never was monolithic. Scotland's right to its own law was enshrined in the Act of Union of 1707. Scotsmen abroad in the empire, serving with Scottish regiments, firms, or missions, might have assumed that Scottish personal law applied to them. It did not.[58] They were governed by English law and, later, laws written specifically for India. Whilst England and Wales' courts took cognisance of Scots law, and were willing to apply it to Scots in England and Wales, it was considered 'almost impossible' to do so in India. Despite a large body of Scottish lawyers and judges there, it was thought unreasonable to apply two systems of law for Europeans.[59] Since so many Scotsmen served in India, it is worth noting some of the differences in Scots, English, and British-Indian personal law.

Scottish law recognized marriages in the established (Episcopalian) Church of Scotland, in the Free (Presbyterian) Church, and, until 1939, irregular marriage remained legal. Irregular marriage took three forms: declaration (spousals) before witnesses, sexual relations after a marriage promise, or publicly living together as man and wife. Irregular marriage remained legal for so long because it was considered preferable to 'living in sin'. As late as 1914, 12 per cent of all Scottish marriages were irregular, and so Scots in India would likely have behaved similarly.[60]

The Indian Christian Marriage Act recognized only marriages performed by clergymen ordained by bishops, and so Free Church marriages were illegal[61] – as were all irregular marriages acceptable to and common amongst Scots. Thus, a wife and child recognized and perfectly respectable amongst Scots would be considered a mistress and illegitimate child in India.

Divorce in the nineteenth century was rare, but there were striking differences between Scottish and English divorce laws. Scots law allowed men or women to petition for divorce on grounds of adultery, but under English law this was grounds only for a man to divorce a wife. English divorce, mid-century, cost about £2,000, whereas in the 1890s a Scottish one could cost as little as £12.[62] There was also a jurisdiction conflict. In 1861:

> Lolley, having married an English wife, went across the border and procured a divorce in Scotland. If he had married again in Scotland, the second marriage would have been lawful, and his children legitimate; but, returning to England and marrying here, he was convicted for bigamy and sentenced to transportation, and his children of the second marriage were illegitimate.[63]

Illegitimate children in England and Wales had no automatic right to inherit their father's property. In Scotland, legitimate and illegitimate children enjoyed identical inheritance rights provided the father had acknowledged his paternity. Illegitimate birth in English law was a burden for life that could not be undone, whereas in Scottish law illegitimate children became legitimate on their mother's marriage.[64]

INDIAN CUSTOMS AND THE *LEX LOCI*

The Chittys maintained that any form of marriage in India that was according to the *lex loci* (or law of the place) had to be recognized in England and Wales as valid. Therefore prior to the 1872 Marriage Act, if Europeans entered into Islamic or Hindu marriages that satisfied Indian legal and doctrinal experts, then those marriages should be considered valid (if not legal) even when not conforming in English law. Instead, such relationships were frequently diminished, bracketed together with relationships with sex workers, and dismissively labelled 'convenient arrangements'.

Islamic Rites

Before the 1753 Hardwick Act, there was no legal definition of what constituted marriage in England and Wales. Before the 1872 Indian Christian Marriage Act, there was no legislation to prevent British subjects in India marrying non-Christians. There was therefore nothing, in English or British-Indian law, to prevent or void interfaith marriage prior to 1872. Any proscription was therefore either doctrinal or social. Evangelical Christians arrived in early nineteenth-century India with a mission to save 'heathens', not to marry them. Whether through their influence or that of the increasing number of European women present, interfaith marriage, though its legal status remained uncertain,[65] became effectively void in the eyes of the British ruling elite. This was not necessarily the case when viewed from a Muslim perspective, or that of the British working classes, or even outside of Calcutta 'society'.[66]

Muslim marriage customs included two types of *nikah* contract, one temporary (now rare) and one permanent, both of which were legally binding under Islamic law. Rizvi's 1988 explanation of Muslim marriage in India is informative:

> Marriage is a contract in Islam. At its core is *nikah* – it comprises:
>
> 1. Incantation of holy verses (*segha*)
> 2. Seeking permission of intended bride in front of 2 witnesses (*wakil*)
> 3. A prenuptial financial guarantee to the bride (*mehr*)
>
> *Nikah-e-daimi* was permanent, conferred property rights (both ways) and divorce, though possible, was difficult.
>
> *Nikah-e-inqatai* [or *mutah*] was less binding and without property rights. It still needed all elements of *nikah* but a pre-arranged term was agreed – anything from hours to life. A man could buy out early on payment of *mehr* to his wife but remained responsible for his children's upkeep. Neither party had rights over the other's property.[67]

It does not appear that both parties had to be Indian, or even Muslim. Local experts interpreted Muslim law, and, for many, marriages between 'people of the book' – Muslim, Jewish, or Christian – were possible. The substance of *nikah* has not changed during or since colonial times, although the common ground shared by the Abrahamic religions has shrunk. In the nineteenth century, Europeans and Hindus alike are known to have entered into such contracts with Muslims.[68]

Indian women undergoing a *nikah* ceremony would have considered themselves married, although European men who married by *nikah-e-inqatai* might be excused if they considered their temporary 'spouses' to be mistresses. However in British-Indian society, a *nikah* marriage of either description was generally portrayed as neither legal nor binding if the man was a European. We know of some European men who exploited differences in understanding between different faiths and cultures. Dyce Sombre, a Eurasian heir to a large fortune, was shocked to find in the late 1830s that a European employee, General Ventura, 'disavows his marriage & says she was only kept by him; and an Armenian priest just mumbled over something which he did not recognise'.[69] But, whilst European men may have exploited legal loopholes to deny they had ever married, we also know of others who insisted they were married regardless of what British opinion, and later British-Indian law, said. Colonel Gardner protested to the editor of the *Mofussil Akhbar* in 1835 that those who questioned the legality of his marriage were in error: 'a Moslem lady's marriage with a Christian is as legal in this country as if the ceremony had been performed by the Bishop of Calcutta; a point lately settled by my son's marriage with the niece of the Emperor'.[70]

Although his viewpoint was not attuned to the *milieu* of British society, in 1835 Gardner correctly assessed the legal status of his marriage. But after the 1872 Act, the only valid and legally binding marriages involving Europeans were those between two Christians. Officially, interfaith marriage did not exist, but amongst the working-classes and soldiers marriage was often defined by cohabitation rather than by contracts sanctioned by church or state. There were very few European women of their class, and so they continued to take Eurasian and Indian 'wives'. Even amongst the elite, a few men continued to defy convention to form 'mixed' marriages.

In 1900, before Henry Waterfield of the Afghanistan Geological Survey married May Majeedie Wahiduddin, she (the daughter of a Muslim) was baptized Christian.[71] Waterfield belonged to an elite family; his father wrote the 1871 census report, his brothers were Bengal Lancers, and all were ICS men. Waterfield had also been Assistant District Superintendent of Police, Peshawar.[72] His family, in India for at least three generations, returned home for education and retirement but, like their wives, were India born. This record of intermarriage was only evident because his wife (on baptism) did not change her name to a European one. It is tempting to conclude that name changes, and Victorian biographers' reticence, may have hidden many more intermarriages amongst the elite.

Hindu Rites

Before the 1872 Act, the legal status of interfaith marriage between a European British subject and a Hindu was ambiguous. Hindu marriage, rather as English marriage had been prior to 1753, was a community affair. Even today, in India, legal registration is not necessary to validate a Hindu marriage:

> Sect. 7. Ceremonies for a Hindu marriage.
>
> 1) A Hindu marriage may be solemnized in accordance with the customary rites and ceremonies of either party thereto.
> 2) Where such rites and ceremonies include the *saptapadi* ... the marriage becomes complete and binding when the seventh step is taken.
>
> Sect. 8. Registration of Hindu Marriages.
>
> 5) ... the validity of any Hindu marriage shall in no way be affected by the omission to make the entry.[73]

Caste rules would usually have proscribed intermarriage because communities were unlikely to accept Europeans as equals or converts.[74] But amongst those of low or no caste, with more to gain than to lose (such as widows), the same cannot be said. Ambitious fathers may also have balanced a daughter's loss of caste against a European son-in-law's connections and patronage, and some Hindu women underwent Christian baptism to marry Europeans. Maria Suffolk, a converted 'Hindoo', was baptized the day before her marriage to John Wakefield, Lieutenant in the 17th Bengal Native Infantry. This may have been an example of a political marriage, since she was ward of the Rana of Kumasin and her father had been *Wuzeer* [sic] to the Rajah of Busseher.[75] Their son George, baptized two months before their Christian marriage, was not described as illegitimate.[76] This case is strongly suggestive of a pre-existing 'marriage', acceptable to both a well-placed Hindu family and to the British. Strange's interpretation of Hindu law was that a son born of parents from the same caste was legitimate because sex between equals was the same as a marriage.[77] Wakefield and a Rana's ward were obviously not of the same caste but could have been considered equals, validating a prior Hindu 'marriage' and their son's legitimacy.

Records are less detailed for Mary Meeran, described as Hindu on her marriage in 1834 to Private Henry Life of the 1st Bengal European Regiment.[78] Their baby, born six weeks before his parents' Christian marriage and baptized days after the event, was declared illegitimate.[79] This couple was of a lower social status and the clergyman who conducted their son's baptism did not recognize that, in Hindu law, the conception of a son by a man and woman of equal status was a marriage.

Whilst considering Islamic rites I noted that the *milieu* of British society in India had changed by the 1830s. There was scope for European men to deny *lex-loci* marriages with non-Christians and, after 1872, British-Indian law voided the concept. But the law did not always work that way. Interfaith (therefore *de facto*) marriages were occasionally recognized, as an 1879 divorce case illustrates.[80]

In 1856, Edward Fowle left his Burmese 'wife' Mahkin, travelled to Europe, and married Charlotte Webster.[81] They travelled to Burma in 1859, but Charlotte left for England in 1861. Returning to Burma in 1876, she sued for divorce citing Fowle's adultery with Mahkin, with whom he had lived for 16 years. The appeal judge said it was:

> a case of the clearest and most systematic adultery ... it amounts in fact to a putting by the respondent of Mahkin for many years together, as completely as possible, into the place of his wife. She managed his house, she bought and sold for him, and was ... the 'lady of the house'; she bore him children, she left her money in his hands and 'helped him generally in his business in everything', and this without any disguise whatever. Mr. Fowle says, indeed, that he had quarrels with her, but he had also quarrels, at least as bitter, with his [British] wife, and perhaps these differences may be taken as making the position more completely quasi-conjugal ... we doubted ... that Mr. Fowle would have consented to sacrifice a woman who was useful to him, and to whom he had become used, in favour

> of another who had never made him happy, and to whom years of separation had made him indifferent.[82]

This shows that an irregular, interfaith, and interracial relationship such as this one had some standing under British-Indian law as a form of marriage. The judge said that 'such convenient arrangements were very common amongst his [Fowle's] class in India', but he also seemed to recognize it (as completely as possible) as a *de facto* marriage of more merit than his *de jure* marriage.[83]

OTHER CONSIDERATIONS

Slavery?

Chatterjee asserts many interracial relationships were between master and slave.[84] Many relationships were not formal 'marriages', and so are absent from ecclesiastical returns, but the evidence in wills, baptisms of 'natural' children, and published work throughout the nineteenth century suggests that many of these relationships were quite different from the master–slave scenario. Chatterjee claims historians have brushed aside the political and economic context in which Indian women, held in a state of slavery by a European 'plantocracy', should be considered productive labour – producing further generations of slave labour.[85] I agree that interracial relationships have often been either ignored or romanticized; however, Chatterjee's portrayal of Indian women as 'sex slaves', her discussion of which she confines to 'the first century of colonial rule in India', is not universally applicable in the nineteenth century.[86] The conditions of Chatterjee's 'slaves' are not sufficiently different from those of contemporary Indian or European women in endogamous marriages to justify this categorization; all women and children were subordinate to men, except in matrilineal societies, regardless of their status as slave, wife, or family member.

Indian wives could be required to embrace practices such as *purdah,* polygamy, and even *sati*, to address their husbands by title, eat only their husband's leftovers, and produce sons. Their purpose, in essence, was to enhance their husband's experience of this life and the next. European women gave up all property rights on marriage, were expected to produce heirs, and had no legal rights over their own children. Women who showed too much disobedience, emotion, or intelligence to irritated husbands could be incarcerated for life as 'insane'. Husbands had 'conjugal rights', making rape within marriage perfectly legal. Whether Indian or European, a man might chastise or violently abuse his wife with impunity. If husbands chose to disinherit them, European, like Hindu, widows were reduced to menial labour or begging for charity to survive. This is not to say that husbands of either nation did not generally respect their wives and treat them well, but simply to point out that all women, slave or free, were subject to laws that upheld the whim and will of men.[87]

Chatterjee also overstates her case by imbuing terminology with slave significance. She sees lock hospital women as slaves because they are described as *belonging* to a regiment, but the men *belonged* to a regiment too. Her discussion of the purchase of Indian child slaves by European 'rescuers', extending into the 1840s, is overly cynical. Children did need to be rescued, and not only in India. Whilst acknowledging that eighteenth-century Europeans had kept slaves in India, 'slave' was not a legal status that survived far into the nineteenth century. Slavery, as a legal status, was abolished throughout the British empire in 1833,[88] and, for at least two decades before that, Indian courts had been unwilling to enforce slave contracts.

Class and Social Mores

Besides legal and religious considerations, social mores constrained personal agency, but for different classes of Europeans in India – and even within the same class, in India rather than Europe – expectations were different.

The median age of marriage in England and Wales differed according to class and occupation: in 1884–5, the average age at which miners married was 23.5 years, whereas for professional men it was 29.6 years.[89] In India, evidence that European men of all classes were marrying younger than they were at home caused concern (see previous chapter). Women married much younger in India, with girls of 14 frequently discharged from orphanages on marriage. Company regulations and marriage legislation for India were enacted to constrain early or inappropriate marriage, but the fact that such measures were necessary shows there was a continued desire for such marriages. The result, inevitably, was to drive such relationships underground and, if anything, to increase the incidence of *de facto* marriage.

'Gentlemen' were expected to maintain a foothold in metropolitan Britain, to uphold family name, character, public image, and the gravitas of their offices. They cared for their children and provided for their futures, and if they could not then their colleagues, families, and peers stepped forward. The archives suggest that most were willing to conform, or at least to be discreet, but this was not always the case; Waterfield and Wakefield (see above) married Indians against public opinion. Richard Birch, Military Secretary in Bengal from 1852 to 1861, was married to 'an aged half-caste of vast rotundity'.[90] All three held senior posts, despite the character flaws shown in their choice of 'unsuitable' wives, but all three could afford to be 'eccentric' because they were well connected.

The lower classes were expected to get drunk, to wench, to disrespect and upset the natives, to avoid work, and to catch venereal diseases. Archive evidence of these behaviours will not disappoint but, like the assumption that Eurasian women were all 'easy', it is an exaggerated Victorian middle-class stereotype.[91] Amongst working-class soldiers and civilians, there were respectable, god-fearing men who, contrary to the opinions of their betters, felt the full gamut of emotions, took responsibility for their own actions, and both raised and nurtured their families.

Knowing the racial sensitivity of contemporary Britain, Stanley says many with Eurasian or native wives felt they could not return there.[92] Working-class British men were no less prejudiced than their superiors but, in India, had less reason to avoid intermarriage. Quinney noted many men had nothing to go home for, their prospects were better in India: 'Foreign service seems to me to be the most desirable for various reasons; two of which are, that a soldier is more respected abroad than at home, and generally finds himself better provided for; in India, especially, this is the case.'[93] So intermarriage was not preventing a return home; rather, settling in India was an attractive alternative. There were opportunities for discharged soldiers to gain employment, as subordinates in governmental and quasi-governmental employ. A high proportion of Company soldiers had a pre-enlistment skill to offer,[94] and even skills developed in the army could transfer to civilian employment as gunners and guards on trains, in supervisory roles, and in the police. A Eurasian or Indian wife was an additional reason to stay but not the cause of continued exile.

Racist attitudes, present in all British classes in India, seem to have been a less effective obstacle to interfaith or interracial 'marriage' for the working classes, and for the best-connected British-Indian families, than amongst those who were most anxious to make themselves a name. Pressure from government, social equals, or employers to conform to particular codes of behaviour could only be effective if two conditions were met. Firstly, failure to comply with social norms had to promote fear of adverse consequences. Secondly, there had to be exposure to a steady input of drip-fed cultural propaganda. Both of these behavioural modifiers became less effective when applied to the extremes of British-Indian society.

For the upper strata of British men, a mistress was not a wife and in writings, thoughts, and the legislation they produced, these men projected their values onto a class who did not necessarily share them. Working-class economics would have been enough to restrict most to one woman in one household. If he had a wife already, but chose to live with another, then, in working-class thinking, she became his *de facto* wife and wife number one would choose another man and become his *de facto* wife. Even for a sailor with 'a girl in every port', relationships may have been concurrent over time but they were also in a monogamous cycle since he could not be in two ports at the same time. The upper echelons whose marriages failed could turn to divorce before a second legal marriage. The middle classes understood discretion and might afford a separate *pied à terre* for a mistress.

EFFECTS ON THE EURASIAN COMMUNITY

Besides the regulatory and legislative difficulties, interracial or interfaith marriage presented social and moral dilemmas for the British elite in India. Discretion (or deceit), anonymizing Indian wives, and keeping them outwith the boundaries of 'society' might protect a man's reputation and promotion prospects, but there remained a moral imperative to acknowledge any children. The ecclesiastical records are littered with the names and ranks of men christening 'natural' children, who were occasionally European but more often Eurasian. This represents a striking difference between metropolitan and colonial culture. In Britain, parish officers often had to chase reluctant fathers and serve bastardy orders to get an admission of paternity. Birth registration or baptismal documentation of illegitimate children in Britain usually bore only a mother's name and a blank where the father's details should have been, a situation that was reversed in India.

European men were encouraged by both Portuguese and British authorities to formalize their Indian marriages by payments to have their children baptized and raised as Christians.[95] This is the evidence on which writers base the assertion that intermarriage was, in effect, a deliberate policy.[96] The counter-argument is that the authorities sought not to increase the number of interracial liaisons, but merely to acknowledge their inevitability and to support those willing to put the arrangements on a formal and moral basis. Certainly the argument falls flat after 1835, when such payments were abolished.[97] But whilst payments were in place they worked in two ways; they provided some financial support for the families of poorer European men and they tore those families apart.

The need for elite British-Indian society to part with children at an early age, sending them to Europe for education, is well and sympathetically documented. Officers with Eurasian children, even those not sent to Europe, also parted company at an early age. Chatterjee highlighted European men's legal rights to stipulate the removal of their children from the influence of native mothers, and said it was 'commonplace to stipulate that a son born of a concubine be handed over to the Orphan Fund, together with the property, and a pension to be granted to the mother during her lifetime by the Fund'.[98] Much less has been said about the vastly poorer European soldiers, and their Indian and Eurasian 'wives', who also parted with their children at a tender age. The Bengal Military Orphan Society agreed in 1784 to care for the children of other ranks.[99] The objectives were:

> ... to encourage the European soldier to enter the marriage state; to relieve him from the heavy burden of rearing a large offspring with very scanty means; and by the comfortable maintenance and education of the children, to attach him to the service [Company army] by ties which did not previously exist; to rescue the children themselves from the vice and intemperance of the barrack, at a tender age in which they have not yet imbibed evil habits; and having saved them from profligacy, distress, and premature decay, to render them useful members of the community by rearing them up in the principles of the Christian religion, and by educating, and respectably settling them in life.[100]

'Orphan' included not only children who had lost one or both parents, but any child of an enlisted European soldier. The removal of Eurasian and 'poor white' children from their families, sanctioned by Company regulation, was never a subject of legislation; theoretically, it was voluntary and a Company benefit enabling soldiers to educate their mostly Eurasian children as Europeans. On death, hardship, or a distant posting, this would no doubt have been a lifeline, but orphanage education was both an entitlement and a requirement.

Other ranks, rather than thoughtlessly abandoning their children, were compelled to abandon them into the care of military orphanages. Madras had paid its men a pagoda, on christening of their mixed-race children, since 1678,[101] and the Bengal Military Orphan Society adopted a similar practice (for European enlisted men and NCOs), with government contributing Rs 3 per month (from birth) for each child, but it was on the understanding that the children were to be given up:

> The Orphan School Allowance having been granted by Government, for the Children of European Non-Commissioned Officers and Privates, borne on the School Rolls, upon the express condition of the Children being sent to the Orphan School at the Presidency on reaching the age of three years.[102]

If parents refused to comply:

> the Station Committee [was] to enforce the Regulation or to strike the Children off the Rolls; discontinuing in such case to draw their Orphan Allowance, and putting the Guardians or Parents of Children thus unauthorizedly detained beyond the limited age, under stoppages, until the whole Allowance which may have been issued to them be recovered.[103]

Families who refused to part with children were placed under considerable financial pressure. The payment from birth to age three, at Rs 3 per month, represented at least Rs 108 per child to pay back, the equivalent of £437 today.[104] In addition, the parents lost the on-going monthly Rs 3, and had to maintain and educate their children without any further assistance.[105] A European infantryman received pay of 1s 1d per day in 1856, and his stoppages could amount to a maximum of 7s per week. A rupee was reckoned to be the equivalent of 2s. Thus, rather than abandoning children without a second thought, soldiers were forced to give them up into state-sponsored institutions because they could not afford to disobey.

Removal of the children of poorer Europeans is entirely consistent with similar arrangements in Britain and in other colonies. Middle-class concerns for the welfare of children born poor or of mixed race were widespread. Like children and adults admitted to workhouses in Britain, education would redeem soldiers' children. They could be 'turned into useful members of society' if removed before they began 'imbibing the evils of barrack life'. Thomas Coram's Foundling

Hospital had been rescuing the 'exposed and deserted' children of London since 1739, though it had never sought to force parents to give them up. Like the Bengal orphanage, it reared them as Christians and, through education, hoped to settle them respectably in life.

The removal of children to orphanages was not, at the time, unique to India, but the element of compulsion was perhaps tested there as a similar system is later found, justifying the removal of working-class children in Britain and of Euro-Aboriginal children in Australia. Between 1869 and 1939, 100,000 British 'Home Children' were removed from working-class families, orphanages, workhouses, and the streets of Britain and sent to Canada. Many more were sent to Australia, New Zealand, and Rhodesia. In 1931, the Australian government passed the Aborigines Act, which allowed any Aboriginal child to be removed from his or her family and given a 'white' education. All 'half-castes' were to be similarly educated and encouraged to marry whites, such that by the third generation no trace of native origin would be apparent. That Act was not rescinded until the1970s![106] The fact that black and 'half-caste' children in Australia and working-class children in England were subjected to the same treatment shows that Eurasians in India were not removed solely because their mothers were Indian or half-caste, but also because their fathers were working class.

Maintaining family ties over a decade or more of separation was difficult or impossible. Orphanage records, such as those of the Madras military orphanage, frequently claimed that mothers' whereabouts, even names, were unknown. Fathers' names and occupations were normally listed, but their whereabouts were often 'dead' or 'gone to Europe' by the time a child was discharged. With such scanty information, the high mobility of troops, and the sheer distances often involved, it would have been almost impossible for many discharged inmates to find their parents.[107]

Mothers had little opportunity to intervene for several reasons. If a soldier's wife (legal or otherwise) and her husband had received the orphan allowance there was little chance she could have changed his mind or been in a position to pay it back. In the absence of a father, if she had no marriage certificate, or proof she was an Anglican, with a suitable education, lifestyle, and sufficient means, she had no right of access to her child.

We can now see that the removal of Eurasian and 'poor white' children was fundamentally different from the middle-class or elite experience of separation. For parents, the Company benefit that assured their children of some kind of care and education would sometimes have been as welcome as the free Company doctor on the other end of a bone-saw. It is true that orphanages relieved financial hardship, were the only safety net for many military families, and that the army's logistics and efficiency improved by removing child camp followers. This does not alter the fact that the system destroyed families.

If European officers' families suffered because they were separated from children undergoing European education, at least they could anticipate the prospect of being reunited eventually. That was less likely for soldiers' families. Their children were to be moulded into second-class Europeans. Without their native or Eurasian mothers, they were to imbibe European values and cultural mores. Without their lower-class fathers, they were to be protected from barrack-room evils. The skills they were taught were determined by what government thought would make them useful. Since they were also removed from parental influence for perhaps a decade, they also lost their families and, with them, much of their own identity.

With so many obstacles to marriages between Britons and Indians or Eurasians, removal of children to orphanages, anonymizing of mothers, and the peripatetic nature of many fathers' lives, it is no surprise that family life was markedly less secure in mixed families than those of endogamous European or Eurasian families.

Irregular 'marriages' were as much the result of necessity as of immorality. Within British India, there were insurmountable obstacles to legal marriages between Christians and Muslims or Hindus. Secular marriages were possible in England and Wales from 1837, but in official British India there was no such thing as a secular marriage until the 1872 Special Marriages Act, and even then it required both parties to renounce any religious persuasion so it still did not provide any legal way (under British law) for two people professing any faith to marry.[108]

Immorality was a concept often used by the British elite to describe the behaviour of their 'other ranks', to characterize interracial relationships, and to assume the illegitimate ancestry of all Eurasians. But applying values prevalent among the working classes in Britain, the 'failure' to marry legally was an acceptable part of working-class culture. It was also, at least in part, a failure on the part of British-Indian legislators who did not provide the means to realize legal interfaith marriage.

Regardless of laws and regulations, relationships akin to marriage were sometimes able to survive as long as formal marriages, and ties of kin could be maintained for several generations. Whilst it is difficult to identify which 'marriages' survived until death in sources that often fail to name or even mention specific women, examples can be found. Durba Ghosh has identified several relationships between European men and Indian women that had grown from master–slave or master–servant arrangements into what she termed 'conjugal' relationships. Whilst Ghosh sees the men's claims to hold the girls in great affection as attempts to justify their exploitative behaviour, they could equally well have been genuine expressions of affection.[109] Either way, they were long-term relationships in which men provided for their 'companions' as they would have provided for wives. Ghosh describes the equitable 15-year relationship with Punna Purree that Thomas Pearce described as a marriage. John Deane's will noted a 20-year relationship with Mussumaut Matloob Brish.[110] The relationship between William Palmer and Faiz Baksh lasted 35 years, that of William Gardner and Mah Munzel Ool Nissa 40 years.[111] None of these appear exploitative.

Stability was a notable feature of some European and Eurasian families of pre-annexation Lucknow and Hyderabad. Speirs highlights the freedom of choice the nawab's award of a large pension gave to one Eurasian family in Lucknow.[112] Llewellyn-Jones found that under the nawabs the average stay of Europeans there was 14 years. Multiple members of the same family were often employed by the *durbar*, or in running commercial ventures such as 'Europe' shops. Good pay and pensions, granted to those in the nawab's favour, enabled family stability. Families such as the Bragancas stayed for about 50 years, the Orrs about 60 years, and the Quieros family for 115 years.[113] Here, Company rules and social pressures that adversely affected the stability of interfaith and interracial families under the British were less effective.

CONCLUSIONS

This chapter is not about endogamous marriages between Eurasians. Other than finding a clergyman, and the complication that half of Eurasians were Catholics, such marriages were relatively unproblematic. The problems for Eurasians who married Indians were broadly similar to those of Europeans; their relationships would have been *de facto* marriages. Unlike intermarriage between European men and Indian or Eurasian women, the children's nationality would have followed that of the fathers. Eurasian women who married rich, senior, and well-connected European men could expect to become second-class Europeans, excluded from 'society' but able to anticipate a decent education for their children and retirement in Britain. Social pressure worked, with increasing efficiency to diminish their numbers.

Eurasian women who married working-class Britons did not move up the racial hierarchy. If anything, military regulations – Company and Crown – destabilized their families and enforced a Eurasian identity on their children. Working-class European husbands who chose to stay in India became 'domiciled European', a category barely discernible from Eurasian.

I do not draw any conclusions about the 60 per cent of Europeans who neither married nor lived *de facto* marriages. Men looking for purely temporary arrangements had plenty of options: they could visit the bazaars, overawe a comely servant, 'rescue' a girl being sold into slavery, pay a mother for her daughter, or find a *bibi* through a servant's recommendation. Many women might also have been resigned to temporary arrangements, or even permanent but limited relationships, if their goal was financial security. My interest in this and the previous chapter is in the 14 per cent of European men in India likely to have chosen to live as married men with Eurasian or Indian women towards the end of the nineteenth century.

On-going intermarriage between Europeans and Indians created new first-generation Eurasian lineages, and on-going intermarriage with Eurasians also fed into and out of existing lineages. British men entering established Eurasian families reinforced the community's cultural connections to Britishness.

Of the 14 per cent, half were in documented legal marriages. The difficulties inherent in divorce meant legal marriages were long-term arrangements; regardless of whether both parties continued to share a home they remained legally bound. The other half, those in *de facto* marriages, has been the subject of this chapter. I have found a myriad of marriage forms and, whilst specific examples are few and quantitation impossible, I found hard evidence of such long-term relationships. The effect of the peripatetic nature of soldiery was the same for soldiers in Britain and India, although the increased mortality rate in India would have shortened many relationships further – but that does not alter intent. I feel perfectly justified in extending the 'marital' behaviour of British men in Britain to their equivalents in India.

Whilst my approach to marital behaviour makes no allowance for racism, I contend that other characteristics, peculiar to women, would have tempered the effects of prejudice. External agency, such as family objections, threats to promotion, or social 'death', would only ever have modified the behaviour of men who had something to lose. Most did not.

For much of the nineteenth century there was no specific legislation defining legal marriage for India's Europeans and Eurasians. In the three presidency towns, the *lex loci* was English law, but only as it stood when those settlements were founded. In the *mofussil*, there was no relevant English law until the final decades of the century, and even then it was unclear to whom it applied. I conclude that interfaith marriage was kept as difficult as possible even though mechanisms existed in Britain, and amongst some Indian communities, which could easily have facilitated it – such as

English civil registration after 1837 and Scotland's traditional marriage forms, which remained valid until 1939. Muslim imams and communities in India were sometimes willing to sanction marriages between 'people of the book'. Admittedly, caste laws would have precluded many marriages between Europeans and Hindus, and Catholic marriage was a sacrament, but, with these exceptions, there need have been no impediment to interfaith marriage.

British and European marriage forms have been explored, showing how Europeans behaved at home and, by extension, were likely to have behaved abroad. Besides British law, custom, and practice, I also looked at some marriage customs acceptable in Indian societies, by which Indian and, to some degree, Eurasian women would have been guided. The views of legal and religious authorities on what constituted a marriage, and their attitudes to interracial and interfaith relationships, have been considered. I have shown that there was no one marriage form for all, and that relationships not recognized by British-Indian law or by the clergy could, perhaps should, have been considered valid *de facto* marriages.

Government acted *in loco parentis* to control the behaviour of young men whose choice of wife would in England have been subject to parental pressure. In line with orders of precedence, cantonment Acts and less formal social norms such as 'clubability', restricting interracial marriage shored up the racial boundaries between the rulers and the native population, and kept British employees' loyalties firmly focused on Britain. Of paramount importance was the need to protect the imagined superior character of the English nation from racial and cultural contamination.

I conclude that government discouraged interfaith and interracial marriage by narrowing the concept of marriage to a degree that did not apply in England. There were many conditions under which an irregular marriage would have been held valid in Britain and in India too, had they not involved Europeans. By making interracial relationships temporary in the eyes of the law, bonds of kinship and even nationality were weakened. The labels 'mistress', 'illegitimate', and even 'orphan' were thereby imposed on many Eurasian and Indian spouses and descendants. Besides these labels, lack of access to a full European education, and pressure to live like Europeans on a fraction of their salaries, further lowered their status relative to Europeans.

Finally, I conclude that the legal and social difficulties of interracial relationships would eventually have led to increased Eurasian endogamy. Up to now, this has been portrayed as a British tendency over time to shun Eurasians as potential wives, but perhaps the fall off of interracial relationships also marked an under-acknowledged example of Eurasian agency. Sometimes, at least in personal relationships, it must have been the Eurasians who turned away from the unwelcoming and unreliable Europeans.

CHAPTER 6

EMPLOYABILITY

A major focus of British concern for Eurasians in the nineteenth century was how to ensure that they became 'useful citizens'. Laws, directives, and usages introduced at the end of the eighteenth century had severely curtailed their employment opportunities, adding to the numbers living in the bazaars, impoverished, uneducated, and unemployed. That could not be permitted to continue because their predicament made it obvious that Europeans were not all 'heaven born' *and* because they exposed a ruthless side of the British – as a people who did not always look after their own. Also, left unaided, Eurasians might challenge British hegemony: either, like their counterparts in North America, they might challenge (or help to challenge) the British for authority in the colony; *or* their poverty and weakness, by demonstrating European vulnerability, could encourage Indians to rebel. Properly handled, they could show Indians the advantages to be had from a European-style education, Christian morals, and cooperation with the British. There was also an increasing diversity and number of jobs that needed people whose European blood meant they could be trusted, without the expense of importing large numbers of British working-class men and women. For these reasons, Eurasians were encouraged to live and work in a manner considered appropriate to those of European descent and yet remain excluded from the power and status of the European elite.

At the century's beginning, some Eurasians were being raised by their parents to live by Muslim mores and conventions; even when Christian, many were schooled for employment or marriage within Asian rather than European society. Eurasian and European men in positions of authority in independent Indian states were employed to bring European knowledge to the durbars or to be intermediaries between the state and the Company. Eurasian-owned businesses and estates could thrive as well as any in native territory; the intermediate ethnicity of their owners might even have proved advantageous. But there were also numerous uneducated Eurasians in the bazaars, unscrupulous fortune hunters, adventurers, and paupers.

By the end of the century, most identifiable Eurasians were employed under the British or were dependent on government or Christian charity. Half the community were dependent on railway employment. Military service involved comparatively few, but was a highly contentious issue throughout the century. Money earned by women made a significant difference in a community required to maintain a European lifestyle on smaller salaries than Europeans. Each of these culturally or numerically significant sectors is explored in a separate, following chapter.

This chapter aims to illustrate how towards the start of the century, Eurasians could exercise agency in their choice of lifestyle and employment and, as the century progressed, how that agency was constricted or alienated. This transition is explored in terms of the provision and aims of education and training, increasing British influence over the affairs of native states, and the moulding of Eurasians in British India for public service employment. Whilst I include lists of occupations, my aim is to explore perspectives on appropriate employment and culture for a community forced into the middle ground between colonial British and Indian identities.

EURASIAN AGENCY

For most Europeans at the beginning of the nineteenth century, elements of an 'Indian' lifestyle remained superficial and easily discarded when fashions changed. Herbert Edwardes posed in native clothes and sported a heavy beard but remained essentially British.[1] Even Richard Burton was able to slot back into a European lifestyle. Some may have needed re-education, such as an early ward of the first Lawrence Asylum: 'a small European boy who was lately found up in Cabal, and is supposed to be the son of some soldier of the destroyed army. He has been brought up as a Mussulman, and made to believe his father was such, and is a very bigot.'[2] For any Eurasian brought up amongst native communities, with little contact with Europeans, it might be argued that the European elements of their lifestyle were the more readily discarded.

Early on, many Eurasians lived a lifestyle that freely mixed Indian and European cultural influences. Hyder Jung Hearsey, coyly described as a close relation of British Lieutenant-Colonel Andrew Hearsey,[3] was close to his British relatives. He was educated at Woolwich before serving Awadh and the Marathas under Perron, but from 1803 brought an army of 5,000 men he had raised over to the British. His large pension stands testimony to the respect he commanded of the British, and yet he had concurrently several Indian wives and, as MacMunn recorded, 'he had a *Pachesi* board tattooed on his abdomen and ... his wives played *Pachesi* (Homeward Bound) thereon while he slept!'[4]

As British influence spread, annexing many native states, imposing its 'protection' on others, and keeping all under scrutiny, lifestyle choices narrowed; people were to be native *or* European, not both. Eurasians came under pressure to choose. In Bellary, for example, as British influence grew Mallampalli has said: 'Race consciousness ... as in other colonial settings, was generated structurally, through the ordering of the urban landscape and through relationships of power and economic dependence.'[5] But in princely states when British influence was less profound, racial zoning of towns unknown, and Eurasians economically dependent on native employers or customers, there was no reason for them to eschew Indian mores and customs. Indeed, according to Grey, it was a condition of employment in the Punjab, under Ranjit Singh's patronage, that Eurasians and Europeans adopt the local culture.[6]

Their descendents would, naturally, have been more conversant with Punjabi than European mores.

Saksena's study of Eurasians and Europeans immersed in Indian literary culture shows that about 90 per cent of these men and women were Eurasians.[7] He includes biographical sketches of members of many of the better-known and independent Eurasian families, mostly dating from the first half of the century, showing that their lifestyles were as much Indian as European.[8] James Skinner is a good example. A first-generation Eurasian, he served both the Marathas and the British as a soldier. He was known by the Mughal title Nasir-ud-Daula 'Sikandar' Bahadur Ghalib Jang and by his British rank, Lieutenant-Colonel James Skinner, CB. He was a Christian, with 14 Indian wives, whose three sisters all married British 'gentlemen'. He spoke English and several Indian vernaculars, and wrote his memoirs in courtly Persian.[9] He wrote on the castes of India (*Kitab-i tasrih al-aqvam*), on the rulers of the Punjab, *Tazkirat al-umara*, and he composed Persian poetry.[10] He was a philanthropist who built a church, a mosque, and, reputedly, a Hindu temple, and a generous host serving Indian food, offering *hookahs*, and hosting *nauches* for European, Indian, and Eurasian guests.[11] Skinner was treated with respect by all communities despite his 'hybrid' race and culture. Yet he felt that his race, no obstacle to his Maratha service, was a major obstruction to progress amongst the British.[12]

Europeans and Eurasians chose English, Indian or mixed names for their children. The descendants of a British colonel (William Gardner) and an Awadhi nawab included his great-grandson Suleiman Shikoh Gardner, the brothers Arthur and Jehangir, and Suleiman's sister, known as both Ellen Christina and Ruqqia or Razia Sultan Begum.[13] The Gardners, with a large estate, an established reputation, sufficient funds, and royal connections, could afford a degree of independence. But later in the century, the Indian and mixed names of the family given in the 1820s and 30s had given way to more uniformly European names such as James, Maggie, John, and Marguerite. The same was true of lesser-known families: Padavartha Frederick, born at the beginning of the century, named his son, born 1840, Peter Kingsley.[14] Whether Eurasians began to empathize more with European culture or needed to fit British perceptions of how Eurasians should behave is unclear.

Eurasian interest in Indian cultures survived longer in native states than under the British. Shadwell Plough, from the fourth generation of his family to serve Alwar state, was nominated captain by the raja at the tender age of ten, and was still writing Persian poetry 40 years later in 1897.[15] He was able to hold rank only because he was a native of a princely state and his ties to the British were minimal; Eurasians dependent on British approval for their employment had long since learned to drop or hide Indian cultural links. 'Going native' was a character fault, and government employees had to be of good (i.e. British) character.[16] Lawyer Alexander Speirs, earlier a schoolmaster at the prestigious Oak Grove School in Mussourie, at the turn of the twentieth century felt it necessary to conceal his Muslim 'wife' and two illegitimate daughters from his employers and most of his family.[17] Hill schools had been established to save European children from degradation and Indian immorality, and so public knowledge of his home life would likely have led to dismissal. Eurasians in British India well understood the part they were required to play: one as close to the European ideal as possible. Medical subordinates in Madras, for example, were required to produce testimonials 'as to character and respectability', and those who achieved the higher ranks were reminded 'they are expected to live as, and to associate with gentlemen of their own station in life, and at all times to maintain the honor [sic] and dignity of their profession'.[18]

A Eurasian identity under the British was not simply a matter of ancestry; individuals had to be Christian,[19] have a European-style education, and be literate, moral, and European in lifestyle and tastes. Maintaining an acceptably European lifestyle might be difficult as Eurasians' generally lower earnings presented practical dilemmas: 'So far as he strives to conform himself as the "European Christian" of government and ecclesiastical rule, he has to starve his belly to cover his back.'[20] Thurston noted a government service rule, under which men in chronic debt should be sacked, and he lambasted the poorest Madras Eurasians, some earning as little as Rs 6 a month, for want of thrift: 'clothes must of necessity be forthcoming – no mere dhoti, *languti*, or sari, but clothes of European device, if not of the latest fashion'.[21] For Thurston, Eurasians were poor and in debt not because they were low paid but because they were stupid, irresponsible, and unable to 'subordinate animal appetite to reason, forethought and prudence'.

If born in native states, or the remote *mofussil*, Eurasians were sometimes able to continue living lifestyles that elsewhere were discouraged or made impossible. In the first half of the century, large numbers of Eurasians were living in native states free from the proscriptions of British India. Besides those in or reliant on military service, native *durbars* employed Eurasians and Europeans in various capacities. An 1848 MP lists 29, comprising 11 military officers and NCOs, two astronomers, eight medical personnel, a civil engineer, two teachers, a forester, an artist, a commercial and a political agent, and an agent in England.[22] At that time returns of Eurasians employed by *durbars* were not consistently demanded but, as early as 1830, in a petition to parliament, Eurasian community representative John Ricketts claimed that rules governing the movements of Europeans and Americans were also applied to them, meaning they could not be employed without special permission of 'the Supreme Government'.[23] By the 1880s, *durbars* and British officials were still confused about whom to report and who required government sanction, though durbars were more uniformly expected to request the permission of the British administration before employing anyone who was not wholly native in their own state.[24]

Eurasians were entitled to live in their natal states provided they could prove they were not British subjects, but even so treaty clauses sometimes forbade not only *durbar* employment but any work or even residence by foreigners within the state. The meaning of 'foreigner' was disputed, as was its application to Eurasians, but, when the British complained, native rulers sometimes placed maintaining peaceful relations above individual rights or treaty stipulations. Hyderabad, for example, dismissed a Mr Butler 'as if the fact of his being Eurasian was sufficient explanation in itself'.[25] Conversely, mindful of the *Nizam's* power and strategic importance, the British were careful not to appear too proscriptive in their dealings with him;

they claimed to be protecting the *Nizam* from 'scamps and loafers' by insisting on prior British sanction for all European and Eurasian *durbar* appointments.[26]

Another obstacle to Eurasian agency within native states was the Vagrancy Act of 1849. Intended to discourage European deserters, adventurers, arms dealers, drunks, and undesirables from becoming an embarrassment by entering native states or outstaying their usefulness in India, it was sometimes applied to Eurasians by local British officials.[27] It exacerbated Eurasians' difficulties in finding work. Rumours of opportunities between Bombay and Madras, perhaps in the *Nizam's* territories through which they passed, prompted unemployed men to travel in search of work. Without visible means of support, they were technically vagrants. Forcible removal of those who had committed a crime (a rarity) also extended to the unsuccessful who had exhausted local charity, and to beggars. Magistrates and Residents scrimped on the cost of removing vagrants, shunting them onto the next district to save funds rather than facilitating their removal to major cities where there may have been work.[28]

John Ricketts outlined specific difficulties affecting Eurasians in an 1830 address to parliament,[29] some caused by, and others that might be solved by, the spread of British influence. Inconsistent application of restrictions on *mofussil* employment caused difficulties for those in native states. Their status as European or native was inconsistent; those employed by the Marathas in 1803 were considered traitors if they did not return to the British lines, and yet the Company refused Eurasians responsible employment because they were the sons of natives. In the *mofussil*, they were Christians subject to Muslim criminal law, without recourse to the Supreme Court at Calcutta, and with no civil law governing their marriages, inheritance, or property. Eurasian doctors and lawyers educated in Europe found it difficult to practise in India because of British prejudice, though they were able to do so in Britain. Natives did not distinguish between 'East-Indians' and Europeans, and other European powers (Dutch, French, Spanish, and Portuguese) were much more liberal in their treatment of Eurasians.

James Skinner died in 1841, but already European ancestry, education, and lifestyle were conflated (by the British) with competence, respectability, efficiency, and trustworthiness. Skinner, and others, such as the Calcutta shipbuilder James Kyd, were seen as exceptional, not examples of Eurasian potential. In fact, Skinner's father, a Scottish officer with the Company, bound him in 1794 for seven years as apprentice to a printer. His brother-in-law, a 'gentleman in Company service', saved him from the bazaars into which he had retreated by placing him as a *writer* with a law firm. But for the intervention of his godfather, who introduced him to General De Boigne and Maratha military service, he had been destined to become another anonymous Eurasian *cranny*.[30] The British had many such places for Eurasians, increasingly so after 1833, but it was rarely in native states or the army. Eurasians were to become a pool of cheap 'semi-European' labour for the Raj.

MOULDING USEFUL CITIZENS

Schools and orphanages for the descendants of Europeans had a long but patchy history in India. The Catholic Church, various Protestant missions and congregations, and the government of Portuguese India had always made some provision. Well-to-do families had kept governesses and teachers for their own children until the latter could be removed to Europe. Some in native states entrusted the education of their children to *munshis*. There were also small schools, run by chaplains, attached to European regiments. To these, the domiciled European and Eurasian communities added schools to provide a British-style Christian education in India; modest 'free schools' served the poorer children, and, for the better off, institutions like the Parental Academical, Doveton's College, and La Martinière mimicked English public schools.[31]

Military and Civil Orphan Schools at Bombay, Madras, and Calcutta were established with some support from the Company specifically for orphans of the *official* British community – soldiers and civil servants – from 1784 onwards. These began with serving officers, concerned for their own children, making regular payments to care for their deceased comrades' orphans.[32] The scheme was later extended to 'other ranks' and funded jointly by government, the officer's fund, the men, and charitable donations.[33] The officers felt they and the Company owed a duty of care to children awaiting passage to Britain and those who were to stay in India.[34] Bengal's Military Orphan Upper School began in 1784, Madras' Military Orphans' Asylum in about 1789, and the Bombay 'Central Schools' effectively in 1826.[35] Each had different criteria for admittance, care varied according to rank, race, gender, and legitimacy, and the children were classified accordingly. Places were allocated in separate establishments for boys and girls, for officers and other ranks, for the disabled, and for babies 'at nurse'.[36] Eventually children were placed in apprenticeships or positions that varied according to their fathers' status.

Officers' children and their mothers received generous pensions, and from 1820 were returned to Britain.[37] Despite the rule forbidding it, some of those returned appear to have been Eurasians; the five children of Major Henry Bellew were accompanied to England by their mother Anna, but she was only permitted to remain until 1856 when her youngest turned 18, which implied that their mother was either Eurasian or native.[38] After Bellew's death in March 1842, his eight-year-old son Henry was immediately enlisted into the Garrison Band at Madras, which also implies that the boy was Eurasian. Presumably the family secured their pension and passage after a few months, since he was discharged in October and the family travelled to England. He returned to India in 1855 as an assistant surgeon. His elder brother Patrick had done the same a year previously and was also an assistant surgeon.[39] Company officers' sons could expect to follow their fathers into civil or military service if they were European and so wished; otherwise, pension provision was sufficient to provide a British education appropriate to their class. Early in the century, Eurasian boys could not gain Company employment in India[40] but were able to work in Britain or elsewhere in the East. Ghosh claims boys of the upper school '... might be sent as writers to Eastern Company outposts such as Bencoolen (Sumatra) or Batavia. The prohibition in 1791 on accepting Eurasians into the Company's covenanted service did not preclude sending them farther eastward.'[41]

Officers' daughters were raised in the expectation of a good marriage to a British civil or military officer. Later, when marriage to Eurasians became a character flaw in men of rank, these girls were left indefinitely in the orphanages, sometimes becoming teachers to younger girls.

Other ranks' children received care and education appropriate to their class and race; they were prepared for subordinate positions and employment in India.[42] Many boys in the Madras Military Male Asylum in July 1835 were being prepared for 'employment in the public service'. Bengal boys in 1784 were expected to stay until, at about 12, 'they are fit for, and obtain admission into, the Service, as Privates, Fifers, Drummers, Marines, Overseers, or otherwise'.[43] In 1796, the Military Orphan Press was founded (at Calcutta) to train boys in printing trades. Any profits were to be used to provide girl orphans with dowries when they married. The press printed much of the government's materials, but rarely made a profit until taken over by the colonial authorities in 1863.[44] The Madras government established the Madras Asylum Press at Egmore in 1800. It printed the *Madras Asylum Almanac*: 'a valuable source for the history of Madras'.[45]

There had to be flexibility on the age at which a boy left, and those who could not be placed stayed indefinitely.[46] William Pendleton's father died when he was four years old, but after 16 years in the Madras Asylum he was still there because he was blind. Cornelius Fisk had been there just as long because he was 'weak and debilitated'.[47]

The fathers of these boys were all European other ranks, from privates to sergeant-majors. Their mothers' race could be European or native, but was mostly Indo-British and the children a mix of legitimate and illegitimate. They were often not orphans at all; barrack life, ignorant fathers, and native mothers were all considered unsuitable for raising Christian children, and, though the fathers' pay was enhanced when they had children, they were required to give them up to the orphan schools.

Ghosh portrays the education of Eurasian and European children for government employment as affirmation of 'the class and race positions of the children'.[48] No doubt that was one aim, but it was also a deliberate nullification of parental and personal agency. A Eurasian boy born to a private soldier had to be given up to an orphanage and would become a military drummer. Neither parent nor daughter could decide which British soldier a Eurasian girl would marry. Her only escape was to become a seamstress. Orphan boys without military fathers were educated for clerking or trades such as printing, and later as railway fitters, as the government deemed necessary. All would speak English, wear European clothing, and be Christians. Many parents did not see the orphan schools as an affirmation of anything; some hid their children with relatives, or deserted their posts, or pretended their children had died rather than part with them.

If duty motivated those who set up the orphan schools, and advancement motivated the fee-payers of Doveton's and La Martinière, government and clergy also had distinct priorities for the children. Clergy, the evangelical lobby, and missionaries believed children had to be educated to become good moral practising Christians. Military and civil orphanages were Protestant institutions because the British presence early in the century was largely restricted to those in government service. The Company acknowledged that many of its lower ranks, especially soldiers, were Catholics and paid some Catholic priests to minister to them, but provision for Catholic orphans was initially left to that Church.[49] The spiritual care of orphans of European descent was of variable importance to government, but the production of useful subordinates represented a return on their investment.

The change from Company to Crown rule prompted a restructuring and re-examination of expenditure and expectation, but duty to dead colleagues and their children was still a factor: 'when the [children] are left helpless, their fathers dying on the battle-field, sealing with their blood their country's dominion, the charge of such children becomes a sacred duty of the State'.[50]

Throughout the century, British India had grown in geographical reach, political hegemony, and population. By mid-century, there were substantial numbers of poor and orphaned children, many of them several generations removed from their European ancestry, whose future was under scrutiny. Walker estimated in 1861 there were 2,160 such poor or orphaned children, aged over eight, being educated in India. His suggestion was to remove them all to Britain, where they could be 'well fed, clothed, and educated in a fine healthy part of Yorkshire ... rosy as pippins and merry as crickets'.[51]

There were other suggestions too. An experiment in 1854 took several Madras orphans, trained as compositors, to Australia as farmers.[52] Events in the 1857 Mutiny led some who presented evidence to the House of Commons during the Fourth Report on Colonisation and Settlement (India) in 1858 to suggest that European military pensioners and their Eurasian families should form the nucleus of colonies dispersed throughout the *mofussil*, who could be called to arms rapidly in times of crisis.[53,54] The government's preference, whether because of old fears of racial degeneration in Britain or the pragmatic need to fill subordinate posts with loyal Eurasians, rather than encouraging European settlement, remained educating Eurasians in India to become useful citizens of that country.

Experimental communities were set up eventually, and some comprised groups of Eurasians rather than European pensioners. Examples include a colony near Bangalore, at Whitefield, Sausmond, and Duckworth in the 1880s, and later at McCluskiegunge. They would be separate and self-sustaining,[55] but their role as a local source of emergency militia was superseded by the spread of the railways, whose Eurasian and European staff provided a well-dispersed and highly mobile militia 'volunteer' force. But suggestions for Eurasian colonies continued to appear. One helpful lady, writing to *The Deccan Post* in 1898, pleaded with the Eurasian community to consider mass emigration to America or Mexico, where they would found a colony and get rich. Instead of:

> sitting and sponging upon some friend or relative. Such a man in the Western hemisphere is always advised in the Western vernacular to 'hustle.' [My] heart longs to free you from the

> bondage of social distinction that binds your people. In America each one of you have equal rights, moral, social and civil, with every other citizen. As your wife can tell you, it only depends upon individual worth the position a man occupies.[56]

Whilst the century saw the government's remit expanding to encompass improved communications, transport infrastructure, health, and education, all of which increased demand for European expertise, the intention to limit the European presence (especially the working classes) remained intact. This meant limiting European recruitment to ready-trained and experienced men; encouragements for them to return home, such as pensions paid at a relatively young age; free passage; short-service enlistment in the army; and short-term contracts with railways; alongside the introduction of specialist training within India. But, even after 'Indianisation' and the creation of the provincial service in the 1880s, domiciled Europeans and Eurasians continued to be an important source of subordinate staff. Until the end of the Raj, they remained in situations for which Indians were considered untrustworthy (such as engine driving) or in departments where they represented a European (or part-European) presence. Various discourses, appeals, reports, enquiries, and government-sponsored publications give a flavour of the roles for which Eurasians were deemed suitable, how these changed over time, and the significance of race-based employment strategies.

EMPLOYMENT IN BRITISH INDIA

John Ricketts' evidence to parliament in March 1830 described the contemporary Calcutta Eurasian community.[57] The majority were employed as government clerks but he believed there were about 500 Eurasians who, but for the proscriptions barring them from covenanted or commissioned posts, were perfectly qualified for more responsible Company employment. He gave examples of Eurasians still in Company service and occupying commissioned and covenanted posts, and a handful in the 'King's Army', taken into the services before the proscriptions of the 1790s.[58] There were also many who had left Maratha armies to serve the British in irregular units, and in the recent Nepal war. He named successful businesses that were Eurasian owned and run,[59] and mentioned Eurasians employed as preachers, missionaries, architects, indigo-planters, carvers, gilders, and teachers.

If, as Hawes suggests, for the British in India 'official employment took the place of birth, wealth and land at home'[60] as a signifier of self-worth, then it is unsurprising that educated Eurasians wanted greater inclusion and opportunity within government employment. A British officer talking about Indian appointments (those made in England, but the sentiment holds true for appointments in India too) said:

> I hear that the new system for India is to throw open Addiscombe and Haileybury to public competition: that this public competition will be fair and open, and free from jobbery and patronage, I suppose no sane person in the 19th century, acquainted with public morals and public bodies, would believe [that] for an instant.[61]

Nevertheless, Eurasians were an important part of the machinery of state in the mid-century and until Indianization began to take effect. Forbes-Mitchell, writing about the Eurasian poor, said in 1900:

> in 1857 beyond the Presidency Towns ... the majority of the [Customs and Surveys] posts now held by Natives were held by Anglo-Indians & Eurasians, & many of those posts carried good salaries, ranging from Rs 150 to Rs 500 per month.; ... the Rupee was then worth 2/2d, whilst living in the upper provinces cost less than half what it does now.[62]

Railway employment is considered in a following chapter because 'railway people' became such a complete alternative identity for a vast swathe of the Eurasian community, to the extent that it replaced the early nineteenth-century stereotype of the Eurasian *cranny*. The occupations filled by Eurasians were, in fact, very diverse. The *crannies* remained, although pressured by Indian competition once Macaulay's education reforms[63] and 'Indianisation' of the provincial service began to produce results. In 1840, 90.56 per cent of clerks in Calcutta's government offices had been Eurasians and only 0.44 per cent were Indian. By 1890, only 18.17 per cent were Eurasians and 81.85 per cent were Indian.[64] But the community's flexibility is illustrated by a description of the Madras community in Risley's 1901 Indian Census report:

> The most noticeable point about the statistics is the great variety of the occupations in which Eurasians are engaged. None of the other communities selected approach them in this respect. The list gives 52 callings followed by seven persons or more and 6.3 per cent. of the community live by others which are followed by even less than this number. Excluding subsistence on endowments and scholarships (most of the persons comprised under which are the inmates of the orphan and other asylums . . .), there is no occupation in the list which is followed by as many as 8 per cent. of the community. The popular idea that Eurasians are mainly employed as fitters or clerks or on the railways is therefore clearly inaccurate.[65]

Thurston had studied Madras Eurasians three years before and listed the occupations of a sample of 130 men. There were 69 distinct occupations (see Table 6.1 below).[66] Elsewhere in Madras presidency, Thurston found less variety in their occupations: in Calicut, his sample of 96 men (including 29 tailors) followed 18 occupations[67] but even that statistic shows flexibility. Stereotypes such as 'Eurasian fitter' were locus specific; the Madras fitter, the Calicut tailor, the Calcutta clerk are no more valid than looking at an army camp and stereotyping the British as soldiers.

Even though Eurasians diversified greatly in the work they undertook, it is undeniable that, for many, government and public service remained the goal. Diversification in work done did not mean a move away from government-sponsored employment. Firstly,

Table 6.1 Occupations of Madras Eurasians in 1898.[68]

Accountant	Fitter	Railway: Auditor
Attendant lunatic asylum	Hammerer	Railway: Block-signaller
Baker	Harness-maker	Railway: Carriage-examiner
Bandsman	Jewel-smith	Railway: Chargeman
Bill-collector	Joiner	Railway: Engine-driver
Blacksmith	Labourer	Railway: Engineer
Boarding-house keeper	Livery-stable keeper	Railway: Goods-clerk
Boatswain	Mechanic	Railway: Guard
Boilersmith	Moulder	Railway: Locomotive inspector
Carpenter	Painter	Railway: Parcel clerk
Chemist's assistant	Petition-writer	Railway: Prosecuting inspector
Clerk, government	Police inspector	Railway: Shunter
Clerk, private	Porter	Railway: Signaller
Commission agent	Printer	Railway: Stationmaster
Compositor	Proof-reader	Railway: Store-keeper
Compounder	Reporter	Railway: Ticket-collector
Contractor	Rivetter	Railway: Tool-keeper
Copper-smith	Saddler	
Crane attendant, harbour	Schoolmaster	
Draftsman	Sexton	
Electric-tram driver	Spring-smith	
Electric-tram inspector	Stereotyper	
Engine-driver, ice factory	Steward	
Evangelist	Telegraph-clerk	
Filer	Watch-maker	
Fireman	Watchman	

Eurasians were educated to believe British rule was essential to India and that public services and utilities were to everyone's benefit, bringing modernity, wealth, and progress.[69] Secondly, government

Table 6.2 Occupations of Anglo-Indians in British India, 1931.[70]

Occupation	Males (per cent)	Females (per cent)
Agriculture	3.05	2.38
Domestic service	2.93	6.61
Exploitation of minerals	1.70	0.21
Industry	10.26	6.89
Own means	4.75	6.72
Professions and liberal arts	8.07	38.15
Public administration	9.89	3.81
Public force[71]	5.35	0.12
Trade	9.03	6.33
Transport	32.07	4.61
Insufficiently described, unproductive or unaccounted for	12.90	24.16
Totals	100	100

wanted to employ them. Eurasian employment in 1931 (see Table 6.2 above) dovetailed with the needs of government.[72]

Continued reliance on government employment made the community particularly vulnerable to the effects of changes in British policy and attitudes. Caplan noted: 'Anglo-Indians were . . . alternately preferred and promoted or thwarted and victimized. This kind of oscillation was especially evident in the occupational realm.'[73]

Risley's 1901 census report states that 'practically the whole Eurasian community can read and write in English'. The report also shows that almost 30 per cent of Madras' Eurasians were illiterate, a contradiction that could be explained away because 'Native Christians have in some cases returned themselves as Eurasians.' There was also a regional difference in the occupations followed by Eurasians, with those of Madras and the Malabar *mofussil* providing 'most of the tailors, carpenters, agriculturalists and coffee estate employés [sic] in the list'.[74]

Beyond the nineteenth century, the liminal position of Eurasians, caught between ruler and ruled, trapped many in an unenviable position. Their association with Europeans meant that concessions designed to appease nationalists excluded them. Their status as statutory natives of India also excluded them from benefits attached to being British. The use of the community made by the state in times of unrest further alienated them from other Indian communities. The most damaging problem for them was their ill-defined and flexible dual status at a time of enmity between the colonial British and the Indian peoples. In a Commons debate in 1925, the Under Secretary of State for India, when asked to clarify the status of Eurasians (by then termed Anglo-Indians) answered:

> For purposes of employment under government and inclusion in schemes of Indianisation members of the Anglo-Indian and Domiciled-European community are Statutory Natives of India; for purposes of education and internal security, their status, so far as it admits of definition, approximates to that of European British Subjects.[75]

He admitted that defining the community had 'always been a matter of some difficulty', but would neither admit it caused the community any difficulty nor was prepared to discuss the effect it had on their eligibility for the Indian Medical Service.

The 1880s' reforms created the provincial service as a separate arm of government, in which Indians were to play a major role in their own government. The imperial service, recruited in the UK and with the British monopolizing all the senior grades, remained intact. The provincial service was numerically dominated by Indians but still largely headed by Europeans. Since it was open to all, some Europeans who failed entry examinations in the UK travelled to India, crammed, and sat local examinations there. In 1887, the House of Commons was reminded that the promise of employment irrespective of colour or caste was not being met. Appointments to superior posts in the Registration, Telegraph, Police and Public Works Departments went almost exclusively to: 'persons of British birth, whose only qualifications appeared to be that they were poor relations of high officials ... promotion is alleged to be by

Table 6.3 Provincial Civil Service.[76]

	Year	Indians	Eurasians
Deputy Magistrates and Deputy Controllers	1862	145	67
	1922	319	12
Sub-judges and *Munsiffs*	1862	56	23
	1922	293	0

favouritism, and to the almost entire exclusion of Eurasians and Natives from higher posts'.[77]

Eurasians were once again in a difficult position because, as one author noted, Indianization, meant de-*Anglo*-Indianization.[78] In 1857, most customs and surveying posts in the *mofussil* were monopolized by Eurasians; by 1922, the majority were held by Indians.[79] Also by 1922, the Bengal Provincial Service employed 91.5 per cent Indians and 6 per cent British, but just 2.5 per cent Eurasians.[80] It was not simply rapid expansion, beyond the rate of expansion of the Eurasian community; Younger found (Table 6.3) that absolute numbers decreased too, as the number of Indians rose. Dual status did not help Eurasians to gain jobs in competition with Europeans or Indians. This was understood in the 1880s but the India Office, even in 1925, found no evidence that Anglo-Indians (Eurasians) or domiciled Europeans 'suffer[ed] any disabilities' because of their classification.[81] Caplan had more success in explaining why the Eurasian community appeared to be suffering downward social mobility:

> in the 'early' colonial period, Anglo-Indian males were relatively free to follow a range of activities. For a time from the end of the eighteenth century they were excluded from many civil and most military services under the government, but by the middle of the nineteenth century they were allowed favoured if restricted access to positions of intermediate responsibility in central government sectors (such as railways, telegraphs, and customs) and, from the early years of the

twentieth century, in the wake of nationalist pressures, they were increasingly exposed to competition from members of the wider society in virtually all areas of their 'traditional' employment spheres. These last developments exacerbated the extent of poverty within the Anglo-Indian fold.[82]

THE POOR, PAUPERS, AND VAGRANTS

Arnold notes a tendency in Raj historiography to portray the European community as consisting 'almost entirely of civil servants, army officers, planters and businessmen'. The truth was very different. He defined nearly half the European and Eurasian population of India as poor whites, and divided these into three categories:

1. Soldiers and sailors.
2. Semi-skilled workers, intermediaries in government departments, private European enterprises and those in some kind of service relationship with the dominant whites.
3. Orphans, vagrants, prostitutes, convicts and lunatics.[83]

I would add that there is a tendency in Raj historiography to ignore Eurasians altogether, to include them as a footnote, or to unwittingly accept a Victorian perspective of their insignificance. Arnold is an exception, but when concentrating on the Eurasian community, in which considerably more than half were both poor by Arnold's categorization and second-class white-*ish*, it is even more important to explore the world of the poor and the pauper.

Despite infrastructural development, reserved occupations, government measures to improve education and training for Eurasians and 'poor whites', and community self-help initiatives, the 1901 Census of Madras indicates poverty was still a problem in the Eurasian community: '17.8 [per cent] of the "actual workers" in the list live on endowments, on their relatives and friends, in convents, in lunatic asylums, in jail or by begging ...'.[84] Bombay still had problematic poverty and unemployment, for which churches, the Anglo-Indian Association, and government offered some help; the association had an 'Anglo-Indian Temporary Relief fund' – to provide suitable clothing for those found employment by Council – and who were in straitened circumstances'.[85] Poverty in Calcutta had always dogged the ill-educated 'poor white' communities, but offices in the Raj's capital had provided significant employment for the educated. By the end of the century, the availability of cheaper Indian clerks, or *babus*, spread unemployment to a broader section of the Eurasian community.[86]

Besides the impact of the Vagrancy Act of 1849 on Eurasian vagrants seeking work,[87] difficulties were presented by rulebooks, laws, and social pressures that sought both to separate Europeans from the 'degenerate half-caste' and to ensure that Eurasians' European descent and lifestyle would be rewarded. Those who solved their own problems by choosing to live amongst Indians, by Indian standards, doing 'native' work for Indian pay, *became* a problem; they had let the side down.

From the end of the eighteenth century when exclusion forced the community into being, and into downward social mobility, the racial divide became an economic reality. Eurasians were a separate racial category, restricted to working-class labour. From the outside, Victorian working-class communities divided only into 'deserving' and 'undeserving' poor, but, from within, self-worth and wealth did not always equate. Many in the Eurasian community accepted and welcomed work as railwaymen; it was not particularly well paid, but they took pride in their technical skills and roles as public servants. Nor was it always true that it was more acceptable to live on charity than to live as a native might, building a humble home, and maintaining both family and independence. James Skinner came from a well-connected family, but life in the bazaar, performing odd jobs for a pittance, was more palatable to him than the printer's apprenticeship, one of the stock trades for Eurasian boys, that his father had arranged. 'I worked with anyone who would hire me well. For several days I got my living by carrying loads, or pulling the driller for the native carpenters, at the rate of two *annas* a day . . . thus supporting myself.'[88] Skinner was trying to run away to sea, but he was not too proud to work in the bazaar doing whatever he could. The concerns frequently expressed about Eurasians and poor whites living like natives in the bazaars show that, whether through choice or necessity, Skinner was far from unusual. These men and families were not paupers but poor, and an embarrassment to British imagining of the European male.

Poverty was often blamed on the individual, but sources from the 1820s and 1830s on indigent British subjects at Anjengo near Cochin illustrate the dramatic effects Company policy and political events could have on a community. The Company had set up a factory there in 1693, hoping to break the Dutch monopoly in locally grown pepper.[89] Wars disrupted trade for many years and the factory closed in 1813. The British deserted, leaving an enlarged population, including many Eurasians, destitute of commerce.[90] Within months, the Resident at Travancore began funding poor relief at Rs 80 a month, supporting 60 destitute British subjects, two schools, and a native doctor, expenses that fell to government only from 1827.[91] Anjengo had become a backwater with serious health issues: 'sinking rapidly from the absence of all commerce and the consequent total want of employment for the population . . . [it is] impossible to convey a faithful idea of the present state of disease, poverty and filth'.[92]

That government agreed to continue payments[93] is of interest because it was so unusual. Two lists of recipients of government aid, a total of 60 adults and 27 children, were prepared. Listed by the Resident in 1827 as either 'common poor' or 'secret poor', almost all had Portuguese names.[94] The 'common poor', mostly listed without surnames, included men, women, and children. The 'secret poor' were all female, many of them elderly (eight aged between 60 and 80) or listed with dependent children. Of 58 'secret poor', no fewer than 19 were described as widows, 17 as children, nine as orphans plus two church beggars and a 'Musselwoman'. The remaining 10 were not described. Almost all 'secret poor' had Portuguese forenames, but unlike the 'common poor' they also had surnames. That the Resident, and later government, felt an obligation to support these 'poor' indicates that they were somehow considered 'deserving'. Since all secret poor were women and children, the term may indicate they were either the families of dead or departed company servants or had been abandoned as the effluvia of a redundant military brothel.[95]

Nearby Cochin also suffered economic depression as a result of Company policy. Dutch Eurasian families there, who were asked to swear allegiance to Britain so that they could continue in private trade, were reduced to penury by the destruction of the fort and diversion of shipping elsewhere. Those who asked for permission to move to Serampore were refused travel permits. Eurasians' poverty in Anjengo and Cochin was not the result of their own ineffectiveness, but of Company policy.[96]

Eurasian poverty was also a matter of perspective, to be seen by comparison with the European community rather than with the mass of the people of India. If Europeans were genetically superior, and Eurasians had a share of that advantage, then there had to be something inherently wrong with them to explain their poverty. Thurston blamed 'the evil of early marriage', a proposition countered by the Bombay EAIA: 'we believe this is open to question. It is challenged, if not flatly denied, by the Pastors of these poor people.' They found Thurston's suggestion of celibacy as a cure for hordes of children brought up in poverty, hunger, and dirt 'strangely flippant'.[97] The association did not deny that poverty was a major problem, and it apportioned blame to some members of the community. It counselled against the 'man-nets' of costly court cases, living beyond one's means, and alcohol abuse. This was a call for self-help and temperance to cure poverty.[98] Thurston did not stop at cultural contributors to the problem of Eurasian poverty. Military service was often posited as the cure-all for poverty, but Thurston physically assessed Eurasian subjects and, extrapolating his findings to the whole Eurasian community, pronounced them inadequate, physically and inherently, for military service. Even the Eurasian insane were portrayed as an inevitable consequence of miscegenation.

Insanity was believed to be especially prevalent amongst Eurasians and Parsis. Measured in the 1891 census, the average rate of insanity amongst Eurasian men was 112 in 100,000 compared to an average for India of 33 in 100,000. For Eurasian women, the insanity rate of 69 in 100,000 compared with an Indian average of 21 in 100,000. Both Eurasians and Parsis were literate, including the women, and both had 'a distinct and predominant foreign strain in their blood'. This was not all bad news, however, since it placed them between the 'high ratios . . . that prevail in Western countries and the dead level of sanity amongst the masses of the ... East'.[99] European sanity statistics were not measured in India because sufferers were routinely shipped back to Europe to 'recover their sanity' and to keep them beyond the eyes of natives.[100]

Class was an issue, since an expression of anger from an official or his *memsahib* might be interpreted as irritation and the same anger from an enlisted man could be deemed evidence of an unsound mind.[101] Eurasian insanity had a cultural element too. The charge of lunacy against David Dyce Sombre in 1840s' London hinged on whether he was predominantly Asiatic or European; his belief that his wife was having affairs (considered impossible for a high-born European woman) would be entirely normal in an Asiatic, but profoundly irrational (and insane) in a European.[102] Similarly, religion played a part. Mrs Jane Cheetham, the 'half-caste' widow of a British officer, also in London, was declared a lunatic and incapable of managing her own affairs because she professed beliefs consistent with Roman Catholic dogma: that her husband's death was only a temporary separation.[103] It was relatively easy for Englishmen to have troublesome people locked up with little proof that they were insane.[104] From perceptions of the Eurasian as 'other' to the Eurasian as mad was not a great leap for a Victorian mind to take.

Gilchrist pronounced on the Eurasian daughters of officers in the Calcutta orphanages of 1825, strongly advising his readers against marrying them: 'it is probably owing to reflection, as much as to their arriving at puberty, that so many of these unfortunate girls become insane'.[105] An anonymous novelist was more insightful:

> A thousand slights – an infinite succession of those butterfly-kicks which wear the spirit to death ... brought constantly

> before her the misfortune of her birth. Enchained by the strong links of prejudice, even the intelligent and the good looked down on the girl as one of a race born of shame.[106]

It did not occur to many Europeans who observed Eurasians that rather than suffering from racial degeneration, some may have been driven mad when subjected to a toxic combination of racial prejudice, hopelessness, and economic hardship.[107]

We cannot know what the Eurasian community's expectations were, nor whether they were as distressed as their leaders claimed in the press and in petitions, because, as Stevenage put it, 'a blanket of anonymity was spread over the "other ranks," except for the hero and the villain'.[108] Some of those labelled insane were clearly just distressed.

The educated Eurasian elite believed their community was unfairly denied parity with Europeans. One might expect that those who worked alongside highly paid Britons were aggrieved by the disparity in their rewards and the unlikelihood that they would receive equal consideration for promotions. But many Eurasians worked alongside natives who were equally aggrieved by similar issues, including the unlikelihood of receiving equal consideration against Eurasian and European competition. Low pay, and the difficulties that it presented to those Eurasians who lived as they thought Europeans should, was distressing only if judged against the standards of the British elite in India. Eurasians were most unlikely to have had much everyday contact with the latter, and they ignored the plight of their Indian co-workers. The pay of Eurasians and 'lesser' Britons was ostensibly the same, though Britons enjoyed better 'fringe' benefits and prospects of promotion, so the potential for tension and dissatisfaction was less pronounced than might be expected. We know that at no point, even in times of crisis, did the Eurasian associations ever attract more than a tenth of that community, though they supposedly represented the interests of the whole Eurasian population. British and Eurasian community leaders may have been more distressed by the poverty of those Eurasians and Europeans who lived in the bazaars than were those who experienced it.

CONCLUSIONS

The nineteenth century was a period of great change for the Raj and for India's Eurasians. Beginning with official exclusion from all but the lowliest employment under the British, Eurasians ended it under increasing competition from Indians educated to serve the state and prepared to work for less pay. There were reserved occupations at the beginning and at the end. However, the type of work Eurasians undertook, its variety, and their preparation for it (education and training) had all changed.

Eurasian agency with regard to both work and culture decreased as British hegemony spread. Legal obstacles to Eurasian employment were largely removed, but subtler obstacles remained as insurmountable barriers to the better-paid positions. Access to education and work required conformity to a culture and lifestyle accepted by the administration and British society; the Raj had to be peopled by British gentlemen, brown or white. At the same time, British society excluded Eurasians, ridiculed their imperfect 'mimicry', and believed them to be inferior. The very poor could always be redesignated native Christian by Europeans who reasoned that no Eurasian could possibly accept the lifestyle of a native. If caught young enough, Eurasians could be removed from their parents, educated, and utilized.

Infrastructural change and growth in the state had created many more jobs under government than ever before. Eurasians were needed to fill those considered too lowly for Europeans but too responsible for Indians. Whilst this presented opportunities for Eurasians to prosper, within limits, it also tied them to the Raj and limited their chance of integrating into Indian society. Confusion over Eurasians' status as British subjects and statutory natives, European for some purposes and Asiatic for others, was never addressed by government. Similarly, whether they were beneficiaries of empire or its victims is a matter of perspective.

CHAPTER 7

WOMEN'S WORK

Generally speaking, Eurasian men earned less than Europeans in India. After 1833, the higher-salaried covenanted posts were open to them, but most were unable to travel to England for the competitive examinations or the European education necessary to secure them. Even in provincial service examinations in India, Eurasians fared badly against better-educated Indians and incoming European candidates. Their awkward status presented further difficulties where opportunities created for Hindu and Muslim Indian communities excluded them. A European lifestyle, part of Eurasian identity, was expensive: decent housing, servants, Western dress and furnishings, a carriage, and Christian (and European-style) schooling for the children, all added to their cost of living. For these reasons, female employment was important in many Eurasian families.

Eurasian women who might once have expected to join European society now faced prejudice, social exclusion, and, for the lower classes, desertion. If exclusion from pension funds, on grounds of race had created distress in the first decades of the century, short-service army enlistment and short-term contracts for technical specialists served only to perpetuate the financial disincentives to intermarriage and the likelihood of future difficulties.

PREJUDICE

Julia Maitland, one of the 'ladies' who visited the Madras military orphanage expressed the kind of opinion of Eurasian girls we might expect of the expatriate British of the 1830s, but she also claimed the prejudices cut both ways:

> Those half-caste girls are in the depths of ignorance, indolence, and worthlessness, and utterly neglected; they have no ideas but of dress and making love ... scarcely any of them really are orphans; and the half-caste young left-handed ladies look down upon the poor little honestly-born Europeans, and boast of being 'gentlemen's children;' and they go out visiting their relatives without shame or ceremony.[1]

The growth in the number of European women able to travel to India after 1833 coincided with increased prejudice against Eurasian women but was not its cause, which seems to have been a more insidious change across a wide section of British society. Maitland's words illustrate both a class prejudice from the Eurasian girls towards soldier's daughters, and a deflection of 'shame' from the fathers who took 'left-handed' wives (mistresses) onto their illegitimate Eurasian children, as well as obvious racial prejudice directed at Eurasian women. The conflation of Eurasian with illegitimate is a given, even though records from the same orphanage indicate that many girls were legitimate.

For intermarriage to be a source of shame there had to be a race-based prejudice against it, and it was inconceivable to the Victorians that a white woman of sound mind and morals could ever consider a non-European husband. The same could not be said of European men who continued to marry Eurasians or to father 'left-handed' (illegitimate) children. If the law was theoretically colour-blind after the 1833 Charter Act, society was not and the policing of racial boundaries continued by less formal means, backed up by the pen.

Besides advice to *griffins* (to avoid such liaisons) from old India hands such as Gilchrist,[2] there were almost universally negative descriptions of Eurasians in many travelogues.[3] Anglo-Indian genre fiction reinforced acceptable attitudes of mind towards the dangers of miscegenation, although this is mostly a later subject for full novels. Early works stressed the difficulties the children would face. Published in 1833, the short story of Ephraim Middlerace illustrates the difficulties mixed-race children would face; Ephraim goes to England where he marries an 'honorable' lady, but false friends relieve him of his cash and all mock him. Only when he returns to Calcutta, and marries a Eurasian, is he respected and happy.[4] Mid-century, Stoqueler's *Tale of East India Life* featured another Eurasian, Edmund Merton, who was both educated and felt at home in England but 'cast ... into a slough of fearful despond' when, in India, his proposal of marriage to an English girl was rejected because 'English girls had not yet so far forgotten their obligations to society as to form matrimonial connexions with persons of his complexion'.[5]

Later examples stress the damage to English men who miscegenated. Winifred Savi wrote at least two books in which miscegenation had tragic consequences: *Neither Fish nor Flesh* and *Rulers of Men*. In the latter, Derek saves his married friend's reputation, and sacrifices his own, by claiming to be the father of his chum's illegitimate Eurasian child Joseph; he funds the boy's education and, though superstitious Indians think he has sold the boy for vivisection, helps settle him in America. Although Derek's reputation is ruined, the truth eventually comes out and he lives happily ever after with a saintly English wife.[6] Writing slightly earlier but after spending the latter decades of the nineteenth century in India, Maud Driver devoted a series of four books to the subject, beginning with *Lilamani*. She weaves social Darwinism into her narrative; the Indian girl (Lilamani) who married an English man advances because Indians acknowledge Western views and customs as enlightened, but the same relationship represents retrogression for the English man. Their son succeeds in life because he remains British to the core.[7] The constant flow of cautionary tales indicates an on-going need to discourage interracial relationships. Fiction featuring Eurasian women, predatory or tragic, and naive men who formed relationships with them, bolstered prejudice and provided constant reminders of the dangers of miscegenation.[8]

MARRIAGE

Marriage served a similar role for nineteenth-century women as employment did for men, that of providing status, financial security, and a purpose as homemaker. Obviously, within the Eurasian community there were always opportunities to form endogamous marriages; partners might be found amongst friends of brothers, at church services and events, at institute dances, or through family contacts. The opportunities to meet European men changed over time. Early in the century, for the daughters of officers:

> The General Management of the Bengal Military Orphan Society ... having found occasion to form some arrangements for the better regulation of the monthly dance given by the society to the daughters of officers at the Kidderpore school, notice is hereby given that no person whomsoever will, in future, be admitted to this entertainment without producing a printed card of invitation.[9]

These balls provided gentleman of the civil and military services with a marriage 'market'. By 1820, the upper orphanage's European girls (and possibly some Eurasians) were being shipped back to Britain, the twice-monthly balls were discontinued by the 1830s, and gentlemen were actively discouraged from forming relationships with Eurasian women. Emma Roberts noted:

> The progress of refinement has materially altered the condition of these young ladies, but has acted in a manner the very reverse of improvement, as far as their individual interests are concerned. [...]
>
> The prejudices against 'dark beauties' (the phrase usually employed to designate those who are the inheritors of the native complexion) are daily gaining ground.[10]

No longer eagerly sought as wives, orphaned (or abandoned) Eurasian daughters of the higher-ranking Europeans, if without private means or extended families, were left isolated from their own class and seemingly destined to remain at the orphanages. Even in the early decades of the century, Eurasian women and children had been vulnerable and could be left without protection. A few lines from one of Henry Derozio's poems fit that situation well:

There was a youth of expectations high,
Heir to a mighty line, with wealth so vast,
You might have deemed some favouring Genius laid
Earth's treasures at his feet. Her only dower
Was that which nature gave her on her face

But, true to Anglo-Indian genre norms, Derozio penned an unhappy end. Abandoned and caught in a storm with her dead child, she laments:

Where is the home that should have sheltered us,
The arm that should have pillowed me and thee,
The Breast that should have hid us in its folds,
The voice that should have bid the winds be still,
And soothed us in calamity?
. . . Thy father – but I will not dream of him –
And I for thee have nothing, my poor boy!
But a disastrous world of woe before me.
Ah! Now thou'rt cold, cold as thy father's heart;
. . . There is more mercy in th' ungentle wind
Than constancy in man![11]

Derozio might have been describing the plight of girls from the Eurasian community who married Company men; a 'three hundred a year' man, dead or alive, had 'expectations high', and many Eurasian girls had no personal wealth to offer. Frequent postings and retirement 'home', as well as social pressures, enabled unscrupulous men to move on and made it difficult for their Eurasian families to follow. In the early decades of the nineteenth century, pension funds even refused payment to legally married 'half-caste' wives.

The military rank and file continued to seek permission from their commanding officers to marry, and, on production of a good character reference, could choose from the wards of the lower orphan schools. Later in the century as railway communities grew, those near military garrisons routinely invited men of the sergeants' mess to railway institute dances and social events[12] where it was relatively easy to meet a girl and marry 'off the strength'. The results varied; some men sought discharge to remain in India but many left families without long-term security when a regiment was moved on.

ALTERNATIVES

There were alternatives to marriage, as a means of support, and more opened up as the century progressed. The 1901 census showed 1,680 Eurasian women were employed in Madras presidency:[13] 'Of these, 537 are inmates of orphan asylums, etc., 262 are sempstresses [sic] and milliners, 201 school teachers, 107 midwives and hospital nurses, 81 are in domestic service, and 38 are shop assistants and clerks.'[14] These figures suggest that across the Bengal, Madras, and Bombay presidencies, the female Eurasian workforce in 1901 exceeded 5,000.[15] The occupations followed were not necessarily the same in all locations, but since this chapter aims only to explore possibilities and illustrate women's work the main occupations found in Madras will suffice.

Seamstresses

The orphanages had always trained girls as seamstresses: they could make clothing for the inmates, their work could be sold to aid the schools, and they could maintain themselves in adulthood. Extrapolating from the 1901 Census of Madras, there would have been around 800 Eurasian women in India supporting themselves as seamstresses and milliners outside the orphanages, and twice as many within these institutions. Added to this, wives and mothers who were not formally employed could still use their expertise to make up household linen and to clothe their families, and it was a skill that a widow could fall back on later in life.

British newspapers carried advertisements by seamstresses seeking positions in private households, and by potential employers looking for a seamstress for their families.[16] Good needlework was also sought after in female household servants, and in workhouse and hospital servants. In India, the orphanages and missions made good use of their skills.

It would be difficult to put a value on their worth or earnings. Firstly, 'seamstress' encompassed everything from skilled tailoring and high fashion to making up sacks. Secondly, location, skill, and reputation played a part in determining earnings. The income of an orphanage seamstress was not hers to keep; it was for her upkeep and to profit the institution. But skilled seamstresses would have found a ready market in the European community, notoriously anxious to be à la mode and desperate for the latest fashions from Europe. Most tailors were, of course, Indian, but since they were also male the more intimate items of clothing would likely have been the preserve of Eurasian women, even if only as employees in Europe shops selling ready-made items.

Domestic Service

Training for domestic service might have been an obvious choice but for the prejudices of the European community, which debarred Eurasians on two counts. Firstly, they were unsuitable as nannies or governesses because they spoke English with a distinctive accent. According to Emma Roberts: 'their pronunciation is short and disagreeable, and they usually place the accent on the wrong syllable: though not so completely barbarized as in America'.[17] Native *ayahs* were preferred because they would not speak 'degenerated' English to the children. Secondly, Eurasian women were unsuitable as housekeepers because they were stereotyped as sexual predators, without the domestic focus that tempered the sexual threat from native women.[18] They represented unwanted competition for the European women, who excluded them from 'society' and opportunities to meet the most eligible men. They also posed a danger to European men, who, bereft of single European women, might marry them, a situation bound to 'terminate almost always in the degradation of the husband to the level of the wife, of whom he is soon ashamed'.[19]

In consequence, the total number of Eurasian women domestic servants was only about 300 in 1901. Two advertisements in *The Times* for Eurasian nurses in Britain, seeking positions with families travelling to India, suggest that some rose above such prejudices, but we cannot know whether these advertisements led to employment or not.[20] There was, of course, always the possibility that a Eurasian woman might hide any knowledge of English, dress in Indian style, and seek employment as a native *ayah*.

Teachers

Throughout the century many small schools were run by private individuals, such as Henry Derozio's mother,[21] without formal qualifications. Their success depended on the reputation of the individual, and on the curriculum her particular accomplishments allowed her to offer. The discourse on the education of boys (whether to raise good moral Christians, or boys fitted for government service or for trades) was less apparent in the schooling of girls. Rather than 'the three R's', teachers wanted to impart five: adding religion (according to Christian denomination) and refinements for ladies, such as French, music, dancing, and needlecraft. Even in the larger schools teaching Eurasians, many of which did not have grants-in-aid and were not subject to government inspection, many of the Eurasian teachers lacked any formal teacher training.[22] They learned 'on the job' as senior pupils (following Bell's method) teaching younger ones.[23]

Government and missionary efforts to extend native education expanded the jobs market for would-be teachers, and social mores worked in favour of Eurasian women. Many native men did not want their daughters taught by men, there were relatively few European women teachers, and government efforts to recruit Muslim and Hindu women into teaching were slow to take effect.[24] In both native and European families, a woman's place was imagined primarily in the domestic sphere; the married *memsahib* might work outside the home, but her role was ideally one embodying social concern and philanthropy.[25] European society was uneasy about the dangers India presented to single 'white' women, and there is evidence that native society distrusted their influence.[26] All of this worked in favour of Eurasian women by limiting competition. But other prejudices worked against them. Their Christianity was a problem for conservative Hindus, who feared they would proselytize.[27] Some missionaries preferred single European women or Indian widows rather than Eurasians. Jane Johnson, for example, complained in the 1870s that the Eurasian teachers at the Delhi mission 'came to dinner in native dress and the table manners left much to be desired ... Eurasians did not seem to become ladies very easily'.[28]

Formal training spread gradually over the last few decades of the century, at government schools and at colleges run by missions.[29] The Madras government's teacher training college in the late 1870s trained Eurasians alongside *Sudras* and native Christians.[30] In Bengal, there were nine Eurasian women in Kurseong's first batch of student teachers (1901), who trained for one year. Their training was later increased to two years, after matriculation, and the numbers of women seeking places rapidly expanded, but teacher training was still unregulated in the 1880s.[31]

Since as late as 1880 only one in seven schools for Eurasians were inspected by government (those in receipt of grants-in-aid),[32] and formal training came late, it is impossible to get an accurate idea of how many Eurasian women teachers without formal qualifications there were. Also, almost half of schools educating Eurasians were run by Catholic orders, most schools were denominational, and there was no all-India policy on Eurasian and European education until 1905. But Anthony claims 15,000 Eurasian and European children attended Indian schools in 1871,[33] employing many Eurasian women teachers. To these must be added those involved with native education, in girls' schools, at various missions and in *zenana* projects, and those teaching the younger European and Eurasian boys. Eurasian women teachers in Madras presidency alone, in 1901, numbered 201.[34]

For the same reasons, their earnings were not standardized. Some continued teaching in their homes and in private schools whilst others benefited from railway expansion, government, and mission schools. In 1880, the schoolmistress at Jumalpore's railway school, Mrs Annie Kiddell, was paid Rs 80 monthly, but she was European and covenanted.[35]

Nursing, Midwifery, and Medicine

Nursing and Midwifery

Formal training and employment in nursing and midwifery had a longer history than teaching for Eurasian women. Historically, in Britain sicknurses were domestic servants, nuns, and 'ladies' with a social conscience. Indian sick attendants were traditionally male, but a few nuns and English nurses cared for Europeans in eighteenth-century Bombay.[36] British nursing as we understand it today began at London's St Bartholomew's Hospital, but professional training (rather than 'picking up' on the job) started at the Nightingale School at nearby St Thomas' Hospital after the Crimean War.[37]

The Madras midwifery school was founded in 1843,[38] and, although government was dismissive of them, there were older women across India, experienced in childbirth but not formally trained, known as *dais*, functioning as village and neighbourhood midwives. The untutored everywhere were derided as 'sunk in ignorance and superstition'.[39] Discussions in 1871 resulted in improved nursing and midwife training. Nightingale nurses from England trained female pupils, and the duration of instruction was increased to 18–24 months. Nursing pupils were taught by the medical warrant officer and the matron. The training differed from the Nightingale system mainly in producing not only hospital nurses but independent practitioners too.[40] Between 1874 and 1894, 259 students were trained at Madras General Hospital besides others trained at Egmore, the Government Hospital for Women and Children, and the Victoria Castle and Gosha Hospitals.[41]

Besides government-sponsored civil and military hospitals, wealthy individuals (European and native) endowed hospitals where nurses gained practical experience and, from imported

European nurses, formal training. The Armenian community sponsored several hospitals in Bombay, as did Christian missions to care for the Indian sick. Diverse training regimes and establishments, pay, and conditions sprang up throughout the country, until they came together gradually between the 1890s and the 1910s.[42] Prior to this, each nursing school and hospital determined the entry qualifications of nursing students, the curriculum they followed, and, once employed, their pay and conditions. Thus a civilian 'nurse' might be an illiterate Hindu widow, trained 'on the job' by missionary sisters, or a matriculated Eurasian or domiciled European who had undergone three years of practical and theoretical training.[43] By 1910, applicants had to be literate and to have spent three years training as a nurse and an extra year to qualify in midwifery, but short training programmes still appeared in times of pressing shortages.[44]

With so few European women, Eurasians made up the greater part of India's nursing service right up to Independence. Anthony claimed that because they were 'free from Caste and communal inhibitions' 80 per cent of India's nurses, military and civilian, were Eurasian.[45] An 1865 list of 80 European and 'East-Indian' midwives who qualified in Madras during the 1850s and 1860s classified 60 of them Eurasian.[46] All were married women, whereas in Britain, until the mid-twentieth century, nurses were single and left their positions on marriage. A longer list, dating to 1879, includes 192 names: 133 (almost 75 per cent) were East-Indians, 29 European, four described as Mahomedans, and a further 26 as natives. The marital status of the Indian women is not given, but only seven of the European and East-Indians were unmarried. A total of 73 remained within Madras, the rest having dispersed to every province of British India (including Burma), and several are also shown to have worked in the princely states, Singapore and Europe.[47]

The 1879 total of 192 Madras qualified nurses and midwives extrapolated across India would yield at least 600 such women, amongst whom at least 450 were Eurasians. Comparing census returns for India with calculations by Colley for England and Wales, both figures for 1881, is interesting. Colley found 38 women in 10,000 were employed as sicknurses, midwives, invalid attendants, or in subordinate medical services: less than 0.4 per cent of adult women.[48] Of the 62,000 Eurasians identified in the 1881 Census of India,[49] if about a third were adult women there would have been 225 nurses and midwives per 10,000 Eurasian women: over 2 per cent of all adult Eurasian women.

Nurses' salaries were not standardized in nineteenth-century India, but at the Madras Lying-in Hospital and the Lady Curzon Hospital, Bangalore nurses and midwives were fed, accommodated, and paid Rs 15 per month during training. Qualified nurses received Rs 50 per month in Madras government service. They could, however, command higher salaries: from October 1886 to August 1889, Rewah state paid Mrs Talbot, a Eurasian instructress in midwifery, a monthly salary of Rs 130.[50] *The Times of India* reported in 1897 that Anglo-Indian nurses (misreported as native Christians) trained at Sir J.J. Hospital in Bombay were being paid Rs 150 per month plus free accommodation.[51]

Expansions in the number of British nurses were not always welcomed. Late in 1897, the Bombay Anglo-Indian Association's journal carried a short piece questioning why expensive British nurses were being imported for plague duty. Not only would European nurses be useless, it argued, but it was also a slur on the British experts who trained local nurses. There were many qualified Anglo-Indian and native nurses – all trained in India by the British, and acclimatized, the natives having a thorough knowledge of the habits and languages of their 'countrymen'.[52]

Medical and nursing educational and employment practices in Madras presidency often served as a model for later, nationwide government practice. Nursing and female medical students were willing to travel to Madras from all over India. Mary Scharlieb, one of the first female medical students in India, and Madras trained, helped pave the way for others – and for the concept of women doctors to become acceptable.

Beyond basic training, Madras Lying-in Hospital offered 15 months' further training to experienced Eurasian and European nurses in both sicknursing and midwifery. Successful pupils were awarded certificates in sicknursing and diplomas in midwifery. Six months sicknurse training was followed by a further six to nine months of midwifery instruction. Students were paid travel *batta*, were accommodated and fed, and received an allowance of Rs 15 per month for a year. There was also a 'native class', and a list of qualified nurses and midwives for the same year indicates that 30 out of 192 were Indian.

Besides the ability to read and write (in Hindi, Urdu, or English) and converse (on any common subject), candidates had to produce testimonials showing their race and that they were of good character, morals, and respectability. The rules allowed for some candidates, with no previous nursing experience, to train over 15 months. Details of age, marital status, and age of youngest child were also requested. Single women had to be over 25, and married women between the ages of 20 and 35. Comparing this requirement with 1865 and 1879 lists of practising nurses and midwives qualified at Madras, single women were exceptional; none appear in the 1865 list and only seven in 1879. This would indicate either that the colleges preferred to train married women or that qualified nurses (and their earnings) were much sought after as wives.

Medicine

Medical training for women met with initial resistance. In the 1870s, about 70 million Indian women had no access to an all-male medical profession unless closely related to a doctor. An American mission at Bareilly began training native Christian women as health workers in 1870, and several other missionary doctors began training Indian women soon after – at Allahabad, Jabalpur, Central India, Lucknow, Sialkot, and Ambala, for example.[53]

Government-sponsored training of European and Eurasian female doctors began at Madras in the late 1870s. Doubts were expressed as to whether 'females of any kind are fit to be doctors'. In the 1880s, the physical and moral stamina of native women trainees was also being questioned. Bengal began admitting Eurasian women to Calcutta Medical School in 1885. Bombay began training women in 1887, and had 17 women of several communities training together at Grant Medical College. Though leading to a prestigious career, medical training was uncommon in India for women of any community and, as late as 1913, there were still only 81 female medical students across the whole subcontinent.[54]

The Lady Curzon Hospital, Bangalore

The Lady Curzon Hospital for Women and Children catered to the needs of the civil and military families of Bangalore. Table 7.1 shows the relative numbers and salaries of the various grades employed when its establishment was revised in 1902–3. Several interesting points emerge. Nuns worked alongside lay nurses and were not restricted to mission hospitals. Native nurses were paid little more than the pupil nurses, and considerably less than Eurasians or Europeans. The salary of a Eurasian nurse (Rs 50 per month) was not insubstantial. Elsewhere in this source, the change in job title from Assistant Surgeon to Lady Doctor was thought appropriate because the incumbent Ada Niebel 'holds a European medical qualification'. The changed designation from 'Eurasian nurse' to 'charge nurse' was a more pragmatic one: 'Difficulties have been experienced from the claims of the holders of the appointment of "Eurasian Nurses" to be regarded as Europeans.'[55]

Captain Standage, Bangalore's residency surgeon, was in charge of the male hospital (Bowring Civil Station) and had some input into the Lady Curzon. Here, too, there were nuns and Eurasian nurses; however, there were neither pupil nurses nor any native nurses. Standage (already paid an IMS captain's salary) received an extra Rs 200 for hospital duties, Rs 50 allowance, and house rent of Rs30, all per month. Ada Niebel, with a European MD qualification, was paid a total of Rs 300 per month.

Independent Agency

The case of Malka Jan Benareswali and her daughter Gauhar Jan of Calcutta is an interesting one. Firstly, it illustrates a cultural 'grey' area, in which females who did not conform to European norms might find themselves classified as prostitutes. Secondly, it demonstrates Eurasian cultural agency at a late date. Malka was a successful entertainer in Benares and Calcutta, and her Urdu poetry

Table 7.1 Establishment for Female Hospital for Women and Children.[56]

	PRESENT cost Rs/m	PROPOSED cost Rs/m	INCREASE Rs/m	DECREASE Rs/m
1 Assistant Surgeon → 1 Lady Doctor	300	300	–	–
2 Hospital Assistants 2 (50)	100	scrap	–	100[(a)]
House rent to do 2 (6)	12	scrap	–	12
→ 1 Lady Assistant Surgeon	–	75	75[(b)]	–
1 Sister of Charity @ 40	40	–	–	–
→ 2 Sisters of Charity 1(40) 1(25)	–	65	25[(c)]	–
1 Matron and Head Nurse	60	scrap	–	60[(d)]
House rent to do	15	scrap	–	15
2 Eurasian Nurses 2 (50)	100	–	–	–
→ Change to 3 Charge Nurses @50 ea.	–	150	50[(e)]	–
→ 3 Pupil Nurses @ 15 ea.		45	45[(e)]	–
3 Native Nurses 2 (20) 1 (15)	55	–	–	–
→ 4 Native Nurses 2 (20) 2 (15)	–	70	15[(f)]	–
1 Compounder	10	10	–	–
4 Ward attendants 4 (7)	28	28	–	–

(Continued)

4 Cooks 1 (10) 1 (9) 2 (8)	35	–	–	–
→ 3 Cooks 1 (9) 2 (8)	–	25	–	10[g]
3 Peons 3 (7)	21	21	–	–
1 Dhoby (pay increase)	16	20	4[h]	–
8 Toties 8 (7)	56	56	–	–
2 Sweepers 2 (6)	12	12	–	–
1 Masalchy	8	8	–	–

a) Decrease owing to the abolition of the appointments of two hospital assistants on Rs 50/m each.
b) Increase to provide for the entertainment [sic] of one Lady Assistant Surgeon on Rs 75/m for the Lady Curzon Hospital.
c) Increase to provide for the entertainment of one extra Sister of Charity, it being found impossible for one Sister to carry out all the work of supervision of the linen, washing, and cooking for the Lady Curzon Hospital.
d) Decrease owing to the abolition of the appointment of the Matron and Head Nurse.
e) Increase to provide for the entertainment of one Charge Nurse and three Pupil Nurses in place of the two Hospital Assistants.
f) Increase to provide for the entertainment of one extra Native Nurse on Rs 15/m.
g) Decrease owing to the reduction of one Servant Cook on Rs 10/m.
h) Increase due to the great difficulty experienced in securing a man on less pay to carry out efficiently the laundry work.
n.b. Decreased expenditure due to the abolition of the appointments of 2 Hospital Assistants on Rs 50 + Rs 6 house rent per month each, and the Matron and Head Nurse on Rs 60 and her house rent of Rs 15.

and song collection, introduced by a descendant of Tipu Sultan, was eventually known throughout India. Sachdeva identifies her as a *tawa'if*, a formerly high-status courtesan who had entertained elite men in north India with poetry, dance, and music. By the 1870s when Malka's career began, they were more often considered to be little different to prostitutes. She seems to have avoided that fate by her talents, and was both well regarded and wealthy. Gauhar Jan followed her mother into entertainment as a *tawa'if*, her career coinciding with the early days of gramophone records, and was a successful popular entertainer.[57]

It is not obvious who their target audience was; Sachdeva notes that their *diwans*, or song-books, were popular with 'working-class *babus*, *munshis* (clerks), railway employees and small time *writers*', but the praise of Tipu's descendant suggests a wider appeal. Gauhar Jan was recorded as an example of 'native' talent. British difficulties in distinguishing prostitutes from female entertainers eventually affected conservative indigenous groups who 'began to prohibit performances by women such as the *tawa'if*'. What is clear is that Malka Jan (Edilian Imangus or Victoria Hemmel) and her daughter Gauhar Jan (Angelina Eduard or Yeoward) exercised agency by immersing themselves in Indian culture and disguising their European ancestry.[58]

Prostitution and Destitution

Derozio's 1827 poem 'The Orphan Girl' is full of language suggesting that without help a soldier's orphaned daughter would inevitably become an erring woman, wretched, scorned, and filled with sorrow, guilt, and shame.[59] He meant prostitution. How many Eurasian women followed that path in Derozio's time is unknown, but statistics for Calcutta in 1880 show that amongst 2,458 brothel keepers and 7,001 prostitutes, only 46 Eurasians and 65 Europeans were identified.[60] From the early nineteenth century, the fate of the daughters of Europeans was a grave concern. When the Company prohibited their return to Britain, the Bengal Orphan Fund managers wrote:

> Almost every consideration that opposes the idea of prohibiting their removal to the Mother country, appears to claim a more

> than ordinary attention in the case of the female Orphans. – To excite this attention in the man of delicacy and of feeling – in the parent – or in the soldier, the bare mention of their sex must be sufficient.[61]

Destitution of single European and Eurasian women was feared more than male destitution because of the risk they would become prostitutes. The prospect of native male clients was particularly abhorrent to European sensibilities. The nineteenth-century 'Englishwoman in India' was a performance. The obedient wife of the domestic sphere personifying a feminine and racial ideal, she was also 'an ambassador for British imperialism'.[62] Prostitution, indeed any miscegenation involving European women, was emphatically *not* part of the performance.[63] The more European a Eurasian woman was, the more this applied to her too – so extended family, government-sponsored orphanages, missionaries, and church congregations mopped up poor European and Eurasian girls and women.

Until 1833, to control who could enter India, the Company required bonds of around £200. Typical amongst thousands of examples is Miss Maria Sharman, who, after posting a bond for £200 and finding two people willing to be responsible for her care and behaviour, was granted permission to travel to India in 1822.[64] India-born, English-educated, and with a brother in indigo production, she married a Company surgeon in the same year. This was the behavioural norm for European women. Those who remained single were expected to leave.

For the India-born, officers' European orphan daughters were sent to Britain. Eurasian and European daughters of other ranks were equipped with a dowry, accoutrements for domestic service, placed as schoolteachers, or set up as seamstresses. Those who remained in the orphanages, some for life, helped care for younger children, made clothing, and 'besides being taught to read, [were] instructed in knitting, spinning, and all kinds of plain work'.[65]

Some women did still fall into destitution, including Eurasians. Anthony quotes Henry Gidney's impassioned descriptions from

The Statesman in 1923 of unemployed, homeless, and starving Anglo-Indian families in Calcutta, a situation Gidney blamed on Indianization policies within government services.[66] Whether destitute Eurasians were to be seen in 1860 is harder to say. Bishop Cotton was horrified by the thought (rather than the sight) of 'degenerate' European and Eurasian orphans on the streets of Calcutta, and Governor-General Lord Canning contemplated a future 'floating population of Indianized English, loosely brought up, and exhibiting most of the worst qualities of both races', but it is not certain either man actually saw such sights.[67] Given the circumstances later described by Gidney, the low count of Eurasian prostitutes appears unrealistic, probably because Eurasians who fell far enough were recategorized as natives (see Chapter 3).

CONCLUSIONS

Eurasian women in nineteenth-century India experienced social and economic changes at least as great as those affecting their male counterparts, but their position was, arguably, more completely altered by social prejudices than was that of men. In the earliest decades, the view of Eurasian women as potential brides for expatriate Britons is as clichéd as that of Eurasian men as *crannies*, but, just as for Eurasian men, infrastructural developments opened up alternatives. British men had always been able to desert their Eurasian families. If they were now actively discouraged from marrying Eurasian women, there is no evidence that the women were complaining about the change.

More alternatives to marriage as a means of support opened up as the century progressed. The 1901 census of Madras presidency showed 1,680 Eurasian women in employment. Almost a third of these were within orphan asylums, institutions that in the early decades had tried to bar them entry. Many had been taught useful skills, helping them to care for their families or allowing them to support themselves as seamstresses and milliners. Many more were well enough educated to work as schoolteachers, midwives, and hospital nurses. By the early twentieth century, the community's women had a dominant role in these spheres. Extrapolated Madras figures suggest that, across India, between a fifth and a quarter of adult female Eurasians were employed. Married women, most evidently in nursing and midwifery, often continued in employment and contributed to their family's income.

CHAPTER 8

EURASIANS AND THE MILITARY

'E would skip with our attack,
An' watch us till the bugles made 'Retire.'
An' for all 'is dirty 'ide,
'E was white, clear white, inside
When 'e went to tend the wounded under fire!

A chapter on military Eurasians in nineteenth-century India ought to be a brief affair; after all, the proscriptions designed to demilitarize and disarm the community had been in place, and added to, since 1791. But the stanza, above, from Kipling's 'Gunga Din', feting the bravery of a native *bhestie*, could just as well be applied to Eurasians. Throughout the century, the buglers would likely have been 'half-castes'; so, too, were many medical orderlies. Both of these were, essentially, reserved occupations for Eurasians within the British military.

In times of crisis Eurasians were suddenly reclassified as Europeans, so they could be enlisted as combatants; there were Eurasian regiments, regular and irregular, when the need arose. Besides these, Eurasian men born in native states were not necessarily British subjects, and the British had difficulty preventing their employment in native armies. Government and railway employees were also expected to join the volunteer regiments that provided a first line of defence in districts without nearby garrisons. Lastly, for boys attending the elite academies modelled on the English public schools, there was cadet force training. There were even claims from within the Eurasian community that their fairer men, of a military disposition, posed as Europeans and joined up against regulations.

That part of the Eurasian community most closely associated with the British resented the rules forbidding them from combatant roles in the military. The majority of Europeans in India were military men, and naturally in this period sons expected that their relatives' service or patronage networks would secure them a military role too. Eurasian associations petitioned Company and Crown governments, and took their grievances directly to Westminster, citing the service of their forefathers – and the poverty and unemployment that dogged the community – in support of their appeal. They could not accept that men of European descent could not be trusted to defend the empire when native Indians could. Community leaders, anthropologists, ethnographers, and civil, military, medical, and churchmen all posited arguments for or against Eurasian soldiers. Meanwhile, prompted by pragmatism and undermanning, a creative interpretation of rules knowingly allowed some Eurasians into military roles from which they were officially barred. An unknown number, through subterfuge or influential connections and the good fortune to be born with fair skin, were also able to circumvent inconvenient rules to the contrary and take up commissions.

There is, in fact, quite a lot to say about Eurasians and the military.

ARMIES OF NATIVE STATES

In 1897, the strength of the native states' combined armies was estimated to be 400,000 men, including 18,000 troops for 'imperial service' under British command supplied and paid for by the princes.[1] From 1885, imperial troops and the states supplying them were said to benefit because the system 'brought the best class of *sirdar* into touch with the best class of British officer'.[2] The remaining 90 per cent of the princely armies were considered by

MacMunn to be a waste of resources, as 'protection' was provided by contingents that were part of the British military.[3] Always uneasy about native states' armies, the British administration sought to control anything it considered especially dangerous, including artillery, Europeans and Eurasians. But the vast majority of princely armies served only within their own states under their own officers, and so would have been difficult to 'police'. Many *durbars* continued employing Eurasians in their armies, sometimes openly but many others covertly.[4]

In the eighteenth and early nineteenth century, many princely states had welcomed European and Eurasian men and officers. They took commands, taught European-style discipline and tactics, and provided artillery expertise. These men offered an answer to any threats posed by European armies and a potential advantage in engagements against other more traditional native forces. The British administration encouraged native *durbars* to dismiss Europeans and Eurasians who might increase French influence, and to employ men of use to British interests.[5] Individual British fathers also used their influence and connections in native *durbars* to place their Eurasian sons in the 'gentlemanly' employment not generally open to them in British India.

The number of Eurasians (and Europeans) serving in the princely armies is largely unknown. Grey estimated 1,500 men.[6] Kumar's data shows Scindhia had five brigades in 1801, each of 6,000 men, under European and Eurasian command. Each brigade had at least 65 Eurasian and European officers, NCOs, and gunners. Haydar Ali fielded 70,000 in Madras, and the Peshwa fielded 20,000.[7] Both included European, American, and Eurasian officers. If they were in the same ratio as in Scindhia's armies, that would give about 1,500 Eurasians and Europeans in just these three armies. Many princely armies were large and similarly staffed to the aforementioned, such as those of the Punjab and Awadh, before the British were able to enforce their influence. Grey's may therefore be an underestimate. There were also perhaps greater numbers who served in the ranks.[8] A total of 1,500 officers and perhaps the same number of 'other ranks', plus an equal number of wives and children, represented a significant proportion (perhaps 6 to 10 per cent) of India's Eurasian population in the early 1800s.

Threats and fear of the consequences of treaty non-compliance encouraged the princes' *durbars* to consider British insistence on prior sanction before employing any European, but this does not mean they always complied; even the British were unsure about whether they should or could interfere in Eurasian employment. The meaning of a circular of 1831 was still being debated in 1885 because the position of a single comma changed its meaning; it was unclear whether government wanted returns of 'all Europeans and East Indians in Native States, or only such persons when also British subjects, or of all Europeans but only of East Indians being British Subjects'.[9] Some of the British, such as the 1882 Agent to the Governor-General (Central Indian States), simply dismissed Eurasians as a military threat: 'East Indians being British Subjects have, in no case, any Military training, and would be useless to the armies of Native States'.[10] An occasional military Eurasian could still surface, however, even where the British had annexed a state, such as Felix Rotton who had served Awadh, and his seven sons who fought against the British in 1858, as did Sarwar Khan, a Muslim *sepoy*, whose father was Irish.[11]

Grey believed that because of concerns about treaty violations, many Eurasians and some Europeans hid their identities behind native names or titles.[12] It is not possible to identify the successfully hidden, but a few have been identified. Louis Balthazar Reinhard, Eurasian son of a German mercenary, was known as Zaffar Yab Khan, a title given to him by the Mughal emperor.[13] William Leigh, of Irish descent, served 20 years at Khorassan as Mahomet Khan, and was serving Ranjit Singh at Lahore in 1825.[14] Mahomed Sidiq, who served the Nawab of Bahawalpur for many years, was either Eurasian or European.[15] Native names, more fully considered in Chapter 6, may also have indicated their religious beliefs.[16] Some rulers insisted that Eurasians and Europeans outwardly adopt the local culture, possibly only to naturalize them more fully but the effect was to disguise their presence. Grey cites John Holmes, who like all Europeans and Eurasians serving Ranjit Singh had to agree to grow a beard, marry locally, give up beef, neither smoke in public nor offend the Sikh religion, and (if required) fight his erstwhile countrymen.[17]

Even towards the end of the century when most states were bound by treaty obligations or 'directed' by British political agents and residents, some did not hide Eurasians or Europeans because they were too powerful for high-handed insistence on rules. The Political Agent to Hyderabad was advised in 1884 to 'tread carefully and see if [the *durbar*] will readily agree' before he interfered in its employment of 271 Europeans and Eurasians there.[18] Not only was Hyderabad powerful and strategically important, but the *Nizam* had the ear of the viceroy and so could afford to ignore lesser officials.[19]

Other *durbars* believed there were no restrictions on their employment of Eurasians or Europeans. Samthar durbar, for example, said:

> the Durbar begs to point out that the practice of employing Europeans and Christian East Indians in the service of this State has been in force since 1852 or for the past fifty years and during that period ... no objections whatever were ever raised ... no applications have ever been submitted from this State either to the Central India Agency or to the Bundelkhand Political Agency for sanction to the employment of Europeans and East Indians.[20]

Military service in native *durbars* attracted Eurasians anxious to carve out a more rewarding military career than was possible in British India, but avoiding the administration's influence became increasingly difficult as the century, and British hegemony, progressed. Samuel Clarkson was employed by Ajangarh durbar in 1891 to help with the suppression of *dacoity*. Within months, the political agent was reprimanded because no permission had been sought prior to this appointment; the agent was ordered to report on both Clarkson's fitness for the place to which he had been appointed *and* his antecedents. He had previously served the British as a bandsman with the 14th Bengal Lancers and had 'exceptionally smart soldierly qualities', but 'the fact of his being a Eurasian Christian appears to have closed the door to advancement which he otherwise deserved in the service'. The political agent claimed that neither he nor the states in Bundelkhand agency had ever been informed that they needed the governor-general's sanction to employ Eurasians. Clarkson was not dismissed, but the imperative to control the movements and influence of Europeans and Eurasians was of central importance to government, regardless of treaty conditions. To affect a compromise, the political agent suggested that the *durbar* might 'contribute' his services to the combined states' forces loaned to government for suppression of thugs and dacoits.[21]

At the start of the nineteenth century, many Eurasians had gained military employment with native states through the patronage of fathers serving the British administration, but, as the century wore on, British officials were less likely to be so closely related. Treaty conditions were more widely enforced and Eurasians were more likely to be noticed and vetted than before. More states were annexed, making more Eurasians British subjects. The Eurasians likely to obtain and retain positions of authority in the armies of native states were those who could remain unnoticed and/or those who least identified with their European heritage, particularly those with non-European names and lifestyles.

THE COMPANY'S ARMIES

Musicians

Greene cites a general order dated 14 June 1798 that all fifers and drummers for *sepoy* regiments should come from military orphan schools, joining when they were 13 or 14.[22] This is probably the first example of an occupation reserved for Eurasians.[23] Between 1782 and 1820, 693 boys were employed from the Bengal Lower Orphan School, three quarters as military fifers and drummers.[24] The order applied to all presidencies, which would mean over 1,660 military orphan boys available throughout India.[25] The sons of Eurasian military musicians were also educated and placed in the same way. Thus, the military bands became the most common form of

Table 8.1 Military Musicians.

Year	No. of battalions (native infantry)	No. of men[26]	Number of posts for musicians (3 per cent)
1795	–	57,000	1,710
1824	144	115,200	3,456
1857	–	311,538	9,346
1863	–	135,000	4,050
1911	138	110,400	3,312

employment for Eurasian sons of soldiers. An idea of the number of positions available can be calculated from known examples.

In 1804, the Scots Brigade numbered 1,024 men, with 26 drummers on its muster.[27] In 1868, Charles Dickens reported that the French army fielded 50 to 60 musicians for 2,400 soldiers.[28] In 1857, the 28th Bengal Native Infantry's band comprised 30 Christian Eurasian bandsmen,[29] and so the Company deployed bandsmen across its presidency armies in a similar proportion to the British and French armies: between 2.5 and 3 per cent of its strength.

Table 8.1 shows that, given the early requirement that bandsmen for native regiments should come from military orphanages, these bands employed a significant number of Indo-British Eurasians.[30] We know their opportunities within Company armies were limited, so many would serve their whole careers as bandsmen, supporting at least an equal number of relatives. If there were between three and four thousand bandsmen (an estimate for 1824) plus an equal number of dependants, they might represent between 6 and 14 per cent of all Indo-British Eurasians.

That Eurasian bandsmen were officially restricted to non-combatant roles did not preclude battlefield duties. Troop Sergeant-Major Charles Thompson's race is not specified in the few extant records, but he must have been Eurasian. He was a bandsman with dark hair, dark complexion, and black eyes, born at 'Beawur' in 1825, and enlisted in the Company's Bengal army in 1839. A band corporal by 1843 serving with the 9th Bengal Light Cavalry, he was awarded a medal for action at Hyderabad in 'Scinde'.[31] He was a sergeant in 1857, and was robbed when the 9th mutinied at Sealkote. Transferring to the Lahore Light Horse (disbanded in 1863), he saw further action at Lucknow. He rose to the rank of troop sergeant-major when awarded a long-service and good-conduct medal in 1866. He had served until 1865, when he was discharged to pension.[32] Thompson's record shows that, though a non-combatant, he was in battle at least three times. It also shows that, contrary to Company standing orders, he was of a rank supposed to be closed to Eurasians: a sergeant-major serving with a native corps. Thompson was not the only Eurasian to achieve a high non-commissioned rank within the Company's armies.

The prospects of bandsmen may have varied by regiment. Master Sergeant Whiley of the 47th Bengal Native Infantry believed that his two bandsmen sons would do better if granted transfers to a European regiment.[33] He did not elaborate on how their prospects might be improved by such a move; he would have been aware that in European regiments bandsmen were combitants or he may simply have wished to ensure that his sons mixed with Europeans and Eurasians rather than natives.[34] Given the 'family' ethos of regimental life, bandsmen would have developed close bonds within their own regiment. If that was a native regiment, the bandsmen would have developed a strong alliegance to their native peers. That was certainly true of the 30 Eurasian bandsmen of the 28th Bengal Native Infantry, who stood with their regiment when it mutinied and who were all killed by Hodson's Horse at Delhi.[35]

A Company bandsman's post has been portrayed as a job with security but no prospects of improvement. However, Samuel Clarkson's 'soldierly qualities' allowed him to move to service with Ajangarh durbar. His move was prompted by lack of prospects in the Company's service, but the latter also helped the political officer to support him when his role was challenged by the governor-general.[36] Lewis Groves made a similar move, from drummer with the 73rd Native Infantry to sergeant-major with Bandar durbar.[37]

Besides military marches, army bands played dance music for social events such as mess and residency balls. Bandsmen who left the military thereby gained a useful transferrable skill; there was work for civilian musicians at dances at the railway institutes, Eurasian weddings, and other community events. Potential employers, particularly those who fielded a volunteer regiment, may also have valued their skills and service record, and considered them worthy of employment on that basis.

Farriers

Farriers, who made horseshoes, acted as grooms, and assisted veterinary surgeons with horse care, were an essential part of any army. Artillery and transport corps used horses alongside the camels and bullocks used to move equipment between encampments. Officers and their wives kept horses for leisure, sport, and to pull their carriages; they carried dispatch riders, and cavalry regiments had more horses than men. The animals were inspected at least twice a day and horseshoes had to be replaced regularly, about once in six weeks, so there was plenty of work for army farriers. Often Eurasian, they too gained skills transferrable to civilian life.

Thurston found a student farrier in his ethnography of poor Madras Eurasians, Samthar durbar employed a Eurasian in its stables on such a low wage (Rs 10 a month) that the political agent presumed he must be 'nothing more than a Native Christian'.[38] There were native farriers with whom they had to compete, but the prejudices of the European elite in particular would have worked in a Eurasian's favour, as would his European heritage in some native *durbars*. Given the care of valuable Arabs, a contract with a stud, or proximity to a racecourse, there would have been steady work. It was a specialist trade that took some years as an apprentice to learn. Gilchrist advised his readers not to bring European coachmen to India because they could easily desert their masters and set up business as farriers.[39] A skilled and trusted farrier sergeant, on leaving the army, could set up as a master with his own journeymen and apprentices. From a working-class perspective, it was a respectable trade.[40]

The Madras Sergeant-Majors

Metcalf noted: 'In India, the young British officer found his ideas shaped by his choice of service and the nature of his work.' He also pointed out: 'In Bengal, the aristocratic sentiments of Lord Cornwallis still dominated the civil service 75 years after the Permanent Settlement.'[41] Thus, the British did not have a single approach to the everyday administration of India. What was unacceptable in Bengal might be viewed differently in the *mofussil* or in another presidency. Such was the case with Eurasian sergeant-majors in the Company's Madras army.

In 1835, 41 of 63 sergeant-majors serving with Madras native regiments were Eurasians. Often drawn from the Military Male Asylum and the free schools, seven were sons of 'old soldiers' and conductors, and two sons of commissioned officers. Others, recruited as adults, had previously been bandsmen, farriers, or clerks, and several had seen battle.[42] The governor-general complained that these appointments were against regulations, and that such posts should go to 'deserving' Europeans. But Madras' military department stood its ground, insisting only the Madras commander could alter the number, organization, pay, clothing, and equipment of his troops. Eventually, it was agreed in writing that Eurasian sergeant-majors would be dismissed.[43] However, in 1843, the East India Register announced the birth of a son to the wife of F. Mergler, one of the Eurasian sergeant-majors from 1835, still with the 35th Madras Native Infantry,[44] with which he had already served for 21 years. Several others were also still in post.

Crises

Military crises also expanded opportunities for Eurasians to serve in a military capacity. Irregular corps, Company and even British army units sometimes needed to expand rapidly, and at such times would accept Eurasians. There was a Eurasian regiment in 1857 Bengal[45] and the 98th Foot had a Eurasian corps in 1858.[46] The EAIA also said the 1st Madras Fusiliers, which 'gave a good account of itself during the Mutiny of 1857-8 might fairly be claimed a Eurasian Regiment'.[47] Allen's *Indian Mail* published a revised establishment for the Lahore Light Horse in February 1860, which declared 'All soldiers enlisted to be of European or Eurasian parentage.'[48] There were even Eurasian artillery men in 1866.[49]

The Indian Subordinate Medical Department

In the Company armies, and later the Indian army, thousands of Eurasians served in the Indian Subordinate Medical Department (ISMD). This was an integral part of the military with its personnel attached to Company and Crown units.[50] Known initially as apothecaries and later as assistant surgeons, European and Eurasian subordinates served with European or native units, either under the direction of a surgeon of the Indian Medical Service (IMS) or alone. Although in theory the IMS was open to 'all natural born subjects of Her Majesty', it was recruited entirely in Europe.[51] All of its members were covenanted or commissioned, but the expense of travelling to Europe and attending medical school there was beyond the reach of most Eurasians, domiciled Europeans, and Indians, who were left with little choice but to join the ISMD.[52] Indian native subordinates, sometimes apothecaries but more usually hospital assistants, served only native units, civil and military.[53]

The ISMD was drawn from graduates educated together with civilians at government medical colleges,[54] government hospitals and in the field. Candidates for apothecary or assistant surgeon posts, already qualified after several years as hospital apprentices, faced further competitive examinations for postings.[55] Those appointed were sent to military stations to care for servicemen and their families.[56] They progressed by seniority through four grades (classes) until they achieved senior apothecary or assistant surgeon grade. All held warrant officer rank, but could not progress beyond senior warrant officer or honorary commissioned officer rank. A few determined individuals managed to get to Britain, gain further training, qualifications and professional registration, and take the necessary examinations there to join the more prestigious and remunerative IMS, a step that also led to increased exposure to racism.[57]

By 1829–31, the Madras ISMD already recorded 200 men in its pension rolls.[58] The total number of apothecaries, assistant apothecaries, and others aspiring to those grades (which included stewards in Bengal and Bombay) across India was 327 in 1841[59] working alongside 846 surgeons and assistant surgeons of Crown forces and the Company's IMS.[60] By the 1860s, there were about 490 apothecaries and assistant apothecaries across British India working alongside about 745 IMS men.[61] In 1908, the subordinate department had in post 664 Eurasian and domiciled European assistant surgeons.[62] In 1914, the IMS establishment was 646, half of whom were doing civil duties; there were 360 medical officers of the Royal Army Medical Corps (RAMC);[63] and the ISMD fielded 2,142 assistant (mostly Eurasian) and sub-assistant surgeons (including Indians).[64] Whatever the criticism of their training and abilities, the proportion of imported European doctors required reduced as the proportion of ISMD men increased, a considerable saving to government since the salary rates of the ISMD (Table 8.2) were much lower than those of the former.[65]

Besides diplomas for apothecaries, Madras, Calcutta, and Bombay medical schools also offered more extensive training courses leading to medical degrees. Madras awarded full medical degrees to 24 students between 1852 and 1867; the school's degrees thereafter were validated by Madras University.[66] Bombay and Calcutta medical colleges also offered full medical degrees validated by universities.[67] These qualified men to work as doctors in India, although those wishing to practise in Britain had to undergo further examinations there for a British licence.[68] The 1869 Madras medical college report noted that, although the Senior Department's men were fully qualified as doctors, 'there are no outlets in this Presidency for those who cannot afford to test the value of their professional training in England'.[69] A similar complaint was made by Dadabhai Naoroji, who noted that native holders of LM degrees (Licentiate in Medicine) were stuck in sub-assistant surgeon positions, unable to progress because examinations for IMS entry up to the 1870s were held only in Britain.[70] Both these complaints ignored the fact that there were no restrictions on private practice,[71] other than racism from European patients[72] and mistrust in Western medicine from many Indians.[73] However, the General Medical Council, with which British doctors had to be registered, and the Indian medical colleges compounded the difficulties. Petty power struggles over validation of qualifications and the powers of a proposed all-India inspectorate, meant that until 1934 anyone commencing their medical education in India could not be sure their qualifications would be recognized by the time they qualified.[74] Whether by intent or neglect, the law forbidding discrimination in government employment on grounds of race, creed, or place of birth was effectively circumvented. Highly trained and qualified Indians, Eurasians and domiciled Europeans in government service were confined to the ISMD, and the IMS remained a European stronghold.

The ISMD was not reserved for Eurasians but, from its inception, they were well represented;[75] a general order of 1812 approved the selection of 24 boys from the Upper and Lower Orphan Schools and the Free School at Calcutta 'to serve as Compounders, Dressers, and ultimately as Apothecaries and Sub Assistant Surgeons'. As pupils, boys were supported by the surgeons training them. As compounders and dressers they got free accommodation and Rs 35 monthly, and as apothecaries or sub-assistant surgeons they were paid Rs 100 monthly.[76] Madras started early in the formal medical education of apothecaries, and the other presidencies followed suit with structured syllabi, regular examinations, and clinical training.[77] Boys aged 16 to 18, who passed the entrance examinations in India, studied for between three and six years with annual examinations. Younger boys were also taken into the service: a year into his training, 15-year-old Andrew Fitzgibbon, a Bengal hospital apprentice, won a Victoria Cross in 1860 whilst serving with the 67th Regiment in China.[78]

Madras Medical College was firmly routed to learning through clinical practice: 'it gives the student a familiarity with the physiognomy and course of disease, which books cannot bestow'.[79] Madras offered three routes to qualification: as a licentiate, an assistant apothecary, or a hospital assistant. The Senior Department, including private scholars and boys who had won scholarships, graduated as licentiates after five years' study; Second Department boys, all military entries, graduated after three years, equipped for employment as assistant apothecaries. Junior Department boys, after two years, could become hospital assistants.[80] New rules introduced in 1865 specified that hospital training had to be undertaken prior to commencing formal studies, to ensure that boys understood both medical terminology and English.[81] By 1870, hospital assistant training had been extended to include more subjects, and the College wanted to lengthen academic training to three years.[82] The grade of hospital assistant had been created to replace a rank being phased out – dressers – but the college principal considered the assistants' training inadequate except to produce 'superior compounders and dispensers of medicines'.[83] In 1866, two Junior Department students were fee paying, five Second Department boys had lost their stipends, and two of the seniors were private (fee-paying) students.[84] By 1869, final-year Second Department and Senior Department students were participating in the training and disciplining of students in the lower years and in the Junior Department.[85] All three departments at Madras included students with European and Indian names, but those of the Junior Department were predominantly Indian. Those with European names at this time were Eurasians, with possibly a few Indian Christians in the Junior Department,[86] since local enlistment of young men for the Medical Department had excluded those of European ancestry on both sides, a condition only removed in 1867.[87]

The full syllabus at Madras in 1865, undertaken by Senior Department boys, comprised anatomy, physiology, surgery, minor surgery, medicine, *materia medica* (pharmacology), ophthalmology, midwifery, chemistry, medical jurisprudence, hygiene, botany, diseases of women and children, organic chemistry, comparative anatomy, dissection, pathology, and microscopy. The Second Department did not study botany or pathology, instead concentrating on practical pharmacy.[88] The Junior Department were taught elementary medicine, surgery and anatomy, *materia medica*, compounding, and minor surgery. In Madras in the 1860s, Indian students trained in the same subjects and were ranked in examinations alongside Europeans and Eurasians.[89] All Madras annual reports included a table showing how many lectures (including practical demonstrations and clinical instruction) or examinations were held for each subject; every third class was an examination. Students also sat annual and final examinations. Those who failed badly were dismissed. Those capable of improvement could repeat a year at their own expense.

Race certainly affected employment and promotion prospects. Naoroji suggests that Bombay's Indian students were excluded from, or disadvantaged in, training as apothecaries and doctors.[90] Of the Senior Department boys at Bombay, Naoroji claimed Indians had to pay to train for medical degrees, whereas Europeans were paid by government, and had to be better qualified to join the college.[91] In Madras in the mid-1860s, two of the ten boys in the final year of Second Department (apothecary) training had Indian names. All were military students on monthly allowances of Rs 10 to 16 and Rs 10 *batta* for rations.[92] M. Pursooramen Naick and Dhanakoti Rajoo had been Senior Department scholars at Madras in 1866, and both had received scholarships.[93] Government scholars, of any race, received a Rs 20 monthly allowance, rising to 30 and then 40 as they progressed over five years.[94] Madras also offered a Lane Scholarship, open to any race, which started at Rs 30 and rose to Rs 50 per month.[95] Naoroji was, of course, writing later and about a different presidency, and so may have been correct in his analysis of the reality, if not the regulations. In Madras, moreover, the Lane Scholarship may have been colour-blind but it was restricted to Protestants. A medical journal in 1905 specified that military medical students there were paid a monthly allowance, but it mentions only Europeans and Eurasians. It is unclear whether Indian students were excluded from training or from the allowance,[96] but it is evident from their names and appearance that the Bengal military medical graduates in 1915 were all Eurasians.[97]

Turning to pay and conditions, we know ISMD personnel were paid considerably less than IMS doctors (effectively Europeans), but training, remuneration, and conditions of service differed within the ISMD too, by grade, over time, and between presidencies.

The early ISMD included Indian and Eurasian 'dressers'. Eurasian dressers drawing monthly salaries of Rs 35 in 1812 Bengal were expected to rise, over time, to become apothecaries.[98] 'Dresser' was, however, a career grade for Indians. A general order in March 1827 established a Madras corps of Indian dressers, paid, whilst pupils, Rs 7 monthly allowance and 1 *anna* 3 *paise* per day *batta* for two years. In 1838, all students of the Lower Department training as dressers were 'natives' and not Indo-Britons.[99] Once qualified, dressers had been equivalent in rank to privates[100] but by 1866 native dressers were being phased out altogether.[101]

Stewards were also low paid and of low status, and in 1868, though the posts remained, they were removed from the ISMD establishment. Their monthly salaries in 1868 Bengal were Rs 20 to 45.[102] The grade was first identified in a general order of 1812, as part of the Bengal ISMD to be trained by IMS men. They were listed in the ISMD rolls for Bengal and Bombay prior to 1868.[103] A description of stewards and assistant stewards in 1855 describes them as warrant officers responsible for 'food, clothing, and similar internal economy of military hospitals' besides aiding 'the surgeon in the preparation of official reports and statements'. Their duties could equally have been carried out by sergeant-majors without the expense of medical training – the route Madras had always taken, using hospital purveyors from the Commissariat Department.[104]

On graduating and entering the service as fourth-class assistant apothecaries, Eurasians and Europeans were ranked as sub-conductors, the forerunners of today's warrant officers, and occasionally held honorary junior commissioned ranks.[105] Cornish gave extensive information, based on the 1868 rules. Hospital apprentices trained for five years 'if the exigencies of the service permit',[106] including two years in a hospital prior to collegiate training. In 1905, the separate presidencies' ISMDs were consolidated into an India-wide service and the European and Eurasian medical students were paid a monthly allowance of Rs 26.4, a flat rate regardless of year of training.[107] Once qualified, they entered the service as fourth-class assistant surgeons,[108] progressing through seniority to become first-class assistant-surgeon, spending about five years in each of the lower grades. Their rates of pay are given in Table 8.2.

The service was again reorganized during the 1920s and early 1930s. The IMS was absorbed into the Royal Army Medical Corps

Table 8.2 Grades and Salaries: Indian Subordinate Medical Department, 1908.[109]

Grade	Monthly salary, Rs	Annual salary, £
4th-class Assistant Surgeon	85	68
3rd-class Assistant Surgeon	110	88
2nd-class Assistant Surgeon	150	120
1st-class Assistant Surgeon	200	160
Senior Hon. Lieutenant	300	240
Senior Hon. Captain	400	320

(RAMC), from which British medical officers were provided for both the Indian army and the civil provincial service; the British population had a protected right to consult a European doctor. The RAMC entrance examinations were in England. RAMC medics' pay had trebled from pre-war levels and they could retire after six years' service with a gratuity of £1,000. The civil provincial service recruited in India and Britain, but was headed by British qualified doctors; half of its medical establishment was reserved for RAMC men. The subordinate service was renamed and absorbed into the Indian Medical Department (IMD), military and civil provincial, with an Indian and a British cadre. IMD assistant surgeons were still attested as soldiers under the Army Act, but those seconded for civil duties came under civil authority. Their pay and conditions, often reduced, were set locally.[110]

THE IRREGULAR CORPS

Although Eurasians were officially excluded from the Company's military, in combative or covenanted posts, there were few reservations over their utilization in times of crisis in irregular corps. Some of the best of these were officered and raised by Eurasians, for example those under Hyder Hearsey and James Skinner.[111] Irregular corps were comparatively cheap since they came with their own arms, accoutrements, and, if cavalry corps, their own horses,[112] and, unlike Company and Crown troops, no pension entitlements.[113]

Irregular corps were not governed or ordered by military regulations. As late as 1857, the Company made use of irregular cavalry, infantry, and artillery corps. MacMunn noted: 'The Company hardly knew what its stock of irregular troops was, for they had been raised as emergency demanded and opportunity offered, on authority which, even if existing at one time in writing, was often not forthcoming afterwards.'[114] They were offered by native rulers, brought over to the British by their officers, or raised by individuals anxious to help.[115] In 1824, there were at least five regiments of irregular horse and several local corps and legions in Bengal, three local battalions in Madras, and two regiments of irregular horse in Bombay.[116] Before 1857, the Bengal irregular cavalry rose from five to 18 corps,[117] but in the 1860s these were reduced to eight regiments.[118] They were, however, a permanent adjunct to the armies serving the government.

Their commanders were charismatic soldiers who had often served native states and were well known to their fiercely loyal men. MacMunn claimed that 'the irregular system especially developed the initiative and responsibility of the native officer'. This made the corps particularly useful in wars that did not follow European rules of engagement, such as hill fighting in Afghanistan. They also brought local knowledge, invaluable in Nagpur and Awadh after their annexation where 'there were scores of reiving barons and robber chiefs to be dealt with' and against the Pindaris in Central India.[119]

VOLUNTEER MILITIAS

Eurasian militias were often raised in cities in times of unrest, and as the century progressed highly mobile railway militias could be deployed wherever there was a railway line. Militias were paid only when on military duties and, with the same conditions as regular infantrymen, would have been required to pay for their own equipment and uniforms through stoppages.[120]

In 1798, Calcutta mustered 'for the Security and Defence of this Presidency, about 1,157 Europeans [including Eurasians], 1,029 Portugueze [sic], and 150 Armenians enrolled themselves to serve in the Corps'.[121] In 1799, Madras mustered two companies of 'First

Class Europeans' (civil servants and other gentlemen), three companies of 'other Europeans' (including Eurasians), one of Armenians, a Black-Town European Militia, and three companies of Portuguese.[122] Whether the Eurasians formed a separate corps from the Europeans or served in joint units with the 'other Europeans' is not recorded.

In the second half of the century, as the railway network grew, railway 'volunteer' militias spread throughout the country and Eurasian employees were required to 'volunteer' for these.[123] Other locally based volunteer forces abounded, such as the Meerut Light Horse, the Bengal Yeomanry Cavalry, and the Lucknow and Lahore Volunteers. By 1897, there were 29,000 Eurasian and European volunteers in India.[124]

After serving in European units during the First World War, or volunteering for the Indian Defence Force, which replaced the many European regulars who were displaced from India to fight elsewhere, Eurasians were still not considered suitable for military service and yet were still required to 'volunteer', making up a large part of the 30,000 strong Indian Defence Force.[125] Military training was also part of the education of boys at the 'better' schools. At the Lawrence asylums and any military orphan schools, there was a strong military ethos.[126] All had their cadet forces, and although these were directed towards character building and not military action they could provide defensive support when troops were stretched or overtaken by events.[127]

CROWN ARMIES

From Cornwallis' arrival in India in 1786, through to the 1833 Charter Act, the sons of natives of India could not serve as European commissioned officers in Company armies, or in Crown armies right up to the end of British rule in India. An unknown number of fair-skinned, European-educated, and well-connected Eurasian men are thought to have covertly entered both without their mixed-race ancestry coming to light, despite a requirement for 'country-borns' to produce a certificate showing that both parents were European. By definition, these individuals are difficult to distinguish with any certainty; a covert Eurasian would not have deliberately identified himself. We also know that Victorian biographers of the 'great and the good' were careful to give full details of antecedence and family connections, so the absence of any maternal ancestry record may signify their wish 'to sustain a respect for the nation's political and intellectual elite'.[128] Sensitivity about miscegenation would have led some to omit any reference to Eurasian or native mothers, and indeed I have found that biographies of the India-born omit maternal ancestry more often than those of British-born officers.

Well-known Eurasian commissioned officers, whose ancestry was not hidden, can occasionally be identified. James Skinner, whose mother was a Jat, never succeeded in gaining a Company commission, serving only in an irregular corps, but was (eventually) rewarded with a royal commission, though not as a serving officer. Another example was Captain George Hipkin Walters, 'the son by a Native Woman of the late Mr Walters, Surgeon ... by his own account, an Officer in His Majesty's Service [11th Light Dragoons] on half-pay'.[129] Lieutenant-Colonel Sir Robert Warburton, founder of the Khyber Rifles and son of an Afghan mother – another exception – joined the Royal Artillery in 1862 and remained a serving officer and political agent until 1899.[130] Frederick William Forjett, son of the Eurasian Commissioner of Bombay Police, was also commissioned; he was a staff corps lieutenant in 1875.[131] All of the examples in this section were the sons or grandsons of a British-born father, and all but Skinner were educated and appointed in Britain. As such, their connections to their European relatives (and patronage) were stronger than for most Eurasians.

Commenting on British attitudes to Eurasians in 1835 India, an anonymous author noted that 'society' was 'willing to admit the abstract truth that the human mind is formed by education and habit' but was unwilling to apply that principle to Eurasians.[132] The few examples given above might contradict that conclusion, but for the fact that they are so few.

THE DISCOURSES

Several themes run through nineteenth-century discourses on the subject of military employment for Eurasians. Their loyalty was questioned, particularly in the early years of the century. Their genetics were probed, measured, and debated. Their martial qualities were proved by their ancestry and disproved by the stereotypes of spare physiques and propensity for *cranny* work. The effects of climate, nutrition, and environment were explored, as were the economic effects of enlistment on the community. The continuous involvement of Eurasians with the military has been explored (above), but discourses on the subject illuminate how and why their exclusion from regular enlistment and the commissioned ranks continued, and why it mattered to the community.

Loyalty

One of the first concerns to emerge was Eurasians' 'hybridity', and how that affected their loyalty. Cornwallis' distrust of settlers, which he brought with him to India, and later the part played by mulattos in West Indies' slave uprisings were discussed earlier. Continued questions about Eurasians' loyalty, whether to Britain, to India or to themselves, were fatuous, and fears were unfounded. Nineteenth-century Eurasians possessed neither power, nor unity, nor followers sufficient to bring about 'regime change', even had they wished to do so. Inciting revolt against the British would, in any case, have adversely affected them too.

Their ill-defined, multiple national status was an on-going problem. During the Maratha wars, the British threatened to treat Europeans and Eurasians as traitors if they continued in the service of what were (or had become) their home states.[133] Early in the century, those serving in hostile *durbars'* armies may have represented a military threat, but portraying those who refused to go over to the British as traitors was inaccurate. Baptiste Filoze, son of an Italian father and a local woman, rose to command the 30,000-strong Gwalior state army. By 1848, he had served Scindia and his home state for 47 years.[134] He owed no allegiance to British interests, was not a British subject, and would not have been allowed to serve the Company except (possibly) as an irregular. Yet he still felt it necessary to withdraw his immediate services whenever the enemy was Britain, to avoid being treated as a traitor. Where they could not be portrayed as traitors, or ignored by history,[135] Eurasians and Europeans serving native states were described dismissively as mercenaries or self-serving adventurers. They 'were sustained by no patriotic spirit, inspired by no national sentiment, bound together by no common cause, and as often opposed to men of their own creed or caste as allied with them. They were merely a hireling soldiery risking their lives for stipulated payment.'[136] The British appeared to think that anyone of European descent who fought for a native state was either a traitor to Britain or a mercenary, but surely a Eurasian might have fought for his native state precisely because he was loyal.[137]

Reduced opportunities for military service in the late eighteenth and early nineteenth century, whether in Company, Crown, or native service, did not preclude the expectation of loyalty to British interests in the Maratha wars, Punjab campaign, or during 1857 when civilian volunteers, including Eurasians, were welcomed. Some believed the community should have been rewarded for its loyalty, particularly after 1857 – a view that was rejected,[138] but it continued to be stressed by Stark near the end of the Raj and, later and more guardedly (because it might easily be misunderstood in an independent India) by Anthony.[139] But this perspective does not appear to have been common in contemporary documents. Exceptions might be Captain William Nicolls, who, after the Mutiny, suggested the formation of a Christian infantry regiment at Madras.[140] Suggestions from the Select Committee on Colonisation and Settlement (India) in 1858 that pensioner soldiers should settle and raise many more children, albeit Eurasians,[141] were motivated by considerations of how to improve the security of British rule rather than any concern to reward the Eurasian community for its loyalty.

Martial Races

Discussions of Eurasians' martial qualities became more common and more frequent as the century progressed, either to establish or deny their presence. British recognition of martial qualities always appears related to the degree to which a group was a threat or rival. Thus, Rajputs, Muslims, Sikhs, and Gurkhas, who had all been difficult to subdue, were declared 'martial races'. It was safer to respect them and offer financial security.

It is ironic that the British could argue soldierly attributes were heritable, and then refute that argument when used by the descendents of soldiers who had delivered the Raj. Eurasian authors believed that the case for Eurasians as soldiers had already been made. Anthony believed in an 'indelible impress the Community [had] left on the military annals of British-Indian history', and that the 'fighting qualities exhibited by the Community' in 1857 had proved that Eurasians possessed martial qualities.[142] Racial degeneration was the riposte; either the admixture of 'Asiatic' blood had resulted in inferior offspring or the climate was inimical to their European blood.

Blood

Most Eurasians were the descendents of European soldiers and so, some claimed, must have inherited martial characteristics. John Crawfurd, an ethnographer writing in 1865, expressed the opinion that the Indo-British were a great improvement over the Hindus: 'In the first generation they have produced men of mark, and with one more infusion of European blood, men of distinction, scarcely, if at all, to be distinguished from the pure European.'[143] At the other extreme were damning indictments from, for example, Canning, Savi, and Darwin: Eurasians combined the worst of both races or had reverted to a savage state.[144] The prevaling prejudice was that Eurasians lacked the courage and physique for military service. George Evatt, a brigade surgeon, contested that by citing their military service in previous crises and comparing underfed urban Britons with underfed Eurasians, both, he believed, would improve with country air, good food, and drill.[145] Dover, a trained biologist and a Eurasian, cited the physical prowess of Eurasians in railway employment 'where hard labour and physical strength are essential'. He rather spoils an otherwise scientific approach to Eurasian genetics, implying their superiority by claiming they possessed 'hybrid vigour' and were destined to 'astound the world'.[146]

The British government and colonial society acted as though Darwin's opinions were proven facts, discouraging miscegenation to prevent degeneration of the English race and providing Eurasians with moral Christian guidance and cosseted locales where European values were encouraged, learned, and even enforced.[147] If the British really believed Eurasians were a degraded form of humanity, one wonders why they bothered.

Environment, Diet, and Climate

The climate on India's plains was popularly believed to damage Europeans; no settlers could survive more than three generations. The environment, physical, mental, and moral, could only be withstood by the most fervent Christians whose education had fully developed their sensibilities and ability to resist depravity. There was also the question of whether poor diet had made the Eurasians permanently unsuitable for fighting.

Evatt blamed the weak physique of many Eurasians on poverty, lack of fresh air, and unordered exercise. The Lawrence asylums, and hill stations for Europeans, had come about because of the belief that the climate in plains India was damaging to Europeans. So it is anachronistic that Evatt in the 1890s and Dover in the late 1920s felt it necessary to offer proof that Eurasian boys, when educated in hill stations, 'showed the potential to be as strong as any westerner, when removed from the debilitating effects of tropical climate and economic distress'.[148] The question of Eurasian military service was raised time and again, right to the end of the century.[149] The Eurasian associations sent a deputation to London in 1897, pleading for a Eurasian regiment to help alleviate poverty within the community.[150] This may have been the prompt for Thurston's 1898 anthropological study of the poorest Eurasians in Madras, which found that their physiques did not compare with that of *sepoys* and they were not suitable for military service.[151] The result came as no surprise to a Eurasian reporter who summed it up: 'Thurston really proves that the Eurasian is not fit for military service when *growed* like Topsy, in a bad climate, in squalor, and in semi-starvation.'[152]

Crawfurd believed the races differed widely 'in physical form and in mental endowment', 'facts' explained by the availability of good staple foods and a good climate. Europeans and 'Hindus' were both hardy races. Heat sapped energy and stunted industry, but did not cause racial degeneration. Almost everyone was intellectually inferior to the European, but 'the skill and forecast necessary to the production of cereals would seem to be both a cause and effect of civilisation'. Northern Europeans and Indians had mastered cereal production, but Europeans were more industrious and questing because they had benefited from a temperate climate over time.[153] This kind of argument, utilized by those who believed in climatic determinism, could mean that Eurasians' European heritage could be redeemed in the hills.

Economics

There was an economic discourse on whether military service would alleviate or exacerbate community poverty. Evatt's interest in the community was genuine, but he was careful to couch his arguments in terms that would appeal to the military and civil administration. Eurasians were thus presented as an underused resource and a problem that might easily be solved. As soldiers they would save the government money, as military hospital attendants they would improve hospital conditions, and military service would instil self-discipline, transferrable to civilian employment. Evatt said money would also be saved, by obviating the need to transport alternative European staff back and forth to Britain. He also argued all tax-paying classes had an 'equitable claim in the personal division of that taxation by drawing a soldier's pay'.[154]

Eurasian community leaders viewed enlistment in a similar light, though besides thinning the ranks of Eurasian paupers they were also interested in helping their own sons into posts with rank. They stressed the large number of fine strong lads anxious to serve their country, and the potential of the physically weak to improve with army diet and discipline. The India Office dismissed any economic advantages of Eurasian enlistment.[155] They were already entitled to enlist as *sepoys* or into non-combatant enclaves reserved for them. European regiments were in India to defend the empire and balance out any renewed threat from mutinous *sepoys* post-1857; Eurasian units would muddy the water. Evatt's taxation argument was also turned around: a Eurasian regiment would replace a *sepoy* one and burden Indian taxpayers with a more expensive Eurasian unit. The community leaders' view that the community stood to benefit economically was also reversed: even on European rates, soldiers could not afford to keep families, and Eurasian women and children would therefore be thrown back onto charity.

Mizutani concludes that the idea of a Eurasian regiment was refused because the terms under which the Eurasians wanted it threatened the 'boundaries of whiteness'.[156] Mizutani's revisioning of the economic arguments claims the Eurasian associations' demands for pay on European scales would have tacitly raised the status of the community to that of the white British. Mizutani's argument is weak because many government jobs already offered the same basic pay (theoretically) to Eurasians and Europeans. It would have been easy for government to sanction a Eurasian regiment with unimpeachably European-British officers in all the upper ranks. Also, government argued that a Eurasian regiment would displace a native regiment – so even had one been formed, the perception of Eurasians as non-European would have continued.

CONCLUSIONS

Even after the Company employment ban was lifted in 1833 (it remained in place for the British army), few Eurasians are known to have succeeded in gaining permanent military employment apart from those discussed above. Besides bandsmen and farriers in Company armies, the British army traditionally employed colonial subjects amongst its bandsmen. Eurasian apothecaries were also part of the military. Local recruitment from orphanages, despite the ban, also included Eurasian NCOs serving with native regiments.

The topic of wider military service was never dropped. There were constantly recurring arguments – about whether Indo-British

Eurasians might have untapped 'martial' qualities or be born clerks, whether military employment might improve the community or whether they were too 'degenerate', and whether as soldiers they might prove an adjunct or a danger to the British. Despite all this, there remained a Eurasian military presence in the British and Company armies (including combatants), in princely armies, as irregulars, or mustered as militias. Frequently ephemeral, often unremunerative, and usually undervalued, military service nonetheless remained important to the Indo-British community and to Eurasians in the native states.

If the British military was an instrument of oppression in colonial India, it was also the means by which tens of thousands of Britons and hundreds of thousands of Indians earned a living, fed their families, and kept themselves in old age. For officers, commissioned and non-commissioned, military rank brought pride and status. For the men, the army was a family, offering the possibility of improvement, of education, and of adventure. On many occasions, Eurasians demonstrated their willingness to undertake military service. Only occasionally were they welcomed without restriction, and yet they were always present in one capacity or another.

Eurasian loyalty to the British Raj is a contentious issue, and I have no wish to emphasize this by portraying their interest in military service as an expression of that sentiment. Other Indian communities could be criticized retrospectively for their loyalty to the colonial state through civil or military service. But many men had little choice other than military service as a livelihood. Even Irish republicans, who detested their British overlords, were willing to take 'the King's shilling' rather than see their families starve.

Eurasian community leaders stressed their British heritage and credentials, emphasized their ancestors' loyalty and service, and eschewed their Indian heritage because that was their best hope of gaining the military service opportunities open to other Indian communities. Encouraged and perhaps even formulated by the British, the strategy worked for Eurasians in many other spheres of government employment. The demilitarization of their community was therefore viewed not only as an economic loss, but also a status loss and an insult to their heritage.

CHAPTER 9

EURASIANS AND THE RAILWAYS

This chapter examines Eurasians' association with Indian railways, particularly those belonging to the East India Railway Company (EIR). European and Eurasian railway personnel in late nineteenth-century India lived primarily in railway 'colonies' or 'lines'. Besides accommodation, larger colonies included railway workshops and offices, churches, clubs, hospitals, schools, sports, and recreational facilities, and their own police and militia. They were built to protect European and Eurasian personnel and their families from the 'degenerating' influence of Indians, and to promote European cultural mores. Many people spent their entire working lives on the railways, as did their sons and grandsons. Thus Eurasian and European 'railway people' lived in geographically, institutionally, and culturally identifiable 'communities'.

Eurasians made up less than 3 per cent of railway employees in the 1870s,[1] but were a large part of the railway colonies; about a third of EIR's upper subordinate posts in 1880 were held by Eurasians,[2] and many European men also had Eurasian wives and families. In 1926, railways employed at least 25 per cent of all the Eurasian men of India:[3] 14,007 men, representing just 1.84 per cent of the railway workforce.[4] According to Caplan, Younger, and Kerr, the quarter of the community employed represented a decline in Eurasian railway employment because of 'Indianization'. At some earlier dates, half of those identified as Eurasian were employed by or dependent upon the railways.[5] However, whilst the 1881 census enumerated 62,085 Eurasian men, the Railways Report of 1877–8 identified only 3,319 Eurasian railwaymen.[6] So there was a massive increase in Eurasian railway employment after 1880 that tailed off by the 1920s. Examining the lives of railway personnel in the late nineteenth century will, therefore, offer insights into the lives and aspirations of a substantial proportion of a British-orientated Eurasian community at a time of some optimism.

Railway companies were subject to strict government control, so general conditions of service in one company largely apply to all and I have chosen EIR because it was the largest employer throughout the latter decades of the nineteenth century. I use railway staff returns and reports, periodicals, maps, genealogical data, contemporary descriptions, and secondary sources to paint a mass demographic picture of railway communities, and to draw out individual cases. It is not possible to say with certainty whether the Eurasian railway community was happy with railway life. There were Eurasian community leaders who sporadically fought official and unofficial racial barriers,[7] and, from the twentieth century, personnel records include numerous complaints from individual Eurasian railwaymen and families.[8] However, it is not certain that, in the nineteenth century, the majority of the Eurasian 'rank and file' assessed their situation relative to anyone outside their immediate neighbourhood. They would have been taught in school, and reminded in church, of their station in life, whether class or race based, and most had little alternative but to accept it. Not everyone would have felt thwarted ambition or discontent. Surely most would have been content with a job that enabled them to meet the basic requirements of life. The railway offered secure employment and a living wage. It also offered important perks such as education and financial support in illness, infirmity, and death.

In half a century, the Indian rail network grew from nothing to 23,627 miles of track.[9] In 1878, Indian railways formally employed 132,040 men, and double that number within 20 years.[10] It became an important source of employment for all communities, although the more technical and responsible posts were, for many years, open only to Europeans and Eurasians. The EIR ran its first passenger train on 15 August 1854 and laid 1,200 miles of track in less than a decade.[11] It was the largest company, with a little under a third of all railway staff in India.[12] It was a private enterprise that began in February 1849. Capital was raised from British investors, some of which was lodged with the East India Company government which underwrote a guaranteed 5 per cent per annum return. Whether or not the railway made a profit, investors were paid from taxation. The EIR was taken over by the state in 1880,[13] but government had always exerted tight control over private railway companies.

Government demanded returns from all railway companies on such subjects as progress and growth, running costs, staffing, and goods and people carried. Detailed returns were required on all European and Eurasian staff but there were contemporary doubts about the accuracy of race data,[14] as well as protests about collecting such information. The EAIA believed distinguishing between Eurasians and Europeans reinforced Eurasian 'disabilities' associated with darker skin colour.[15] Such disabilities undoubtedly existed, and were not confined to the railways.[16] Complaints that Eurasians were treated unfairly because of their race were still found several decades later in petitions held in EIR archives examined by Laura Bear.[17] Regardless of accuracy, however, the race data collected by EIR, together with statistics on position, length of service, salaries, and location, allows the effects of Eurasian racial classification to be assessed.

Methodology

A slim volume, published by the EIR press, lists 1,479 European and 'East Indian' employees, in post on 30 June 1880.[18] The data, presented in tabular form, include length of service, name, race, occupation and grade, station and department, salary, any amount paid in Britain, provident fund details, and remarks such as resignations, dismissals, or discharge and/or re-employment. This information has been entered into a database for comparative analysis against race categorization, minimizing subjective input, and allowing general trends to be identified and quantified. Most railway personnel records remain in India and are not easy to access,[19] so tracing individual career trajectories was problematic; however, further detail of some men has been added by reference to earlier editions of the EIR's returns,[20] to Thacker's Indian Directories, the three presidencies' ecclesiastical records, the OIOC biographical index, and web-based databases such as fibis.org, ancestry.com and familysearch.org.[21] This allowed some career paths and families to be recovered over time. Background information on EIR occupations, training posts, and regimes has also been assembled, although extant sources are patchy.[22]

There were irresolvable difficulties in distinguishing between domiciled Europeans and Eurasians, but in some respects both were disadvantaged when compared with Europeans temporarily resident in India. Throughout the century, there were advantages available to the European (including the domiciled) but not the Eurasian population in India, some of which are evident from my analyses of railway staff records, and so there is justification in examining Eurasian railway society as though it were a distinct community of itself.[23] Eurasians' wealth, position, and prospects can be compared directly to the Europeans who lived and worked alongside them, but there is no distinction in these sources between Europeans permanently or temporarily resident in India, except that a small number were covenanted and likely to have been appointed in Britain.[24] Further, 'race' identified as such in employment records does not single out the Eurasian families of European employees who may have enjoyed some advantages over the sons of Eurasians, but few from such families have been identified and the data is insufficiently detailed to draw any conclusions.[25]

This study concerns only railway people, and so tells us nothing about the half of Eurasians with no railway association. Even in Calcutta, 22 per cent of Eurasians were 'destitute' in 1892,[26] and even had they once been railway people they could not have remained in railway colonies since such housing was tied to jobs. Non-railway Eurasians are considered only briefly, since the identity most strongly and ubiquitously associated with Eurasians by the end of the nineteenth century was 'railway people'.

By exploring data and noting trends that co-locate with race, it is possible to identify factors likely to have promoted satisfaction or dissatisfaction with railway employment and to assess the extent to which the railways met the needs of a considerable part of the Eurasian community. At its most basic, exchanging labour for wages is a means by which to satisfy our basic need for food and shelter, but occupation is a significant aspect of self-identity too. Railway employment unquestionably provided the basics: wages, a degree of job security, and a sense of belonging. The questions of whether there was also a safe environment, good working conditions, and a chance for fulfilment of potential was, we already know, particularly problematic for nineteenth-century Eurasians. In the following sections, I look at factors directly related to occupation, at some railway colonies and their associated institutions, and then discuss more generally the advantages and disadvantages for Eurasians of railway life.

EUROPEAN AND EURASIAN EMPLOYMENT CONDITIONS

The vast majority of EIR's employees were, of course, Indians; returns for 1877–8 show the company employed 38,912 men, 37,383 of whom were 'natives'.[27] As such, they are not the main subject of analysis but do provide comparative data. Separate returns were made of all others; 1,487 names appear in the 1881 European and Eurasian staff list of June 1880, which, oddly, includes an American, and 15 West Indians. The remaining 1,471 men on the list comprised 936 Europeans, both domiciled and imported, and 535 East Indians or Eurasians. The overall figure encompasses 273 apprentices and probationers, but these are not included in the following general analysis by occupation; these were temporary positions and are considered separately. This leaves 754 Europeans and 460 Eurasians, 62 per cent and 38 per cent respectively, as full employees.

Recruitment

Figure 9.1 is drawn from data on those still employed in 1880. The curves are not quantitative, since no allowance can be made for those

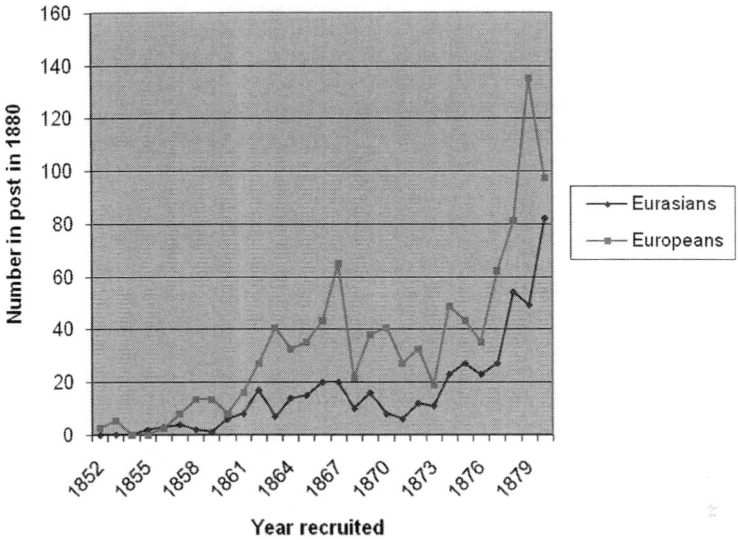

Figure 9.1 1880 European and Eurasian Employees by Recruitment Year.

recruited in earlier years who were no longer in post in 1880, but they are likely to be proportionate to each other. Though Eurasians outnumbered Europeans in India 2:1, Europeans were recruited at around twice the rate of Eurasians. Of course, the European population had a disproportionately large number of employable males[28] and the Eurasian population figures included all the elderly, infirm, females, and children. Therefore, railway European populations might have been proportionate to the numbers of European and Eurasian men available. Further, the network and its staff were growing, so there was a constant need to recruit experienced personnel, and for some trades these men were easier to find in Britain than India. At no point during this period did Eurasians in post outnumber Europeans.

Communal Earnings

Monthly salaries ranged from Rs 13 to Rs 2,000.[29] Some individuals with 20 years' service earned below Rs 100, and some with over ten

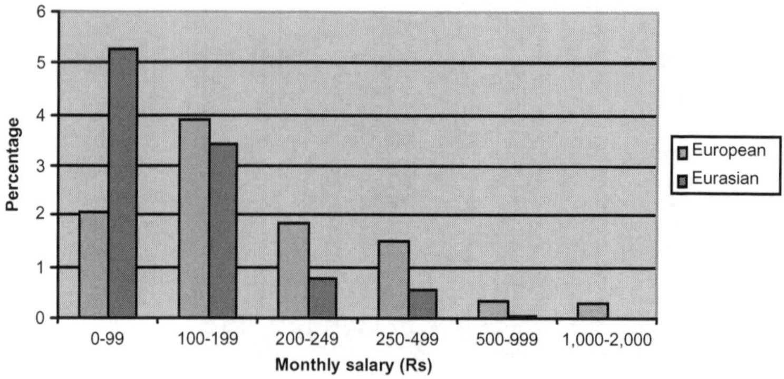

Figure 9.2 Monthly Salary by Race Classification.

years earned just Rs 35. Excluding apprentices and probationers, European average monthly earnings of Rs 226 were double those of Eurasians at Rs 113. Small numbers of posts at the margins, often the covenanted men, could cause severe distortions, and so, taking the middle 90 per cent, Europeans' average earnings were Rs 190, whereas those of Eurasians averaged Rs 103. So there was a difference in wealth between these two racial categories, as shown in Figure 9.2.

Over half of the Eurasian employees, but only a fifth of Europeans, had a monthly salary below Rs 100. A further third of Eurasians, and two-fifths of Europeans earned between Rs 100 and Rs 199, with 8 and 19 per cent respectively on salaries of Rs 200 to Rs 249. Arnold, writing about the best schools available to Europeans and Eurasians in nineteenth-century India, noted that they attract 'the wealthier class ... usually those with incomes above Rs 250 per month'.[30] By this measure, less than 6 per cent of EIR's Eurasian employees, but over 21 per cent of the Europeans, are classified as wealthy men. No Eurasian earned above Rs 700, whereas 31 Europeans earned between Rs 800 and Rs 2,000, drew an average of £13, 5s in England (equivalent to Rs 135), and enjoyed generous furloughs.

Eurasians could also be subdivided: 34 with German/Dutch/Danish names earned the same as those with British names, Rs 113; but 100 men with Portuguese names earned an average of Rs 98. Rather than different rates of pay for the same job determined by race, Europeans were more likely to occupy higher-paid posts in management, engineering, and other professions and, as already noted, trained personnel came from Britain until later in the century, when skilled India trained men began to trickle through.[31] Also, for lesser-paid posts, locally trained personnel, whether European or Eurasian, were already available in India. For that reason, it is likely that Europeans earning smaller salaries were already domiciled. The lower pay of Portuguese Eurasians may also reflect the economic conditions of the community from which they were drawn.

Whilst the Eurasian community was not so well off as the European, Indians' pay shows that railway Eurasians were comparatively prosperous. Mukherjee notes that pay for native railway labourers would have been about Rs 10 per month.[32] Similarly, figures from Sleeman indicate a pensioned *sepoy* got 'four rupees a month, that is about one-fourth more than the ordinary wages of common uninstructed labour throughout the country'; a subadar, the native rank equating to major, earned Rs 92 per month.[33] EIR paid masons, carpenters, and bricklayers 6 pence (or 2 *annas*) per day,[34] and the few native engine drivers were paid Rs 20 per month.[35]

Railway Schools

The children of wealthy Europeans had always been expected to return to Britain for their school years but the pay of most rail men would not meet that cost, and provision for the education of poorer Europeans and Eurasians in India had always been problematic. The army provided regimental schools for their own children, or had sent them to orphanages, but the less well-off domiciled and Eurasian communities had been left largely to their own devices to found and fund Christian English-medium schools. These, however, were mainly in the presidency cities and government grants-in-aid, where they were available, had to be matched with fees charged, putting them geographically and economically out of the reach of many railwaymen.

English-medium government-funded education provision, including grants paid to children who regularly attended, concentrated on secular provision to attract the Hindu and Muslim communities. Mission schools were unpopular with some Eurasians, anxious to maintain a distinction between themselves and native Christians. Government help for Eurasian education was minimal although periodic reviews led to some local initiatives and funding, such as small government grants to encourage brighter children to stay in school for longer.[36] Numbers of Eurasian and European children grew rapidly as the rail network, and Raj infrastructure more generally, expanded during the second half of the nineteenth century. The railway's geographical spread only exacerbated the problem of education for Eurasians and poorer Europeans. Danvers' 1877 and 1878 reports identified 3,399 European and Eurasian railway employees' children. Almost half were the children of EIR's staff, spread across 42 stations, only 13 of which had schools, leaving 600 children at the remaining stations with no railway schools. Even had the lowest paid been willing to send their children to schools outside the railway colonies, an enquiry in 1876 found that a third of children of railwaymen earning over Rs 100 per month did not attend any school. Concerns were raised by the Church, India Office, government, and the EAIA. The India Office wanted children trained 'in a manner which would give them the best opportunity of becoming good citizens in the land of their adoption'.[37] The EAIA wanted local schools so that parental influence could be maintained.[38]

Railway schools were relatively new in 1880; Jumalpore's large boarding school for European and Eurasian children was amongst the first, but Danvers' 1877 report had noted: 'the mechanical class ... will reside many years, if not all their lives, in India, and raise a progeny there'. If left in the plains, they would 'be reduced to a feeble and flaccid condition'.[39] The EIR founded a hill school (Oak Grove) at Musoorie in 1888;[40] its high fees ensuring exclusivity. Before this, rail companies and existing hill schools (such as La Martinière) already worked together to place boys as apprentices.[41] The sons of the wealthiest were schooled in Britain. For the majority of Eurasians, earning salaries insufficient for either of these options, railway schools on the plains, though not free, were a major benefit.[42]

The hill schools discourses provide interesting insights into the ramifications of providing education targeted at the wealthier railwaymen's children. From a European perspective, the bracing air of the hill schools would improve the children 'physically and morally'. The EAIA had a different perspective; far from helping the situation, more hill schools would damage existing independent boarding schools in the plains. Wealthier children would be relocated, the existing schools would lose their fees and close, further reducing provision for the less well off. They said government was underestimating the value of parental guidance for non-boarders, and, since there was no state church in India, said all schools should be ecumenical.[43] Schooling was an important concern, but the paternalistic attitudes of the railway company, the state, and the Anglican Church were resented by some Eurasians. Their responsibility for and connection to their own children was being undermined, their opinions ignored, and their philanthropic efforts in support of independent schools in the plains undervalued and damaged.

The provision of railway schools, however, was a valuable perquisite. In providing English-medium Christian education, it offered a high level of security to families concerned for their children's future, with the hope that, through education, they would secure employment and status.

Provident Funds

Pensions were also offered to EIR employees. A provident fund scheme, proposed in 1864 but not fully implemented until January 1868, was a welcome addition, offering economic security in sickness and old age. It was designed to 'allow clearing of higher appointments, and [for] those past their best years to retire'. At first it was divisive, since it rewarded Europeans more than others. Europeans paid higher contributions but Eurasians and Indians, paying half as much, had to work twice as long. The final reward was a pension of a quarter of average salary after 15 or 30 years, according to race. Contributions were set at 5 and 2.5 per cent of salary respectively. The company's promise to make contributions from profits was not initially kept. New employees earning over Rs 30 per month were compelled to join. Those already employed who wanted to join the scheme had to contribute for the years already worked. They were given two years to do so, but charged 10 per cent interest on monies outstanding. Conditions of redundancy 'for meritorious service' also differed by race, with Europeans awarded up to a year's salary and Eurasians and Indians limited to six months' maximum. The dismissed 'idle or vicious' were not pensioned but had their contributions returned, with interest but without company contributions.[44]

That conditions differed by race was a source of dissatisfaction, particularly as the position of domiciled Europeans was not spelt out. The unanswerable question is whether domiciled Europeans were pensioned as Europeans or Eurasians. Rule changes in 1881 abolished the distinction between European and non-European members, and thenceforth all who earned at least Rs 15 per month were required to contribute 5 per cent of salary. The fund rules were not changed again until 1903.[45]

Accommodation

Housing for European and Eurasian railway employees was built, maintained, policed, and subsidized by railway companies within 'colonies'. Like other European settlements (civil, military, and hill station) these were racially exclusive. Housing for Indian employees was not provided in the nineteenth century, so the inclusion of Eurasians was an affirmation of their European-ness. There was barrack-style accommodation for travelling staff (e.g. drivers and line inspectors), apprentices, single men, and even families. However, cottages and bungalows with individual gardens were increasingly provided for families, senior staff, and small groups of single men.[46] The environment was rigidly European and the railway police, in their role of curbing immorality, could be intrusive, but rents were affordable at about a tenth of salary.[47]

Tied railway housing was a bonus, but on dismissal through retirement, fault, or periodic restructuring, whole families were uprooted and evicted from the colonies that had provided not only home but many community institutions. This was less traumatic if they were near a large town, since there would have been alternatives available nearby. But at dedicated railway towns such as Jumalpore, it meant relocation over a considerable distance, and loss of much that was central to daily life and identity.

OCCUPATIONS

Besides the general conditions of railway service, the nature of work undertaken had an influence on how men felt about the rewards of railway employment. This section explores the occupations in which most Eurasians were employed.

Variety of Occupations

Figure 9.3 shows the proportions of Europeans to Eurasians employed. Large variations from this picture may indicate occupations in which race-based 'disabilities' might have been an issue. Europeans and Eurasians held at least 55 different railway occupations. Few of these were exclusive to either racial category except engineering and covenanted positions, all of which were occupied by Europeans, and gunners, who were almost all Eurasian or West Indian. There were 1,307 employees in the 19 most common occupations whose numbers were in double figures (see Table 9.1).

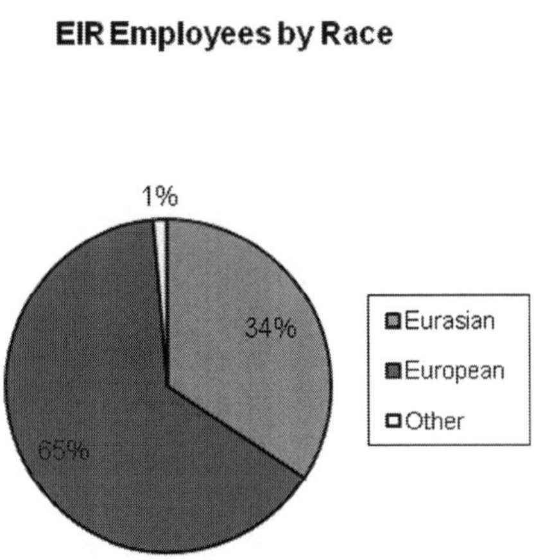

Figure 9.3 Non-Indian Employees of EIR by Race.

Table 9.1 Number of Men and Monthly Salary by Occupation and Race.

Occupation	No. of Europeans	Rs/m	No. of Eurasians	Rs/m
Accountant, Auditor, Assistant	16	350–2,000	5	180–400
Agent and Chief Engineer	1	3,500	0	–
(Secretary to Agent)	2	1,200–1,200	0	–
Assistant Surgeon	0	–	2	300–325
Boilermaker	16	80–210	0	–
Bookkeeper, Paymaster	5	350–500	2	290–700
Carriage Trimmer	2	0	0	–
Checker	0	–	1	40
Clerk, Record Keeper, Writer	59	40–400	63	20–400
Commander (Steamer)	1	400	0	–
Compositor, Printer, Pressman	0	–	8	18–80
Draughtsman	0	–	2	90–120
Driver	219	120–240	43	120–260
Engineer, Engineering Manager	35	350–1,500	0	–
Examiner	14	140–200	9	120–200
Finisher	1	175	0	–
Fireman	59	60–70	30	40–70
Fitter (and assistant)	59	40–220	33	35–210
Foreman	43	180–400	7	80–400
Godown- or Warehouse-keeper	3	300	6	30–270
Guard	203	85–150	50	50–150

Gunner	1	40	58	40–115
Gunner – West Indian	15	50–65	0	–
Inspector	46	50–400	15	50–350
Loader	0	–	4	40–110
Mechanic	22	120–250	16	110–275
Medical Officer/Physician	22	100–600	0	–
Mine Inspector	2	350	0	–
Plate-layer	5	275–400	1	200
(Assistant Plate-layer)	0	–	1	70
Schoolmistress/master	1 + 1	80–150	0	–
Shunter	16	90–100	14	80–100
Signaller	0	–	20	25–130
Spring–Maker/Moulder	1 + 1	160–170	0	–
Station–Master	43	175–400	10	150–240
Superintendent	22	370–2,000	2	300–400
Ticket Collector	16	40–90	21	30–175
Timekeeper	5	90–100	1	160
Tool Keeper	3	80	0	
Turner/Carpenter	2	140–170	1	20
Wagon/Body Maker	2	175	0	–
Watch- and Clockmaker	1	250	0	–
Writer	0	–	1	30

Other than apprentices and probationers, several occupations were, in effect, training posts. For this reason, some occupations are considered in logical groupings. Specific occupations in which the greatest number of Eurasians was represented are discussed below.

Clerks

An enduring stereotype of Eurasian men in India was the clerk, or *cranny*. Government clerks were paid relatively well, for India, and government service brought status. In the early nineteenth century, this was the practical limit to which Eurasians could aspire.[48] Younger found that in 1840 over 90 per cent of clerks in Calcutta's government offices were Eurasians; by 1890, these posts were 82 per cent Indian.[49]

Eurasian clerks predominated in the early years because there was an embargo on importing European clerks, and Indians were not thought suitable. Eurasians were frequently accused of being unwilling to take up trades.[50] The largest single group of Eurasians employed by EIR in 1880 was indeed clerks. Out of 122 clerks listed, 63 were Eurasians but, even so, 59 were Europeans. The remaining 477 Eurasians occupied, or were training for, 27 trades and occupations other than *crannying*.

Clerks (Table 9.2) earned between Rs 20 and 400 per month,[51] but only five Eurasians earned Rs 200 or more and only two were wealthy by Arnold's estimate. Europeans were four times more likely to draw larger salaries. However, including these few, almost a third of Eurasian clerks earned Rs 100 or more and their average salary was Rs 82. The vast majority of EIR's *crannies* were, in fact, Indians, who were paid considerably less. Most clerks received incremental salary increases for a few years and then their salaries levelled off, but the skills of clerks were transferable to other employers so staff turnover would be expected in cities. Only 11 of 63 remained in post for more than a decade.

Table 9.2 Clerks.

	Europeans	Eurasians	Total
In post 10 or more years	17	11	28
Salary Range Rs	30–400	20–400	
Paid ≥ Rs 200	22	5	27
Paid Rs 201–250	14	2	16
Paid Rs 251–400	4	1	5

Gunners

Of 81 gunners and gunner guards in 1880, 60 were Eurasians, eight Europeans, and 13 West Indians. A quarter of gunners stayed with the company for many years. Gunners' average pay (Rs 60 per month) was lower than that of clerks, and opportunities for promotion, whilst remaining gunners, were also less. Even after a decade of service, average pay was still only Rs 81. Only three gunners (5 per cent) earned Rs 100 or more, and none more than Rs 115.

There was a high incidence of Portuguese and other European surnames; less than half appear to be of British origin. The 13 West Indians are likely to have arrived in India with European regiments, as black drummers were quite common at this time. Low pay, lack of an obvious path to promotion, paucity of Europeans, predominance of Indo-Portuguese and West Indians – all suggest gunners and gunner guards were of low status within the EIR's heirarchy. They provided, however, important support for the security of company property.[52]

Guards and Station-Masters

There was a ceiling of Rs 150 on the pay of guards, but 70 per cent of them earned Rs 100 or more and 36 per cent drew the maximum. It was possible to reach the top salary in four years after starting at Rs 70. Only a quarter spent their careers as guards, serving a decade or more with EIR. Some of the higher-paid guards in 1871 became station-masters by 1880, with considerable pay rises. Kipling said that EIR '... has a weakness for recruiting from the Army for its guards ... after depositing twenty pounds to pay his home passage [he can] enter the Company's service on something less than one hundred rupees a month and rise in time to four hundred as a station-master'.[53] Though not offering particularly high pay, competition for these posts, from European soldiers retiring in India, meant they outnumbered Eurasians three to one. Clusters of European recruitment, such as late in 1879 when 17 Europeans were appointed, likely coincided with a regiment leaving India. No such clusters are found amongst Eurasian recruits.

Firemen and Drivers

Firemen, shunters, assistant shunters, and drivers are considered together (Table 9.3) because they constitute a career path; drivers would have been firemen and shunters earlier in their careers.[54] Drivers' training lasted four years; a few had less than four years' service but most of these were reappointments. No fireman earned over Rs 70 and no driver less than Rs 100. Drivers' pay increased in line with length of service. More than 143 of 241 drivers earned Rs 200 or more, with five (three Europeans and two Eurasians) exceeding Arnold's 'wealthy' level.[55] In 1880, 80 per cent of drivers were Europeans. A total of 41 per cent of Eurasian drivers earned over Rs 200,[56] whereas 64 per cent of European drivers earned this much per month. The gap was substantial, but the pay of native drivers a decade later was a paltry Rs 20 per month![57]

Table 9.3 Drivers.

	European	Eurasian	Total
Fireman	52	30	82
Asst. Shunter	6	4	10
Shunter	11	11	22
Driver	194	46	240

Most drivers had been recruited from Britain but they stayed in post for many years, 70 per cent having served the EIR for more than a decade. Eurasian drivers, though fewer, were equally loyal and, once employed, were no slower to progress. Most firemen had less than two years' service, assistant shunters up to three years', and shunters four to six years', regardless of whether they were Eurasian or European.

There were much higher-paid posts with EIR, but engine driving in 1880 had other attractions such as status, responsibility, and reputation. Drivers might cover 300 miles in a day. Keeping an engine for two or three years, effectively, 'she must belong to him'.[58] Mail train drivers were considered to be 'somebody'. By the late 1880s, few drivers were being imported, leaving more opportunities for Eurasians but there was competition from cheaper native drivers, '... supposed to be good enough for branch work and shunting',[59] who undermined Eurasian drivers' sense of job security and stability.

Fitters

Excluding assistants, fitters earned up to Rs 210 monthly, averaging Rs 107, and since about half (including covenanted Europeans) remained in post for over a decade this was a career-level post. Assistant fitter, too, could be a long-term post, not always resulting in promotion. In contrast to clerks, half of fitters remained in post for over a decade. Both had similar prospects with EIR: fitters could become workshop foremen and clerks could become chief clerks, both drawing up to Rs 400 per month. But fitters' skills were less transferable. Up to 17 per cent of railway staff, including fitters and foremen, were employed in the workshops.[60] Most worked at Jumalpore, Allahabad and Assensole. Only three in seven fitters were Eurasians, but the proportion varied by location (Table 9.4).

The average Eurasian fitter's salary was Rs 119, and, for non-covenanted Europeans it was Rs 130. Covenanted European fitters averaged Rs 197 plus an average of £3, 5s in England (about another Rs 33 monthly). Excluding covenanted men, who may have brought greater experience with them, the difference in earnings between these race categories was not great, but there were a higher

Table 9.4 Fitters.

Station	European	Eurasian	Total
Allahabad	9	11	20
Jumalpore	31	9	40
Assansole	1	6	7
Howrah	1	5	6
Other	4	0	4

proportion of long-service men amongst the Eurasians (60 per cent) than amongst the non-covenanted Europeans (32 per cent).

Apprentices and Probationers

Amongst the 1,504 European and Eurasian and other non-Indian staff listed, there were 145 apprentices and probationers, 94 of whom were Eurasians. That two-thirds of men were European but two-thirds of apprentices and probationers were Eurasian is not surprising; Eurasians were recruited in India, where they outnumbered Europeans two to one, and EIR still recruited ready-trained men in Britain. By 1880, half of newly appointed non-Indian staff were Eurasian, compared with just a quarter of those who had been in post since the 1850s. Eurasian railway employment had increased, and their prevalence amongst apprentices and probationers indicates they were increasingly being prepared for better-paid posts. Since the 1850s, EIR had also provided local training at a survey school in Calcutta, and engineering colleges at Calcutta and Roorkee,[61] but not all apprentices were trained in centralized colleges.

EIR's 18 apprentice plate-layers in 1880 were in the engineering department, but spread between ten stations as plate-laying was learned 'on the job'. The apprentice plate-layers had all been in post less than two years, showing that their apprenticeship was short. They were paid Rs 30 per month, with just two paid Rs 50 who were (with a single exception) the longest serving. Two-thirds were Eurasians. Once qualified, plate-layers earned Rs 175 to 400 monthly.

Table 9.5 Apprentices.

Locomotive Department		Coaching and Wagons Department	
Year	Pay Rs/m	Year	Pay Rs/m
4	45	4	30
3	40	3	20
2	30	2	15
1	20	1	10

Apart from plate-layers, the data do not indicate the trades of any other apprentices, but some apprentices in 1871 had become fitters and mechanics by 1880. Almost all were stationed at Jumalpore, Allahabad, or Howrah. It is likely that most of the 50 in Jumalpore and Allahabad's locomotive departments, and the 30 in Howrah's coaching and wagons department, were destined to become fitters after five years as apprentices, earning Rs 80 to 210 monthly. Apprentices earned Rs 10 to 45 monthly (Table 9.5), increasing with length of service and, probably, trade (since locomotive department apprentices at Jumalpore and Allahabad earned more than those of Howrah's coaching and wagons department).

With few exceptions, 'probationers' earned more than apprentices, and more than many other employees. Once qualified, probationers became mechanics drawing Rs 110 to Rs 275 monthly. Length of service, for 32 probationers in coaching and wagons and six in the traffic department, varied between four months and 15 years, indicating promotion from amongst existing employees rather than the duration of probation. Their remuneration, Rs 60, 80, 90, or 99 per month, may indicate a four-year probationary period. Three-quarters were Eurasians. Amongst qualified mechanics the proportions were roughly equal, which, again, indicates increasing opportunities for Eurasians to gain better-paid positions.

By the 1920s, fitters' apprenticeships had been shortened to three years; apprentice mechanics spent four years in training; and 'special apprentices' trained for four years at Jumalpore, and then took an engineering degree in England, before appointments at entry level as assistant mechanical engineers or assistant works managers.[62]

Kipling wrote about Jumalpore's apprentices in 1889. He attended night school three times a week, where 'M Bonnaud ... teaches him mechanics and statistics so thoroughly that even the awful Government Inspector is pleased.' But much of the apprentice's instruction was in workshops, often undertaken by his own father.[63] Even today, Indian Railways maintain a quota of jobs reserved for the sons of railwaymen.[64] A nineteenth-century railwayman expected no less.

RAILWAY COLONIES AND COMMUNITIES

For a community to exist, there have to be sufficient numbers present. A community's sense of identity, place, cohesion, and worth is affected by its numerical strength relative to other communities, its wealth and power, its status, and its relationship to those other communities. The railways' efforts to maintain old communal identities created new ones by concentrating European and 'allied' races together.[65] By providing institutions that could be used to manipulate cultural identity, and by exclusion and punishment, they enforced an idealized European-ness whilst creating a corporate camaraderie and common purpose in railway employment. Arnold has described railway colonies as the main instance of white colonization.[66]

Up to a third of the residents were Eurasians, about half of the Eurasian population of India, making railway colonies highly significant for this study. Bear concluded that a covert function of the EIR's railway colony was social engineering. Europeans and Eurasians were housed in a controlled 'European' environment to minimize Indian influences and to reinforce an idealized European lifestyle. Her comment that 'Railway police patrolled the streets as much to monitor the residents' behaviour as to protect them from crime' echoes Rudyard Kipling's description of Jumalpore a century earlier: 'No one can flatter himself that in the multitude he is overlooked, or believe that between 4pm and 9am he is at liberty to mis-demean himself.'[67]

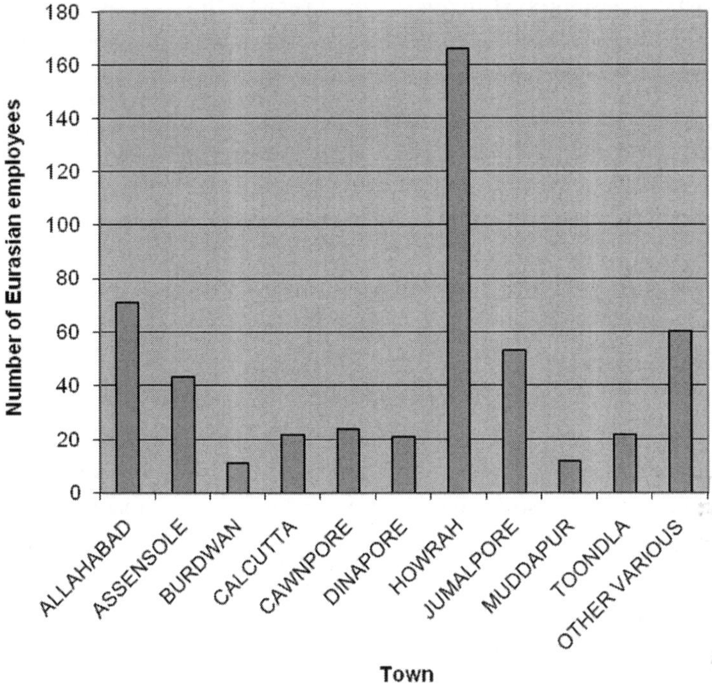

Figure 9.4 East Indian Railway's Eurasian Employees by Location.

This section examines three railway locations: Howrah, Allahabad, and Jumalpore. Chosen because each had a large Eurasian contingent (see Figure 9.4), they were also geographically and functionally distinct from one another, and, for each, descriptive data was readily accessible.

Numerical strength

Most entries in the staff lists represent breadwinners, including apprentices and probationers; Eurasians often married young or may have had other less fortunate family members to support.[68] Thus, each may represent a family. Families may have averaged five persons, the figure used by clergy in population estimates for census returns, or three, as suggested in *The Times*, although this smaller estimate applied to the destitute.[69] I have taken the middle road, and assumed a family unit to comprise four persons.

Howrah

Howrah had been a shipbuilding area for several decades before the EIR established its station in 1854.[70] The chief engineer thought employees were endangered by proximity to Calcutta's distractions. He observed that Bobby Dean's hotel attracted men away from their work with drink and billiards, and drivers and foremen enjoyed themselves 'in rather a boisterous manner' at Wilson's Coffee Room.[71] Jumalpore was chosen as a workshop site to avoid such distractions. But Howrah's location, adjacent to deep water and shipping, was indispensable for transporting imported manufactured goods and exporting grain, merchandise, and raw materials. Howrah's work was exceptionally diverse with huge goods traffic, coach and wagon workshops, large stores, and quays, besides passenger traffic from Calcutta to the rest of India. The European and Eurasian staff list for 1880 gives 316 names at Howrah: six West Indians, 178 Eurasians and, 132 Europeans, including a third of EIR's trade apprentices and half of the probationers.

Howrah had the largest concentration of Eurasians of any EIR station. There was also a large established Eurasian population in Calcutta, so, although some staff lived outside the colony proper, extended families of greater size than I have suggested may have lived together in colony housing. A number of the 132 Europeans (and perhaps also the half dozen West Indians) also had Eurasian families, and so Howrah's railway Eurasians could easily have numbered 1,000. Whether through employment or domicile, Eurasians were numerically superior to Europeans at Howrah. At Toondla, a major garrison town, European employees outnumbered Eurasians four to one, and at Bankipore (near Patna) there was a solitary Eurasian station-master and no European employee in 1880 – although there were many European civil servants and indigo planters in the vicinity, and three European EIR men at Patna.

Class, trade, and civil condition determined where, within colonies, employees were housed (see Allahabad, below). There was a conscious effort, from 1876 onwards, to reinforce 'Britishness' in government-funded elementary schools,[72] which brought younger Eurasians and Europeans into closer physical and cultural proximity. Howrah was large enough for a Eurasian to have multiple communal identities to choose from: through location, by occupation or trade, as an EIR man, as a breadwinner, or by family and church as well as ethnic categorization. Only nine Europeans earned more than the highest paid Eurasians, but, even after excluding these and the apprentices and probationers, Howrah's Europeans earned 36 per cent more overall. Even if Eurasian railwaymen at Howrah did not protest at this differential, it was an issue the EAIA raised with the EIR, with government, and with Westminster.[73]

Allahabad

Allahabad colony also had a large Eurasian community because of the proximity of the railway to the town. It was a major commercial centre, it had a garrison, was the seat of the Upper Provinces government, and other railways (such as Oudh and Rohilkhand) intersected the East India Railway line there. In was the hub for traffic between the North-West Provinces, Simla, Bombay, Central India, and Calcutta. Allahabad's 81 EIR Eurasian employees worked alongside three West Indians and 151 Europeans, but the total Eurasian and European population of the town (including the military and cantonments) was about 3,000.[74] Maps of Allahabad's railway accommodation give an indication of how they were housed.[75] Although there was a railway colony, many employees lived elsewhere. Some senior staff lived in the North Cantonment, the old civil lines, at Kutra, and in the 'new' civil and commercial cantonment to the north-west. The Cline and Heymerdinger families owned and occupied houses in the last-named location; the deputy agent rented a North Cantonment bungalow from an indigo planter; and Mr Barnett, an accountant, was living with the Dumbleton family at Kutra. 'Lesser mortals' are harder to trace, but Farnworth, a

Eurasian ticket collector in 1880, earning only Rs 40 per month, likely chose to live with his family who owned and occupied property in the old civil station at Colonelgunge.

The colony's site, just north of the native city, abutted the south-western aspect of the civil and commercial centre. Its siting, according to Bear, was chosen to take full advantage of the availability of native labour.[76] It was thoroughly regimented in its layout of roads, barrack blocks, terraced cottages, and bungalows. Its specific occupants were rarely recorded because staff constantly moved between stations, but buildings were allocated by department, occupation, and civil condition.

Four large bungalows, separated off by the rails and a level crossing at the southern limits, belonged to the engineering department. One was an office and the remaining three were allocated to the clerk of works, district engineer, and barrack master. Rows of six-room ranges (barracks) to the west were occupied by 'assistants' of the locomotive and engineering departments including, amongst others, drivers, guards, and fitters. The central ranges housed the railway press, library, and hospital. Four bungalows in the centre were allocated, with two sharing, to five senior men in the traffic, locomotive, and engineering departments. One of these – John Strachen, a covenanted European – was a district superintendent in 1880, earning Rs 1,000 per month. His neighbours in 1863 were an uncovenanted European, James Martin, who in 1880 was a foreman earning Rs 340 per month, and his Eurasian family. Across a road to the east were three more bungalows, one vacant and the others occupied by an accountant and a station-master.

Three barrack blocks at the eastern edge housed 'assistants', grouped together by department. The largest housed married men and 'La Martinière boys' in 34 rooms. The other two, each of 17 rooms, housed 'assistants' from all departments as well as Mr Casey, superintendent of the EIR Press, who occupied two rooms. Besides the Press, the hospital, and the library mentioned above, the colony provided a theatre, a railway cooperative shop, and a larger hospital south of the Jumna. Other than these, local amenities in Allahabad included a distillery; Anglican, Roman Catholic, and Presbyterian churches; a European club; bazaars; hotels; banks; a post office; and a racetrack. Allahabad did not have a railway school, but several schools nearby provided an English-medium education. The presence of La Martinière boys suggests they were already gaining the kind of education that government, and company, wished to promote, but even in 1880 the EIR itself employed only two schoolteachers and they were both based at Jumalpore.

As at Howrah, a difference in communal wealth was evident at Allahabad. Excluding the covenanted staff, earning a monthly average of Rs 498, Europeans averaged Rs 163 per month, 40 per cent more than the Eurasians' average pay of Rs 116, but West Indians drew only Rs 58 monthly.

Jumalpore

We have contemporary detailed descriptions of Jumalpore that include layout, purpose, staff, and facilities. Founded by the EIR in 1862, it was (and is) amongst the largest railway workshops in India. In 1889, it was 'a station [town] entirely made by, and devoted to, the use of those untiring servants of the public, the railway folk'. No other line passed through Jumalpore, so all of these were employees (and dependents) of the EIR. Including Indians, total railway manpower at Jumalpore by 1889 was around 3,500, continuing to rise as the company grew, to 9,428 employees by 1906. The non-Indians in 1880 comprised 127 Europeans, 'recruited from Manchester and the Clyde ... homes of the great ironworks of the North',[77] and 55 Eurasians.[78] There were 141 in the locomotive department, repairing and refurbishing engines; 22 in the traffic department; 14 audit and accounts staff; two teachers; a doctor; a nurse; and a handful of supra-departmental district staff.[79] Besides the manufacture of components, and iron salvage from worn-out parts, each of three sheds (covering 40 to 50 acres in 1889) could accommodate 50 engines under repair 'without pressure, and on occasions as many again'.[80] The workshop also manufactured engines, and by 1906 Jumalpore's sheds were known as 'the Crewe of India'.[81] Sites of heavy industry, workshops like Jumalpore were noisy, dirty, and dangerous. Unlike the stereotypic image of British Raj personnel, railway employees comprised skilled and semi-skilled working-class men, with both gentlemen and *crannies* in the minority. The vast store department, 'as clean as a new pin, and stupefying in its naval order', stocked everything necessary for 'the due and proper workings of a long line'.[82] Like a mill or mine town in Britain, the town ran to the company's schedule: 'The Buzzer howls, for it is nearly tiffin time. There is a rush from every quarter of the shops ... the tiffin hour has ended. The buzzer blows ... and the shops take up their toil.'[83]

Chief Engineer D.W. Campbell selected the site in part because it was remote enough to keep European and Eurasian staff from the distractions and dissipations of a large town.[84] Kipling mentioned only 'a dreary village' in the neighbourhood, where many native railway employees and their dependents lived.[85] Huddleston noted that this was problematic; it soon become necessary to run daily workmen's trains to bring labour from 19 miles away. The native quarter of Jumalpore and other railway colonies attracted concern, about both sanitation and security, but remained largely unplanned until the turn of the century.[86] The village was said to 'make the most of any cholera that may be going'.[87] The absence of an entry for Jumalpore in the 1881 census indicates that its total population was below 10,000. Kipling found the colony 'specklessly and spotlessly neat' with 'a holy calm about the roads – totally unlike anything in an English manufacturing town'.[88] It was laid out, like Allahabad, with military precision, bounded on three sides by a ring of hills and enclosed by the company's sheds, offices, and workshops.[89]

Its facilities, by 1889, included accommodation, a church,[90] a freemason's lodge, infirmary, school, apprentices' quarters, bandstand, firing range, the mechanics' institute, six tennis courts, swimming pool, and library. Huddleston reported in 1906 that it also had a Catholic chapel, hospital (including separate isolation facilities), boarding school for European and East Indian children, apprentices' boarding house, the company volunteers' armoury and headquarters, and gymkhana, cricket, football, and tennis facilities.[91]

As there had been neither a civil nor a military presence at Jumalpore, railway personnel governed it themselves until the introduction of the provincial (largely native) service, a move greatly resented by the Europeans and Eurasians:

> we administer ourselves ... or we did – till we had local self-government in – and now the [Club] racket-maker administers us ... The introduction of local self-government ... to a place made by, and maintained for, Europeans ... a board largely composed of Babus, ... since that day Jumalpore's views on government have not been fit for publication.[92]

This did not prevent Europeans and Eurasians making their authority patent, in and out of working hours. The 150-strong Railway Volunteer Force (and band) paraded twice a week, drilling, practising rapid deployment (by train), and honing marksmanship.[93] They were uniformed, carried Martini-Henry rifles, and some were ex-army. In 1889, there were 'no regulars between Howrah and Dinapore',[94] and so volunteers were the military presence. In the workplace too, Europeans exercised authority. In 1880, all foremen were Europeans, three-quarters of them covenanted.[95] They allocated work to teams of three Europeans or Eurasians (fitters and their apprentices), who in turn directed eight or nine Indians.[96] European and Eurasian foremen fitters and apprentices in 1880 Jumalpore numbered approximately 100.[97] Their numbers grew to about 240 by 1906, proportionate to overall staffing growth.

In Jumalpore's 1880 workforce, Eurasians were outnumbered by Europeans more than two to one. The average monthly pay for Europeans was Rs 241 and for Eurasians just Rs 89. The largest European salary was Rs 2,000 per month plus £25 monthly, whereas the highest-paid Eurasian drew Rs 400 per month. District-level staff, based at Jumalpore (exclusively European), drew huge salaries, averaging Rs 1,400 monthly. Accountants and auditors, again all European, were paid an average of Rs 550, and foremen, 'captains of five hundred or more',[98] drew monthly salaries of Rs 200 to 500.[99] Fitters, around a quarter of whom were Eurasians, drew Rs 80 to

280 a month. Eurasians and Europeans received the same basic pay for the same grade and length of service, although other conditions differed.[100] Sharp differences in pay between these communities in Jumalpore illustrate a widespread source of tension and protest but also reflect pre-existing expertise and training that railway artisans brought with them from Britain, and the EIR's determination that senior posts be filled from Britain. Eurasian and domiciled European employees were considered 'second best', but native fitters were paid even less, about Rs 30 a month, a third to a ninth of the rate paid to Europeans and Eurasians.[101]

The accommodation provided to Europeans and Eurasians at Jumalpore comprised a railway bungalow (with single men sharing) or cottage, which 'cost him [no] more than one ninth of the pay of his grade'.[102] Each bungalow or cottage had a garden and, by the 1900s, electric lighting and fans.[103] There was a boarding school for European and Eurasian children on site. Apprentices lived together in barracks, except for a quarter who lived with their families. Churches, both Anglican and Catholic, catered for spiritual needs. Kipling thought the atmosphere of the mechanics' institute the:

> best and prettiest of the many good and pretty things in Jumalpore . . . of a Saturday when the Volunteer Band is playing and the tennis courts are full and the babydom of Jumalpore – fat sturdy children – frolic round the band-stand. The people dance . . . they act, they play billiards, they study their newspapers, they play cards and everything else, and they flirt in a sumptuous building, and in the hot weather the gallant apprentice ducks his friend in the big swimming-bath. Decidedly the railway folk make their lives pleasant.[104]

SUMMARY OF FINDINGS

In this chapter, I have looked at occupations, opportunities to progress, salaries, perquisites, and the built and cultural environment associated with the railways in India, and attempted to identify differences in the experience of railway life that co-locate with racial categorization. My findings clarify what Eurasians gained and lost by becoming railwaymen. The reasons Eurasians were keen to join railways are clear, but so too are factors that would have engendered a sense of grievance.

Railway employment allowed Eurasians to satisfy their basic needs with a regular wage, but it would have been obvious that many Europeans with whom they lived and laboured were wealthier. The provident fund and long service promoted security and stability, but, again, Europeans were rewarded more generously. As the single largest employer of Eurasians, India's railways physically drew together a small and dispersed minority into communities with a common (or similar) purpose and status. Even tiny railway communities were a free train ride away from larger ones. Company and government policy with regard to education, lifestyle, provision of institutions, and remuneration also shaped a distinct identity and affiliation ('the railwayman') that to some extent masked the unwelcome categorization of 'Eurasian'. But deployment across the network also meant that regular postings and high mobility disrupted family life. In addition, policing and supervision of lifestyles was intrusive, restricting personal agency and invading privacy. Respect came with government service, but, undermining this, 'glass ceilings' and regulations based on racial hierarchies were demeaning. The Eurasian associations' complaint that Eurasians' promotion and salary compared unfavourably to Europeans' appears fully justified. However, compared to Indians they were rewarded far more generously for their labour. This and the railways' use of Eurasians as militia caused ill-feeling towards them; whether this concerned them is a moot point. The numbers in long-term employment suggest there was a high level of satisfaction for most.

Education treated Eurasians and domiciled Europeans the same; rather than race, class and denomination provided dividing lines. Had prospects of promotion and pay been as equal in practice as they were on paper, then the Eurasian and European railway communities might have merged completely. As it was, Eurasians lived amongst Europeans whose aspirations they shared but could not quite achieve unless individually re-categorized as European. Living outside the railway colonies may therefore have been preferable for some. If there was a family home nearby there may have been a financial incentive for living there, but a less regimented, more mixed locale may also have offered relief from the railway colony's relentless 'European' cultural constraints.

DISCUSSION

The pleasant picture of railway life, such as he described in Jumalpore, was, Kipling noted, less than perfect. Company and government policies shaping racial hierarchies in the workforce would have led to employee dissatisfaction amongst all but the white elite, and even they found reason to be dissatisfied on occasion. There was no encouragement, beyond the chance of promotion, for the kind of inventiveness that could benefit the company and develop an employee's potential. 'Would it ruin the richest Company in India', Kipling asked, 'to lend their model-shop and their lathes to half a dozen, or, for the matter of that, half a hundred, abortive experiments?'[105] Government policy too could cause great dissatisfaction. Engineers were incensed when in 1869 the governor-general accused 'all civil engineers' of taking bribes and commissions, and of regarding them as 'legitimate sources of emolument' when awarding contracts. The engineers conceded that some probably were dishonest but objected to Lord Mayo's 'unfounded accusations' and sweeping generalization.[106]

But railway employment did offer status in the wider community of India, simply because it was quasi-official and anything associated with government carried status. Kipling noted that men came to believe their work made them 'the real pivots on which the Administration turns'. But the administration portrayed itself as of central importance in India, its covenanted and officer cadres were 'heaven born', and such an attitude would have filtered down to every level of that administration. Kipling gave an instance:

> A half-caste clerk was ruling forms in a Pay Office. He said to me, 'Do you know what would happen if I added or took away one single line on this sheet?' Then with the air of a

conspirator, 'It would disorganize the whole of the Treasury payments throughout the whole of the Presidency Circle! Think of that!'[107]

The reader was meant to see such a belief as ridiculous because the work of a clerk was inherently unimportant. But the clerk was not completely deluded. Just as, in Kipling's *The Man Who Would be King*, freemason regalia elevated the deserter Dan Dravot to the status of a god, government employment elevated the status of a humble clerk because he represented government.

Eurasians diversified widely in their search for employment and, contrary to the picture of Eurasians as uninterested in education to better their lot, many had served long apprenticeships to develop valuable specialized skills. Contrary to stereotyping of Eurasian indiscipline and unreliability, 30 per cent had been with the EIR for a decade or more. Excluding apprentices and probationers, that figure rises to nearly 40 per cent.[108] Some had served the same company in the same town for over 25 years; C.W. Clarke, for example, an auditor employed since 1860, had been at Jumalpore since 1869 and was still there in 1895![109] With monthly salaries averaging over Rs 100 (about £10), the Eurasian railway community was poorer than its European counterpart in India but was better off than Indian railwaymen, British soldiers,[110] or even Scottish farm labourers.[111]

Bear provided insights into how the EIR company shaped the 'bio-moral' character of European and Eurasian staff by deliberately indoctrinating them with European culture, housing them in colonies from which 'India' had been hygienically removed, invading every aspect of their private and family lives to ensure that their behaviour was 'approved', and by the constant fear of dismissal. The accommodation, education, and leisure facilities of EIR's colonies represent an experiment in which compliance was demanded. There was no room in railway colonies for a Eurasian who, elsewhere in place or time, might have had a Muslim wife, donned a *kurta* after work, or written Urdu poetry. Company policy for Europeans and Eurasians demanded their British-ness and penalized inappropriate behaviour. To quote Bear: '[the colony] did not reflect culture; it helped to produce the reality of national, racial, and cultural difference.'[112]

Part of that culture involved 'volunteering' for the militia, a policy that reinforced the dichotomy of natives as potential threat and Europeans and Eurasians as defenders of British interests.[113] With an average wage almost six times that of an Indian train driver, living beside his European colleagues in good housing it would hardly be surprising if the Eurasian felt privileged. He gained status, cameraderie, and the means to keep his family housed, fed, healthy, entertained, and educated. These were clear rewards. To keep these rewards, however, he paid a heavy price; forever a second-class 'Britisher' and alienated from the people and cultures of the only country he would ever know – India.

Railways brought massive change to the landscape of India, to the logistics of trade, and to colonial military deployment. They also offered new opportunities for India's Eurasians from the middle of the nineteenth century until, despite 'Indianization' and later Independence, about 1960.[114] If, as Kerr claims, the railways were 'engines of change [that] shaped the making of modern India',[115] then a large section of the Eurasian community must surely number amongst the pioneers of modern India.

CHAPTER 10

CONCLUSIONS

There are many dimensions to the Eurasian 'problem' in nineteenth-century India. Eurasians' existence and proclivities were a concern to the British, as were their interactions with other communities. For Indians, the Eurasian problem was that they monopolized reserved occupations and were indistinguishable from the colonial presence. The British themselves constituted Eurasians as a problem: first excluding and stereotyping their Eurasian kin, then constraining their roles and ambitions, whilst insisting they acculturate to British norms. British hegemony also displaced other Europeans, notably the Dutch, Portuguese, and French, leaving their Eurasian populations with even bigger cultural hurdles to overcome. Eurasians came to occupy a liminal zone, permanently suspended between the numerical power of the Indian population and the political and economic power of the British. Thus, the wants and needs of these neighbours, and changes in their relationship to one another, had consequences for all Eurasians. The lived experience of Eurasians in British India necessitated the near-impossible separation of their roles and allegiances into British *or* Indian according to context: employed as statutory natives, educated as Europeans, largely excluded from military service as statutory natives of India, and yet required to take up arms as a second line of European defence against their fellow Indians.

By the mid-nineteenth century, a gulf had formed separating the colonial British from their Indian subjects. Whilst the British were happy to encourage Indians to cross the cultural divide, become *brown sahibs*, and adopt western civilization, the crossing could not be bi-directional; the British were meant to believe there was nothing in Indian culture of benefit to them. Racial 'crossing' also became inimical to the racial justification for a British empire and colonial rule, but Eurasians had already been born, in simpler times when ruling had not yet become a racially determined competence. Already, early in the century, the pre-existing Eurasians could not be seen to take a wrong cultural direction because, since they had European blood, they would serve as a bad example to Indians. They could no longer be assimilated into the British population, where their blood 'might debase the succeeding generations of Englishmen'.[1] Nothing could be done about their existence; their numbers were such that the population had proved to be self-perpetuating.

The British solution to this dilemma was two pronged. Firstly, the British put psychological distance between themselves and the Eurasians, briefly by proscription but mainly by social pressures; treated them as a class (or race) apart; and educated their own to abhor miscegenation. Secondly, Eurasian agency resulted in lifestyles that mixed cultures in a way the British considered dangerous to their own prestige, and so Eurasian cultural life had to be encouraged down a European route. Once British hegemony was likely, those who had assimilated into Indian life were of little further concern and could be categorized as native Christians. A residuum persisted in mixing with Indians; these Eurasians were often poor, but with cultural mores that distinguished them as part-European. But once reminded of their place, those 'Anglo-Indians' who were anglicized by inclination and schooling had the potential to become 'useful citizens'. The proscription decades had already reduced most Eurasians to a state of economic dependence in which opportunities for employment, albeit in subordinate roles, could not easily be refused.

I have used the term Eurasian throughout this monograph, although aware that it may cause a degree of discomfort but with good reason. The more acceptable term, Anglo-Indian, would have been both ahistorical, since it applied to a different population in the nineteenth century, and too exclusive. Today's Indian constitution uses the term Anglo-Indian to define a minority Indian community with European paternal ancestry; but those who have left India and settled elsewhere, those born or living in Pakistan, Bangladesh, or Burma (Myanmar), and those with only maternal European ancestry are excluded by this usage. The still-active All India Anglo-Indian Association would also exclude the non-Christian and the non-anglophone. Though use of the term necessitates a geographic limiter to restrict the discussion to South Asia, 'Eurasian' can encompass anyone whose ancestry was both European and South Asian. It allowed my remit, to a lesser degree, to extend to others who were known to have straddled the racial divide between the colonial British and South Asia's non-European population. Nirad Chaudhuri's 1965 diatribe against their influence lumped together genetic and cultural 'half-castes', though perhaps, coming from an Indian Oxford don famed for being a very English gentleman, he metaphorically shot himself in the foot when he labelled them all as 'dangerous'![2] But Chaudhuri's conception is my justification for using data that did not distinguish between domiciled Europeans and Eurasians, implying as it does that both 'blood' and 'culture' contributed to the community. The distinction between these two imagined communities was always ephemeral, and I have left it so.

A fundamental difficulty in any understanding of the Eurasians of South Asia is, and always was, delineation. This affected the nineteenth-century censuses and other head counts. Indians merged into the Eurasian community through marriage, education, conversion, and for employment purposes. Government recognized some communities (Parsis, Armenians, and Jews) in the odd category of 'European and allied races' or employed them as Eurasians. Eurasians married, lived, and worked amongst Indians probably as much as they did amongst themselves or with Europeans. Europeans continued to marry Indians and Eurasians, or otherwise linked themselves with India, its cultures, and its people. William 'Oriental' Jones, Mrs Meer Hassan Ali, and Richard Burton all swam against the political, biological, or cultural currents, but all exercised the option to retain their British identity. Similarly, some Eurasians, by virtue of family connections; education; and, of course, wealth were able to leave the liminal zone and make their way inside the European pale. Thomas Carlyle was smitten with one wealthy Eurasian heiress, Kitty Kirkpatrick, who was accepted into English high society. Begum Johnson was prominent in Calcutta society, despite being Eurasian. Her grandson Robert Jenkinson, 2nd Earl Liverpool, became prime minister of Britain despite his mixed ancestry. These were exceptional individuals, one way or another, but, as has been shown in other instances, a degree of acceptance could be achieved by many early in the century, when wealth, education, or deeds provided sufficient bedrock on which to build a British identity.[3] Later, as race theories successfully peddled inherent racial competencies, such a shift could only be achieved through subterfuge.

Central to my analyses have been the lives and concerns of those who remained in the space they were allocated, between Europeans and Indians; but to understand that space it was necessary to look at the construction and policing of its perimeters because, like the margins of a sand dune, they enable the existence of the whole. Changes to the margins also change the shape of the whole, and this phenomenon was apparent in Eurasian communal development, in individual prospects over time, and in the ever-changing attitudes to and utilization of Eurasians by the colonial state. The concept of 'community' presented further problems, which is why I have endeavoured to limit its use in this monograph to areas where it was unquestionably appropriate. Just as Englishmen were by default Church of England, many Eurasians were, by default, members of a Eurasian community, and neither default position says much about its presumed members. There undoubtedly were Eurasian communities that functioned as such: large populations in a stable geographical locus, with work and their own institutions. But communities could be ephemeral, pragmatic responses to stimuli that forced their existence: tied housing, boarding schools, and political campaigns that neither commanded nor defined complete identity, although choosing to join a body that represented a Eurasian community does imply some degree of identification. I doubt, for example, that there was a distinct Eurasian community in Awadh before the British told them they were such, although shared religion and lifestyle might have given them that appearance. Even kinship does not need to equate to community; the Skinner family today has both a Christian and a Muslim branch, only one of which would be recognized by many Anglo-Indians as part of their community.

In this monograph, I have shown that the Eurasian population of India grew to possibly 300,000 by 1911, and, in exploring this, I was able to bring out the heterogeneity of Eurasian ancestry and the artificiality inherent in British attempts to classify them. I have demonstrated that whilst Eurasian historiography written by members of the community exhibited a strong sense of injustice and reflected the local politics, it did not adequately explore external issues that affected them. I have examined proscriptions enacted around the 1800s to show how they contributed to 'othering' Eurasians. Then in line with more recent developments in historical research that, however, left Eurasian history largely untouched, I have explored its global and personalized context. I have suggested that much of the legislation inimical to Eurasian interests was really directed at Europeans. The aim was reforming the administration of India, and merging minorities and marginalized groups in Britain into an emergent British identity.

I went on to examine intermarriage and conceptual understandings of marriage. I have shown, by a mass demographic approach, the degree to which intermarriage between the British and Eurasians continued, despite formal and informal attempts to discourage miscegenation. I have demonstrated that by discarding the strict middle-class Victorian understanding of this concept in favour of a broader interpretation, more akin to the customs and practices of the diverse people involved, an equally large cohort of irregular relationships, marriages in all but name, might be added to the official total. This point was important for two reasons. Firstly, it countered Victorian stereotyping of both Eurasians and working-class Britons as immoral. Secondly, intermarriage was an effective method of acculturation that reinforced Eurasians' self-image as British.

Self-identity has many facets, including upbringing, ethnicity, faith, home, and nationality, but employment is still a primary identifier for most people; what you do is who you are. This fact was not lost on the British administration. Thus, linking employment opportunities to supposed racial competencies, making them contingent on culture, controlling the environment in which employees lived, and providing appropriate facilities and cultural institutions enabled Eurasians and the British to reach a working compromise. In reserving some occupations for Eurasians, or favouring them, government and quasi-government enterprises benefited from the cheaper labour and semi-European loyalty of Eurasians. Eurasians gained a range of livelihoods; financial security for their community; and alternate, more welcome, identities defined by occupation. I have explored some of these occupations and, in the process, the racial and class logic behind what was considered suitable or acceptable, showing that subordination was always maintained and often resented.

The zenith of Eurasian anglicization has to have been railway employment. The accommodation, education, and leisure facilities of railway colonies epitomized a social-Darwinian experiment in which compliance was demanded and there was no room for Eurasians who might otherwise have chosen a more Indian lifestyle. It is this cultural heritage, with its colonial baggage, that has handicapped Eurasians' assimilation. If race, or miscegenation, were the main issue, then there would have been an equally disparaged group of Eurasians whose culture was more conventionally 'Indian'.

Eurasians' need for secure work was no different from that of many thousands of Indians who worked for the colonial state, except that government employment was the only door open to many of the former. An important factor that marks Anglo-Indians out as different, besides their part-European ancestry, is that they were often the face of government in everyday life, and when people opposed the colonial state this made them the enemy. They occupied only subordinate posts, but even junior government employees exercised power. Kipling tells a tale of a lowly Eurasian telegraph signaller, earning just Rs 35/month. He was no imperial master but when inter-communal rioting broke out at his sub-station, 'until the Assistant Commissioner came, he, the Telegraph Signaller, was the Government of India'.[4]

For many Anglo-Indians, participation in volunteer regiments was a condition of employment. They were deployed whenever there was a disturbance and regular troops were unavailable, provoking further hostility towards them and associating them even more with colonial oppression. Yet, hundreds of thousands of Indians served the colonial state and most of them were paid to bear arms. Nowadays, neither Bengalis nor Sikhs are treated as colonial collaborators simply because their ancestors served the colonial state as *babus* and soldiers.

The Anglo-Indians' foreign culture marks them as different but many Indians now incorporate elements of foreign culture into their lifestyles too. English-language proficiency, technical skills, and familiarity with foreign cultures are a passport to employment in, for example, the media, in the burgeoning IT sector, and in technical support and call centres throughout India. The departure of half the Eurasian community since Independence has been taken to signify disloyalty, but many millions of Indians and other South Asians have emigrated too.

I have shown a route by which Eurasians' personal agency was removed by the colonial state so that many Eurasians, those later identifiable as Anglo-Indians, came to conform to and perform an assigned role, living by the European cultural norms demanded of and inculcated in them, as aliens in their own country. If they were, as Nirad Chaudhuri would have it, pale imitations of both the British and the Indian, then that reflects British policy far more than Eurasian agency.

In my discussions of employment I have perhaps paid too little heed to the non-official sector, and would like to have expanded my discussion of women's work. Similarly, I am aware that religion was, and remains, of great importance to many Eurasians and most Anglo-Indians; it is, like the English language, at the core of their self-identity but, for reasons of space, I have addressed it only as a secondary issue. Three questions might be addressed in future research: why was religion so important, how did Eurasians participate, and did it dictate their behaviour? My hypothesis, supported by glimpses of these issues in this monograph, is that such investigation would confirm my conclusions about Eurasian agency and the basis of their Europeanized culture.

I began this research thinking its focus would be an examination and reassessment of nineteenth-century stereotypes about Eurasians. Instead, I came to analyse some of the conditions that made Eurasians as they were. I have ended by asking how these findings relate to the stereotypes today: the choices made for and by India's Eurasians have had an unfortunate legacy. In appearing to give up their personal cultural agency they lost part of their own identity, their Indian-ness. It is proving difficult for today's Anglo-Indians to reclaim it. My own experience of Anglo-Indian culture would suggest they never did lose touch with either their European or their Indian culture, but merged the two into an amalgam that was new and distinctive. Much of the experience of being Eurasian in colonial India has resonance today for populations whose sense of belonging is questioned by others. Minorities such as non-Jewish Israelis; non-Muslim Pakistanis; Muslim Britons; white Zimbabweans; US communists; and, still, Anglo-Indians in India are all in some way outsiders in their own country. This monograph has examined the background to that status for India's Eurasians. One response to the situation, exercised by half of the Anglo-Indians and many Portuguese and French Eurasians, was to leave in search of a new homeland. In the twenty-first century, that may still be a last resort. But the more any minority knows of its own history and contribution to its homeland, the better equipped it is to deal with prejudice; to assert its right to exist; and, put simply, to belong.

NOTES

Introduction

1. The Portuguese in India were mostly male, and their intermarriage with Indians dated back to the beginning of the sixteenth century. The *mestizos* were Catholics, and their culture largely European. Subcategories of Portuguese along racial lines were never definitive, but the elite were always European born. To the British all Portuguese were a 'mongrel' race, and the terms Indo-Portuguese, *mestizo*, and Portuguese were often used interchangeably. 'Luso-Indian' was reserved for those the British thought were Indians masquerading as Portuguese.
2. Some Eurasian Catholic women were known to prefer the stigma of remaining 'mistresses' rather than relinquish control of their children's Catholic faith to Protestant husbands.
3. J.B. Gilchrist, *The General East India Guide and Vade Mecum . . . a Digest of the Work of the Late Capt. Williamson*, Kingsbury, Parbury & Allen, London, 1825, p. 186.
4. Richard Burton, *Goa, and the Blue Mountains*, Richard Bentley, London, 1851, p. 97.
5. Given the many derogatory references made to 'half-breeds' in the American colonies before this date, this is quite surprising. Numerous examples of this can be found, in reference to dealings and relations with the Iroquois confederacy in New England over several decades prior to the American Revolution, in Fintan O'Toole, *White Savage: William Johnson and the Invention of America*, Faber & Faber, London, 2005.

6. Frank Anthony, *Britain's Betrayal in India: the Story of the Anglo-Indian Community*, Allied Publishers, New Delhi, 1962, pp. 2–3.
7. Anthony, Betrayal, pp. 2–3.
8. Environmentalists believed European settlement of India was impossible because climate could modify racial characteristics. Since environment also encompassed education, it was normal practice for the elite's children to be schooled in Britain to compensate for the racial 'degeneration' caused by environment or mixed parentage. This theory, premised upon European superiority, at least offered a prospect of redemption; Indians could be turned into 'Brown Englishmen' and Europeans could take steps to minimize 'Indianization'. See T.B. Macaulay, 'Minute on Education, February 2 1835', in H. Sharp (ed.), *Selections from Educational Records, Part 1 (1781–1839)*, Superintendent of Government Printing, Calcutta, 1920, reprinted Delhi, NAI, 1965, pp. 107–17; Peter Robb, 'Children, Emotion, Identity and Empire: Views from the Blechyndens' Calcutta Diaries (1790–1822)', *Modern Asian Studies*, 2006, vol. 40 (1), pp. 175–201. Though it was superseded by Social Darwinism and Galtonism, environmental determinism never completely disappeared from British thinking.
9. A flavour of this can be found throughout Kipling's *Plain Tales*; matrons and 'chums' were expected to keep a chap in order. Men who mixed with natives came to a bad end, were passed over for promotion, and ruined by drink. Rudyard Kipling, *Plain Tales from the Hills*, 1887 (reprinted Penguin, London, 1987).
10. Typifying this attitude, Valentia warned that 'half-cast [sic] children ... [were] creating a link of union between the English and the natives'. George Viscount Valentia, *Voyages and Travels to India and Ceylon, 1802–6*, vol. 1, Rivington, London, 1811, p. 197.
11. Kenneth Ballhatchet, *Race, Sex and Class under the Raj, Imperial Attitudes and Policies and their Critics, 1793–1905*, Weidenfeld & Nicolson, London, 1980, p. 131; Christopher Hawes, *Poor Relations: the Making of a Eurasian Community in British India, 1773–1833*, Curzon, Richmond, 1996, p. 61.
12. The Charter Act of 1833 made the theoretical concession that natives of British India and natural-born subjects of His Majesty could no longer be disabled from holding any place, office, or employment under the Company by reason only of his religion, place of birth, descent, colour, or any of them. *The Charter Act of 1833,* section 87, 3rd and 4th George VI, Cap. 83; *The Indian Criminal Procedure Act Amendment Bill, 1883* (The Ilbert Bill) proposed dropping the law requiring that British subjects could only be tried by European judges. It was soon modified (1884) so that only the most senior native judges could try a European, and the accused could demand a half-European jury.
13. Race and racial hybridity are, of course, disputed concepts. I use 'hybridity' only in its historical context.
14. Valentia, *Voyages*, p. 197.
15. The Wallace deputation to parliament had just returned to India, and Mr M.T. Carroll was addressing a meeting of the newly renamed 'Anglo-Indian

Association of Western India.' *The Anglo-Indian Journal*, vol. 1 (2), 1897, pp. 7–9.

16. Laura Roychowdhury, *The Jadu House: Travels in Anglo-India,* Black Swan, London, 2001, p. 48.
17. As early as 1789, Innes Munro had been concerned that Anglo-Indian numbers in England were a threat to racial purity. Innes Munro, *A Narrative of the Military Operations on the Coromandel Coast*, privately printed, London, 1789, p. 50.
18. David Arnold, 'European Orphans and Vagrants in India in the Nineteenth Century', *Journal of Imperial & Commonwealth History*, vol. 7 (2), January 1979, pp. 104–27.
19. The work of each of these authors covers many topics relevant to this monograph, and full details are given in the bibliography under secondary sources: Noel Gist, V.R. Gaikwad, Glenn D'Cruz, Elizabeth Buettner, Michael H. Fisher, Durba Ghosh, David Arnold, Laura Bear, Lionel Caplan, Alison Blunt, and Ann Laura Stoler.
20. Collingham shows how issues of health and genealogy, as well as choice of food, dress, and sexuality, all became of interest to the state in legitimizing British rule. E.M. Collingham, *Imperial Bodies: the Physical Experience of the Raj, c. 1800–1947*, Blackwell, Malden, USA, 2001.
21. Dorris W. Goodrich, *The Making of an Ethnic Group: The Eurasian Community in India,* PhD thesis, University of California, Berkeley, CA, 1952; Christopher Hawes, *Eurasians in British India 1773–1833: the Making of a Reluctant Community,* SOAS PhD Thesis, London, 1993; and Hawes, *Poor,* 1996.
22. See, for example, Frederick Cooper and Ann Laura Stoler (eds), *Tensions of Empire: Colonial Cultures in a Bourgeois World*, University of California Press, Berkeley, CA, 1997; Kathleen Wilson (ed.), *A New Imperial History: Culture, Identity, and Modernity in Britain and the Empire, 1660–1840*, Cambridge University Press, Cambridge, 2004.
23. For an in-depth study of identity formation in Britain and India during this period, see Sudipta Sen, *Distant Sovereignty: National Imperialism and the Origins of British India,* Routledge, London, 2002.
24. Several Indian census reports confirm that many Eurasians returned themselves (or were returned by others) as Europeans. For examples, see W. Chichele Plowden, *Report on the Census of British India Taken on the 17th February 1881*, Eyre and Spottiswoode, London, 1883, p. 32; Jervoise Athelstane Baines, *General Report on the Census of India, 1891,* HMSO, London, 1893, p. 177; J.A.B. (ed.), 'The Census of India, 1911: Christians by Race and Sect', *Journal of the Royal Statistical Society*, vol. 75 (4), March 1912.
25. The earliest, Stark, wrote or co-authored eight books, including Herbert Alick Stark and Walter Madge, *East-Indian Worthies*, n.p., Calcutta, 1892; Stark, *India under Company and Crown: Being an Account of its Progress and Present Administration*, Macmillan & Co., Calcutta, 1914; and Stark, *Hostages to India, or the Life Story of the Anglo-Indian Race*, 2nd edn, Star Printing Works, Calcutta,

1936. Dover's most relevant works are: Cedric Dover, *Chimmerii? Or, Eurasians and Their Future,* Modern Art Press, Calcutta, 1929 and *Half-Caste*, Martin Secker and Warburg Ltd, London, 1937; see also Anthony, *Betrayal*. Two authors outside the community offer a more dispassionate analysis: Hawes, *Eurasians* and *Poor*; and Goodrich, *Making*.

26. Darcus Howe identified the lasting effects of a British 'empire' identity, imbibed from British schoolmasters in Trinidad, that leaves him feeling foreign in the now independent land of his birth. Darcus Howe, 'I returned to Trinidad and just stared at my parents', *New Statesman*, 23 April 2001, p. 24.

Chapter 1 Eurasian 'Othering'

1. Frank Anthony, *Britain's Betrayal in India: the Story of the Anglo-Indian Community*, Allied Publishers, New Delhi, 1962; Cedric Dover, *Chimmerii? Or, Eurasians and Their Future*, Modern Art Press, Calcutta, 1929; Dorris Goodrich, *The Making of an Ethnic Group: The Eurasian Community in India*, PhD thesis, University of California, Berkeley, CA, 1952; Christopher Hawes, *Eurasians in British India 1773–1833: the Making of a Reluctant Community*, SOAS PhD Thesis, London 1993; Christopher Hawes, *Poor Relations: the Making of a Eurasian Community in British India, 1773–1833,* Curzon, Richmond, 1996; Herbert Stark, *Hostages to India, or the Life Story of the Anglo-Indian Race*, 2nd edn, Star Printing Works, Calcutta, 1936.
2. Many such 'usages' were referred to by Ricketts when he was questioned by MPs, peers, and the Board of Control. Hansard, 'Petition of Indo-Britons to House of Commons', in *Hansard's Parliamentary Debates*, vol. XXIV, 4 May 1830, pp. 377–87.
3. 13 Geo. III, Cap. 63 (Regulating Act 1773) in *The Law Relating to India and the East-India Company*, 4th edn, Allen & Co., London, 1842, pp. 26–38.
4. Hawes, *Poor*, p. 56; Goodrich, *Making*, p. 138.
5. Those informally referred to as half-castes or country-born were designated 'country-born' in March 1827, and, after protests from Eurasian organizations, 'Indo-Briton' for all public documents from 30 November 1827. Continued protests from various groups highlighted disunity rather than a single Eurasian community. IOR/F/4/1115/29907, *Eurasian wives of European soldiers eligible for admission to Lord Clive Fund*, 1828.
6. References for Table 1.1: (i) 13 Geo., *The Law*, 1842, pp. 26–38. (ii) IOR/B/102, *Court Minute Book*, 14 March 1786; n.a., *Original Papers Relative to the Establishment of a Society in Bengal for the Protection of Orphans – 1784*, Joseph Cooper, London, n.d., pp. 29–34. (iii) WO4/297, *War Office Out-letters*, 6 May 1790, from George Younge to Lord Cornwallis, pp. 113 and 138. (iv) Govenor-General-in-Council Fort William to Court of Directors, 6 March 1793, in Charles Ross, *Correspondence of Charles, First Marquis Cornwallis*,

vol. 2, John Murray, London, 1859, p. 562. (v) IOR/B113, *Court Minute Book*, 19 April 1791 and 9 November 1791, Standing Order, p. 17. (vi) A.C. Bannerjee (ed.), *Fort William – India House Correspondence and Other Contemporary Papers Relating Thereto, 1792–1796*, vol. 20, (Military Series), National Archives of India, Delhi, 1969, p. 391. (vii) Cornwallis to Henry Dundas, 7 November 1794, in Ross, *Cornwallis*, vol. 2, Appendix LXXIII, p. 581. (viii) Uncertainty and confusion over the eligibility of Eurasians for jury service, resulting from the Regulating Act of 1773 resolving as they are by now classed as natives – at least for this purpose: n.a., *The Law*, 1842, pp. 26–38. (ix) Arthur Wellesley of Wellington and John Gurwood (eds), *The Dispatches of Field Marshal the Duke of Wellington, during his various Campaigns...*, vol. 1, Parker, Furnivall and Parker, London, 1844, p. 769. (x) Madras Military Fund, *East India Register and Directory*, 1825, p. 471; Bombay Military Fund, *ibid.*, p. 484; Bengal Military Fund, *ibid.*, p. 463; Bengal Civil Fund, Charles Lushington, *The History, Design and Present State of the Religious Benevolent and Charitable Institutions ... in Calcutta,* Hindustanee Press, Calcutta, 1824, Appx 14, pp. lxviii–lxxii; Bengal Mariners and General Widows Fund, *East India Register*, p. 286; King's Military Fund, *ibid.*, p. 275. (xi) No primary source was found for this, but it appears in several secondary texts – see below. (xii) The Charter Act, 21 July 1813, in n.a., *The Law*, 1842, pp. 167–99 (pp. 190–5 for references to British subjects).

7. IOR/B/102, *Court*.
8. Legitimate meant born in Christian wedlock only, a concept the nature of which still varied according to location, class, and creed in the UK. See Chapter 5: Law and Marriage.
9. Letter from the managers to Eyre Coote, 18 November 1782, *Original Papers, 1784*, pp. 29–30.
10. *Original Papers, 1784*, pp. 30–4.
11. Anthony, *Betrayal*, p. 20; Hawes, *Poor*, pp. 55 and 138; Goodrich, *Making*, pp. 123–4 and 129; Dover, *Chimmerii?*, p. 21; Stark, *Hostages*, p. 55.
12. WO4/297, *War Office Out-letters*, 6 May 1790.
13. Burke was referring to 26 Geo. III, P.J. Marshall, *The Writings and Speeches of Edmund Burke; India: The Launching of the Hastings Impeachment 1786–1788*, vol. VI, Clarendon Press, Oxford, 1991, pp. 66–73.
14. Quoted in Hawes, *Poor*, p. 64.
15. Senior army officers and civil servants working for the Company (or, later, for the government or many commercial ventures) had to enter into a covenant, or indenture, and two witnesses had to guarantee (with a large deposit) that they would do their duty and refrain from taking bribes or seeking personal enrichment.
16. George Viscount Valentia, *Voyages and Travels to India and Ceylon, 1802–6*, vol. 1, Rivington, London, 1811, p. 197; Stark, *Hostages*, p. 55; Hawes, *Poor*, p. 64.
17. In 1793, Cornwallis elaborated on a prior order, dating from 1790, in an order banning even residence for British subjects outside the Calcutta area without explicit permission from government. The Governor-General in Council Fort

William to the Court of Directors, 6 March 1793, in Ross, *Cornwallis,* 1859, vol. 2., p. 562; Hawes, *Poor*, p. 38; Zoe Yalland, *Traders and Nabobs: the British in Cawnpore, 1765–1857*, Michael Russell, Wilton, UK, 1987, p. 89.

18. Anthony, *Betrayal*, p. 18; Stark, *Hostages*, p. 64; Hawes, *Poor*, p. 38.
19. Ross, *Cornwallis,* 1859, vol. 2., p. 203.
20. *Ibid*., p. 562.
21. James Baillie Fraser, *Military Memoir of Lieut.-Col. James Skinner,* vol. 2, Smith Elder & Co, London, 1851, pp. 98–102.
22. 53 George Cap. 155, in *The Law,* 1842, pp. 194–5.
23. Hawes, *Poor*, p. 38.
24. 'I have to apprize you that I am not an European . . . there are no objections to a person born in this Country settling in any part of the British dominions it will not be requisite for me to obtain previous permission from Government.' From George Sinclair to the Agent of the Governor-General, Saugor and Nerbudda Territories 22 May 1832, in NAI, Foreign Dept./Pol.Cons. No. 86, 30 July 1832, *Discourage Mr Sinclair–an East Indian From Settling in Oocheyrah Jugeer as an Indigo Planter.*
25. From 1833 a natural-born subject of His Majesty could buy, hold, and profit from land in British-held territory, provided he was authorized (by the Governor-General) to reside there. *Charter Act of 1833*, section LXXXVI.
26. n.a., Act No. IV of 1837, in *The Law*, 1842, p. 672.
27. NAI, Foreign & Political/Notes/Proc. nos.18–54, *Employment of . . . East Indians by Native States, 1854–1885*, Orders issued to Punjab Government, 1876.
28. *Ibid*., Hyderabad.
29. IOR/B113, *Court Minute Book,* 19 April 1791, p. 17. John Turing nominated as a Cadet for Madras – refused.
30. Anthony, *Betrayal*, p. 21; Dover, *Chimmerii?*, p. 21; Stark, *Hostages*, pp. 57 and 63; Hawes, *Poor*, pp. 62–6; Goodrich, *Making*, p. 130.
31. Hawes, *Poor*, pp. 62–6.
32. J.W. Ricketts, *Report of Proceedings Connected with the East Indians' Petition to Parliament Read at a Public Meeting Held at Calcutta Town Hall, 28th March 1831*, Baptist Mission Press, Calcutta, 1831, Appx 14, p. 35.
33. Amales Tripathi (ed.), *Fort William – India House Correspondence and Other Contemporary Papers Relating Thereto*, vol. 12, Public series, 1793–1795, NAI, Delhi, 1978, p. 1.
34. IOR/B113, *Court Minute Book*, 19 April 1791, p. 17. Pitt's India Act of 1784 (24 Geo. III Sec. 2 Cap. 25) had established dual control and rule of British India between the Company and the Crown.
35. Stark, *Hostages*, p. 58; Anthony, *Betrayal*, p. 21
36. Letter to Fort William, 25 February 1793, Reply 27 October 1793, in Bannerjee, *Fort William – India House Correspondence, 1792–6*, p. 391; Hawes, *Eurasians*, p. 210.
37. Hawes, *Poor*, p. 68.

38. 'On the strength' meant that a soldier's commanding officer was willing to allow his wife and children to travel and live with the regiment, to draw rations, and to live in the barracks. Married men were later paid more than single men and allocated married quarters. When a man was posted without his family, they might be paid a travel allowance so that they could reach his home town and be supported by parish relief. Wives and children 'off the strength' were ignored by the army and the men treated as single.
39. IOR/F/4/557/13666, *Whether European Soldiers Should be Allowed to Send to England Half-caste or Native Wives or Illegitimate Offspring by Such Women*, 26 May 1817.
40. IOR/L/AG/23/2/1, quoted in Durba Ghosh, 'Making and Un-making Loyal Subjects: Pensioning Widows and Educating Orphans in Early Colonial India', *Journal of Imperial and Commonwealth History*, vol. 31 (1), 2003, pp. 1–28.
41. Letter to Fort William, 25 February 1793 and reply 27 October 1793, in Bannerjee, *Fort William – India House Correspondence, 1792–6*, p. 391.
42. IOR/F/4/211/4716, *Eurasian and Indian Wives and Widows of Soldiers,* Military Consultations, Fort St George, 22 April 1805.
43. In 1823, the vestry supported 7,623 persons, half described as Portuguese, a third as Musselmen, 540 Hindus, 573 Europeans, and 734 dependents of Europeans, who, by exclusion, would have been Eurasian and native wives and children. Its funds were donated by the congregation and three large legacies from Claude Martine, whose wife was Indian; the Indo-Portuguese John Barretto; and the Indo-British Charles Weston. Lushington, 1824, Appx 13, Lord Clive's Fund, p. 341; IOR/F/4/211/4716, *Eurasian*.
44. Lushington, *The History,* Appx 13, Lord Clive's Fund, pp. liv–lvi.
45. Ghosh, *Making and Un-making*, p. 5.
46. IOR/F/4/1115/29907, *Eurasian Wives*.
47. Letter from Nailor, Fonseca, Wilson and Jeremiah to the Governor in Council, *ibid*.
48. No one has cited an original directive from London, though all but Dover cite the year and the action taken in India to debar Eurasians from any combatant role. Anthony, *Betrayal*, p. 21; Stark, *Hostages*, p. 58; Hawes, *Poor*, p. 64; Goodrich, *Making*, p. 131.
49. This was probably the first example of an occupation reserved for the Eurasian community. William Sheppey Greene, *A Code of the Pay Regulations of Various Military Establishments under the Presidency of Fort William*, Military Orphan Press, Kidderpore, 1810, p. 210.
50. Dundas to Cornwallis, London, 17 September 1792, in Ross, *Cornwallis,* vol. 2, pp. 215–17.
51. Cornwallis to Dundas, 7 November 1794, *ibid*., Appendix no. LXXIII, p. 581.
52. Eurasians were still being appointed to and serving in the Madras Army in 1835. IOR/F/4/1544/61371, *Proposed Abolition of the Appointment of Sergeant Majors to Native Regiments of the Madras Army,* February 1835.

53. Anthony, *Betrayal*, p. 21; Stark, *Hostages*, pp. 58–9 and 64; Hawes, *Eurasian*, p. 186; Goodrich, *Making*, pp. 130–3.
54. Cornwallis to Dundas, 7 November 1794, in Ross, *Cornwallis*, vol. 2, p. 574.
55. One father sought the Commander-in-Chief's help in getting his two sons transferred from his regiment because they would have a chance of doing better in a European Corps. See IOR/Mss/Eur/F133/176, *Humble Petition of Master Sergeant Whiley*, 47th Regiment Bengal Native Infantry, 1857.
56. The ruling of 1822 established that illegitimate Eurasians were not British subjects, it did not explicitly say that legitimate Eurasians were British Subjects. n.a., Charles Reed v. Byjuant Sing, *The Asiatic Journal and Monthly Register*, vol. 13, February 1822, pp. 178–9; Goodrich, *Making*, p. 139; Hawes, *Poor*, p. 138.
57. Hawes, *Poor*, p. 138; 7 George IV. Cap 37, *The East Indies Juries Act*, 1826.
58. Wellington and Gurwood, *Dispatches*, p. 769.
59. NAI: Foreign Dept. Political Branch, 17 May 1804 Cons. no. 78–9, *Daniel Murrey asking for consideration* on same footing as officers included in 1803 Proclamation; Foreign Political, 12 July1804, Cons. no. 18, *Mr K B Stuart Scindia Service*; Foreign Political, 9 August 1804, Cons. no. 17, and 13 September, Cons. no. 12, *Thos Lloyd Marhatta Service*; Foreign Political, 2 May 1805, Cons. no. 108, *John Beckett Letter.*
60. James Skinner, Hyder Hearsey, John Holmes, Henry Forster, and William Palmer are amongst the most well known.
61. Charles Grey and H.L.O. Garrett (eds), *European Adventures of Northern India, 1785–1849*, J. Jetley (for AES), New Delhi, 1929 (1993 Reprint), pp. 1–11 and 212.
62. IOR/F/4/215/4746, *List of European and Eurasian Mercenaries Serving with the Nizam's Army*..., vol. 2, 1806–7.
63. Once the Maratha emergency had passed, the government remembered that Eurasians had been barred from covenanted and commissioned posts since 1791. Stark, *Hostages*, pp. 83–4.
64. Such as Captain James Lloyd, who successively served Scindia, the *Nizam*, and then as a British Irregular. IOR/F/4/215/4746, *List*.
65. Hawes, *Poor*, p. 113.
66. NAI, F & P/*Proceedings Nos 18–54*.
67. Letter to Captain Sydenham from Secretary to Government, Fort William, Bengal Secret Cons., 8 January 1807, in IOR/F/4/215/4746, *List*.
68. The *Nizam* was encouraged to dismiss Salvador Rodriguez, Antony Martine, and Terribio, in *ibid*.
69. Hawes, *Poor*, pp. 66–70; Goodrich, *Making*, pp. 134–6; Lushington, *The History,* Appx 14, pp. lxviii–lxxii.
70. Lushington includes examples of correspondence on this matter: Lushington, *The History*, Appx 14, pp. lxviii–lxxii.
71. *East India Register and Directory*, 1825, p. 471.
72. Thomas Munro, 'Minute On the Eurasian Population, 24th November 1824', in Sir A.J. Arbuthnot, *Selections from Minutes and Other Official Writings of*

Major-General Sir Thomas Munro, Higginbotham & Co, Madras, 1886, pp. 558–60.

73. The sicca rupee contained more pure silver than a Company rupee in the ratio 16 to 15.
74. *East India Register and Directory*, 1825, pp. 463 and 484; Lushington, *The History*, p. 286.
75. Lushington, *The History*, p. 275.
76. Hawes, *Poor*, pp. 68–70.
77. Goodrich, *Making*, pp. 134–6.
78. Anthony, *Betrayal*, p. 22.
79. Stark, *Hostages*, pp. 83–4.
80. Hawes, *Poor*, p. 66.
81. See section on Madras sergeant majors in Chapter 8.
82. Ricketts, *Report, 1831*, Appx 14, p. 34
83. Goodrich, *Making*, p. 138.
84. NAI, Foreign/ Internal/Part B/ Proc. nos 464–465, May 1906, (A), *Whether Application for Divorce from East Indians are to be Treated Similarly as these from European British Subjects in Gwalior*; NAI, Foreign Dept./Pol. Cons. no. 210, 18 July 1838, *Whether Rule of International Law Observed in Hyderabad State Should be Observed in Travancore & Cochin*; NAI, Foreign Dept./Judl. (A) Branch, Consultations Collection, March 1867, No. 5/7, *Whether Political Agents with Consent of Native Sovereigns in Central India, Rajpootana, &c., Should Adopt Measures for Removal of European Vagrant*; NAI, Bundelkhand Agency/ English Files/ Part I/ File 8/ 1866 to 1908, *Employment of Europeans and Eurasians in Indian States.*
85. NAI, F & P/*Proceedings Nos 18–54.*
86. Malcolm Speirs, *The Wasikadars of Awadh*, Rupa, New Delhi, 2008, pp. 19–20.
87. Thomas Munro, 'Minute On the Eurasian Population, 24th November 1824,' in Arbuthnot, *Selections*, pp. 558–60.
88. Metcalf quotes Cornwallis, who described Indian officials as 'cruel instruments of rapine and extortion'. Metcalf says the British 'sought to make of the Indians a people uniquely predisposed to corruption, extortion and mendacity'. Thomas R. Metcalf, *Ideologies of the Raj*, Cambridge University Press, Cambridge, 1994, pp. 23–4.
89. *The East Indian*, for example, was established by Henry Derozio, the Eurasian poet, teacher, journalist and Bengal nationalist.
90. This would primarily have been because Eurasians and the better-off Europeans lived in different areas served by different churches.
91. For greater detail on the emergence of Eurasian communal institutions and activities, see Anthony, *Betrayal*; Dover, *Chimmerii?*; Stark, *Hostages*; Hawes, *Poor*; Goodrich, *Making.*
92. IOR/F/4/211/4716, *Eurasian.*
93. Lushington, *The History*, Appx 13, Lord Clive's Fund, p. 341.

94. See discussions regarding a school for Eurasians in Karachi: NAI, Home/Public/Proc. no. 52, *Bombay Govt. has Consented to Contribute Half the Expense of Erecting a School for children of English and Indo-British Inhabitants at Kurrachee*, October 1855.
95. Stark, *Hostages*, p. 91.
96. Referred to in a letter from John Jebb and James Pattison to Rt. Hon. George Canning, dated 27 February 1818, in 'Report from the Select Committee on the Affairs of the East India Company', *House of Commons, Parliamentary Papers*, 1832, vol. 1, General Appx, p. 258.
97. There was a Madras association representing Indo-Britons in 1827; IOR/F/4/1115/29907, *Eurasian Wives.*
98. The Calcutta Association was formed in 1822. Hawes, *Poor*, p. 143.
99. Directives, standing orders, and regulations had the force of law even though not the result of legislation.
100. Ross, *Cornwallis*; Richard Wellesley and Robert Montgomery Martin (eds), *The Dispatches, Minutes, and Correspondence, of the Marquess Wellesley*, W.H. Allen & Co., London, 1836 and 1837. There is no similar contemporary collection of Dundas' correspondence. Probably because his impeachment had caused so much controversy, his descendants held his papers privately for over a century. The Cornwallis and Wellesley collections, however, contain many examples of Dundas' correspondence.
101. See: Catherine Hall, *Civilising Subjects; Metropole And Colony In The English Imagination, 1830–1867*, Polity Press, Cambridge, 2002; Catherine Hall and Sonya O. Rose, *At Home With The Empire: Metropolitan Culture And The Imperial World*, Cambridge University Press, Cambridge, 2006; Peter J. Marshall, *'A Free Though Conquering People,' Eighteenth Century Britain and its Empire,* Ashgate Publishing, Aldershot, 2003.

Chapter 2 Hidden Agendas

1. 'Britain is an invented nation, not so much older than the United States.' Peter Scott, *Knowledge and Nation*, Edinburgh University Press, Edinburgh, 1990, p. 168.
2. They had to be major shareholders before they could be elected as directors.
3. Peter J. Marshall, *'A Free Though Conquering People,' Eighteenth Century Britain and its Empire*, Ashgate Publishing, Aldershot, 2003, Ch. XVI, p. 9.
4. *Ibid.*, Ch. III, p. 191.
5. In Ireland and India, in addition to civil duties he was also commander-in-chief of the army. He was appointed, alongside Lord Liverpool, minister plenipotentiary of Addington's administration, negotiating a short-lived peace with Napoleon in 1802.

6. Cornwallis to Major-General Ross, 1 July 1798, in Charles Ross, *Correspondence of Charles, First Marquis Cornwallis*, vol. 2, John Murray, London, 1859, pp. 357–8.
7. Dundas pressed the court to cooperate and allow the governor-general to make his own decisions. Cornwallis was criticized in parliament for engaging in war with Tipu Sultan, and ignored calls to conclude it rapidly. Philips cites 'permanent settlement' as an example of 'the futility of attempting to conduct the Company's external policy from London'. Philips believed Dundas' role was to sell Cornwallis' plan to the EIC directors. Sir Cyril Henry Philips, *The East-India Company 1784–1834*, Manchester University Press, Manchester, 1940, p. 63 and pp. 68–9.
8. That Cornwallis arrived in India with a bundle of instructions from the directors does not diminish this point. Dundas, Cornwallis, and the prime minister are known to have met several times and corresponded regularly before his departure, and to have 'steam-rollered' the directors into passing resolutions in accord with their own political and economic agendas.
9. Eurasians of non-British descent, e.g. French and Portuguese, were already 'othered'. There is also evidence that the prospects of British Eurasians were beginning to diverge from those of their European kin prior to his arrival, but there had been no *official* attempts to differentiate between them.
10. C.A. Bayly and Katherine Prior, 'Cornwallis, Charles, first Marquess Cornwallis (1738–1805)', *ODNB* (accessed June 2010).
11. *Ibid.*
12. Cornwallis to Ross, 23 February 1786, in Ross, *Cornwallis*, vol. 1, p. 215.
13. Raymond A. Callahan, 'Cornwallis and the Indian Army, 1786–1797', *Military Affairs*, vol. 34 (3), 1970, pp. 93–7.
14. The regular army and the Company armies of Madras, Bombay, and Bengal were effectively independent of one another.
15. Cornwallis to Dundas, 14 August 1787, in Ross, *Cornwallis,* vol. 1, pp. 269–72.
16. *Ibid.*, vol. 2, pp. 193 and 201–2.
17. R. Kumar (ed.), *Military System of East India Company*, Ajay Verma for Commonwealth Publishers, New Delhi, 2004, p. 171.
18. Cornwallis to Court of Directors, 6 March 1789, in Ross, *Cornwallis*, vol. 1, pp. 550–2.
19. See previous chapter.
20. IOR/B/102, 14 March 1786; n.a., *Original Papers Relative to the Establishment of a Society in Bengal for the Protection of Orphans – 1784*, London, Joseph Cooper, n.d., pp. 29–34.
21. The Governor-General in Council Fort William to Court Of Directors, 6 March 1793, in Ross, *Cornwallis,* vol. 2, p. 562.
22. WO4/297, *War Office Out-letters*, 6 May 1790.
23. IOR/B/113, *Court Minute Book*, Standing Order, 19 April 1791, p. 17, and 9 November 1791.

24. Cornwallis to Dundas, dated 7 November 1794, in Ross, *Cornwallis*, vol. 2, Appx LXXIII, p. 581.
25. A.C. Bannerjee (ed.), *Fort William – India House Correspondence And Other Contemporary Papers Relating Thereto, 1792–1796*, vol. 20, Military Series, National Archives of India, Delhi, 1969, p. 391.
26. This can be contrasted with the situation under the Dutch in Batavia, where even amongst civilians intermarriage could be prevented by law. Ann Laura Stoler, 'Rethinking Colonial Categories; European Communities and the Boundaries of Rule', *Comparative Studies in Society and History*, vol. 31 (1), 1989, pp. 134–61.
27. Although he died soon after, his return to India was assumed even before he went to Ireland. He wrote to Ross on the subject in April 1797. Cornwallis to Major-General Ross, 23 April 1797, in Ross, *Cornwallis*, vol. 2, p. 326.
28. *Ibid.*, pp. 357–8.
29. *Ibid.*, pp. 329–30.
30. This included the army, navy, volunteers, and fencibles. J.E. Cookson, *The British Armed Nation, 1793–1815*, Clarendon Press, Oxford, 1997, p. 95.
31. Several abortive attempts were made to land French forces in Ireland in 1797 and 1798.
32. Cornwallis to Pitt, in Ross, *Cornwallis*, vol. 2, pp. 414–16.
33. Bayly and Prior, Cornwallis, *ODNB*.
34. C.A. Bayly, 'Wellesley, Richard, Marquess Wellesley (1760–1842)', *ODNB*, (accessed March 2009); *Imperial Gazetteer of India*, New edition, Oxford, Clarendon Press, 1908–31 [1909]; Hugh Chisholm (ed.), *The Encyclopaedia Britannica*, 11th edn, vol. 28, Cambridge University Press, Cambridge, 1911, pp. 506–7.
35. Wellesley to Liverpool, 21 May 1812, Robert Rouiere Pearce (ed.), *Memoirs and Correspondence of Richard Marquis Wellesley*, vol. 3, Richard Bentley, London, 1846, p. 238.
36. Richard Wellesley, *The substance of the speech of the Marquis Wellesley on the 31st of January, 1812, in the House of Lords, on the motion of Earl Fitzwilliam, respecting the present State of Ireland*, Longman Hurst, London, 1812.
37. Pearce, *Memoirs*, vol. 3, p. 212.
38. Minute of Mr Canning's Communication [as spokesman for Wellesley] to Earl Liverpool, 23 May. *Ibid.*, p. 241.
39. *Ibid.*, Chapter XVI.
40. Debate in House of Lords on 10 June 1828, *ibid.*, pp. 395–400.
41. *Ibid.*, p. 406.
42. Ian Heath, *The Irish Wars, 1485–1603*, Osprey Publishing, Oxford, 1993, p. 1.
43. Harman Murtagh, 'Irish Soldiers Abroad, 1600–1800', in Thomas Bartlett and Keith Jeffery (eds), *A Military History of Ireland*, Cambridge University Press, Cambridge, 1996, pp. 294–314.
44. It was a commonplace that the Irish were a Celtic people, inferior to the Anglo-Saxon but, nonetheless, European and therefore superior to everyone

else! Pearce said that, given better government, they would gradually improve, but he was also careful to caution that it would be 'worse than vain, to seek to depreciate the Saxon race, whose robust manhood, perseverance, energy, skill, indomitable courage, and dignity of character have made the English name respected in the remotest corners of the Earth'. Pearce, *Memoirs*, vol. 1, pp. XIV–XVI.

45. Protestants were more likely to have been kept in Ireland, as yeomanry. The Anglo-Irish land and office holders relied on them to maintain law and order at home. Cookson, *British*, p. 164.
46. *Ibid.*, p. 126.
47. *Ibid.*, pp. 177–8 and 153–5.
48. Wellesley claimed, in an 1803 letter to Castlereagh, to have reined in his own support for private trade, except where absolutely necessary, and complied with the directors' wish to assert the Company's monopoly. Richard Wellesley and Robert Montgomery Martin (eds), *The Dispatches, Minutes, and Correspondence, of the Marquess Wellesley*, vol. 3, W.H. Allen & Co., London, 1836 and 1837, pp. 54–60; Philips, *East-India Company*, pp. 120–1.
49. Company's General Court of Proprietors' Quarterly Meeting, 17 March 1841, in Pearce, *Memoirs*, vol. 3, pp. 438 and 443.
50. *Ibid.*, p. 445; St Johns was completed in 1787, a decade before Wellesley arrived. n.a., *The Bengal Obituary*, Holmes & Holmes, Calcutta, 1851, p. 1; There were pre-existing Armenian and Greek Orthodox Churches (built in 1724 and 1781), *ibid.*, pp. 310 and 313. A Catholic one was completed the year before he arrived, *ibid.*, p. 302.
51. Pearce, *Memoirs*, vol. 1, pp. 351–6.
52. Lushington includes examples of correspondence on this matter: Charles Lushington, *The History, Design and Present State of the Religious Benevolent and Charitable Institutions ... in Calcutta*, Hindustanee Press, Calcutta, 1824, Appx 14, pp. lxviii–lxxii.
53. Letter from Mornington (Wellesley's title) to Dundas, Cape of Good Hope, 23 February 1798, in Wellesley and Martin, *Dispatches*, vol. 1, 1836, pp. 1–15.
54. Letter from Mornington (Wellesley) to Dundas, Cape of Good Hope, 23 February 1798, in *ibid.*
55. Memorandum of conversation between Meer Allum and Arthur Wellesley, September 1800, in 1st and 2nd Duke of Wellington, *Supplementary Despatches and Memoranda of Field Marshal Arthur, Duke of Wellington*, John Murray, London, 1858, vol. 2, p. 180.
56. William Dalrymple, 'White Mughals', in Indrani Chatterjee (ed.), *Unfamiliar Relations: Family and History in South Asia*, Permanent Black, New Delhi, 2004, pp. 122–60.
57. Edward Ingram (ed.), *Two Views of British India: the Private Correspondence of Mr Dundas and Lord Wellesley, 1798–1801*, Adams Dart, Bath, Somerset, 1970, p. 12.

58. Michael Fry, 'Dundas, Henry, first Viscount Melville (1742–1811)', *ODNB* (accessed March 2009).
59. Noam Chomsky, 'Crises and the Unipolar Moment', *The Globalisation Lecture Series*, SOAS, 27 October 2009.
60. Henry Dundas quoted in Cookson, *British*, pp. 67–8.
61. *Ibid.*, pp. 34–5, 133–7 and 180.
62. Ingram, *Two Views*, page preceding Introduction.
63. James G. Parker, *The Directors of the East India Company, 1754–1790*, PhD thesis, University of Edinburgh, 1977, p. 434; Philips, *East-India Company*, p. 34.
64. Parker, *The Directors*. p. 434.
65. Philips, *East-India Company*, pp. 34–5.
66. *Ibid.*, p. 35.
67. Chisholm, *Encyclopaedia Britannica*, vol. 18, pp. 102–3.
68. James A. Lovat-Fraser, *Henry Dundas, Viscount Melville, 1742–1811*, Cambridge University Press, Cambridge, 1916, pp. 13–14, 67, 135.
69. This viewpoint is also expressed in Cookson, *British*, p. 133. Philips, however, found the Scots already disproportionately prevalent in Company service long before the Board was formed. Philips, *East-India Company*, p. 35.
70. Parker, *The Directors*, p. 444; John Michael Bourne, *The Civil and Military Patronage of the East India Company, 1784–1858*, PhD thesis, University of Leicester, 1977, pp. 176–8.
71. As President of the Board, Dundas could personally nominate only four to six *writers* or cadets annually.
72. Cookson, *British*, p. 133.
73. Philips, *East-India Company*, p. 36.
74. Bourne, *Civil*, p. 178.
75. Lovat-Fraser, *Dundas*, p. 19.
76. Marshall, *Free*, Ch. XVI, p. 9.
77. Dundas discussed the involvement of Ireland in empire trade with Lord Hobart, Secretary of State for Ireland, before his appointment as Governor of Madras. Castlereagh, who followed Dundas as President of the Board, had also served as Secretary for Ireland. Philips, 1940, pp. 70 and 118.
78. He raised emancipation of Scottish Catholics as an MP in 1778, and of the Irish when Home Secretary in 1781. Lovat-Fraser, *Dundas*, pp. 6 and 38.
79. Marshall, *Free,* Ch. III, p. 191.
80. Ingram, *Two Views*, p. 4.
81. Kumar, *Military System*, p. 170.
82. Dundas had been recommending Cornwallis as early as 1783. He had chosen Shore as a safe pair of hands to continue the reforms until Cornwallis could return to India. In the event Cornwallis' return was delayed, so Wellesley, Pitt's first choice and Dundas' second, was made governor-general in his stead. Lovat-Fraser, *Dundas*, p. 13.

83. Dundas intimated a willingness to serve as governor-general himself, but claimed Pitt wanted him to remain in England. Dundas to Cornwallis, 20 January 1797, in Ross, *Cornwallis*, vol. 2, p. 321.
84. Disagreements between the Board and the Company were frequent, but governor-generals were appointed by the Board to do its bidding. Philips, *East-India Company*, pp. 69–70.
85. From Govenor-General Marquis Wellesley to the Court of Directors, n.a., *On the Trade of India*, Fort William, dated 30 September 1800, Richardson & Budd, London, 1812.
86. Dundas' son Robert served on the Board of Control between 1797 and 1802.
87. The Irish were drawn exclusively from the Protestant ascendancy at this time.
88. Parker, *The Directors*, p. 442; Bourne, *Civil*, pp. 174–82.
89. Dundas' patronage of his kin was not particularly unusual in the late eighteenth and early nineteenth century, but I raise the subject to illustrate how effective it could be.
90. Ingram, *Two Views*, p. 10.
91. *Public Advertiser*, London, 2 January 1783, Issue 15, p. 162.
92. As minister in charge of the colonies from 1791, this was within his remit. He also believed that Highlanders were particularly suited to military service.
93. The Highland and Lowland clearances of 1750–1850 left many thousands of Scots without work, disaffected, and a potential threat to law and order. The Act of Proscription of 1746, which had banned 'Highland garb' (except for the army) was repealed in 1782. The rehabilitation of barbarous clansmen as noble savages in Highland regiments and the widespread adoption of tartan as Scotland's national dress followed. Magnus Magnusson, *Scotland; the Story of a Nation*, Harper Collins, London, 2001, pp. 653–4.
94. *The Inverness Advertiser*, 26 July 1853.
95. For a detailed consideration of Scottish military recruitment and Dundas' role in this, see Cookson, *British*, pp. 126–52.
96. *Ibid.*, pp. 137–8.
97. *Ibid.*, pp. 135–6.
98. n.a., 'Parliamentary Intelligence, House of Commons', *Morning Chronicle and London Advertiser*, London, 1 February 1783, Issue 4,278.
99. n.a., 'House of Commons', *General Evening Post*, London, 28 January 1783, Issue 7,636.
100. Maria Graham, *Journal of a Residence in India*, 2nd edn, Archibald Constance & Co., Edinburgh, 1813, p. 128.
101. George Viscount Valentia, *Voyages and Travels to India and Ceylon; 1802–6*, vol. 1, Rivington, London, 1811, p. 197.
102. Thomas Williamson, *East India Vade Mecum*, vol. 1, Black, Parry, and Kingsbury, London, 1810, p. 459.
103. J.B. Gilchrist, *The General East India Guide and Vade Mecum . . . a Digest of the Work of the Late Capt. Williamson*, Kingsbury, Parbury & Allen, London, 1825.

104. In one example, a white woman marries 'a black' and her half-caste daughter later visits havoc on her younger European sibling, in n.a., 'Reminiscences of a Returning Indian', *The Asiatic Journal and Monthly Register*, London, Parbury & Allen, vol. 18 (new series), September 1835, pp. 17–29 and 81–94.
105. More than one author suggested half-castes could only be happy with their own kind: 'A Lady', 'Reminiscences of a Half-Caste', in *The East India Sketch-Book*, vol. 1, Richard Bentley, London, 1833, pp. 1–95.
106. Jon E. Wilson, *The Domination of Strangers: Modern Governance in Eastern India, 1780–1835*, Palgrave Macmillan, Basingstoke, 2008.

Chapter 3 Population Statistics

1. Rev. Claudius Buchanan, *Colonial Ecclesiastical Establishment; Submitted to the Consideration of the Imperial Parliament*, 2nd edn, Cadell & Davies, London, 1813, pp. 117–19.
2. *Ibid.*, p. 159.
3. Henry Waterfield, *Memorandum on the Census of British India 1871–72*, Eyre and Spottiswoode, London, 1875, p. 9.
4. Robert Montgomery Martin, *History of the Possessions of the Honourable East India Company*, vol. 1, Bengal, Madras, and Bombay, Whittaker & co., London, 1837, p. 262.
5. *Ibid.*, footnote 5, p. 275.
6. The number of Indo-French was small compared to the Indo-Portuguese, so they are disregarded as a separate entity.
7. These proportions come from William Walker (from *The Times of India*, 25 Novenber 1861), reprinted in Walker's *Tom Cringle's Letters on Practical Subjects, Suggested by Experiences in Bombay*, Education Society's Press, Byculla, 1863, pp. 111–13. Buchanan actually used the ratio 5:4:2 for Eurasians and 2:3:1 for European Protestants; the latter ratio varied with the distribution of Irish (Catholic) regiments. Buchanan, *Colonial*, pp. 158–9.
8. 'Bombay Education Society', *The Asiatic Journal & Monthly Miscellany*, vol. 28, September 1829, p. 353.
9. Martin, *History*, vol. 1, pp. 366–7.
10. Ricketts estimated there were 800–900 Eurasian children in the Upper and Lower military orphanages of Calcutta in 1830. Herbert Alick Stark and Walter Madge, *East-Indian Worthies*, n.p., Calcutta, 1892, p. 54.
11. Cuthbert Finch, 'Vital Statistics of Calcutta', *Journal of the Statistical Society of London*, vol. 13, (2), 1850, pp. 168–82.
12. Calcutta was home to 60 per cent of Bengal's Eurasians by 1931, but this percentage included all the suburbs, which the 1837 census did not. Cuthbert Finch, 'Vital Statistics of Calcutta', *Journal of the Statistical Society of London*, vol. 13 (2), 1850, pp. 168–82.

13. Buchanan, *Colonial*, pp. 158–9.
14. The term 'East-Indian' was more or less synonymous with 'Eurasian.'
15. NAI, Home/Public/Proc. no. 52, *Bombay Govt. has Consented to Contribute Half the Expense of Erecting a School for children of English and Indo-British Inhabitants at Kurrachee*, October 1855.
16. The number of Indo-Portuguese claiming Portuguese nationality would have been small, since there were only 426 returned as Portuguese in British India. Waterfield, *Memorandum*, p. 29.
17. *Ibid.*, p. 28.
18. n.a., *Annual Report of the Eurasian and Anglo-Indian Association* [EAIA], Calcutta, 1879, Appx E, p. 32.
19. W. Chichele Plowden, *Report on the Census of British India Taken on the 17th February 1881*, Eyre and Spottiswoode, London, 1883, p. 38.
20. Letter to the Secretary to Government of India, Home Dept., No. 81, Calcutta, 17 July 1880, reprinted in n.a., EAIA, *Annual*, 1880, pp. 34–40.
21. Plowden, *Census Report*, pp. 38–9.
22. *Ibid.*
23. I found that 100 of 535 EIR employees in 1881, described as Eurasian or Indo-British, still bore Portuguese names. See Chapter 9.
24. Jervoise Athelstane Baines, *General Report on the Census of India, 1891*, HMSO, London, 1893, p. 307.
25. *Ibid.*, p. 170.
26. *Ibid.*, p. 187.
27. *Ibid.*, p. 178.
28. *Ibid.*
29. Anne Booth, 'The Colonial Legacy and its Impact on Post-Independence Planning in India and Indonesia', in Lionel Blussé, Anne Booth, et al., *India and Indonesia from the 1920s to the 1950s: the Origins of Planning*, E.J. Brill, Leiden, 1987, p. 2.
30. Baines, *Census of India*, pp. 177–82; H.H. Risley and E.A. Gait, *Report On The Census Of India*, 1901, Government Printing Press, Calcutta, 1903, p. 219; Dorris Goodrich, *The Making of an Ethnic Group: The Eurasian Community in India*, PhD thesis, University of California, Berkeley, CA, 1952.
31. References for Table 3.2: (i) These are raw figures, with no allowance made for exogamy and no attempt to count Eurasians other than those classified as of Portuguese or British descent. Other than figures extracted from census returns and other sources, all calculations are based on an annual population growth rate of 0.4 per cent until 1920 and 1.5 per cent thereafter. These low rates of growth are in line with the growth rate for India. Blussé and Booth, India and Indonesia, p. 2. (ii) These columns are calculated from the 1871 census return, annually reduced by 0.4 per cent for earlier dates, increased annually by 0.4 per cent after 1871 until 1920, and thereafter increased by 1.5 per cent in line with Blussé. Waterfield, *Memorandum*, p. 52; Blussé and Booth, *India and Indonesia*, p. 2. (iii) This column is calculated from the 1881 census return, annually

reduced by 0.4 per cent for earlier dates, increased annually by 0.4 per cent after 1881 until 1920, and thereafter increased by 1.5 per cent in line with Blussé. Plowden, *Census Report*, p. 33; Blussé and Booth, *India and Indonesia*, p. 2. (iv) Lionel Caplan, *Children of Colonialism: Anglo-Indians in a Postcolonial World*, Berg, Oxford, 2001, pp. 67–8; see also Elizabeth Buettner, *Empire Families: Britons and Late Imperial India*, Oxford University Press, Oxford, 2004, pp. 82–4. (v) The figures in this column are calculated from the 1826 census of Bombay published in Martin. Martin reported that of 50,000 Roman Catholics in Bombay, 8,020 were identified as Portuguese and the rest as converts. He reported that there were 600,000 Roman Catholics in India as a whole, so, if the ratio of Portuguese Eurasians to native converts remained the same, this would give the figure of 96,240 Indo-Portuguese for 1826. This figure is increased annually by 0.4 per cent from 1826 until 1920, and thereafter increased by 1.5 per cent in line with Blussé. Martin does not recognize that there would be Indo-French and Indo-British amongst the Catholics. Martin, History, vol. 1, p. 262; Blussé and Booth, *India and Indonesia*, p. 2. (vi) Buchanan reported there were 100,000 Indo-British 'Protestants' in 1813 India. He implied an equal number of Roman Catholics, which would give a starting figure much higher than this. He took no account of the Indo-Portuguese. Whilst Buchanan's estimate appears high when compared with later censuses, his other figures (for the number of European residents and troops) are consistent with other contemporary sources. Buchanan, *Colonial*, p. 117. (vii) Lionel Caplan, *Children of Colonialism: Anglo-Indians in a Postcolonial World*, Berg, Oxford, 2001, p. 67. (viii) Caplan, *Children*, p. 67. (ix) Caplan, *Children*, p. 68.

Chapter 4 Europeans and Miscegenation

1. Rudyard Kipling, *Plain Tales from the Hills*, 1887 (reprinted Penguin, London, 1987), p. 186.
2. Although aimed at prostitutes, the English 'Contagious Diseases Acts' from 1864 allowed any woman to be arrested, examined for venereal disease, and detained until 'cured'. It applied in 18 towns with an army or navy presence, and included fortnightly examinations for registered prostitutes, and up to nine months' incarceration. The moral argument in Britain, that the law treated women severely while 'allowing men to sin with impunity', seems to have been less persuasive in India. It was repealed in England and Wales in 1886.
3. This issue is explored in greater detail in Kenneth Ballhatchet, *Race, Sex and Class under the Raj, Imperial Attitudes and Policies and their Critics, 1793–1905*, Weidenfeld & Nicolson, London, 1980.
4. Durba Ghosh disagrees with this interpretation, citing an increase in the number of wills filed by indigenous women, the partners of European men, after

1800. Durba Ghosh, *Sex And The Family In Colonial India; The Making Of Empire*, Cambridge University Press, Cambridge, 2006, p. 136.

5. *Ibid.*, p. 130.
6. n.a., 'Report from the Select Committee on Colonisation and Settlement (India); [1st–4th reports] with Minutes of Evidence taken before them, 1858', *The North British Review*, vol. 30, February–May 1859, Article VII, pp. 441–6.
7. Excluding officers and their wives, 329 women accompanied 9,554 men on troop-ships to India. A total of 9,452 men and 581 wives returned to England. 'Statement no. 141, Showing the Particulars of the Troops Conveyed to and from India, Year to 31st March 1882', in India Office, *Statistical Abstract Relating to British India From 1876/7 to 1885/6*, vol. 21, Her Majesty's Stationary Office, London, 1887.
8. 'Abstract no. 130, Strength and deaths of the European Army, 1881', and 'Abstract no. 132, Terms of Engagement of Non-Commissioned officers and men', in India Office, *Statistical Abstract*, pp. 202 and 206; R. Holmes, *Sahib; The British Soldier in India*, Harper Collins, London, 2005, p. 216.
9. The National Archives of the UK (TNA): Public Record Office (PRO), *Census Returns of England and Wales, 1881*, [database online], http://search.ancestry.co.uk/search/grouplist.aspx?group=1881uki; W. Chichele Plowden, *Report on the Census of British India Taken on the 17th February 1881*, Eyre and Spottiswoode, London, 1883; India Office, *Statistical Abstract*.
10. Joachim Hayward Stocqueler, *The British Soldier: an Anecdotal History of the British Army, from its earliest formation to the present time*, Wm. S Orr & Co., London, 1857, p. 274.
11. These age limiters were chosen because boys of 14 could marry and could serve as soldiers, whilst men over 60 were unlikely to have been fit enough to continue as serving soldiers.
12. The marriage rates I have found for the general population of England and Wales in 1881 differ from those quoted by Plowden. His figures, however, would have been based on a sample, whereas mine are the totals from the whole census, and our decadal groups differ; I have taken 21–30, 31–40, etc., whereas Plowden's groups are 25–34, 35–44, etc. See Abstract XXXVII, England and Wales, 1881 – Percentage on Civil Condition, in Plowden, *Census Report*, p. 92.
13. Ballhatchet, *Race*, p. 35.
14. Absolute numbers are from source data. Percentages and the predicted number of married soldiers in India are my calculations. TNA, *Census*, 1881; figures for soldiers in India are taken from 'Abstract no. 130, Strength and Deaths of the European Army, 1881', in India Office, *Statistical Abstract*, p. 202.
15. This figure is for army pensioners. Plowden, *Census Report,* vol. 1, p. 470.
16. Of 684,094 males born 1861–3, only 20,568 are indexed as married in the 1881 English census. There is also a substantial error rate, illustrated by the 3,000 'married' boys under 14. TNA, *Census*.

17. The average British military presence was 58,780 p.a. between 1876 and 1886: see 'Abstract no. 135, Regiments and detachments of all arms embarked for service in India from the United Kingdom and from the Colonies', and 'Abstract no.132, Terms of engagement of the non-commissioned officers and men of the different arms among British troops in India', in India Office, *Statistical Abstract*, p. 206.
18. In 1881, 375 wives arrived with the army's 'other ranks'. Allowing six years for complete military turnover at 10,000 troops and their wives per year, and excluding officers, this represents 2,250 soldiers' wives from Britain in India at any given date.
19. It is highly unlikely that many wives of ordinary soldiers, left behind in England, could have afforded to make their own way to India.
20. 9,524 men were accompanied home by 581 women on troop-ships from India. 'Statement no. 141, Particulars of Troops Conveyed to and from India, Year to 31st March 1882', in India Office, *Statistical Abstract*.
21. Other ranks seeking a wife had two main routes; they might have approached the orphanages or met girls when invited to 'socials' at the numerous railway institutes.
22. Charles Allen, *Plain Tales from the Raj*, Abacus, London, 1975, pp. 191–2.
23. Currently, half an armoured reconnaissance regiment will be NCOs, but only two in seven in an infantry battalion. General Sir Mike Jackson, 'The Role of the Non Commissioned Officer in the British Army', *UK Defence Forum*, cream paper no. 46, June 2003, http://www.ukdf.org.uk/assets/downloads/CP46TheRoleoftheNonCommissionedOfficer.pdf (accessed February 2013).
24. Muster Roll of Scots Brigade, 1804, FIBIS, http://search.fibis.org/frontis/bin/aps_browse_sources.php?mode=browse_components&id=418&s_id=178 (transcription, accessed February 2013).
25. 'Abstract no. 134, Past Services of Non-Commissioned Officers and Men ... amongst British Troops in India'; troopships in the years before and after 1881–2 carried similar numbers. 'Statement no. 141, Particulars of Troops Conveyed to and from India, Year to 31st March 1882', India Office, *Statistical Abstract*, pp. 208–9.
26. 'Ages of the British-Born Population', in Plowden, *Census Report*, Abstract XCV, pp. 469–70.
27. I have chosen this age range because so few European men in India were over 60, and a disproportionately low percentage was under 21.
28. Samuel Brown, 'On the Rates of Mortality and Marriage amongst Europeans in India', *Journal of the Statistical Society of London*, vol. 27 (4), 1864, pp. 566–79.
29. Some would have been Indian not European, but the number is so small it can be ignored.
30. This was the average of surviving children living with parents in 1881, excluding those deceased or living apart who would have added considerably more. Francis M.L. Thompson (ed.), 'People and Their Environment', in *The*

Cambridge Social History of Britain, 1750–1950, vol. 2, Cambridge University Press, Cambridge, 1996, p. 34.

31. Some were with other relatives, a few in children's homes or working, but most were school boarders.
32. The 23,100 British women in India with 19,608 children gives a different ratio of women to children, but I only counted those women resident in England living with their children so there is no direct comparison. In India, about a thousand were unmarried, others had children boarding in England, some had adult children, some were childless, and others had not yet completed their families.
33. This proportion is a calculation from the figures in Tables 4.2 and 4.3 based on the small proportion of civilians and the much higher proportion of soldiery, all corrected for age and rank.
34. 'Ages of the British-Born Population,' in Plowden, *Census Report*, Abstract XCV, p. 469.
35. These data are taken from *ibid.* Where a figure is my estimation, derived from such data, this is clearly indicated.
36. With only a single figure (25,000) for the total number of women and children, the figures in this row were calculated by splitting that total in the same ratio as for the British-born population: 54 per cent women to 46 per cent children, and amongst children 59 per cent boys and 41 per cent girls – the gender disparity amongst the children was caused by including girls over 14 as adults.
37. Only total numbers of male and female were available under this head. So the numbers in this row were calculated by splitting the total of females in the same ratio as for the British-born women and girls; 12,897 women and girls = 26.6 per cent (3,430) girls, so for European others girls = 26.6 per cent of 6,498 females = 1,728. If boys and girls were present in same ratio as British-born girls and boys, then they were in the ratio of 59:41. Girls numbered 1,728 = 41 per cent of children, so boys = 1,728/41 × 59 = 2,487.
38. This percentage is that needed for troops in India, corrected for age, to match marriage rates amongst soldiers in the 1881 census for England and Wales.
39. This percentage is that needed for civilians and officers in India to miror marriage rates amongst the general population in England and Wales.
40. Suresh Chandra Ghosh, *The Social Condition of the British Community in Bengal; 1757–1800*, Brill, Boston, MA, 1970, pp. 64–5.
41. Thomas Williamson, *East India Vade Mecum*, vol. 1, Black, Parry, and Kingsbury, London, 1810, pp. 173–5 and 414–15.
42. Innes Munro quoted in S.C. Ghosh, *The Social*, pp. 70–1.
43. n.a., 'The Bengal Military Orphan Society', in *The Calcutta Review*, vol. 45 (90), 1867, p. 303.
44. Stone's conclusion that the English practised a 'very high degree of social and economic endogamy' is apt. Lawrence Stone, *The Family, Sex and Marriage in England, 1500–1800*, abridged edition, Penguin, London, 1979, p. 50.

Although Stone was writing about England in the seventeenth century, the concepts of class and race overlapped in the colonies. Satoshi Mizutani, *The Meaning of White; Race, Class, and the 'Domiciled Community' in British India 1858–1930*, Oxford University Press, Oxford, 2011, p. 4. Those women who did not find a match at home in Britain were referred to as the 'fishing fleet' when they arrived in India looking to 'catch' a suitable husband, but working-class women could not afford to join the 'fishing fleet'.

45. n.a., *North British Review*, 1859.
46. Bedfordshire had the highest marriage rates and the highest rates of women 'earning money in industrial occupations'. In Herefordshire, the rate of marriage was half that of Bedfordshire, and of paid industrial employment for women less than half. W. Ogle, 'On marriage Rates and Marriage Ages with Special Reference to the Growth of Population', *Journal of the Royal Statistical Society*, vol. 53, 1890, pp. 253–89.
47. Peter Stanley, *White Mutiny: British Military Culture in India, 1825–1875*, Hurst & Co., London, 1998, p. 14.
48. Thomas Quinney, *Sketches of a Soldier's Life in India*, David Robertson, Glasgow, 1853, p. 94.
49. For further examples of this in Plymouth, see Judith Walkowitz, *Prostitution and Victorian Society; Women, Class and the State*, Cambridge University Press, Cambridge, 1982, pp. 199–204.
50. J.B. Gilchrist, *The General East India Guide and Vade Mecum ... a Digest of the Work of the Late Capt. Williamson*, Kingsbury, Parbury & Allen, London, 1825, pp. 184–5.
51. Stanley, *White Mutiny*, p. 67.
52. Frank Anthony, *Britain's Betrayal in India: the Story of the Anglo-Indian Community*, Allied Publishers, New Delhi, 1962, p. 16.
53. *Madras Military Female Asylum Records*, transcription at http://search.fibis.org/frontis/bin/aps_browse_sources.php?mode=browse_components&id=387&s_id=229 (accessed February 2013); n.a., 'Marriage Announcements', *East India Register*, vol. 1, 1835.
54. Quinney, *Sketches*, p. 52.
55. Charles Lushington, *The History, Design and Present State of the Religious Benevolent and Charitable Institutions ... in Calcutta*, Hindustanee Press, Calcutta, 1824, pp. 257–65.
56. Allen, *Plain Tales*, pp. 191–2.
57. 'Statement no. 141, Particulars of the Troops Conveyed', and 'Statement no. 140, Numbers conveyed since 1866–67', India Office, *Statistical Abstract*. The latter gives only a ten-year summary of total numbers without a breakdown to show relative numbers of men, wives, and children.
58. The number of marriages returned was obtained by a manual count of entries in the ecclesiastical indexes.
59. Stanley, *White Mutiny*, p. 67; Brown, 'On the Rates,' pp. 566–79.

60. The women would have been at least nominally Christian to have been married under the laws underpinning the ecclesiastical returns.
61. The Indian Christian Marriage Act XV of 1872 (Rule 6) defined a British Subject as (1) A subject of Her Majesty, born, naturalized or domiciled in the United Kingdom of Great Britain and Ireland, and (2) the child or grandchild of any such person by legitimate descent. Everyone else was, by default, either foreign or native. Nothing is said in the Act about Eurasians further removed from direct British ancestry than a grandfather. Native marriages were (by Rule 7) recorded in a separate register, and certified entries were sent to district registrars but not forwarded to Britain.
62. This figure is the English-speaking total minus those classed as British. Plowden, *Census Report*, vol. 2, p. 14.
63. Plowden does not break down the Eurasian population by age, but there is other data showing that Eurasian children had a higher mortality rate than Europeans, resulting in smaller families with one rather than the two or three children characteristic of European families. From this (and from Eurasians not being transient) I divided Eurasians into approximately one-third each adult male, adult female, and children.
64. S.C. Ghosh, *The Social*.
65. Thomas Munro, 'Minute On the Eurasian Population, 24th November 1824', in Sir A.J. Arbuthnot, *Selections from Minutes and Other Official Writings of Major-General Sir Thomas Munro*, Higginbotham & Co., Madras, 1886, pp. 558–60.
66. Lushington, *The History,* Appx 13, Lord Clive's Fund, pp. liv–lvi.

Chapter 5 Law and Marriage

1. Frank Anthony, *Britain's Betrayal in India: the Story of the Anglo-Indian Community*, Allied Publishers, New Delhi, 1962, p. 11.
2. 'They might claim British fathers, but bore the stigma of illegitimacy.' Suresh Chandra Ghosh, *The Social Condition of the British Community in Bengal; 1757–1800*, Brill, Boston, MA, 1970, p. 90.
3. Anthony, *Betrayal*, p. 17.
4. Mr Tucker quoted in John Clark Marshman, *The Life and Times of Carey, Marshman and Ward*, vol. 1, Longmans & Roberts, London, 1859, p. 203.
5. A point made in Lionel Caplan, *Children of Colonialism: Anglo-Indians in a Postcolonial World*, Berg, Oxford, 2001, p. 2.
6. Centre for the History of Medicine, *The Scottish Way of Birth and Death*, at http://www.gla.ac.uk/departments/scottishwayofbirthanddeath (accessed February 2013).

7. Olive Anderson, 'Incidence of Civil Marriage in Victorian England & Wales', *Past and Present*, no. 69, 1975, pp. 50–87, http://www.jstor.org/stable/650296 (accessed February 2013).
8. Legal marriage involving Europeans in British India could occur without church or clergy but was still a Christian affair, and flexible arrangements merely a pragmatic solution to the paucity of clergymen and churches.
9. Beaumont noted that in Jamaica such arrangements had been popular with 'half-caste women but they had latterly found them demeaning'. Beaumont believed the laws and institutions of state were manipulated by powerful men to their own benefit. Augustus Beaumont, 'The Late Fatal Duel in Jamaica', *The Morning Chronicle*, London, 9 August 1833, Issue 19,954.
10. Thomas R. Metcalf, 'Imperial Towns and Cities', in P.J. Marshall, *Cambridge Illustrated History of the British Empire*, Cambridge University Press, Cambridge, 2001, p. 247.
11. Ghosh and Hawes found willing acknowledgement of illegitimate children. Fathers baptizing their illegitimate or natural children abound in ecclesiastical returns; Hawes found 54 per cent of children baptized at St John's, Calcutta between 1767 and 1782 were illegitimate Eurasians. As to abandonment, many European men provided for Indian mistresses when they returned to Europe, either financially or by ensuring that a friend took over their care. Christopher Hawes, *Poor Relations: the Making of a Eurasian Community in British India, 1773–1833*, Curzon, Richmond, 1996, pp. 4–5; Durba Ghosh, *Sex And The Family In Colonial India; The Making Of Empire*, Cambridge University Press, Cambridge, 2006, p. 110.
12. Peter Stanley, *White Mutiny: British Military Culture in India, 1825–1875*, Hurst & Co., London, 1998, p. 285; Rudyard Kipling, 'Mandalay', *Barrack–room Ballads*, Methuen & Co., London, 1892, pp. 50–3.
13. n.a., *Original Papers Relative to the Establishment of a Society in Bengal for the Protection of Orphans – 1784*, London, Joseph Cooper, n.d., pp. 29–30.
14. Ronald Hyam, *Empire and Sexuality; the British Experience*, Manchester University Press, Manchester, 1990, pp. 116–17 and 213.
15. Charles Darwin, *The Variation of Animals and Plants under Domestication*, vol. 2, 2nd edn, D. Appleton & Co., New York, 1892, p. 21.
16. Charles Raikes, *The Englishman in India*, Longmans, Green & Co., London, 1867, pp. 6–7 and 53.
17. '... some gentlemen, of a singular (and I think unnatural) taste, preferring them to white women. For my part, I consider them at best as a filthy inanimate set of creatures, having a strong smell; ... enough to disgust any man with a sound nose.' Innes Munro, *A Narrative of the Military Operations on the Coromandel Coast*, privately printed, London, 1789, pp. 49–50.
18. n.a., *Thacker's Indian Directory*, Thacker Spink and Co., Calcutta, 1895.
19. This figure is a low estimate, derived from partial data on the occupations of British-born men identified in W. Chichele Plowden, *Report on the Census of*

British India Taken on the 17th February 1881, Eyre and Spottiswoode, London, 1883, p. 470.

20. 'Act for marriages in India, 14 & 15 Victoria, Cap. 40, 24 July 1851', in Francis Lestock Beaufort, *A Digest of the Criminal Law of the Presidency of Fort William,* 2nd edn., Part II, Book III, Chapter IV Thacker & Co., Calcutta, 1859, pp. 625–36.
21. Leah Leneman, 'The Scottish Case that Led to Hardwicke's Marriage Act', *Law and History Review*, vol. 17 (1), 1999, http://journals.cambridge.org/action/displayAbstract;jsessionid=A9A5E7DCA9F9DF39AA872B24F2D61F52.journals? fromPage=online&aid=8316716 (accessed February 2013).
22. This anomaly is ironic, given that a Scottish bigamy case had led to the enactment of the new law.
23. Chris Durston, 'Unhallowed Wedlocks', *The Historical Journal*, vol. 31 (1), 1988, pp. 45–59.
24. Rev. Claudius Buchanan, *Colonial Ecclesiastical Establishment; Submitted to the Consideration of the Imperial Parliament*, 2nd edn, Cadell & Davies, London, 1813. Buchanan was also Vice-Principal of Fort William College.
25. Richard Burn and George Chetwynd, *The Justice of the Peace and Parish Officer*, vol. 2, 23rd edn, Longman Hurst, London, 1820, p. vi.
26. Although all Indians in British-Indian territory were also British subjects, in this context the term was only applied to those born or naturalized in Britain. It may, or may not, have applied also to Eurasians of British paternal descent, and to other Europeans who had sworn an oath of allegiance to the British monarchy.
27. Joseph and Thomas Chitty, *The Justice of the Peace and Parish Officer*, 28th edn, vol. 5, Lincoln's Inn, London, 1837, p. 248.
28. Emphasis in original.
29. Parliamentary Papers, 1203, East India marriages, '*Second Report of the Commissioners Appointed to Inquire Into the State and Operation of the Law of Marriage, East India Marriages*', 1850, p. v.
30. Another two decades passed before the (still inadequate) Indian Christian Marriage Act of 1872.
31. One of the participants, later accused of bigamy by a British colonial court in Newfoundland, claimed his marriage was void because he had not sought government sanction. Chitty, *The Justice*, p. 250.
32. *Ibid.*
33. *Ibid.*, p. 249.
34. Until the Hardwick Act, English courts accepted that a promise between a man and a woman to live as man and wife constituted a legal contract of marriage. New legislation was slow to alter working-class public opinion. Eve Tavor Bannet, 'The Marriage Act of 1753: "A Most Cruel Law for the Fair Sex"', *Eighteenth-Century Studies*, vol. 30 (3), 1997, pp. 233–54.

35. Theoretically the 1851 Act allowed anyone to marry, but the use of Anglican liturgy, glibly presumed to be inoffensive to all, would have been an obstacle to many in India. Beaufort, *A Digest*, pp. 625–36.
36. J.B. Gilchrist, *The General East India Guide and Vade Mecum . . . a Digest of the Work of the Late Capt. Williamson*, Kingsbury, Parbury & Allen, London, 1825, p. 208.
37. 9 Geo. IV Cap. 31, 1828 Act, in Chitty, *The Justice*, pp. 246–7.
38. *Ibid.*
39. Section 22, Polygamy and Bigamy, in Chitty, *The Justice*, 1837, pp. 246–7.
40. *Ibid.*
41. English marriage law did not apply to 'Gentoos and Musselmans' and nor would the Church have agreed with this technicality.
42. Buchanan, *Colonial*, pp. 189–90.
43. *The Times,* 2 August 1836, Issue 16,171, p. 7, col. B.
44. Hawes, *Poor*, p. 138.
45. n.a., *History of the Church Missionary Society in Bengal*, Church Missionary Society, 1846, p. 74.
46. William Carey, head of the Baptist mission at Serampore and Professor of Sanskrit at Fort William College, married in 1808 in Danish territory. Earlier, he had taken Danish nationality to prevent the British authorities deporting him. This Baptist marriage was invalid in English law.
47. IOR/N/1/10, f. 555, *John Hammerdinger*; IOR/N/1/2, f. 152 and N/1/2, f. 144verso, *Martha Isaacs*; IOR/N/1/66, f. 180, *Paul Raphael*; IOR/N/1/4, f. 85, *John Vendrick*; IOR/N/1/3, f. 9, *John Charles*; IOR/N/1/12, f. 531, *Caustaut marriage.*
48. Malcolm Speirs, *The Wasikadars of Awadh*, Rupa, New Delhi, 2008, pp. xl–xli.
49. Dr Robert Fowler, Bishop of Ossory, 'Roman Catholic Question', *Hansard (Lords Debates)*, vol. 36, 16 May 1817, p. 636.
50. James Stuart Olson and Robert Shadle, *Historical Dictionary of the British Empire*, Greenwood Publishing, Westport, CT, 1996, p. 7.
51. George IV, 'A Bill for the Relief of His Majesty's Roman Catholic Subjects,' *Hansard*, 24 March 1829.
52. With the Treaty of Tordesilles (1494), Pope Alexander VI had divided up the non-Christian world into 'East' and 'West', 370 degrees west of the Azores. The West (except Brazil and Newfoundland) was in Spainish care. Portugal was to care for the East, including India. Both were obliged to prosletyze Catholicism and were therefore entitled to appoint clergy without reference to Rome. Robert Bruce Mullin, *A Short World History of Christianity*, Westminster John Knox, Louiseville, KY, 2008, p. 150. The British government did not recognize the treaty and refused to support one side more than the other. Kenneth Ballhatchet, *Caste, Class and Catholicism in India 1789–1914*, Curzon, Surrey, 1998, pp. 2–5.

53. British Library, India Office Records: *Family History, Ecclesiastical Records*, http://www.bl.uk/reshelp/findhelpregion/asia/india/indiaofficerecordsfamilyhistory/ecclesiastical/eccrecords.html (accessed February 2013)
54. Ballhatchet, *Caste*, pp. 14–15.
55. Those I have classed as British subjects had British names and reserved occupations (such as commissioned officers) or were their children. *Chandernagore Civil marriage index*, Centre d'Archives d'Outre-Mer at Aix-en-Provence, France, http://search.fibis.org/frontis/bin/aps_browse_sources.php? mode=list_sources&source_class=169 (accessed February 2013); *IOFH*, http://indiafamily.bl.uk/UI/ (accessed February 2013).
56. *Marriage register of St Patrick's R.C. Church, St Thomas Mount* http://search.fibis.org/frontis/bin/aps_browse_sources.php?mode=browse_components&id=125&s_id=55 (accessed February 2013).
57. Ballhatchet, *Caste*, p. 20.
58. This was still the case in 1926. Earl Winterton, 'Indian and Colonial Divorce Jurisdiction Bill – 2nd reading (Lords)', House of Commons Debate, *Hansard*, 1 December 1926, vol. 200, pp. 1,212–14.
59. *Ibid.*
60. Recent research by Probert has suggested that the English conformed strongly in seeking marriage by Anglican rites. However, her research was not concerned with the mobile communities of seaports or garrison towns, did not explore regional differences, and specifically excluded Scotland and Scottish law. Rebecca Probert, *Marriage Law & Practice in the Long Eighteenth Century*, Cambridge University Press, Cambridge, 2009.
61. When the Free Church broke away from the established church in 1843, a third of all Scots became dissenters. Its ministers were considered laymen because they were not ordained by bishops. In India, they could perform irregular marriages within British lines, if authorized by a commanding officer. Such marriages 'would be good for some purposes only, but not for all, especially as relates to real estate'. Parliamentary Papers, 1203, *East India marriages*, pp. v–vi and 24.
62. The cost of an English divorce dropped after the Matrimonial Causes Bill of 1857. John D. Baird, 'Divorce and Matrimonial Causes: An Aspect of "Hard Times" ', *Victorian Studies*, vol. 20 (4), Summer 1977, pp. 401–12; Centre, *The Scottish Way*.
63. House of Lords Debates, *Hansard*, 11 March 1861, vol. 161, p. 1,690.
64. J.A. Haythornthwaite, *Scotland in the Nineteenth Century; an Analytical Bibliography of Material Relating to Scotland in Parliamentary Papers, 1800–1900*, Scholar Press, Aldershot, 1993, p. 167.
65. The commissioners posed the question: 'what is the status of mixed-marriages?', Parliamentary Papers, 1203, East India marriages, p. VII.
66. Washbrook has shown British 'rule' was more informed by local custom and practice in Madras than elsewhere. David Washbrook, 'South India 1770–

1840: The Colonial Transition', *Modern Asian Studies*, vol. 38, (3), 2004, pp. 479–516.

67. B.R. Rizvi, 'Marriage system among the Muslims of Kargil', in B.B. Goswami, J. Sarkar and D. Danda (eds), *Marriage in India: Tribes, Muslims, and Anglo-Indians*, Anthropological Survey of India, Calcutta, 1988, p. 236.
68. Ghazi-ud-din Haidar's fifth wife, Mumtaz Mahal, was a Hindu although she had been converted to Islam before her marriage: Speirs, *Wasikadars*, p. 15. Mrs Meer Hassan Ali agreed a *nikah* contract to marry her Muslim spouse, and remained Christian: Rosemary Cargill Raza, 'Meer Hassan Ali, Mrs (*fl.* 1832)', *ODNB* (accessed May 2008), and Colonel William Gardner (also a Christian) insisted that his Muslim marriage was perfectly legal: William Lineus Gardner, 5 March 1835, quoted in William Dalrymple, *Begums, Thugs & White Mughals: the Journals of Fanny Parkes*, Sickle Moon, London, 2002, p. 220.
69. Armenians were, of course, Christian, but the example would hold true of Muslim marriages too. Nicholas Shreeve, *Nawab to Nabob: The Diary of David Ochterlony Dyce Sombre*, Bookwright, West Sussex, 2001, p. 234.
70. Gardner quoted in Dalrymple, *Begums*, p. 220.
71. IOR/N/2/280, f. 288, *Waterfield marriage entry*, Madras Presidency, 29 March 1900.
72. Henry Waterfield, *Memorandum on the Census of British India 1871–72*, Eyre and Spottiswoode, London, 1875; *Thacker's Indian Directory*, 1895, pp. 207, 504, 841, 914, and 1,641.
73. Sudhir Shah, *The Hindu Marriage Act (Act 25 of 1955), An Act to Amend and Codify the Law Relating to Marriage Among Hindus*, 18 May 1955, http://www.sudhirlaw.com/Marriages.html (accessed February 2013).
74. The Arya Samaj, founded in the late 1860s, had a basic set of precepts that would not have excluded Europeans who wished to convert to Hinduism.
75. IOR/N/1/33, f. 9, *Wakefield marriage*, Barielly, 9 January 1832. *Wuzeer* is an alternate spelling of *Vizier*, a high ranking minister: see Henry Yule and A.C. Burnell, *Hobson-Jobson: The Anglo-Indian Dictionary*, Wordsworth Editions Ltd., Hartfordshire, 1996, p. 967.
76. IOR/N/1/32, f. 19, *George Wakefield baptism*, Barielly, November 1831.
77. Sir Thomas Strange, *Elements of Hindu Law: Referable to British Judicature in India*, Payne and Foss, London, 1825, p. 101.
78. IOR/N/1/39, f. 137, *Life Marriage*, Chunar, 22 October 1834.
79. IOR/N/1/38, f. 269, *Egbert Life Baptism*, Chunar, November 1834.
80. J. Markby, Chief Justice, Rangoon, appeal, *Fowle vs. Fowle Divorce Petition and Judgment*, 14 September 1878, http://indiankanoon.org/doc/1231396 (accessed February 2013).
81. Whilst Mahkin may have been a Buddhist rather than a Hindu, British law classified Buddhists, Jains, and Sikhs as members of Hindu 'sects'.
82. Markby, *Fowle vs. Fowle.*

83. According to Roychowdhury, the court found evidence of infidelity but not of adultery because Mahkin was not a European. Contrary to Bear, I did not find the woman's race to have been used against her, and, if anything, she was assessed by the same standards of behaviour to the foul Mr Fowle, as was his English wife. Laura Roychowdhury, *The Jadu House: Travels in Anglo-India*, Black Swan, London, 2001, p. 152.
84. Indrani Chatterjee, 'Colouring Subalternity: Slaves, Concubines and Social Orphans in Early Colonial India', in Gautam Bhadra, *Subaltern Studies X*, Oxford India Paperbacks, New Delhi, 1999(a), p. 76. Chatterjee's argument is not unlike that of Acton, who saw prostitution in London as akin to a white slave trade. William Acton, *Prostitution, Considered in its Moral, Social & Sanitary Aspects*, John Churchill, London, 1857.
85. Chatterjee, 'Colouring', 1999(a), pp. 49–97.
86. Chatterjee does not specify dates but, from her sources, her first century of colonial rule seems to extend into the 1870s.
87. Amanda Vickery's study of elite women in Georgian England shows that the unhappily married 'boiled with indignation' when subjected to masculine tyranny, but the husband's will was almost always his legal right. Amanda Vickery, *The Gentleman's Daughter*, Yale University Press, New Haven and London, 2003, pp. 72–81 and 285.
88. The Slavery Abolition Act of 1833 gave manumission to all slaves in the British empire.
89. W. Ogle, 'On marriage Rates and Marriage Ages with Special Reference to the Growth of Population', *Journal of the Royal Statistical Society*, vol. 53, 1890, pp. 253–89.
90. Stanley, *White Mutiny*, p. 246.
91. See J.S. Buckingham, *Select Committee on Drunkenness*, Evidence Presented to the House of Commons, Benjamin Bagster, London, 1834; Samuel Couling, *Our Labouring Classes: Their Intellectual, Moral, and Social Condition*, Partridge and Oakey, London, 1851; George Huddleston, *History of the East Indian Railway*, Thacker Spink & Co., Calcutta, 1906, p. 242; or Judith Walkowitz, *Prostitution and Victorian Society; Women, Class and the State*, Cambridge University Press, Cambridge, 1982.
92. Stanley, *White Mutiny*, p. 237.
93. Thomas Quinney, *Sketches of a Soldier's Life in India*, David Robertson, Glasgow, 1853, pp. 145 and 176.
94. Stanley, *White Mutiny*, pp. 12–13.
95. The Portuguese and the British rewarded their men on each child's baptism. The payment of a *pagoda* was sanctioned in a directors' communiqué to the President of Madras on 8 April 1687. IOR, Letter Book no. 8, pp. 290 and 493, quoted in E.L. Hedin, 'The Anglo-Indian Community', *The American Journal of Sociology*, vol. 40 (2), 1934, pp. 165–79.
96. Herbert Stark, *Hostages to India, or the Life Story of the Anglo-Indian Race*, 2nd edn, Star Printing Works, Calcutta, 1936, pp. 2 and 15; Anthony,

Betrayal, p. 12; Austin D'Souza, *Anglo-Indian education; a study of its origins and growth in Bengal up to 1960*, Oxford University Press, Delhi, 1976, pp. 9–11.

97. Kenneth Ballhatchet, *Race, Sex and Class under the Raj, Imperial Attitudes and Policies and their Critics, 1793–1905*, Weidenfeld & Nicolson, London, 1980, p. 99.
98. Chatterjee, 'Colouring', 1999(a), p. 76. In the case of officers, the handover of children was either 1) sometimes dictated by economic hardship, or 2) a condition specified in a will after the officer's death.
99. *Original Papers*, pp. 53–6.
100. n.a., *Bengal and Agra Annual Guide and Gazetteer*, Part III, 1881, p. 331.
101. The *pagoda* payment was not formally abolished until 1835 in Madras. Ballhatchet, *Race*, p. 99.
102. 'General Order of the Governor-General (GOGG), 27 January 1821, Orphan School allowance for Children, how to be drawn', *The Calcutta Annual Register*, 1821, Part III, Public Documents, Military Regulations, p. 32.
103. *Ibid.*
104. TNA, *Currency Converter*, http://www.nationalarchives.gov.uk/currency/results.asp#mid (accessed February 2013).
105. Government had paid money for children on the orphan school rolls, whether old enough to attend or not, to the secretaries of the state orphan committees. These secretaries then credited the school with the allowance for each child already in the school. Monies for children on the school rolls for future admission, but who were under three years of age and still living with their parents, was payable by the secretaries to the parents. The system was cumbersome, since regiments could be many hundreds of miles remote from presidency towns, and resulted in delays. The change instituted in GOGG, '*Orphan School Allowance*', January 1821, was to redirect the money to regimental paymasters who would be nearer to the men and their families, to speed up its distribution to the parents of younger children.
106. Barry McMillan, '24 Frames', *The Furrow*, vol. 54 (11), 2003, pp. 616–18.
107. In this, the Indian orphanages were quite different from Thomas Coram's Foundling Hospital in London. When children were taken in by that institution, careful records were kept, as were keepsakes that might aid an eventual reunion of mother and child.
108. The Special Marriages Act of 1872 demanded an oath that participants were 'neither Hindu, nor Mussalman, nor Christian'. This remained on the statute book until replaced by India's Special Marriage Act of 1954. In the Dutch East Indies (Batavia), mixed marriages involving European men (not women) were sanctioned in 1898. Ann Laura Stoler, *Carnal Knowledge and Imperial Power*, University of California Press, Berkeley, CA, 2002, p. 101.
109. Young men in Britain behaving in the same way with servant-girls and actresses prompted the Hardwick Act of 1753, to prevent young men ruining their family names with unsuitable marriages.

110. D. Ghosh, *Sex*, 2006, pp. 113–18.
111. *Ibid.*, pp. 119–21; Hawes, *Poor*, p. 8.
112. The *Wasika*, or pension, awarded to an ancestor of Speirs has passed down the generations. The paperwork generated by administering this has allowed him to trace his ancestry, the subject of his book: Speirs, *Wasikadars*, 2008.
113. Rosie Llewellyn-Jones, 'A Fatal Friendship; the Nawabs, the British and the City of Lucknow', *The Lucknow Omnibus*, Oxford University Press, New Delhi, 2001, pp. 27–9.

Chapter 6 Employability

1. The National Portrait Gallery, London holds portraits of Edwardes in native dress by both Alfred Crowquill and Henry Moseley.
2. William Hodson and George Hodson (eds), *Twelve Years of a Soldier's Life in India*, John W. Parker & Son, London, 1859, pp. 41–2.
3. They were father and son, although this is not acknowledged in Hugh W. Pearse, *The Hearseys; Five Generations of an Anglo-Indian Family*, William Blackwood & Sons, London, 1905, pp. 38–48.
4. George Fletcher MacMunn, *The Martial Races of India,* Sampson, Low, Marston & Co., London, n.d., p. 269.
5. Chandra Mallampalli, 'Cosmopolitanism in the Hinterland? Bellary District Through Fresh Lenses, 1800–1840', *Indian Economic Social History Review*, vol. 46 (2), 2009, pp. 183–210.
6. Charles Grey and Herbert L.O. Garrett (eds), *European Adventures of Northern India, 1785–1849*, Superintendent of Government Printing, Punjab, 1929, (reprint AES, New Delhi, 1993), p. 12.
7. Ram Babu Saksena, *European & Indo-European Poets of Urdu and Persian*, Newul Kishore Press, Lucknow, 1941.
8. *Ibid.*, p. 30.
9. Skinner's volume of military memoirs *Tazkirat al-umara* was subsequently used as a source for the 2-volume biographical work by James Baillie Fraser, *Military Memoir of Lieut.-Col. James Skinner*, vol. 2, Smith Elder & Co., London, 1851.
10. Saksena, *European*, pp. 95–6.
11. Fanny Eden described him as very black but better society than any of the white colonels she met at Delhi, he was an intimate friend of James Baillie Fraser and his brother, a firm favourite of the British Commander-in-Chief Lord Lake, and the loyalty of his troops was legendary. Janet Dunbar (ed.), *Tigers, Durbars and Kings: Fanny Eden's Indian Journals 1837–38*, John Murray, London, 1988, p. 135. Fraser, *Military Memoir*, vol. 1, Introduction and vol. 2, pp. 99–102. A hookah is a tobacco pipe in which smoke is drawn through water.

12. Hawes points to the financial success Skinner enjoyed, helped by his status as a native, and implied that his complaints were unfounded. Christopher Hawes, *Poor Relations: the Making of a Eurasian Community in British India, 1773–1833*, Curzon, Richmond, 1996, pp. 99–101.
13. Saksena, *European*, p. 103.
14. *Extract from the Register of Marriages*, Church of St Stephen, Ootacamund, 19 April 1876.
15. Saksena, *European*, p. 84.
16. 'Colonial conditions ... put Indian Civilization itself on trial as the principal impediment to modernity and self-rule.' Nicholas Dirks, *Castes of Mind,* Princeton University Press, Princeton, NJ, 2001, p. 255.
17. Malcolm Speirs, *The Wasikadars of Awadh,* Rupa, New Delhi, 2008, pp. 180–2.
18. William R. Cornish, *A Code of the Medical and Sanitary Regulations for the Guidance of Medical Officers Serving in the Madras Presidency*, vol. 1, Government Press, Madras, 1870, p. 78.
19. Exceptions to this were made for Jews and Parsis, who could be treated, for education and employment purposes, as Eurasians.
20. n.a., 'Anthropology and Eurasians', *The Anglo-Indian Journal*, vol. 1 (13), 1898, pp. 3–4.
21. IOR/V/25/900/8, Edgar Thurston, 'Eurasians of Madras and Malabar', *Madras Government Museum Bulletin: Anthropology*, vol. 2 (2), 1898, p. 76.
22. Viscount Jocelyn, 'Return of Europeans in Military or Civil Employment of the Native States of India', *House of Commons Papers*, Accounts and Papers, vol. XLVIII.313 (69), 7 February 1848.
23. Herbert Alick Stark and Walter Madge, *East-Indian Worthies*, n.p., Calcutta, 1892, p. 50.
24. Government sanction to employ a European or Eurasian in any significant post could only be granted by the governor-general. Minor posts could be sanctioned by provincial governors. NAI, Baghelkhand Agency/Political/ English Files, Procceedings no. 23, I, *Annual return of Europeans and Eurasians Employed in Native States*, 1882.
25. NAI, Foreign/Political/Notes, Procceedings no. 29, 'British Resident, Hyderabad, to Foreign Secretary', *Employment of Europeans and East Indians by Native States*, October 1883.
26. NAI, 'Foreign Secy. to Offg. British Resident, Hyderabad', *ibid.*, 29 August 1872.
27. The Act was to apply to 'all British Subjects', which terminology was open to interpretation in the case of Eurasians. Cap. 17 of Act 1, Victoria 28, *The Vagrancy Act*, 1849.
28. See NAI, Central India Agency/English files, no. 355, *Measures to be Concerted With Native States for Removal of Vagrant Europeans*, 6 May 1867.
29. Stark and Madge, *Worthies*, pp. 49–54.
30. Fraser, *Military Memoir*, vol. 1, pp. 106–8.

31. The Parental Academical in Calcutta, founded by Eurasian leader John Ricketts in 1823 and renamed several times, moved to Darjeeling in 1864. It was renamed Doveton's College in 1855, and Doveton's Protestant College was set up at Madras when John Doveton, a Eurasian officer serving Hyderabad, left it a huge legacy. La Martinière schools were founded by the legacy of Frenchman Claude Martin, who had served Awadh and the EIC. La Martinière, Calcutta opened in 1836 and that in Lucknow in 1845. For a detailed history, see Austin D'Souza, *Anglo-Indian education; a study of its origins and growth in Bengal up to 1960*, Oxford University Press, Delhi, 1976.
32. n.a., *Original Papers Relative to the Establishment of a Society in Bengal for the Protection of Orphans – 1784*, London, Joseph Cooper, n.d., 1784.
33. Widely advertised both in Indian and metropolitan newspapers, orphan funds attracted donations from the British, wealthy Indians, and Christian congregations. Fathers received an allowance from the fund on the understanding that they gave up both child and cash by the time the child reached 3–5 years of age. J.B. Gilchrist, *The General East India Guide and Vade Mecum ... a Digest of the Work of the Late Capt. Williamson*, Kingsbury, Parbury & Allen, London, 1825, pp. 208–9.
34. *Original Papers,* pp. 29–30.
35. *Ibid.* The Madras Orphan Asylum grew from the much older support offered by the congregations and communities of Madras. Government help began in about 1787, including property at Egmore granted in 1789: Frank Penny, *The Church in Madras*, vol. 2, Smith Elder & Co., London, 1904, p. 524–6; the Bombay Education Society began in 1815, but the schools did not open until 1826: n.a., 'Bombay Education Society', *The Asiatic Journal & Monthly Miscellany*, vol. 28 (September) 1829, p. 353.
36. The disabled were cared for by the Friend in Need Society at Madras, and babies 'at nurse' at Poonamallee: IOR/F/4/1558/63799, *Military Male Orphan Asylum*, July 1835, pp. 36–7.
37. The families of covenanted civil servants were also well provided for: 'by marrying a member of the Civil Service, she secured a husband with at least £300 a year, and at his death, would be entitled to a pension from the Civil Fund to the same amount'. W.H. Carey, *The Good Old Days of Honorable John Company*, (first published 1882), abridged edition, Quins Book Co., Calcutta, 1964, p. 83.
38. IOR/L/AG/23/7/7, *Alphabetical List of Orphaned Children of Officers of the Bengal Army*, 1820–57.
39. 'Bengal Army Medical List', *New Calcutta Directory*, Military Orphan Press, Calcutta, 1862.
40. Once the official embargo on their employment was removed, social mores maintained the difficulties for Eurasian sons of officers, who, if they wished to remain in India, had to accept subordinate posts or find non-government work.

41. Durba Ghosh, 'Making and Un-making Loyal Subjects: Pensioning Widows and Educating Orphans in Early Colonial India', *Journal of Imperial and Commonwealth History*, vol. 31 (1), 2003, pp. 1–28.
42. The boys were to be 'disposed of, either by settling them as Clerks, or binding them apprentice to Captains of Ships, Tradesmen, Handicrafts, &c.', *Original Papers*, p. 53.
43. *Ibid.*, p. 53.
44. D. Ghosh, *Making*, 2003.
45. A. Ganesan, *The Press in Tamil Nadu and the Struggle for Freedom, 1917–1937*, Mittal Publications, Delhi, 1988, p. 4.
46. Long-term care of the disabled had been anticipated from the start, and was in operation (at Madras) in the 1830s. *Original Papers*, p. 53; IOR/F/4/1558/63799, *Military Male*, pp. 36–7.
47. IOR/F/4/1558/63799, *Military Male*, pp. 36–7.
48. D. Ghosh, *Making*, pp. 1–28.
49. n.a., 'Catholicity in India', *The Rambler*, vol. 8 (XLVIII), December 1857, pp. 385–99.
50. William Walker (from *The Times of India*, 25 Novenber 1861), reprinted in William Walker, *Tom Cringle's Letters on Practical Subjects, Suggested by Experiences in Bombay*, Education Society's Press, Byculla, 1863, pp. 111–13.
51. *Ibid.*
52. Henry Cornish, *Under the Southern Cross*, Penguin, Harmondsworth, 1978 (First Imprint, Madras, 1879), pp. 263–70.
53. Europeans who had served in government employment long enough to draw a pension were thought suitable because they were already in India and they were unlikely to become a burden on the state.
54. House of Commons, *Fourth Report from the Select Committee on Colonisation and Settlement (India)*, no. 3, vol. 7, pt. 2, 1858.
55. IOR/R/2/Box 1/15, File 151, *Settlements of Anglo-Indians and Eurasians near Bangalore*, 1883; IOR/R/2/Box 2/21, File 558, *Settlement of EAIA at Whitefield, Sausmond and Duckworth*, 1885; Kuntala Lahiri-Dutt, *In Search of a Homeland: Anglo-Indians and McCluskiegunge*, Minerva, Calcutta, 1990.
56. Mrs John D. Miles, 'A New Out-let for an Anglo-Indian Colony', *The Anglo-Indian Journal*, vol. 1 (13), October 1898, p. 4.
57. See Stark and Madge, *Worthies*, pp. 49–54; J.W. Ricketts, *Report of Proceedings Connected With the East Indians' Petition to Parliament Read at a Public Meeting Held at Calcutta Town Hall, March 28 1831*, Baptist Mission Press, Calcutta, 1831; Hansard, 'Petition of Indo-Britons to House of Commons', *Hansard's Parliamentary Debates*, vol. XXIV, 4 May 1830, pp. 377–87.
58. These were: Colonel Sir Robert Stevenson, Quartermaster-General of the Bengal Army; Major Hearsey of the Bengal Cavalry; Mr James Achmuty of the Civil Service; and Major Deare, Captain Rutledge and Lieutenant Mullins, all of the Royal Army. Stark and Madge, *Worthies*, p. 51; Hawes, *Poor*, pp. 158 and 169.

59. Traders and mariners in the Calcutta–China trade, Baretto's House, Lackersteens, Brightmans, Bruce, Vrignon, and Allens, besides the Kyd Brothers' dockyard: Stark and Madge, *Worthies*, p. 52. Eurasian-owned businesses would later suffer in competition with increased commerce and trade by Europeans with stronger connections to London, and who were members of racially exclusive Chambers of Commerce. See R.K. Renford, *The Non-official British in India to 1920*, Oxford University Press, Delhi, 1987.
60. Hawes, *Poor*, p. 36.
61. 'Camp, near Peshawur, August 6th, 1853', reprinted in Hodson, *Twelve Years*, p. 136.
62. W. Forbes-Mitchell, *The Gospel of Regeneration of the Anglo-Indian and Eurasian Poor*, Thacker, Spink and Company, Calcutta, 1900, p. 100.
63. Henry Sharp (ed.), *Selections from Educational Records*, Part 1, 1781–1839, Superintendent of Government Printing, Calcutta, 1920 (Reprint: NAI, Delhi, 1965, pp. 107–17).
64. Coralie Younger, *Anglo-Indians: Neglected Children of the Raj*, B.R. Publishing Corp., Delhi, 1987, p. 163.
65. H.H. Risley and E.A. Gait, *Report On The Census Of India, 1901*, Government Printing Press, Calcutta, 1903, p. 219.
66. IOR/V/25/900/8, Thurston, Eurasians, pp. 74–5.
67. *Ibid.*, p. 98.
68. *Ibid.*, pp. 74–5.
69. Stark's short history schoolbook is an example of the way respect for the Raj was taught in English-medium schools. Fisher reiterated this point and its effects on the aspirations of many Indians early in the nineteenth century. Herbert Stark, *India under Company and Crown: Being an Account of its Progress and Present Administration*, Macmillan & Co., Calcutta, 1914; Michael H. Fisher, *Counterflows to Colonialism: Indian Travellers and Settlers in Britain 1600–1857*, Permanent Black, Delhi, 2004, p. 338.
70. Adapted from Dorris Goodrich, *The Making of an Ethnic Group: The Eurasian Community in India*, PhD thesis, University of California, Berkeley, CA, 1952, p. 267.
71. 'Public force' would have included police, militia, and the army.
72. Transport was the huge growth sector for men, as teaching (under liberal arts) was for women.
73. Lionel Caplan, 'Colonial & Post Colonial Hybridities: Eurasians in India', *IIAS Newsletter*, no. 30, March 2003, pp. 16–7, http://iias.nl/iiasn/30/IIASNL30_16.pdf (accessed February 2013).
74. Risley and Gait, *Census Report*, pp. 168, 181, and 219.
75. Earl Winterton, *'House of Commons Debate, 21 December 1925', Hansard*, vol. 189, 1925–6; Sujit Mukherjee, *Forster and Further: the Tradition of Anglo-Indian Fiction*, Orient Longman Ltd, Bombay, 1993, p. 169.
76. Mr Bradlaugh, MP for Northampton, *'House of Commons Debate, 9 September 1887', Hansard*, vol. 321, 66.

77. Ibid.
78. Frank Anthony, *Britain's Betrayal in India: the Story of the Anglo-Indian Community*, Allied Publishers, New Delhi, 1962, p. 3.
79. Forbes-Mitchell, *Gospel*, p. 100.
80. Younger, *Anglo-Indians*, Appx.
81. Earl Winterton, *Hansard*, vol. 189, 1925–6.
82. Caplan, 'Colonial', p. 16, col. 3.
83. David Arnold, 'European Orphans and Vagrants in India in the Nineteenth Century', *Journal of Imperial & Commonwealth History*, vol. 7 (2), January 1979.
84. Risley and Gait, *Census Report*, p. 219.
85. Editorial, 'Anthropology & Eurasians, & Relief fund', *The Anglo-Indian Journal*, vol. IV (3), 1901, p. 6.
86. Younger, *Anglo-Indians*, pp. 163–4.
87. The Act was to apply to 'all British Subjects', which terminology was open to interpretation in the case of Eurasians; *The Vagrancy Act*, 1849.
88. Fraser, *Military Memoir*, vol. 1, pp. 106–7.
89. Anjana Singh, *Fort Cochin in Kerela, 1750–1830: the Social Condition of a Dutch Community in an Indian Milieu*, Brill, Leiden, 2010, p. 20.
90. Anjengo, in the *Imperial Gazetteer of India*, Oxford, Clarendon Press, vol. 5, 1908–31, p. 384 and vol. 24, p. 314.
91. IOR/F/4/1174/30663, *Continuation of Certain Charitable Payments to Indigent British at Anjengo*, 1827–9, pp. 6–7.
92. A.S. Nair and C. Logan, 'Colin Paterson and his Medical Report of Travancore (1842)', *Journal of Kerela Studies*, vol. XXXIII, 2006, pp. 82–113.
93. The payments were questioned again in 1830, but were still in place in 1842. IOR/F/4/1174/30663, *Continuation*; IOR/F/4/1351/53620, *How it Happens That Sixty Destitute British Subjects are to be Found at Anjengo*, 1830–1.
94. IOR/F/4/1174/30663, *Continuation*, pp. 6–7.
95. Patterson reported endemic and chronic leprous and venereal ulcers around Travancore. He blamed the prevalence of virulent syphilis and gonorrhoea on the Rajah of Travancore's *sepoys*, though they were not deployed at Anjengo. Nair and Logan, '*Colin Paterson*', pp. 82–113.
96. Singh, *Fort Cochin.*
97. IOR/V/25/900/8, Thurston, *Eurasians*; n.a., 'Anthropology & Eurasians', *The Anglo-Indian Journal*, vol. 1 (13), 1898, p. 3.
98. n.a., 'Anthropology & Eurasians', *The Anglo-Indian Journal*, vol. 1 (13), 1898, pp. 1–2.
99. Jervoise Athelstane Baines, *General Report on the Census of India, 1891*, HMSO, London, 1893, pp. 241–2.
100. IOR/F/4/1311/52160, '*Bengal Medical Board Suggestion that Experimental Sanatorium at Cherrapunji be Used Only by Eurasian and Native Insane not Europeans,* Report of Asst Surgeon Wm Rhodes, 1830–2, pp. 7–18.
101. Waltraud Ernst and Detlef Kantowski, 'Mad Tales from the Raj', *Society*, vol. 22 (3), 1985, pp. 31–8.

102. See David O. Dyce Sombre, *Refutation of the Charge of Lunacy*, n.p., Paris, 1849.
103. Edmund Burke (ed.), 'Commission of Lunacy to Inquire into the State of Mind of Mrs Jane Cheetham', *Annual Register*, vol. 85, July 1844, p. 11.
104. Peter McCandless, 'Dangerous to Themselves and Others: The Victorian Debate over the Prevention of Wrongful Confinement', *The Journal of British Studies*, vol. 23 (1), 1983, pp. 84–104.
105. Gilchrist, *Vade Mecum*, p. 208.
106. A Traveller (anon.), *The English in India and Other Sketches*, Longman, Rees, Orme & Co., London, 1835, p. 196.
107. An interesting comparison may be drawn with a study of African-Americans, who are more likely to have mental illness than white Americans but, when corrected for socioeconomic status, the apparent racial difference disappears. George J. Warheit, Charles E. Holzer III, and Sandra A. Arey, 'Race and Mental Illness: An Epidemiologic Update', *Journal of Health and Social Behavior*, vol. 16 (3), 1975, pp. 243–56; Porter also addresses issues of power, othering, and helplessness in relation to the Victorians' understanding of madness: Roy Porter, *A Social History of Madness: Stories of the Insane*, Phoenix, London, 1996.
108. P.H. Stevenage, *A Railway Family in India*, BACSA, London, 2001, p. 5.

Chapter 7 Women's Work

1. A Lady (Mrs Julia C. Maitland), *Letters from Madras, During the Years 1836–1839*, John Murray, London, 1846, pp. 131–2.
2. J.B. Gilchrist, *The General East India Guide and Vade Mecum ... a Digest of the Work of the Late Capt. Williamson*, Kingsbury, Parbury & Allen, London, 1825, pp. 207–9.
3. See George Viscount Valentia, *Voyages and Travels to India and Ceylon: 1802–6*, vol. 1, Rivington, London, 1811, pp. 197–8.
4. n.a., 'Confessions of a Eurasian', *The Asiatic Journal and Monthly Register*, vol. 10 (new series), January 1833, pp. 144–52.
5. J.H. Stocqueler, 'A Tale of East India Life', *Ainsworth's Magazine*, vol. 3, 1845, pp. 328–36.
6. Ethel Winifred Savi, *Rulers of Men*, G.P. Putnam's Sons, London, 1922.
7. Maud Diver, *Lilamani*, Hutchinson & Co., London, 1911.
8. For an overview of intermarriage in Anglo-Indian fiction, see Bhupal Singh, *A Survey of Anglo-Indian Fiction*, Curzon, London, 1934 (1975 reprint), pp. 165–94.
9. *The Gazette*, 1 November 1810, quoted in W.H. Carey, *The Good Old Days of Honorable John Company*, (first published 1882), abridged edition, Quins Book Co., Calcutta, 1964, pp. 84–5.

10. Emma Roberts, *Scenes Characteristic of Hindostan with Sketches of Anglo-Indian Society*, vol. 1, Wm. H. Allen & Co, London, 1837, pp. 42–3.
11. Henry L.V. Derozio, 'The Deserted Girl', *The Fakeer of Jungheera, A Metrical Tale; And Other Poems*, Samuel Smith & Co., Calcutta, 1828, pp. 165–72.
12. Charles Allen, *Plain Tales from the Raj*, Abacus, London, 1975, pp. 191–2.
13. This was based only on the three districts with the largest Eurasian populations: Madras City, Malabar, and Chingleput. H.H. Risley and E.A. Gait, *Report On The Census Of India, 1901*, Government Printing Press, Calcutta, 1903, p. 219
14. *Ibid.*
15. There do not appear to have been comparable analyses elsewhere in India, so this total is calculated using the distribution 5:4:3 for Bengal: Madras: Bombay. William Walker (from *The Times of India*, 25 November 1861), reprinted in William Walker, *Tom Cringle's Letters on Practical Subjects, Suggested by Experiences in Bombay*, Education Society's Press, Byculla, 1863, pp. 111–13.
16. Mr Allen, 'Wanted in a small genteel family', *The Morning Post*, London, 27 June 1805, Issue 11,503, p. 1; n.a., 'Wanted by a respectable young person', *The Morning Post*, London, 15 February 1822, Issue 15,888, p. 1.
17. Roberts, *Scenes*, vol. 1, p. 43.
18. English women in India stereotyped Indian women as devoted to family and as sensuous mistresses in need of help from colonial civilizers. Indrani Sen, 'Devoted Wife/Sensuous Bibi; Colonial Constructions of the Indian Woman, 1860–1900', *Indian Journal of Gender Studies*, vol. 8, 2001, pp. 1–22.
19. A Traveller (anon.), *The English in India and Other Sketches*, Longman, Rees, Orme & Co., London, 1835, p. 197.
20. For examples, see 'An Indo-British Nurse', *The Times*, 13 November 1877, Issue 29,098, p. 3, col. B; and 'An Eurasian Nurse', *The Times*, 22 September 1882, Issue 30,619, p. 11, col. A.
21. Thomas Edwards, *Henry Derozio, the Eurasian Poet, Teacher and Journalist*, W. Newman & Co., Calcutta, 1884, p. 179.
22. Austin D'Souza, *Anglo-Indian education; a study of its origins and growth in Bengal up to 1960*, Oxford University Press, Delhi, 1976, p. 111.
23. Bell's system encouraged responsibility in older pupils, but mainly provided cheap teachers. It was widely adopted in India in native and European/Eurasian schools throughout the century. See Joseph Fox, *A Comparative View of the Plans of Education of Dr Bell and Mr Lancaster*, privately published, London, 1809.
24. IOR/V/24/842, *Public Instruction in Madras Presidency*, 1889, p. 102.
25. For a consideration of the role of European women in colonial India, see Alison Blunt, *Domicile and Diaspora: Anglo-Indian Women and the Spatial Politics of Home*, Blackwell, Oxford, 2005; and Alison Blunt, 'Imperial Geographies of Home: British Domesticity in India, 1886–1925', *Transactions of the Institute of British Geographers*, (New Series), vol. 24, (4), 1999, pp. 421–40. Blunt argues that the political significance of imperial domesticity extended beyond home, a point echoed by Denise P. Quirk, ' "True Englishwomen" and "Anglo-Indians": Gender, National Identity, and Feminism in the Victorian Women's Periodical

Press', in J.F. Codell (ed.), *Imperial Co-histories: National Identities and the British Colonial Press*, Rosemont Publishing, Cranbury, NJ, 2003, pp. 167–87.

26. IOR/V/24/839, *Public Instruction in Madras Presidency*, 1882, p. 189.
27. IOR/V/24/840, *Public Instruction in Madras Presidency*, 1884, p. 93.
28. Quoted in Alice Thorner and Maithreyi Krishnaraj (eds), *Ideals, Images, and Real Lives: Women in Literature and History*, Orient Longman Ltd, Mumbai, 2000, pp. 85–6.
29. D'Souza, *Anglo-Indian*, p. 128.
30. Caroline Louise Weaver, *Colonialism and Culture in British India, 1854–1891*, PhD Thesis, Birkbeck College, University of London, 1997, p. 198.
31. D'Souza, *Anglo-Indian*, pp. 134–5 and 111.
32. *Ibid.*, p. 109.
33. Frank Anthony, *Britain's Betrayal in India: the Story of the Anglo-Indian Community*, Allied Publishers, New Delhi, 1962, p. 408.
34. Risley and Gait, *Census Report*, p. 219.
35. S. Gore-Browne, *Alphabetical list of Europeans and East Indians in the Company's Service on 30th June 1880*, East India Railway Company Press, Calcutta, 1880.
36. O.P. Jaggi, *Western Medicine in India: Medical Education & Research*, Alma Ram, Delhi, 1979, p. 132.
37. *Ibid.*, pp. 128–9.
38. H01/ST/NC/018/011/064, London Metropolitan Archives, 'Papers of Henry Bonham Carter', *Saint Thomas' Hospital: Nightingale Collection*, 21 July 1873.
39. Jaggi, *Western*, p. 93.
40. H01/ST/NC/018/011/064, *'Henry Bonham Carter'*.
41. Jaggi, *Western*, pp. 130–1.
42. *Ibid.*, p. 135.
43. *Ibid.*, pp. 134–5.
44. *Ibid.*, p. 137.
45. Anthony, *Betrayal*, pp. x–xi.
46. n.a., 'List of Qualified Midwives, European and East Indian from the Government Lying-in-Hospital, Madras', *The Asylum Press Almanac for 1865*, Lawrence Asylum, Ootacamund, 1865, pp. 489–90.
47. n.a., 'List of Midwives residing at Madras who have received Certificates of Qualification at the Government Lying-in-Hospital', *Asylum Press Almanac 1879*, Lawrence Asylum Press, Ootacamund, 1879, pp. 553–6.
48. Clara E. Collet, 'Utilization of Official Statistics on the Extent and Effects of the Industrial Employment of Women', *Journal of the Royal Statistical Society*, vol. 61 (2), 1898, pp. 219–70.
49. W. Chichele Plowden, *Report on the Census of British India Taken on the 17th February 1881*, Eyre and Spottiswoode, London, 1883, Abstract XIA, p. 33.
50. NAI, Baghelkhand Agency/Political/English Files, Proceedings no. 23, I, *Annual return of Europeans and Eurasians Employed in Native States*, 1889.
51. Quoted in 'Spectator', *The Anglo-Indian Journal*, vol. 1 (3), 1897, p. 4.
52. *Ibid.*

53. Jaggi, *Western*, pp. 93–6 and 101–2.
54. *Ibid.*
55. NAI, Foreign/Internal/Part B/Proceedings, nos 383–4, *Designation of Assistant Surgeon and Eurasian Nurses altered to Lady Doctor and Charge Nurses*, February 1903.
56. Table adapted from *ibid.*
57. Shweta Sachdeva Jha, 'Eurasian Women as Tawa'if Singers and Recording Artists: Entertainment and Identity-making in Colonial India', *African and Asian Studies*, 8, 2009, pp. 268–87; Ram Babu Saksena, *European & Indo-European Poets of Urdu and Persian*, Newul Kishore Press, Lucknow, 1941, pp. 297–8.
58. Sachdeva Jha, *Eurasian Tawa'if*; Saksena, *European*, pp. 297–8.
59. Anon., *The Poetical Works of Henry Louis Vivian Derozio: With a Memoir of the Author*, W. Newman, Calcutta, 1871, p. 14.
60. Kenneth Ballhatchet, *Race, Sex and Class under the Raj, Imperial Attitudes and Policies and their Critics, 1793–1905*, Weidenfeld & Nicolson, London, 1980, p. 133.
61. n.a., *Original Papers Relative to the Establishment of a Society in Bengal for the Protection of Orphans - 1784*, Joseph Cooper, London, n.d., p. 33.
62. For examples, see *The English Woman's Domestic Magazine*, 124, June 1874, pp. 291 and 294; Quirk, in Codell, *Imperial*, p. 177; her 'performance' was also subject to criticism, see *The Queen, the Lady's Newspaper,* London, 7 July 1877, p. 6, col. 3.
63. British women in London did marry Indian men. See Rozina Vizram, *Ayahs, Lascars and Princes: Indians in Britain 1700–1947*, Pluto, London, 1986, pp. 59–63. Real and fictional miscegenation involving white women was a recurring theme. See Nancy L. Paxton, *Writing under the Raj: Gender, Race, and Rape in the British Colonial Imagination, 1830–1947*, Rutgers University Press, New Brunswick, NJ, 1999.
64. IOR/Z/O/19, *Miscellaneous Bonds*, no. 3,338, 1822.
65. *Original Papers*, 1784, pp. 1–4.
66. Anthony, *Betrayal*, pp. 112–13.
67. George Cotton, *Memoir of George Edward Lynch Cotton, Bishop of Calcutta*, Longmans, Green & Co., London, 1872, pp. 168 and 170.

Chapter 8 Eurasians and the Military

1. Joseph Whittaker, *An Almanack for the Year of Our Lord 1897*, Warwick Lane, London, 1897, pp. 455 and 462.
2. The Imperial Service troops included 51 squadrons of cavalry and 84 companies of infantry, together with transport corps of 1,600 carts and 1,200 camels. Contingents (such as the Hyderabad Contingent) were units raised,

trained, and officered by the British but paid for by the princely states in which they were deployed. They were often not native to the states in which they served. George Fletcher MacMunn, *The Armies of India*, A&C Black, London, 1911, pp. 191–207.

3. *Ibid.*
4. Discretion was a prerequisite in smaller states with binding treaties, so there is no way to estimate the number of Eurasians still enlisting in many armies. I make the assertion that they continued to do so for three reasons. Firstly, any Eurasian with military ambitions had no other outlet. Secondly, census reports consistently complained that Eurasian numbers could not be established because they reported themselves as European; it may not have occurred to British administrators but it would have been just as easy to report themselves as natives, especially if born in an independent state. Thirdly, communications between the British administration and the most powerful *durbars* who dared to question them show that Eurasians were still serving as late as the 1880s.
5. This is evident in the reorganization of the Nizam of Hyderabad's armies in 1806. IOR/F/4/215/4746, *List of European and Eurasian Mercenaries Serving with the Nizam's Army...*, vol. 2, 1806–7.
6. Charles Grey and Herbert L.O. Garrett (eds), *European Adventures of Northern India, 1785–1849*, of Government Printing, Punjab, 1929 (reprint AES, New Delhi, 1993), p. 212.
7. R. Kumar (ed.), *Military System of East India Company*, Ajay Verma for Commonwealth Publishers, New Delhi, 2004, pp. 164 and 185.
8. There were, for example, many European and Eurasian rank and file serving the *Nizam*. IOR/F/4/215/4746, *List*, 1806–7.
9. This source also noted that the meaning of the term 'East Indian' was open to different interpretations. NAI, Foreign/Political/Notes, Procceedings no. 29, 'British Resident, Hyderabad, to Foreign Secretary', *Employment of Europeans and East Indians by Native States*, 1885.
10. Agent to Governor-General, Sir L. Griffin, Letter no. 91–217a, 1 July 1882; *A Response to Foreign Department No. 894 G.G.*, dated 27 May 1882.
11. Rosie Llewellyn-Jones, 'The "Other" Victims of 1857', *Mutiny at the Margins*, Conference, Edinburgh, 2007, www.csas.ed.ac.uk/mutiny/confpapers/Llewellyn-Paper.pdf (accessed February 2013). The Rottons were probably descended from Mr W. Rotton, who had been in Marhatta service until 1803 when he was pensioned off by the British. NAI, Foreign/Political/Consultations, no. 91, 2 May 1805; no. 67, 1 January 1807; and no. 77, 22 January 1807, *Re Mr W. Rotton, Lucknow.*
12. Grey and Garrett, *European*, pp. 1–11.
13. Nicholas Shreeve, *The Indian Heir: David Ochterlony Dyce Sombre*, Bookwright, West Sussex, 1999, p. 4.
14. Grey and Garrett, *European*, pp. 75–8.
15. *Ibid.*, p. 11.

16. See section on Eurasian agency in Chapter 6.
17. Grey and Garrett, *European*, p. 12.
18. NAI, Foreign/Political/Notes/Proceedings no. 29, *Employment*, 1885.
19. *Ibid.*, 1884.
20. NAI, Bundelkhand Agency/English Files/Part 1/No. 8, 'Rubakar from the Samthar Durbar, Political Agent's translation', *Return of Europeans and East Indians in the service of Native States*, 24 June 1882.
21. *Ibid.*, pp. 66–71.
22. William Sheppey Greene, *A Code of the Pay Regulations of Various Military Establishments under the Presidency of Fort William*, Military Orphan Press, Kidderpore, 1810, p. 210.
23. Few of the rank and file would have been able to bring a European wife with them and there were few working-class European women in India, so most of their children were Eurasian.
24. Durba Ghosh, 'Making and Un-making Loyal Subjects: Pensioning Widows and Educating Orphans in Early Colonial India', *Journal of Imperial and Commonwealth History*, vol. 31 (1), 2003, pp. 1–28; Charles Lushington, *The History, Design and Present State of the Religious Benevolent and Charitable Institutions ... in Calcutta*, Hindustanee Press, Calcutta, 1824, p. xlvii.
25. The demographic ratio of Bengal 5: Madras 4: Bombay 3 has been applied to calculate the total number.
26. 1824 and 1911 figures are calculated for the number of infantry battalions, allowing a total of 800 men per unit.
27. Muster Roll of Scots Brigade, 1804, FIBIS, http://search.fibis.org/frontis/bin/aps_browse_sources.php?mode=browse_components&id=418&s_id=178 (transcription, accessed February 2013).
28. Charles Dickens (ed.), 'Easter Monday at Portsmouth', *All the Year Round*, vol. 19 (472), 1868, pp. 520–4.
29. Llewellyn-Jones, 'Other'.
30. European boys from military orphanages would not have been placed in native regiments but would have made up numbers in European ones. Alternatively, they may have been disproportionately represented amongst the boys who were apprenticed or returned to their parents. In 1863, there were 62,000 British troops in India with a complement of up to 1,860 bandsmen – European, Eurasian, and even African.
31. Scinde is now known as Sindh.
32. IOR/L/Mil/5/69, *Scinde Medal roll*, 1843; IOR/L/Mil/5/77, *Mutiny Medal Roll*, 1857; Steve Kettle, Scan of *Discharge Certificate, Charles Thompson*, dated 26 June 1865, http://www.britishmedals.us/collections/TB/heic/thompson.html (accessed February 2013).
33. IOR/Mss/Eur/F133/176, *Humble Petition of Master Sergeant Whiley*, 47th Regiment Bengal Native Infantry, 1857.

34. See http://www.bl.uk/reshelp/findhelpregion/asia/india/indiaofficerecords familyhistory/glossary /glossaryb/glossaryb.html.
35. Llewellyn-Jones, 'Other', p. 2.
36. See this chapter, previous section.
37. IOR/F/4/1601/64653, *Europeans and Eurasians in the service of the Nawab of Bandar*, 1834, pp. 12–17.
38. NAI, Bundelkhand Agency/English Files/Part 1/No. 8, *To Agent to the Governor-General for Central India from Political Agent, Bundelkhand*, no. 255, 11 July 1882.
39. J.B. Gilchrist, *The General East India Guide and Vade Mecum . . . a Digest of the Work of the Late Capt. Williamson*, Kingsbury, Parbury & Allen, London, 1825, p. 184.
40. The Worshipful Company of Farriers has been one of the City of London's livery companies for over 400 years.
41. Thomas R. Metcalf, *Forging the Raj: Essays on British India in the Heyday of Empire*, Oxford University Press, New Delhi, 2005, p. 45.
42. IOR/F/4/1544/61371, *Proposed Abolition of the Appointment of Sergeant Majors to Native Regiments of the Madras Army*, May 1829–October 1835.
43. *Ibid.*, 'Extracts from Military Letter from Fort St George', 3 July 1835 (no. 37).
44. 'Birth Announcements', *Madras, Mergler*, 13 July 1843, *East India Register*, 1844.
45. The Eurasian regiment formed during 1857 still existed in 1860, but was later disbanded. Lord Canning's Despatch relating to the Organization of European Forces in India, *Return to an Address of the Honourable The House of Commons*, 29 June 1860, http://www.csas.ed.ac.uk/mutiny/confpapers/PostMutinyDispositi onof EuropeanTroopsinIndia.pdf (accessed June 2010).
46. 'From the London Gazette, Friday, Sept. 24, War Office, Pall Mall, (Official Appointments and Notices)', *The Times*, 25 September 1858, Issue 23, 108, p. 4, col. C.
47. 'To the Hon. Sec., Anglo-Indian Sub-Committee of the East India Association, (letter no. 52, Calcutta, 5th May 1880)', *Fourth Annual Report, EAIA*, Appx C, 1880.
48. *Allen's Indian Mail and Official Gazette*, vol. 18 (428), 18 February 1860, p. 114.
49. F. Warren, 'The Lost Guns In Bhootan', *The Times*, 12 January 1866, Issue 25, 393, p. 5, col. G.
50. MacMunn, *The Armies*, pp. 187–8.
51. IMS candidates also had to hold qualifications in both medicine and surgery, be aged between 21 and 28, be registered to practice in Britain, and have testimonials from a 'person of standing in society' and a minister of religion. n.a., 'Regulations of the General Medical Council and Medical Licensing Bodies', *British Medical Journal*, vol. 2 (1,653), 3 September 1892, pp. 497–559.

52. *The Anglo-Indian Journal*, vol. 1 (3), December 1897.
53. The explanation for this difference was that 'the European or semi-European assistant surgeon has more authority with the British soldier than a native would have'. C. H. Joubert de la Ferté, 'The Indian Subordinate Medical Department', *British Medical Journal*, vol. 2 (2,485), 15 August 1908, pp. 385–8.
54. Madras, Calcutta and Bombay medical colleges were set up in the mid-1830s, but Bombay failed within six years and was later re-established as Grant Medical College. Hyderadad also had a small medical college recognized by government, and another opened in Lahore in 1860. There were 10 recognized medical schools across India by 1911. A.H. Butt, 'The Medical Council of India', *British Medical Journal*, vol. 2 (4,471), 14 September 1946, pp. 369–72.
55. n.a., 'The Indian Subordinate Medical Department, Assistant Surgeon Branch', *British Medical Journal*, vol. 2 (2,343), 25 November 1905, p. 1,435. Less successful students may have been appointed to lesser posts: de La Ferte explained, in 1908, that since military students were educated at government expense they were required to serve the government for many years, and, he said, all successful students were appointed to substantive posts. See de la Ferté, '*Indian Subordinate*', pp. 385–8.
56. Some of the Eurasians and Europeans were seconded for civil duties. See *Ibid.*
57. Lieutenant-Colonel Sir Henry Gidney, one example of this transition, is described in Frank Anthony, *Britain's Betrayal in India: the Story of the Anglo-Indian Community*, Allied Publishers, New Delhi, 1962, pp. 87–90. Racism was more evident for such candidates because IMS doctors were more likely to have to treat European women than were ISMD men, raising concerns with some Europeans. A total of 77 IMS men from the Eurasian and domiciled European community are listed in *The Anglo-Indian Journal*, vol. 1 (3), December 1897, pp. 7–9.
58. These were ranked second apothecary, apothecary, or assistant apothecary. IOR/F/4/1338/53155, *Madras Apothecaries' Pension Fund*, January 1829–October 1831, transcription from http://search.fibis.org/frontis /bin/aps_browse_sources.php?mode=browse_components&id=490 (accessed November 2010).
59. n.a., 'British Foreign Medical Service', *Boston Medical & Surgical Journal*, vol. 26 (1), 9 February 1842, pp. 17–18.
60. *Ibid.*
61. IMS figure: n.a., 'Medical Services of the British Army', *British & Foreign Medico-Chirurgical Review*, vol. 15, April 1855, pp. 411–49 (see particularly pp. 440–1). There were 181 in Bengal's ISMD; the ranks in 1862 Bengal were assistant apothecary, apothecary, or senior apothecary: 'Apothecaries Serving in Bengal, Bengal Army List', *New Calcutta Directory*, 1862. Madras ISMD numbered 197 men: n.a., 'List of Medical Warrant Officers of Her Majesty's Indian Forces', *Madras Quarterly Journal of Medical Science*, vol. 1, 1860, pp. 231–44. There were 105 in ISMD Bombay; this figure's date is unclear but the latest reference used in the source is dated 1869: Dadabhai Naoroji

(Chunilal Lallubhai Parekh, ed.), *Speeches, Addresses and Writings (on Indian Politics) of the Hon'ble Dadabhai Naoroji*, Caxton Printing Works, Bombay, 1887, p. 269–73.
62. de la Ferté, *'Indian Subordinate'*, pp. 385–8.
63. The Royal Army Medical Corps was formed in 1898 and provided medical services to the British army.
64. L.F. Rushbrook Williams, 'India and the War', in H.H. Dodwell (ed.), *The Cambridge History of India, vol. VI, The Indian Empire 1858–1918*, Cambridge University Press, Cambridge, 1932, p. 482.
65. Though Indian doctors would have been even cheaper it was not considered appropriate to allow natives to treat Europeans.
66. Madras government, *Selections From the Records of the Madras Government, Annual Reports of the Madras Medical College, 1866–7 Session*, vol. 4, Gantz Brothers, Madras, 1867, p. 14.
67. Butt, *Medical Council*, pp. 369–72.
68. n.a., 'Regulations of the General Medical Council and Medical Licensing Bodies', *British Medical Journal*, vol. 2 (1,653), 3 September 1892, pp. 497–559.
69. Madras government, *Selections*, 1868–69, p. 14.
70. Naoroji, *Speeches*, pp. 269–73.
71. n.a., 'Proposed Medical Registration Act for India', *British Medical Journal*, vol. 2 (2,486), 22 August 1908, pp. 521–2.
72. Christopher Hawes, *Poor Relations: the Making of a Eurasian Community in British India, 1773–1833*, Curzon, Richmond, 1996, p. 49.
73. Robert Cole (ed.), 'The Madras Medical School', *Madras Quarterly Journal of Literature and Science*, vol. 7, January 1838, pp. 265–8.
74. Butt, *Medical Council*, pp. 369–72.
75. The Madras College apothecaries' class of 1838 were exclusively 'Indo-British', with two or three 'who appeared to be European'. Robert Cole (ed.), 'The Madras Medical School', *Madras Quarterly Journal of Literature and Science*, vol. 7, January 1838, pp. 265–8.
76. n.a., 'GOGG, Fort William, June 15th 1812; Boys from the Upper & Lower Orphan Schools & Free School to Serve as Compounders, Dressers and Apothecaries', published in *Calcutta Gazette*, vol. LVII (1,479), 2 July 1812, http://www.wiki.fibis.org/index.php?title=General_Order_of_the_Governor_General_in_Council,_June_15th_1812 (accessed June 2009).
77. For a description of the examinations and syllabus at Madras in 1838, see Cole, *Madras Medical*, pp. 265–8.
78. P.H. Starling, 'The Youngest Victoria Cross: the Award of the Victoria Cross to Andrew Fitzgibbon', *Journal of the Royal Army Medical Corps.*, vol. 154 (1), March 2008, pp. 81–3.
79. Madras government, *Selections*, 1867, p. 11.
80. *Ibid.*, pp. 29–32.

81. This lengthened study by a year, and students who did not pass annual exams could be held back a year. Government Order no. 1,884, 29 March 1865, *ibid.*, 1866, pp. 11–12.
82. *Ibid.*, 1867, p. 17.
83. *Ibid.*, p. 24.
84. *Ibid.*, p. 17.
85. *Ibid.*, 1869, p. 52.
86. The Junior Department at Madras in 1838 included Indian Christians, some of whom may have adopted European names on baptism. Cole, 'Madras Medical', pp. 265–8.
87. Madras government, *Selections*, 1867, pp. 21–2.
88. *Ibid.*, 1866.
89. *Ibid.*
90. Naoroji, *Speeches*, pp. 269–73.
91. *Ibid.*
92. Madras government, *Selections*, 1867, p. 29.
93. *Ibid.*, p. 56.
94. *Ibid.*, 1868, pp. 49–50.
95. *Ibid.*, pp. 50–1.
96. n.a., 'Indian Subordinate', p. 1,435.
97. Hop Sing and Co., *Military Students, Calcutta Medical School (1911–1915)*, scanned photograph, http://search.fibis.org/frontis/bin/aps_browse_sources.php?mode=browse_picture&id=2552&s_id=815 (accessed February 2013).
98. *GOGG*, 1812.
99. Cole, *Madras Medical*, pp. 265–8.
100. *Ibid.*
101. Madras government, *Selections*, 1867, p. 24. 'Dresser' also described any medical student who, having passed third- or fourth-year examinations, was undertaking a period of clinical work under a senior surgeon to hone practical skills and 'dress' surgical wounds, and was used in that context in Britain and India until the 1950s. N. E. Dudley, 'A Hands on or Hands off Approach to Patients?' *British Medical Journal*, vol. 318 (1,361), 15 May 1999, p. 1.
102. n.a., 'Subordinate Medical Department', *The Indian Medical Gazette*, vol. 3 (7), July 1868, p. 158.
103. *Ibid.*
104. IMS figure. n.a., 'Medical Services of the British Army', pp. 411–49.
105. Cole, *Madras Medical*, pp. 265–8.
106. William R. Cornish, *A Code of the Medical and Sanitary Regulations for the Guidance of Medical Officers Serving in the Madras Presidency, vol. 1*, Government Press, Madras, 1870, p. 83
107. The students got Rs 9.4 per month after deductions for board and lodgings. n. a., 'Indian Subordinate', p. 1,435.
108. *Ibid.*

109. de la Ferté, 'Indian Subordinate', pp. 385–8.
110. The British Medical Association (BMA) advised its members not to work in India until assured that doctors qualified in Britain would hold the chief administrative posts in the provincial services. By 1929, there were 70 unfilled posts and the government was forced to comply. n.a., 'The Indian Medical Service', *British Medical Journal*, vol. 1 (3,573), 29 June 1929, pp. 1,168–9; n. a., 'The Indian Medical Department', *British Medical Journal*, vol. 1 (3,664), 28 March 1931, pp. 565–6.
111. MacMunn, *The Armies*, pp. 22–3.
112. *Ibid.*, p. 13.
113. Pension requests were usually resisted, but were occasionally granted as 'a special case'. Llewellyn-Jones, 'Other', p. 9.
114. MacMunn, *The Armies*, pp. 105 and 113–14.
115. Sardhana state offered troops in 1803, Skinner was followed by 2,000 men on leaving Scindia's service in the same year, and at Madras in 1799 Richard Chase raised and paid for a native militia company. Herbert Compton, *A Particular Account of the European Military Adventures of Hindustan, from 1784 to 1803*, T.F. Unwin, London, 1892, pp. 40–3; IOR/F/4/59/1312, 'Embodying The Militia At Madras, and an independent company of natives raised and paid for by Mr. Chase', *Extract of Military Letter from Fort St George*, 2 January 1799.
116. MacMunn, *The Armies*, pp. 20–1.
117. *Ibid.*, p. 111.
118. *Ibid.*; IOR/L/Mil/7/7244, Coll.156A/9, *Disbandment of East India Regiment, Lahore Light Horse and Eurasian Artillery,* 1863.
119. MacMunn, *The Armies*, pp. 14, 33, 85–6 and 103; Narindar Saroop, *A Squire of Hindoostan*, Palit & Palit, New Delhi, 1983, p. 81.
120. IOR/F/4/59/1312, *Militia at Madras*, 1798–9.
121. IOR/F/4/56/1299, *Corps of Militia at Calcutta, to Consist of Europeans, Armenians and Eurasians*, 1798.
122. IOR/F/4/59/1312, *Militia at Madras*, 1798–9.
123. '... a man must be a volunteer ... or someone will ask the reason why'. Rudyard Kipling, *From Sea to Sea and Other Sketches – Letters of Travel*, first published 1889, republished by Cambridge University Press, Cambridge, 2011, vol. 2, p. 279.
124. Whittaker, *Almanack*, p. 462.
125. Anthony, *Betrayal*, p. 115.
126. Describing the Lawrence Asylum in 1847, Hodson wrote: 'the majority of the boys will, of course, become soldiers'. William Hodson and George Hodson (eds), *Twelve Years of a Soldier's Life in India*, John W. Parker & Son, London, 1859, p. 44.
127. La Martinière cadets were active in the defence of Lucknow in 1857.
128. J. Tosh, *The Pursuit of History*, 2nd edn, Longman, London, 1982, p. 77.

129. IOR/F/4/401/10087, June 1812–August 1813, *George Hipkin Walters, Eurasian merchant, permitted to reside at Lucknow.*
130. E. I. Carlyle (revised by James Falkner), 'Sir Robert Warburton, Army Officer (1842–1899)', *ODNB* (accessed January 2011).
131. 'Domestic Occurrences, Marriage at Surat, Forjett & Faulkner, 9/2/1875', *Times of India*, 16 February 1875.
132. A Traveller (anon.), *The English in India and Other Sketches*, Longman, Rees, Orme & Co., London, 1835, p. 197.
133. Governor-General Wellesley's Proclamation, 29 August 1803, recalling all Britons and Eurasians from the Military Service of Several Indian States, in Arthur Wellesley Duke of Wellington and John Gurwood (eds), *The Dispatches of Field Marshal the Duke of Wellington, During his Various Campaigns*..., vol. 1, Parker, Furnivall and Parker, London, 1844, p. 769.
134. Compton, *Particular*, pp. 352–4.
135. Eurasian 'adventurers' were often described as Europeans in contemporary correspondence; Cornwallis and Wellesley, for example, usually referred to Europeans when they meant Europeans and Eurasians. Eurasians were also hidden by the titles of histories such as Compton, *Particular;* and Grey and Garrett, *European*.
136. A description of DeBoigne's brigades, which included Eurasians. Compton, *Particular*, p. 106.
137. History had been kind enough to remember James Skinner's loyalty to Scindia's salt (sharing salt implied friendship and mutual protection), but such balance is rare.
138. IOR/L/Mil/5/673, *Copy memorandum on European regiments raised during the Mutiny ... inadvisability of admitting Eurasians to the British Army*, 1875.
139. Herbert Stark, *Hostages to India, or the Life Story of the Anglo-Indian Race*, 2nd edn, Star Printing Works, Calcutta, 1936, p. 135; Anthony, *Betrayal*, p. 71.
140. IOR/Mss/Eur D629, *Memorandum by Capt William Thomson Nicolls ... suggestive of the embodying of a Christian Native Infantry*, 10 February 1859.
141. It was suggested that grants of land should be given to demobbed soldiers who would stay in India, intermarry, and increase the Eurasian community, providing a pool of loyal men who could take up arms. n.a., 'Report from the Select Committee on Colonisation and Settlement (India); [1st – 4th reports] with Minutes of Evidence taken before them, 1858', *The North British Review*, vol. 30, February–May 1859, Art. VII, pp. 441–6.
142. Anthony, *Betrayal*, pp. 1 and 85.
143. John Crawfurd, 'On the Commixture of the Races of Man as Affecting the Progress of Civilisation', *Transactions of the Ethnological Society of London*, vol. 3, 1865, pp. 98–122.
144. Lord Canning, in n.a., NAI, Home/Education/Part A/Procs., Nos 31–4, *Education of European and Eurasian Children in India,* October 1882; Ethel Winifred Savi, *Neither Fish nor Flesh*, Hurst & Blackett, London, 1924; Charles

Darwin, *The Variation of Animals and Plants under Domestication*, vol. 2, 2nd edn, D. Appleton & Co., New York, 1892, p. 42.

145. G.J.H. Evatt, 'Military Service for Eurasians', pamphlet reprinted from the *Indian Medical Record*, June 1892.
146. Cedric Dover, *Chimmerii? Or, Eurasians and Their Future*, Modern Art Press, Calcutta, 1929, pp. 34, 57 and 60.
147. See the discussion about railway cantonments in Chapter 9, Eurasians and the Railway. Concern about racial degeneration was often specifically about the English, and their supposed qualities, rather than the British. See for example George Viscount Valentia, *Voyages and Travels to India and Ceylon, 1802–6*, vol. 1, Rivington, London, 1811, p. 197.
148. Evatt, *Military Service;* Dover, *Chimmerii?*, p. 20.
149. Hansard, 'Petition of Indo-Britons to House of Commons', *Hansard's Parliamentary Debates*, vol. XXIV, 4 May 1830, pp. 377–87; IOR/L/Mil/7/12778, Collection 279/1, 1875–6, *Memorial from Anglo-Indian Aid Association of Mysore, praying that Eurasians be admitted into military service*; IOR/L/PJ/6/529, File 149, *Proposed Creation of Eurasian Regiment*, 1900.
150. J.R. Wallace, 'Deputation of the Eurasian & Anglo-Indian Associations to the Sec. of State for India', *The Anglo-Indian Journal*, vol. 1 (1), Bombay, 1897, p. 5.
151. IOR/V/25/900/8, Edgar Thurston, 'Eurasians of Madras and Malabar', *Madras Government Museum Bulletin: Anthropology*, vol. 2 (2), 1898.
152. n.a., *The Anglo-Indian Journal*, vol. 1(13), Bombay, 1898, p. 4.
153. John Crawfurd, 'On the Effects of Commixture, Locality, Climate, and Food on the Races of Man', *Transactions of the Ethnological Society of London*, vol. 1, 1861, pp. 76–92.
154. Evatt, *Military Service.*
155. n.a. 'EAIA: Deputation to the Secretary of State', *The Friend of India & Statesman*, 25 August 1897, p. 21.
156. Satoshi Mizutani, *Loyalty, Parity, and Social Control – the Competing Visions on the Creation of an 'Eurasian' Military Regiment in Late British India*, 2010, http://home.alphalink.com.au/~agilbert/satoshi.html (accessed February 2013).

Chapter 9 Eurasians and the Railways

1. In 1877–8, a total of 3,319 out of 132,040 staff were Eurasians. Juland Danvers, *Report to the Secretary of State for India in Council on Railways in India*, Eyre & Spottiswoode, London, 1878.
2. S. Gore-Browne, *Alphabetical List of Europeans and East Indians in the Company's Service on 30th June 1880*, East India Railway Company Press, Calcutta, 1880.
3. I refer to Eurasians as identified in the decentennial censuses of India, and to n. a., *Reports by the Railways Board on Indian Railways for 1926–7*, vol. II, Appendix C.

4. Coralie Younger, *Anglo-Indians: Neglected Children of the Raj*, B.R. Publishing Corp., Delhi, 1987, p. 164.
5. Lionel Caplan, *Children of Colonialism: Anglo-Indians in a Postcolonial World*, Berg, Oxford, 2001, pp. 29 and 95–6; Ian J. Kerr, *Engines of Change: The Railroads That Made India*, Praeger Publishers Inc., Westport, CT, 2006, p. 81; Younger, *Anglo-Indians*, p. 165.
6. W. Chichele Plowden, *Report on the Census of British India Taken on the 17th February 1881*, Eyre and Spottiswoode, London, 1883, p. 33; Danvers, *Report*, 1878.
7. The Calcutta Eurasian elite sent a delegation and petition to parliament in 1830, and the EAIA lobbied government departments and other employers in the 1870s and 1880s.
8. Existing work on railway personnel concentrates on the twentieth century and is concerned primarily with industrial action and nationalism. An exception is the archival research of Laura Bear on EIR's Anglo-Indians, though even this uses colonial-era data mainly to ground an anthropological study of late twenty-first-century Anglo-Indians. Laura Bear, *Lines of the Nation*, Columbia University Press, Chichester, NY, 2007; Laura Bear, 'Public Genealogies, Bodies and Nations in Anglo-Indian Railway Family Histories', *Contributions to Indian Sociology*, vol. 35, 2001, pp. 355–88.
9. Ian J. Kerr, *Building the Railways of the Raj; 1850–1900*, Oxford University Press, Delhi, 1995, pp. 211–12.
10. Figures include all racial categories, but exclude many thousands employed in construction, as porters and caterers, and secondary employment created by the railway's presence.
11. Kerr, *Building*, p. 31.
12. Danvers, *Report*, 1878, p. 10.
13. George Huddleston, *History of the East Indian Railway*, Thacker Spink & Co., Calcutta, 1906, p. 106.
14. 'Bhagulpore Commissioner to Government of Bengal, 1875', quoted in Bear, *Lines*, p. 78. The category 'East-Indian' was used by the EIR, whilst railway reports from the India Office used the terms East-Indian and Eurasian interchangeably. The EAIA employed the terms Eurasian and Anglo-Indian, sometimes using the latter for domiciled Europeans only but often including Eurasians.
15. '... one brother eligible for special privileges ... because he is fair, and another subjected to special disabilities ... because he is dark'. EAIA Secretary, 'Letter to Secretary to the Govt. India, Public Works Dept., Railway Branch, No 112, Calcutta, 20 November 1880', n.a., *Annual Report of the Eurasian and Anglo-Indian Association* [EAIA], Calcutta, 1880, pp. 27–9.
16. Government figures for covenanted and uncovenanted civil servants showed more than a quarter of those earning over Rs 1,000 perannum were Eurasian. However, 21 per cent of Europeans earned salaries over Rs 10,000 annually but only 0.5 per cent of Eurasians drew such a salary. IOR/L/PJ/6/315, File 291, *List of amounts earned by Europeans, Eurasians and Indians in the ICS*, 31 March 1886.

17. Laura Roychowdhury, *The Jadu House: Travels in Anglo-India,* Black Swan, London, 2001, p. 123; for detailed examples, see Chapter 5 in Bear, *Lines*. Petitions deal exclusively with complaints and are inherently biased toward the disaffected, the dismissed, and the unreliable, offering no insight into the lives of those who neither complained nor were disciplined.
18. Gore-Browne, *Alphabetical List*; Danvers, *Report*, 1878, pp. 10–11; EAIA Secretary, *Annual*, pp. 26–7.
19. Records of covenanted men in the OIOC exclude Eurasians who were not recruited in England. Personnel records in India are now held by the various divisions of today's Indian Railways. None, to my knowledge, has been indexed and only one has been the subject of academic research. It can take many months of persistence and 'networking' to gain access. Roychowdhury, *Jadu House*, p. 118; J.B. Harrison, 'The Records of Indian Railways: a neglected resource', *South Asia Research*, 1987, vol. 7 (2), pp. 105–21.
20. Gore-Browne, *Alphabetical List*; there are extant lists for 1871–9. Not all years include racial status.
21. See bibliography for details of websites.
22. Hena Mukherjee, *The Early History of the East Indian Railway; 1845–1879*, Firma KLM Private, Calcutta, 1994; Blair Williams, *The Jamalpur Gymkhana,* http://home.alphalink.com.au/~agilbert/onjama~1.html (accessed February 2013); William Andrews, *Indian Railways as Connected With British Empire in the East*, W.H. Allen, London, 1884; Rudyard Kipling, *From Sea to Sea and Other Sketches – Letters of Travel*, first published 1889, republished by Cambridge University Press, Cambridge, 2011, vol. 2; Francis J.S. Venner, 'England And Her Eastern Question', *New Monthly Magazine*, vol. 143, 1868, p. 355.
23. Three examples: European station-masters were paid more than others for the same work – H. Mukherjee, *Early History*, p. 111; a European factory overseer was paid up to Rs 150 a month, a Portuguese 'half-caste' was paid Rs 50, and an East-Indian 'half-caste' was paid Rs 100 – n.a., 'Affairs of the East India Company: Minutes of evidence: 21 May 1830', *Journal of the House of Lords*, vol. 62, 1830, pp. 1081–8; 'Adventurous young Englishmen ... naturally obtained preferential treatment, and the Anglo-Indians thereby received a set-back' – Herbert Stark, *Hostages to India, or the Life Story of the Anglo-Indian Race*, 2nd edn, Star Printing Works, Calcutta, 1936, p. 123.
24. East Indian Railways applied the term 'covenanted' to those recruited in Britain on four- or five-year contracts. They could take six months' leave in England and then return to their employment in India on another covenant. Stan Blackford, *One hell of a life: an Anglo-Indian Wallah's memoir from the last decades of the Raj*, Self-published, Sydney, 2000, p. 280.
25. Exogamous marriages between working-class Europeans and Eurasians were not uncommon.
26. n.a., 'European and Eurasian Pauperism in Calcutta', *The Times*, News, 18 July 1892, issue 33693, p. 5, col. F.

27. Danvers, *Report*, 1878.
28. European males in India outnumbered females 3 or 4 to 1. P.J. Marshall, 'British Society in India under the East India Company', *Modern Asian Studies*, vol. 31 (1), 1997, pp. 89–108.
29. Two individuals' salaries were stated to be Rs 0. These have been ignored as probable typographical errors.
30. David Arnold, 'European Orphans and Vagrants in India in the Nineteenth Century', *Journal of Imperial & Commonwealth History*, vol. 7 (2), January 1979, pp. 104–27.
31. Kerr notes engineers imported from Britain, thoroughly trained and experienced there, often lacked specific knowledge needed for work in India. Kerr, *Building*, p. 13.
32. H. Mukherjee, *Early History*, p. 164.
33. W.H. Sleeman, *Rambles and Recollections of an Indian Official*, Hatchard, London, 1844, pp. 447–8.
34. Andrews, *Indian Railways*, p. 165.
35. Kipling, *Sea to Sea*, p. 290.
36. NAI, Financial/Expenditure/Part A/Procs., nos 202–3, June 1867, *Allowances to European and Eurasian Boys in the Central Provinces who Pass Certain Prescribed Examinations*, 1867.
37. Danvers, *Report*, 1878.
38. EAIA Secretary, *Annual*, Appx E.
39. Danvers, *Reports*, 1878 and 1887.
40. Permanent Delegation of India to UNESCO, *Oak Grove School*, 28 January 2009, http://whc.unesco.org/en/tentativelists/5404/ (accessed February 2013).
41. M. DeRosaire, *Index to and Map of the new Civil station and Cantonments of Allahabad showing owners and occupants of houses with names...*, Government Press, Allahabad, 1863; Col. HL Thuiller, *Allahābād Cantonment, Civil Station, City and Environs, 1867–1868, Corrected up to 1875*, Map, Surveyor General's Office, Calcutta, 1876.
42. Even calls for the companies to help out with free travel to and from the existing schools were rebuffed. n.a., NAI, Home/Education/Part A/Procs., Nos 31–4, *Education of European and Eurasian Children in India,* October 1882.
43. *Ibid.*; Danvers, *Report*, 1878; EAIA Secretary, *Annual*, Appx E.
44. n.a., 'East India Railway Leave, Allowances, and fund rules', EAIA Secretary, *Annual*, Appx D, pp. 27–9; Huddleston, *History*, pp. 207–9.
45. Huddleston, *History*, pp. 121–2.
46. *Ibid.*, p. 251.
47. Kipling, *Sea to Sea*, p. 279.
48. Christopher Hawes, *Poor Relations: the Making of a Eurasian Community in British India, 1773–1833*, Curzon, Richmond, 1996, pp. 42–3.
49. Younger, *Anglo-Indians*, p. 163.
50. See, e.g., 'K.E. Wallace, The Eurasian Problem', reviewed by C. Rhodes, *Journal of the Royal Institute of International Affairs*, vol. 9 (4), 1930, pp. 570–2.

51. A solitary European 'Clerk of Works', earned Rs 600/m.
52. Looting was a problem, especially in times of famine or high food prices. David Arnold, 'Industrial Violence in Colonial India', *Comparative Studies in Society and History*, vol. 22 (2), 1980, pp. 234–55.
53. Kipling, *Sea to Sea*, p. 279.
54. This is illustrated by several cases wherein men who were firemen in 1871 were drivers in 1880.
55. David Arnold classed those earning Rs 250 or more per month as wealthy. A further six covenanted European drivers drew above Rs 250 if money paid in England is included. Arnold, 'European', pp. 104–27.
56. In all, 63 Eurasians earned Rs 200 or more working for EIR in 1880.
57. Kipling, *Sea to Sea*, p. 290.
58. *Ibid.*, p. 288–9.
59. *Ibid.*, p. 290.
60. Shugun-Chand Aggarwal, *Industrial Housing in India*, Roxy Press, New Delhi, 1952, p. 233.
61. Mukherjee implies that almost all skilled and semi-skilled employees were sent from Britain in the period to 1879, at great expense. H. Mukherjee, *Early History*, pp. 109–10.
62. Blair Williams, 'On Jamalpur – Anglo-Indian Railway Officers', *The International Journal of Anglo-Indian Studies* Vol. 6, No. 2, 2001, http://home.alphalink.com.au/~agilbert/onjama~1.html (accessed February 2013).
63. Kipling, *Sea to Sea*, pp. 276–80 and 298.
64. Subash Kumar Rain, of Darjeeling was recently employed as an assistant driver under this scheme after his driver father had died. Gerry Troyna, *Monsoon Railway*, DVD, BBC Productions, 2005.
65. The 1901 Indian Census Report refers to Eurasians and Armenians as 'allied races'.
66. David Arnold, 'White Colonization and Labour in Nineteenth-Century India', *Journal of Imperial and Commonwealth History*, vol. 11 (2), 1983, pp. 133–58.
67. Kipling, *Sea to Sea*, p. 299.
68. A quarter of Eurasians at this time were destitute, relying on charities or family. In 1901, a substantial number of unemployed Eurasians were supported by families and friends. H.H. Risley and E.A. Gait, *Report On The Census Of India, 1901*, Government Printing Press, Calcutta, 1903, p. 219.
69. Our Own Correspondent, 'Indian Contrasts', *The Times*, 27 October 1874, Issue 28144, p. 8, col. D.
70. L.S.S. O'Malley and Manmohan Chakravarti, *Bengal District Gazetteers: Howrah*, Bengal Secretariat, Calcutta 1909, p. 165.
71. Huddleston, *History*, p. 242.
72. Bear, *Lines,* 2007, pp. 86–9.
73. For examples of such protests see EAIA Secretary, 3rd *Annual Report, 1879*, Appendix D, Allowances to Wives of Bandsmen, p. 17 and Appendix H, Degradation of Eurasian Railway Guards, pp. 20–1.

74. The 1901 census found 6,000 Christians at Allahabad, half of them Eurasian or European.
75. DeRosaire, *Index and Map*, 1863 and 1876.
76. There was an on-going debate between the advantages of a city location for the procurement of labour and a remote, more readily defensible one. Bear, *Lines*, pp. 38–40.
77. Kipling, *Sea to Sea*, pp. 244, 273 and 283; Huddleston, *History*, pp. 240–51. The two quotes in this paragraph are from Kipling, *Sea to Sea*.
78. Gore-Browne, *Alphabetical List*.
79. Jumalpore was also the headquarters of the EIR's traffic department, later moved to Calcutta. Huddleston, *History*, p. 112.
80. Kipling, *Sea to Sea*, p. 286.
81. Huddleston, *History*, p. 242.
82. Kipling, *Sea to Sea*, p. 298.
83. *Ibid.*, pp. 284 and 287. Tiffin is a light meal, often lunch.
84. Huddleston also pointed to its proximity to Monghyr, the inhabitants of which 'had been mechanics for many centuries'. Huddleston, *History*, p. 242.
85. Kipling, *Sea to Sea*, p. 276.
86. The Chief Engineer of Oudh and Rohilkhund Railway suggested that the construction of small native villages that sprang up near station premises should be systematized, and sanitary issues addressed. Danvers, *Report*, 1877, p. 9. Later discussions on native railway workers' accommodation consider sanitation, security, and promotion of loyalty. See Chapter 4 of Bear, *Lines*, and Nitin Sinha, 'The World of Workers' Politics: Some Issues of Railway Workers in Colonial India, 1918–1922', *Modern Asian Studies*, vol. 42 (5), 2008, pp. 999–1033.
87. Kipling, *Sea to Sea*, p. 276.
88. *Ibid.*
89. *Ibid.*, p. 275.
90. St Mary's was consecrated by the Bishop of Calcutta in 1867. Frances Maria Milman, *Memoir of the Right Rev. Robert Milman*, John Murray, London, 1879, p. 44.
91. Huddleston, *History*, pp. 243–4.
92. Quoted in Kipling, *Sea to Sea*, p. 274.
93. *Ibid.*, pp. 276–7.
94. *Ibid.*, p. 278.
95. Gore-Browne, *Alphabetical List*.
96. Kipling, *Sea to Sea*, p. 286.
97. Gore-Browne, *Alphabetical List*.
98. Kipling, *Sea to Sea*, p. 283.
99. Gore-Browne, *Alphabetical List*.
100. Battles to standardize pension and leave rules and promotion prospects for European and Eurasian staff predated later struggles to win fair treatment for

all, regardless of race. EAIA Secretary, *Annual*, p. 27; Sinha, 'The World', pp. 999–1,033.

101. Venner, 'Eastern Question', p. 355.
102. Kipling, *Sea to Sea*, p. 279.
103. Huddleston, *History*, p. 251.
104. Kipling, *Sea to Sea*, p. 299.
105. Kipling, *Sea to Sea*, pp. 292–3.
106. n.a., 'India and the Civil Engineers', *The Railway News and Joint-Stock Journal*, vol. 11 (306), 6 November 1869, pp. 471 and 476.
107. Wressley of the Foreign Office, in Rudyard Kipling, *Indian Tales*, United States Book Company, New York, pp. 265–71.
108. There were also a dozen firemen and gunners with previous service, discharged (not resigned or dismissed) in periodic reorganizations, but later re-employed.
109. Gore-Browne, *Alphabetical List*; n.a., *Thacker's Bengal Directory*, Thacker Spink and Co., Calcutta, 1869, p. 270; 1870, p. 275; and 1895, p. 560.
110. Soldiers' pay was about £1 10s per month, before stoppages.
111. Farm labourers in West Lothian were paid £5 per month in 1914. Stuart Mitchell, Fay Oliver, and Tim Neighbour, *A Social History of 19th-Century Farm Workers and their Families*..., http://www.sair.org.uk/sair33/sair33.pdf (accessed February 2013).
112. Laura Bear, 'Miscegenations of modernity: constructing European respectability and race in the Indian railway colony, 1857–1931', *Women's History Review*, vol. 3 (4), 1994, pp. 531–48.
113. 'a man must be a volunteer ... or someone will ask the reason why'. Kipling, *Sea to Sea*, p. 279.
114. A quota of posts was reserved specifically for Anglo-Indians for a decade after Independence, to allow the community time to adapt.
115. The network grew in half a century to be the fourth largest rail network in the world. Kerr, *Engines*, 2006, p. 1

Chapter 10 Conclusions

1. Letter from the managers to Eyre Coote, 18 November 1782, in n.a., *Original Papers Relative to the Establishment of a Society in Bengal for the Protection of Orphans – 1784*, London, Joseph Cooper, n.d., pp. 29–30.
2. Nirad C. Chaudhuri, *The Continent of Circe: an Essay on the Peoples of India*, Chatto and Windus, London, 1965, p. 44.
3. See Peter Robb, 'Children, Emotion, Identity and Empire: Views from the Blechyndens' Calcutta Diaries (1790–1822)', *Modern Asian Studies*, 2006, vol. 40 (1), pp. 175–201
4. Rudyard Kipling, *Plain Tales from the Hills*, 1887 (reprinted Penguin, London, 1987), p. 95.

BIBLIOGRAPHY

PRIMARY SOURCES

Private Papers and manuscripts

Hawes, Christopher J., *Unfinished Book on Anglo-Indians, 1750–2004*, IOR/Mss/Eur F531.

Hop Sing and Co., *Military Students, Calcutta Medical School (1911–1915)*, scanned photograph, http://search.fibis.org/frontis/bin/aps_browse_sources.php?mode=browse_picture&id=2552&s_id=815 (accessed February 2013).

Kettle, Steve, *Discharge Certificate, Charles Thompson*, dated 26 June 1865, scan at http://www.britishmedals.us/collections/TB/heic/thompson.html (accessed February 2013).

Nicolls, Captain William Thomson, 24th Madras Native Infantry, *Memorandum Suggestive of the Embodying of a Christian Native Infantry Regiment in the Madras Presidency*, 10 February 1859, IOR/Mss/Eur D629.

Whiley, Master Sergeant J., 47th Bengal Native Infantry, *Petition to the Commander-in-chief, India Requesting the Transfer of his Two Sons from the 47th Native Infantry to a European Regiment*, c1857, IOR/Mss/Eur F133/176.

Archival Sources

London Metropolitan Archives

St Thomas' Hospital: *Nightingale Collection.*

British Library

DeRosaire, M., *Index to and Map of the New Civil Station and Cantonments of Allahabad Showing Owners and Occupants of Houses with Names* ..., Government Press, Allahabad, 1863.

IOR Ecclesiastical returns: Birth, Death and Marriage indexes, 1800–1900.

IOR/B: East India Company: Minutes of the Court of Directors and Court of Proprietors 1599–1858.

IOR/F: Board of Control Records 1784–1858.

IOR/L: India Office Departmental Records: AG – Accountant-General's Records c1601–1974; MIL – Military Department Records 1708–1959; P&J – Public and Judicial Department Records 1795–1950.

IOR/R/2: Crown Representative: Indian States Residencies Records c1789–1947.

IOR/V: India Office Records Official Publications Series c1760–1957.

IOR/Z/O/19, *Miscellaneous Bonds*, no. 3,338, 1822.

n.a., *Allahābād Cantonment, Civil Station, City and Environs, 1867–1868, Corrected up to 1875*, Map, Calcutta, 1876.

n.a., *Imperial Gazetteer of India*, Oxford, Clarendon Press, 1908–31, vols 5 and 24.

National Archives of India

Baghelkhand Agency, Political, English Files, Proceedings, 1882–1907.

Bundelkhand Agency, Political, English Files, Proceedings, 1866–1908.

Central India Agency, Political, English files, Proceedings, 1867.

Financial Department, Expenditure, Proceedings (A), 1867.

Foreign Department, Political Consultations, 1804–38.

———, Political Proceedings, 1854–85.

———, Judicial Branch Consultations (A), 1867.

———, Internal Proceedings (B), 1903–6.

Home Department, Public Proceedings, 1855.

———, Education Proceedings (A), 1882.

The National Archives of the UK

Public Record Office (PRO), *Census Returns of England and Wales, 1881*, http://search.ancestry.co.uk/search/grouplist.aspx?group=1881uki (accessed February 2013).

WO 4/297, *War Office Out-Letters*.

Reports

Danvers, Juland, *Report{s} to the Secretary of State for India in Council on Railways in India*, Eyre and Spottiswoode, London, 1860, 1868, 1877, and 1878.

n.a., *Annual Report of the Eurasian and Anglo-Indian Association* {EAIA}, Calcutta, 1877–82.

n.a., *Reports by the Railways Board on Indian Railways* for 1926–7.

Parliamentary Papers

Buckingham, J.S., *Select Committee on Drunkenness, Evidence Presented to the House of Commons*, Benjamin Bagster, London, 1834.

The Charter Act of 1833, section 87, 3rd and 4th George VI, Cap. 83.

The East Indies Juries Act 7, George IV, Cap. 37.

Hansard, *House of Commons Debates*.

Hansard, *House of Lords Debates*.

House of Commons, Papers, *Accounts and Papers*, vol. XLVIII, 313 (69), 7 February 1848.

House of Commons, Parliamentary Papers, *Report from the Select Committee on the Affairs of the East India Company*, 1832.

House of Commons, Reports, *Select Committee on Colonisation and Settlement (India)*, Fourth Report, no. 3, vol. 7, pt 2, 1858.

The Indian Criminal Procedure Act, Amendment Bill [The Ilbert Bill], 1883.

Journal of the House of Lords, 1830.

The Vagrancy Act 1, Victoria 28, 1849.

Wellesley, Richard, *The Substance of the Speech of the Marquis Wellesley on the 31st of January, 1812, in the House of Lords, on the Motion of Earl Fitzwilliam, Respecting the Present State of Ireland*, Longman Hurst, London, 1812.

Winterton, Earl, 'House of Commons Debate, 21 December 1925', *Hansard*, vol. 189, 1925–6.

Newspapers and Periodicals

Allen's Indian Mail and Official Gazette, 1860.

The Anglo-Indian Journal, 1897–1901.

Annual Register, 1844.

The Asiatic Journal & Monthly Register, 1822–35.

British Medical Journal, 1892–1999.

The Calcutta Annual Register, 1821.

The Calcutta Gazette, 1812.

The Calcutta Review, 1855–67.

East India Register, 1835 and 1844.

East India Register and Directory, 1825.

The Edinburgh Review, 1868.

The Friend of India & Statesman, 1897.

General Evening Post, 1783.

The Inverness Advertiser, 1853.

The London Gazette, 1858.

The Morning Chronicle, 1833.

Morning Chronicle and London Advertiser, 1873.

The Morning Post, 1805–22.

New Monthly Magazine, 1868.

The North British Review, 1859.

Public Advertiser, 1783.

The Rambler, 1857.

The Times Digital Archive, 1800–1900.

The Times of India, 1875.

Books and Articles

Andrews, William, *Indian Railways as Connected With British Empire in the East*, W.H. Allen, London, 1884.

Anon., 'Reminiscences of a Half-Caste', *The East India Sketch-Book*, vol. 1, Richard Bentley, London, 1833.

———, *The Poetical Works of Henry Louis Vivian Derozio: with a Memoir of the Author*, W. Newman, Calcutta, 1871.

Anon. (A Traveller), *The English in India and Other Sketches*, Longman, Rees, Orme & Co., London, 1835.

Anon. (Julia C. Maitland), *Letters from Madras, During the Years 1836–1839*, John Murray, London, 1846.

Arbuthnot, Sir A.J., *Selections from Minutes and Other Official Writings of Major-General Sir Thomas Munro*, Higginbotham & Co., Madras, 1886.

Baines, Jervoise Athelstane, *General Report on the Census of India*, 1891, HMSO, London, 1893.

Bannerjee, A.C. (ed.), *Fort William – India House Correspondence and Other Contemporary Papers Relating Thereto, 1792–1796*, vol. 20 (Military Series), National Archives of India, Delhi, 1969.

Beaufort, Francis Lestock, *A Digest of the Criminal Law of the Presidency of Fort William*, (2 vols), 2nd edn, Thacker, Calcutta, 1857–9.

Bengal and Agra: Annual Guide and Gazetteer, n.p., 1881.

Brown, Samuel, 'On the Rates of Mortality and Marriage Amongst Europeans in India', *Journal of the Statistical Society of London*, vol. 27 (4), 1864, pp. 566–79.

Buchanan, Rev. Claudius, *Colonial Ecclesiastical Establishment: Submitted to the Consideration of the Imperial Parliament*, 2nd edn, Cadell & Davies, London, 1813,

Burn, Richard and Chetwynd, George, *The Justice of the Peace and Parish Officer*, vol. 2, 23rd edn, Longman Hurst, London, 1820.

Burton, Richard, *Goa, and the Blue Mountains*, Richard Bentley, London, 1851.

Carey, W.H., *The Good Old Days of Honorable John Company*, abridged edition, Quins Book Co., Calcutta, 1964 (first published 1882).

Chitty, Joseph and Chitty, Thomas, *The Justice of the Peace and Parish Officer*, vol. 5, Lincoln's Inn, London, 1837.

Cole, Robert (ed.), 'The Madras Medical School', *Madras Quarterly Journal of Literature and Science*, vol. 7, January 1838, pp. 265–8.

Compton, Herbert, *A Particular Account of the European Military Adventures of Hindustan, from 1784 to 1803*, T.F. Unwin, London, 1892.

Cornish, Henry, *Under the Southern Cross*, Penguin, Harmondsworth, 1978, (first imprint, Madras, 1879).

Cornish, William R., *A Code of the Medical and Sanitary Regulations for the Guidance of Medical Officers Serving in the Madras Presidency*, vol. 1, Government Press, Madras, 1870.

Cotton, George, *Memoir of George Edward Lynch Cotton, Bishop of Calcutta*, Longmans, Green & Co., London, 1872.

Couling, Samuel, *Our Labouring Classes: Their Intellectual, Moral, and Social Condition*, Partridge and Oakey, London, 1851.

Crawfurd, John, 'On the Effects of Commixture, Locality, Climate, and Food on the Races of Man', *Transactions of the Ethnological Society of London*, vol. 1, 1861, pp. 76–92.

———, 'On the Commixture of the Races of Man as Affecting the Progress of Civilisation', *Transactions of the Ethnological Society of London*, vol. 3, 1865, pp. 98–122.

Darwin, Charles, *The Variation of Animals and Plants under Domestication*, vol. 2, 2nd edn, Appleton & Co., New York, 1892 (first published 1868).

Derozio, Henry L.V., *The Fakeer of Jungheera, a Metrical Tale; and Other Poems*, Samuel Smith & Co., Calcutta, 1828.

Dickens, Charles (ed.), 'Easter Monday at Portsmouth', *All the Year Round*, vol. 19 (472), 1868, pp. 520–4.

Dover, Cedric, *Chimmerii? or Eurasians and Their Future*, Modern Art Press, Calcutta, 1929.

———, *Half-Caste*, Martin Secker and Warburg Ltd, London, 1937.

Dunbar, Janet (ed.), *Tigers, Durbars and Kings; Fanny Eden's Indian Journals, 1837–38*, John Murray, London, 1988.

Dyce Sombre, David O., *Refutation of the Charge of Lunacy*, self-published, Paris, 1849.

Edwards, Thomas, *Henry Derozio, the Eurasian Poet, Teacher and Journalist*, W. Newman & Co., Calcutta, 1884.

Evatt, G.J.H., Military Service for Eurasians. Reprinted from the *Indian Medical Record*, June 1892, C.J.A. Pritchard, Calcutta, 1892.

Finch, Cuthbert, 'Vital Statistics of Calcutta', *Journal of the Statistical Society of London*, vol. 13, (2), 1850, pp. 168–82.

Forbes-Mitchell, W., *The Gospel of Regneration of the Anglo-Indian and Eurasian Poor*, Thacker, Spink and Company, Calcutta, 1900.

Fox, Joseph, *A Comparative View of the Plans of Education of Dr Bell and Mr Lancaster*, privately published, London, 1809.

Fraser, James Baillie, *Military Memoir of Lieut.-Col. James Skinner* (2 vols), Smith, Elder & Co., London, 1851.

Gilchrist, J.B., *The General East India Guide and Vade Mecum . . . a Digest of the Work of the Late Capt. Williamson*, Kingsbury, Parbury & Allen, London, 1825.

Gore-Browne, S., *Alphabetical List of Europeans and East Indians in the Company's Service, 30th June 1880*, East Indian Railway Press, Calcutta, 1880.

Government of India, *Abstract of Tables Giving the Main Statistics of the Census of the Indian Empire of 1931, with a Brief Introductory Note, Government of India*, Calcutta, 1932.

Graham, Maria, *Journal of a Residence in India*, 2nd edn, Archibald Constance & Co., Edinburgh, 1813.

Greene, Major William Sheppey, *A Code of the Pay Regulations of Various Military Establishments under the Presidency of Fort William*, Military Orphan Press, Kidderpore, 1810.

Grey, Charles and Garrett, Herbert L.O. (eds), *European Adventures of Northern India, 1785–1849*, Superintendent of Government Printing, Punjab, 1929 (reprint, AES, New Delhi, 1993).

Hodson, William S.R. and Hodson, G.H. (eds), *Twelve Years of a Soldier's Life in India*, John W Parker & Son, London, 1859.

India Office, *Statistical Abstract Relating to British India from 1876/7 to 1885/6*, vol. 21, HMSO, London, 1887.

J.A.B. (ed.), 'The Census of India [1911]: Christians by Race and Sect', *Journal Of The Royal Statistical Society*, vol. 75 (4), March 1912.

Kipling, Rudyard, *Plain Tales from the Hills*, 1887 (reprint, Penguin, London, 1987).

———, *From Sea to Sea and Other Sketches – Letters of Travel*, vol. 2, first published 1889, republished by Cambridge University Press, Cambridge, 2011.

———, *Barrack-room Ballads*, Methuen & Co., London, 1892.

Lushington, Charles, *The History, Design and Present State of the Religious Benevolent and Charitable Institutions ... in Calcutta*, Hindustanee Press, Calcutta, 1824.

Madras Government, *Selections from the Records of the Madras Government, Annual Reports of the Madras Medical College, 1865–9 sessions*, Gantz Brothers, Madras, 1865–9.

Markby, J., *Fowle vs Fowle Divorce Petition and Judgment*, 14 September 1878, transcription at http://indiankanoon.org/doc/1231396 (accessed February 2013).

Marshall, Peter J., *The Writings and Speeches of Edmund Burke. Vol. 6, India: The Launching of the Hastings Impeachment 1786–1788*, Clarendon Press, Oxford, 1991.

Marshman, John Clark, *The Life and Times of Carey, Marshman and Ward*, vol. 1, Longmans & Roberts, London, 1859.

Martin, Robert Montgomery, *History of the Possessions of the Honourable East India Company*, vol. 1, Bengal, Madras, and Bombay, Whittaker & Co., London, 1837.

Milman, Frances Maria, *Memoir of the Right Rev. Robert Milman*, John Murray, London, 1879.

Montgomery, Howard and Cornish, William (eds), 'List of Medical Warrant Officers of Her Majesty's Indian Forces', *Madras Quarterly Journal of Medical Science*, vol. 1, 1860, pp. 231–44.

Morris, H., *Anglo-Indian Worthies*, Christian Vernacular Education Society, Madras, 1890.

Muir, W. and Coldstream, W. (eds), *Records of the Intelligence Department of the Govt. of the NWP During the Mutiny of 1857*, vol. 1, T&T Clark, Edinburgh, 1902.

Munro, Innes, *A Narrative of the Military Operations on the Coromandel Coast*, privately printed, London, 1789.

Naoroji, Dadabhai (Parekh, Chunilal Lallubhai, ed.), *Speeches, Addresses and Writings (on Indian Politics) of the Hon'ble Dadabhai Naoroji*, Caxton Printing Works, Bombay, 1887, p. 269–73.

n.a., *Original Papers Relative to the Establishment of a Society in Bengal for the Protection of Orphans – 1784*, Joseph Cooper, London, n.d.

———, 'Bombay Education Society', *The Asiatic Journal & Monthly Miscellany*, vol. 28, 1829, p. 353.

———, 'British Foreign Medical Service', *Boston Medical & Surgical Journal*, vol. 26 (1), 9 February 1842, pp. 17–18.

———, *The Law Relating to India and the East-India Company*, 4th edn, Allen & Co., London, 1842.

———, *History of the Church Missionary Society in Bengal*, Church Missionary Society, Calcutta, 1846.

———, *The Bengal Obituary*, Holmes & Holmes, Calcutta, 1851.

———, *New Calcutta Directory*, Military Orphan Press, Calcutta, 1862.

———, 'Pioneer, 15 April, 1868', *The Indian Medical Gazette*, vol. 3, 1 May 1868, p. 117.

———, 'Subordinate Medical Department', *The Indian Medical Gazette*, vol. 3 (7), 1868, p. 158.

———, 'Table of Fees Charged in the Medical Schools of England', *The Medical Times and Gazette*, vol. 2, 12 September 1868, p. 326.

———, *The Asylum Press Almanac*, Lawrence Asylum Press, Ootacamund, 1865 and 1879.

———, *Thacker's Indian Directory*, Thacker Spink and Co., Calcutta, 1870–95.

Ogle, W., 'On Marriage Rates and Marriage Ages with Special Reference to the Growth of Population', *Journal of the Royal Statistical Society*, vol. 53, 1890, pp. 253–89.

O'Malley, L.S.S. and Chakravarti, M., *Bengal District Gazetteers: Howrah*, Bengal Secretariat, Calcutta, 1909.

Pearce, Robert Rouiere (ed.), *Memoirs and Correspondence of Richard Marquis Wellesley* (3 volumes), Richard Bentley, London, 1846.

Pearse, Hugh W., *The Hearseys; Five Generations of an Anglo-Indian Family*, William Blackwood & Sons, London, 1905.

Plowden, W. Chichele, *Report on the Census of British India Taken on the 17th February 1881*, Eyre and Spottiswoode, London, 1883.

Pope, Rev. George U., *The Lutheran Aggression; a Letter to the Tranquebar Missionaries, Regarding Their Position, Their Proceedings, and Their Doctrine*, American Mission Press, Madras, 1853, http://anglicanhistory.org/india/pope_aggression1853 (accessed February 2013).

Quinney, Thomas, *Sketches of a Soldier's Life in India*, David Robertson, Glasgow, 1853.

Raikes, Charles, *The Englishman in India*, Longmans, Green & Co., London, 1867.

Ricketts, J.W., *Report of Proceedings Connected with the East Indians' Petition to Parliament Read at a Public Meeting held at Calcutta Town Hall, 28 March 1831*, Baptist Mission Press, Calcutta, 1831.

Risley, H.H. and Gait, E.A., *Report On The Census Of India, 1901*, Superintendent of Government Printing, Calcutta, 1903.

Roberts, Emma, *Scenes Characteristic of Hindostan with Sketches of Anglo-Indian Society*, vol. 1, Wm. H. Allen & Co., London, 1837.

Ross, Charles, *Correspondence of Charles, First Marquis Cornwallis* (3 volumes), John Murray, London, 1859.

Sharp, Henry (ed.), *Selections from Educational Records, Part 1, (1781–1839)*, Superintendent of Government Printing, Calcutta, 1920 (reprint, National Archives of India, Delhi, 1965).

Sleeman, W.H., *Rambles and Recollections of an Indian Official*, Hatchard, London, 1844.

Stark, Herbert Alick, *India Under Company and Crown: Being an Account of its Progress and Present Administration*, Macmillan & Co., Calcutta, 1914.

———, *Hostages to India, or the Life Story of the Anglo-Indian Race*, 2nd edn, Star Printing Works, Calcutta, 1936.

Stark, Herbert Alick and Madge, E. Walter, *East-Indian Worthies*, unknown publisher, Calcutta, 1892.

Stocqueler, Joachim Hayward, *The British Soldier: an Anecdotal History of the British Army, from its Earliest Formation to the Present Time*, Wm. S. Orr & Co., London, 1857.

Strange, Sir Thomas, *Elements of Hindu Law: Referable to British Judicature in India*, Payne and Foss, London, 1825.

Tripathi, Amales (ed.), *Fort William – India House Correspondence and Other Contemporary Papers Relating Thereto, 1793–1795*, vol. 12 (Public Series), National Archives of India, Delhi, 1978.

Valentia, George Viscount, *Voyages and Travels to India and Ceylon: 1802–6*, vol. 1, Rivington, London, 1811.

Walker, William, *Tom Cringle's Letters on Practical Subjects, Suggested by Experiences in Bombay*, Education Society's Press, Byculla, 1863.

Waterfield, Henry, *Memorandum on the Census of British India 1871–72*, Eyre and Spottiswoode, London, 1875.

Wellesley, Govenor-General Marquis, *To the Court of Directors: on the Trade of India, Fort William, dated 30 September 1800*, Richardson & Budd, London, 1812.

Wellesley, Richard and Martin, Robert Montgomery (eds), *The Dispatches, Minutes, and Correspondence, of The Marquess Wellesley* ... (5 volumes), W.H. Allen & Co., London, 1836 and 1837.

Wellington, Arthur Wellesley Duke of, and Gurwood, John (eds), *The Dispatches of Field Marshal the Duke of Wellington, during his Various Campaigns* ..., vol. 1, Parker, Furnivall and Parker, London, 1844.

Wellington, 1st and 2nd Duke of, *Supplementary Dispatches and Memoranda of Field Marshal Arthur, Duke of Wellington*, John Murray, London, 1858.

Whittaker, Joseph, *An Almanack for the Year of Our Lord 1897*, Warwick Lane, London, 1897.

Williamson, Thomas, *East India Vade Mecum* (2 volumes), Black, Parry, and Kingsbury, London, 1810.

SECONDARY SOURCES

Theses

Bourne, John Michael, *The Civil and Military Patronage of the East India Company, 1784–1858*, PhD thesis, Leicester University, 1977.

Goodrich, Dorris W., *The Making of an Ethnic Group: The Eurasian Community in India*, PhD thesis, University of California, Berkeley, 1952.

Hawes, Christopher J., *Eurasians in British India 1773–1833: The Making Of A Reluctant Community*, PhD thesis, SOAS, University of London, 1993.

Parker, James G., *The Directors of the East India Company, 1754–1790*, PhD thesis, Edinburgh University, 1977.

Weaver, Caroline, *Colonialism and Culture in British India, 1854–1891*, PhD thesis, Birkbeck College, University of London, 1997.

Websites

(all accessed February 2013)

Ancestry, http://www.ancestry.co.uk – transcriptions and scanned original data: includes directories, telephone books, school and medal rolls, immigration and passenger movements, and newspapers.

FamilySearch, https://www.familysearch.org – transcribed data from extensive collection of microfilmed primary sources, attributed, but also some unattributed (unusable) data.

FIBIS, http://www.new.fibis.org: The Families in British India Society – fully attributed transcriptions, scanned original documents, and photos.

ODNB, http://www.oxforddnb.com: *Oxford Dictionary of National Biography*, H.C.G. Matthew and Brian Harrison (eds), Oxford, Oxford University Press, 2004; online edition, Lawrence Goldman (ed.), January 2008.

IOFH, http://indiafamily.bl.uk/UI/Home.aspx: The India Office Family History Search – data transcribed from the British Library biographical card index. Currently contains about 10 per cent of the biographical sources available in the India Office Records.

Books and articles

Aggarwal, Shugun-Chand, *Industrial Housing in India*, Roxy Press, New Delhi, 1952.

Allen, Charles, *Plain Tales from the Raj*, Abacus, London, 1975.

Andersen, Rev. Rasmus, 'The Church of Denmark and the Anglican Communion', a paper read before the Scandinavian Episcopal Church Association, Department of Missions of the Episcopal Church, n.d., http://anglicanhistory.org/lutherania/denmark.html (accessed February 2013).

Anderson, Olive, 'Incidence of Civil Marriage in Victorian England & Wales', *Past and Present*, no. 69, 1975, pp. 50–87.

Anthony, Frank, *Britain's Betrayal in India: the Story of the Anglo-Indian Community*, Allied Publishers, New Dehli, 1962.

Arnold, David, 'European Orphans and Vagrants in India in the Nineteenth Century', *Journal of Imperial & Commonwealth History*, vol. 7 (2), January 1979, pp. 104–27.

———, 'Industrial Violence in Colonial India', *Comparative Studies in Society and History*, vol. 22 (2), 1980, pp. 234–55.

———, 'White Colonization and Labour in Nineteenth-Century India', *Journal of Imperial and Commonwealth History*, vol. 11 (2), 1983, pp. 133–58.

———, 'Race, Place and Bodily Difference in Early Nineteenth Century India', *Historical Research*, vol. 77 (196), May 2004, pp. 254–73.

Ashcroft, Bill, Griffiths, Gareth, and Tiffin, Helen, *Post-Colonial Studies: Key Concepts*, Routledge, Abingdon, 2000.

Baird, John D., 'Divorce and Matrimonial Causes: An Aspect of "Hard Times",' *Victorian Studies*, vol. 20 (4), 1977, pp. 401–12.

Ballhatchet, Kenneth, *Race, Sex and Class under the Raj, Imperial Attitudes and Policies and their Critics, 1793–1905*, Weidenfield & Nicholson, London, 1980.

———, *Caste, Class and Catholicism in India, 1789–1914*, Curzon, Surrey, 1998.

Bannet, Eve Tavor, 'The Marriage Act of 1753: "A Most Cruel Law for the Fair Sex",' *Eighteenth-Century Studies*, vol. 30 (3), 1997, pp. 233–54.

Bear, Laura, 'Miscegenations of Modernity: Constructing European Respectability and Race in the Indian Railway Colony, 1857–1931', *Women's History Review*, vol. 3 (4), 1994, pp. 531–48.

———, 'Public Genealogies, Bodies and Nations in Anglo-Indian Railway Family Histories', *Contributions to Indian Sociology*, vol. 35, 2001, pp. 355–88.

———, 'School Stories and the Internal Frontiers: Tracing the Domestic Life of Anglo-Indian Citizens', in V. Bénéï (ed.), *Education and Nationalism in Europe, South Asia, China: Manufacturing Citizenship*, Routledge, London, 2005, pp. 236–61.

———, *Lines of the Nation*, Columbia University Press, Chichester, NY, 2007.

———, 'Ruins and Ghosts: The Domestic Uncanny and the Materialization of Anglo-Indian Genealogies in Kharagpur', in Janet Carsten (ed.), *Ghosts of Memory: Essays on Remembrance and Relatedness*, Blackwell, Oxford, 2007.

Blunt, Alison, 'Imperial Geographies of Home: British Domesticity in India, 1886–1925', *Transactions of the Institute of British Geographers*, New Series, vol. 24 (4), 1999, pp. 421–40.

———, 'Postcolonial Migrations: Anglo-Indians in "White Australia"', paper presented at King's College London, 2000.

———, *Domicile and Diaspora: Anglo-Indian Women and the Spatial Politics of Home*, Oxford, Blackwell, 2005.

Blussé, Lionel, Booth, Anne, et al., *India and Indonesia from the 1920s to the 1950s: the Origins of Planning*, E.J. Brill, Leiden, 1987.

Buettner, Elizabeth, *Empire Families: Britons and Late Imperial India*, Oxford University Press, Oxford 2004.

Callahan, Raymond A., 'Cornwallis and the Indian Army, 1786–1797', *Military Affairs*, vol. 34 (3), 1970, pp. 93–7.

Caplan, Lionel, 'Creole World, Purist Rhetoric: Anglo-Indian Cultural Debates in Colonial and Contemporary Madras', *The Journal of the Royal Anthropological Institute*, vol. 1 (4), 1995, pp. 743–62.

———, 'Gifting and Receiving: Anglo-Indian Charity and its Beneficiaries in Madras', *Contributions to Indian Sociology*, vol. 32, 1998, pp. 409–31.

———, 'Iconographies of Anglo-Indian Women: Gender Constructs and Contrasts in a Changing Society', *Modern Asian Studies*, vol. 34 (4), 2000, pp. 863–92.

———, *Children of Colonialism: Anglo-Indians in a Postcolonial World*, Berg, Oxford, 2001.

———, 'Colonial & Post Colonial Hybridities: Eurasians in India', *IIAS Newsletter*, No. 30, 2003, pp. 16–17, http://iias.nl/iiasn/30 /IIASNL30_16.pdf (accessed February 2013).

Centre for the History of Medicine, Glasgow University, *The Scottish Way of Birth and Death*, http://www.gla.ac.uk/departments/scottishwayofbirthanddeath (accessed February 2013).

Chatterjee, Indrani, 'Colouring Subalternity: Slaves, Concubines and Social Orphans in Early Colonial India', in Gautam Bhadra, *Subaltern Studies X*, Oxford India Paperbacks, New Delhi, 1999.

———, *Gender, Slavery and Law in Colonial India*, Oxford University Press, New Delhi, 1999.

——— (ed.), *Unfamiliar Relations: Family and History in South Asia*, Permanent Black, New Delhi, 2004.

Codell, J.F. (ed.), *Imperial Co-histories: National Identities and the British Colonial Press*, Rosemont Publishing, Cranbury, NJ, 2003.

Colley, Linda, 'Britishness and Otherness: an Argument', *The Journal of British Studies*, vol. 31 (4), 1992, pp. 309–29.

Cookson, J.E., *The British Armed Nation, 1793–1815*, Clarendon Press, Oxford, 1997.

Cooper, Frederick and Stoler, Ann Laura (eds), *Tensions of Empire: Colonial Cultures in a Bourgeois World*, University of California Press, Berkeley, CA, 1997.

Dalrymple, William, *Begums, Thugs & White Mughals; The Journals of Fanny Parkes*, Sickle Moon, London, 2002.

Dirks, Nicholas, *Castes of Mind*, Princeton University Press, Princeton, NJ, 2001.

Dodwell, H.H. (ed.), *The Cambridge History of India, Volume VI, The Indian Empire 1858–1918*, Cambridge University Press, Cambridge, 1932.

D'Souza, Austin A., *Anglo-Indian Education: a Study of its Origins and Growth in Bengal up to 1960*, Oxford University Press, Delhi, 1976.

Ernst, Waltraud and Kantowski, Detlef, 'Mad Tales from the Raj', *Society*, vol. 22 (3), 1985, pp. 31–8.

Fisher, Michael H., *Counterflows to Colonialism: Indian Travellers and Settlers in Britain 1600–1857*, Permanent Black, Delhi, 2004.

———, *The Inordinately Strange Life Of Dyce Sombre: Victorian Anglo-Indian MP And 'Chancery Lunatic'*, Hurst & Co., London, 2010.

Gaikwad, V.R., *The Anglo-Indians: a Study in the Problems and Progress Involved in Emotional and Cultural Integration*, Asia Publishing House, London, 1967.

Ganesan, A., *The Press in Tamil Nadu and the Struggle for Freedom, 1917–1937*, Mittal Publications, Delhi, 1988.

Ghosh, Durba, 'Making and Un-making Loyal Subjects: Pensioning Widows and Educating Orphans in Early Colonial India', *The Journal of Imperial and Commonwealth History*, vol. 31 (1), 2003, pp. 1–28.

———, *Sex and the Family in Colonial India; The Making of Empire*, Cambridge University Press, Cambridge, 2006.

Ghosh, Suresh Chandra, *The Social Condition of the British Community in Bengal; 1757–1800*, Brill, Leiden, 1970.

———, *The British in Bengal, a Study of the British Society and Life in the Late Eighteenth Century*, Munshiram Manoharlal Publishers, New Delhi, 1998.

Gist, Noel P., 'Cultural versus Social Marginality: The Anglo-Indian Case', *Phylon*, vol. 28 (4), 1967, pp. 361–75.

Goswami, B.B., Sarkar, J., and Danda, D. (eds), *Marriage in India: Tribes, Muslims, and Anglo-Indians*, Anthropological Survey of India, Calcutta, 1988.

Hall, Catherine, *Civilising Subjects; Metropole and Colony in the English Imagination, 1830–1867*, Polity Press, Cambridge, 2002.

——— and Rose, Sonya O., *At Home with the Empire: Metropolitan Culture and the Imperial World*, Cambridge University Press, Cambridge, 2006.

Hawes, Christopher J., *Poor Relations: The Making of a Eurasian Community in British India, 1773–1833*, Curzon, Richmond, 1996.

Hedin, E.L., 'The Anglo-Indian Community', *The American Journal of Sociology*, vol. 40 (2), September 1934, pp. 165–79.

Holmes, Richard, *Sahib: The British Soldier in India*, Harper Collins, London 2005.

Huddleston, George, *History of the East Indian Railway*, Thacker Spink & Co., Calcutta, 1906.

Hyam, Ronald, *Empire and Sexuality: the British Experience*, Manchester University Press, Manchester, 1990.

Ingram, Edward (ed.), *Two Views of British India: the Private Correspondence of Mr. Dundas and Lord Wellesley, 1798–1801*, Adams Dart, Bath, Somerset, 1970.

Jaggi, O.P., *Western Medicine in India: Medical Education & Research*, Alma Ram, Delhi, 1979.

Kerr, I.J., *Building the Railways of the Raj; 1850–1900*, Oxford University Press, Delhi, 1995.

———, *Engines of Change: The Railroads That Made India*, Praeger Publishers Inc., Westport, CT, 2006.

Kumar, R. (ed.), *Military System of East India Company*, Ajay Verma for Commonwealth Publishers, New Delhi, 2004.

Lahiri-Dutt, Kuntala, *In Search of a Homeland: Anglo-Indians and McCluskiegunge*, Minerva, Calcutta, 1990.

Leneman, Leah, 'The Scottish Case that led to Hardwicke's Marriage Act', *Law and History Review*, vol. 17 (1), 1999.

Llewellyn-Jones, Rosie, 'A Fatal Friendship: the Nawabs, the British and the City of Lucknow', in *The Lucknow Omnibus*, Oxford University Press, New Delhi, 2001.

———, 'The "Other" Victims of 1857', paper presented at 'Mutiny at the Margins' conference, Edinburgh, 2007, http://www.csas.ed.ac.uk/mutiny/confpapers/Llewellyn-Paper.pdf (accessed February 2013).

Lovat-Fraser, James A., *Henry Dundas, Viscount Melville, 1742–1811*, Cambridge University Press, Cambridge, 1916.

MacMunn, Sir George Fletcher, *The Armies of India*, A&C Black, London, 1911.

Mallampalli, Chandra, 'Cosmopolitanism in the Hinterland? Bellary District Through Fresh Lenses, 1800–1840', *Indian Economic Social History Review*, vol. 46 (2), 2009, pp. 183–210.

Marshall, Peter J., 'British Society in India under the East India Company', *Modern Asian Studies*, vol. 31 (1), 1997, pp. 89–108.

———, *'A Free Though Conquering People', Eighteenth Century Britain and Its Empire*, Ashgate Publishing, Aldershot, 2003.

McCandless, Peter, 'Dangerous to Themselves and Others: The Victorian Debate Over the Prevention of Wrongful Confinement', *The Journal of British Studies*, vol. 23 (1), 1983, pp. 84–104.

Metcalf, Thomas R., *Ideologies of the Raj*, Cambridge University Press, Cambridge, 1994.

———, *Forging the Raj: Essays on British India in the Heyday of Empire*, Oxford University Press, New Delhi, 2005.

Mizutani, Satoshi, *Loyalty, Parity, and Social Control – the Competing Visions on the Creation of an 'Eurasian' Military Regiment in Late British India*, 2010, http://home.alphalink.com.au/~agilbert/satoshi.html (accessed February 2013).

———, *The Meaning of White; Race, Class, and the 'Domiciled Community' in British India 1858–1930*, Oxford University Press, Oxford, 2011.

Mukherjee, Hena, *The Early History of the East Indian Railway: 1845–1879*, Firma KLM Private, Calcutta, 1994.

Mukherjee, Sujit, *Forster and Further: the Tradition of Anglo-Indian Fiction*, Orient Longman Ltd, Bombay, 1993.

Nair, A.S. and Logan, C., 'Colin Paterson and his Medical Report of Travancore (1842)', *Journal of Kerala Studies*, vol. 33, 2006, pp. 82–113.

Paxton, Nancy L., *Writing Under the Raj: Gender, Race, and Rape in the British Colonial Imagination, 1830–1947*, Rutgers University Press, New Brunswick, NJ, 1999.

Philips, Sir Cyril Henry, *The East-India Company 1784–1834*, Manchester University Press, Manchester, 1940.

Porter, Roy, *A Social History of Madness: Stories of the Insane*, Phoenix, London, 1996.

Probert, Rebecca, *Marriage Law & Practice in the Long Eighteenth Century*, Cambridge University Press, Cambridge, 2009.

Renford, R.K., *The Non-official British in India to 1920*, Oxford University Press, Delhi, 1987.

Robb, Peter, 'Children, Emotion, Identity and Empire: Views From The Blechyndens' Calcutta Diaries (1790–1822)', *Modern Asian Studies*, 40, 1, 2006, pp. 175–201.

Roychowdhury, Laura, *The Jadu House: Travels In Anglo-India*, Black Swan, London, 2001.

Sachdeva Jha, Shweta, 'Eurasian Women as Tawa'if Singers and Recording Artists: Entertainment and Identity-making in Colonial India', *African and Asian Studies*, 8, 2009, pp. 268–87.

Saksena, Ram Babu, *European & Indo-European Poets of Urdu and Persian*, Newul Kishore Press, Lucknow, 1941.

Saroop, Narindar, *A Squire of Hindoostan*, Palit and Palit, New Delhi, 1983.

Sen, Indrani, 'Devoted Wife/Sensuous Bibi: Colonial Constructions of the Indian Woman, 1860–1900', *Indian Journal of Gender Studies*, vol. 8, 2001, pp. 1–22.

Sen, Sudipta, *Distant Sovereignty: National Imperialism and the Origins of British India*, Routledge, London, 2002.

Shah, Sudhir, *The Hindu Marriage Act, Act 25 of 1955, 18th May, 1955*, http://www.sudhirlaw.com/innermain.htm (accessed February 2013).

Shreeve, Nicholas, *The Indian Heir: David Ochterlony Dyce Sombre*, Bookwright, West Sussex, 1999.

———, *Nawab to Nabob: The Diary of David Ochterlony Dyce Sombre*, Bookwright, West Sussex, 2001.

Singh, Anjana, *Fort Cochin in Kerala, 1750–1830: the Social Condition of a Dutch Community in an Indian Milieu*, Brill, Leiden, 2010.

Singh, Bhupal, *A Survey of Anglo-Indian Fiction*, Curzon, London, 1934 (1975 reprint).

Sinha, Nitin, 'The World of Workers' Politics: Some Issues of Railway Workers in Colonial India, 1918–1922', *Modern Asian Studies*, vol. 42 (5), 2008, pp. 999–1033.

Speirs, Malcolm, *The Wazikadars of Awadh*, Rupa, New Delhi, 2008.

Stanley, Peter, *White Mutiny: British Military Culture in India, 1825–1875*, Hurst & Co., London, 1998.

Stevenage, P.H., *A Railway Family in India*, BACSA, London, 2001.

Stoler, Ann Laura, 'Making Empire Respectable: The Politics of Race and Sexual Morality in 20th-Century Colonial Cultures', *American Ethnologist*, vol. 16 (4), 1989, pp. 634–60.

———, 'Rethinking Colonial Categories: European Communities and the Boundaries of Rule', *Comparative Studies in Society and History*, vol. 31 (1), 1989, pp. 134–61.

———, 'Sexual Affronts and Racial Frontiers: European Identities and the Cultural Politics of Exclusion in Colonial Southeast Asia', *Comparative Studies in Society and History*, vol. 34 (3), 1992, pp. 514–51.

———, *Race and the Education of Desire: Foucault's History of Sexuality and the Colonial Order of Things*, Duke University Press, Durham, NC, 1995.

———, *Carnal Knowledge and Imperial Power*, University of California Press, Berkeley, CA, 2002.

———, 'Affective States', in David Nugent and Joan Vincent (eds), *A Companion to the Anthropology of Politics*, Blackwell Publishing, Oxford, 2004, pp. 4–20.

Stone, Lawrence, *The Family, Sex and Marriage in England, 1500–1800*, abridged edition, Penguin, London, 1979.

Thompson, Francis M.L. (ed.), *The Cambridge Social History of Britain, 1750–1950, Volume 2: People and Their Environment*, Cambridge University Press, Cambridge, 1996.

Thorner, Alice and Krishnaraj, Maithreyi (eds), *Ideals, Images, and Real Lives: Women in Literature and History*, Orient Longman Ltd, Mumbai, 2000.

Vizram, Rozina, *Ayahs, Lascars and Princes: Indians in Britain 1700–1947*, Pluto, London, 1986.

Walkowitz, Judith, *Prostitution and Victorian Society: Women, Class and the State*, Cambridge University Press, Cambridge, 1982.

Warheit, George J., Holzer, Charles E. III., and Arey, Sandra A., 'Race and Mental Illness: An Epidemiologic Update', *Journal of Health and Social Behavior*, vol. 16 (3), September 1975, pp. 243–56.

Washbrook, David, 'South India 1770–1840: The Colonial Transition', *Modern Asian Studies*, vol. 38 (3), 2004, pp. 479–516.

Williams, Blair, 'On Jamalpur – Anglo-Indian Railway Officers', *The International Journal of Anglo-Indian Studies*, Vol. 6, No. 2, 2001, http://home.alphalink.com.au/~agilbert/onjama~1.html (accessed February 2013).

Wilson, Jon E., *The Domination of Strangers: Modern Governance in Eastern India, 1780–1835*, Palgrave Macmillan, Basingstoke, 2008.

Wilson, Kathleen (ed.), *A New Imperial History: Culture, Identity, and Modernity in Britain and the Empire, 1660–1840*, Cambridge University Press, Cambridge, 2004.

Yalland, Zoe, *Traders and Nabobs: The British in Cawnpore, 1765–1857*, Michael Russell, Wilton, Wiltshire, 1987.

Younger, Coralie, *Anglo-Indians: Neglected Children of the Raj*, B.R. Publishing Corp., Delhi, 1987.

INDEX